The Politics of the Miraculous in Peru

Fredrick B. Pike

The Politics of
the Miraculous in Peru
Haya de la Torre and
the Spiritualist Tradition

University of Nebraska Press
Lincoln and London

The paper in this book meets the guidelines for
permanence and durability of the Committee on
Production Guidelines for Book Longevity of the
Council on Library Resources.

Publication of this book was assisted by a grant
from the National Endowment for the Humanities, a
federal agency that supports the study of such fields
as history, philosophy, literature, and language.

Frontispiece: Haya de la Torre in 1979, during the
period when he presided over Peru's constituent
assembly. From the collection of Senator Edmundo
Haya de la Torre, courtesy of Juan Mejía Baca.

Library of Congress Cataloging in Publication Data

Pike, Fredrick B.
The politics of the miraculous in Peru.
Bibliography: p.
Includes index.
1. Haya de la Torre, Víctor Raúl, 1895-1979.
2. Peru – Politics and government–1919-1968.
3. Spiritualism – Peru – History – 20th century.
I. Title
F3448.H3P55 1986   985'.063   85-1162
ISBN 0-8032-3672-7 (alk. paper)

For Helene

Contents

x   List of Illustrations

xi   Preface

1   1. Introduction

12   2. Modernization and the Emergence of Millenarian
     Hopes: Peru from the 1890s to World War I
12   The Fruits and Costs of Peruvian Modernization
21   Modernization in Peru: A Perspective from Trujillo

33   3. Peruvian Opposition to Modernity in the 1920s
     (I): Hispanism on the Right, University Reform on
     the Left
33   The *Oncenio*, 1919–30: The Triumphs and Strains of
     Accelerated Modernization
36   Hispanism: A Traditionalist Challenge to
     Modernization
39   The University Reform Movement: A Utopianist
     Challenge to Modernization

52   4. Opposition to Modernity (II): Indianism,
     Marxism, and Regeneration Mythology
52   Indianism and Regeneration Mythology
63   "Soft" Marxism as Regeneration Mythology

75   5. The Forging of a Prophet: Europe's Impact on
     a Rebel in Exile
75   The Spiritualist Vogue in Europe
82   The Influence of Romain Rolland and Count
     Keyserling on Haya de la Torre
87   Historical Space-Time

94 The English and German Influences on Haya de la Torre

101 The Exile Returns

106 **6. Fundamentals of Aprismo (I): Charisma and Spiritualism**

106 Haya de la Torre: Charisma and Narcissism

117 The APRA: Spiritualism and Millenarian Beliefs

123 Aprismo, Indianism, and Feminism

130 **7. Fundamentals of Aprismo (II): Religion, Regeneration, and Synthesis**

130 The New Religion and Its Promise of Regeneration

138 The East-West and the North-South Synthesis

145 Indo America as the Organic Center of the World

150 **8. The APRA Is Born from Death: Persecution and the Forging of a Mystique, 1931–39**

150 Peruvians reject Haya de la Torre and the New Religion: The 1931 Election

161 The Death and Rebirth of Aprismo: 1931–33

174 Apristas in the Catacombs: 1934–39

184 The APRA as of 1939: Failures, Accomplishments, and Expectations

187 **9. A Convergence of Regeneration Visions: United States and Aprista Intellectuals in the 1920s and 1930s**

187 The Quest for New Beginnings in the United States

189 Latin America as a New Frontier for a Redeemer Hemisphere

193 Waldo Frank's and Aprismo's Visions of Regeneration

199   10. **Emergence from and Return to the Catacombs: Haya and the APRA, 1940–48**

199   The Years of Hope and Visionary Fervor, 1940–44

206   The APRA Returns to Legality: Haya and His Party, 1944–45

220   The Political Arena in Peru, 1946–48

227   The United States and the Frustrations of Visionary Aprismo

230   The Return to the Catacombs: Haya and Aprismo in 1948

234   11. **From Middle Age to Old Age: The Mystical and Political Worlds of Haya de la Torre, 1949–63**

234   Haya in Confinement and Abroad, 1949–57

244   Visions and Politics: Haya de la Torre from 1957 to 1963

258   12. **Success Born of Failure: Haya's Final Years, 1963–79**

258   Apristas Regroup for an Election That Never Came: 1963–68

264   Millennialism New and Old: Peru from 1969 to 1976

271   Haya de la Torre's Last Encounter with the Peruvian Military, 1969–78

278   The Recovery from Narcissism

280   The 1978 Constituent Assembly and the Death of Haya de la Torre

286   The Accomplishments of Haya and Aprismo: A Final Assessment

295   Notes

379   Index

ILLUSTRATIONS

Frontispiece:
ii Haya de la Torre in 1979,
during the period when
he presided over Peru's
constituent assembly

103 Haya in 1931, the year of
his return from exile

222 Haya in 1947

249 Haya delivering a political address in 1961

259 Haya at Oxford, 1964

285 The monument to Haya

Preface

When I began graduate studies in Latin American history in 1950, Víctor Raúl Haya de la Torre had been a legendary figure in the lands to the south for twenty years. Indeed, Haya was clearly the premier bigger-than-life political personage to have emerged since the Mexican Revolution of 1910, with its Emiliano Zapatas and its Pancho Villas—although Nicaraguans would claim this status for Augusto César Sandino. Eva and Juan Perón would shortly challenge Haya's preeminence, and within a dozen or so years Fidel Castro and Ernesto "Che" Guevara would begin to eclipse Haya as leaders of mythic proportions, at least as far as leftists were concerned. At the midpoint of the twentieth century, however, Haya stood supreme as Latin America's greatest living legend.

An article by Ray Josephs that appeared in the October 16, 1948, *Colliers* caught many dimensions of the Haya legend, including that of an electoral victor denied the presidency of his native Peru because of a fraudulent vote tally perpetrated by the oligarchy and the military. An unabashed glorification of Haya, Joseph's article, titled "Uncle Sam's Latin Salesman," is an exercise in journalistic sycophancy. It also happens to reflect widely prevailing opinions among supposedly informed North Americans and provides testimony to the effectiveness of Haya's propaganda efforts in the United States. Certainly the article makes it clear why no young graduate student of Latin American history could ignore the Haya phenomenon. Almost from the time the article appeared, I have been a Haya watcher.

Included in Joseph's short essay are, by my count, nine categories of the Haya legend or myth. These categories are listed below, followed by quotations from Joseph's article. Statements attributed to Haya himself, spoken in the course of his interviews with Josephs, are included in single quotation marks.

The defender of the oppressed. "He's [Haya's] the only man to have been able to organize, and hold, the millions of Latin America's whipped and beaten Indians and mixed-blood mestizos, and to restore some measure of their once fierce pride.... 'The Indians I saw [in Cuzco beginning in 1917] were beaten, whipped, ignorant and living in misery.... Feeling bitter [about] how far they'd fallen since Pizarro's conquest in 1530 [sic], I became a driven man who had to do something.' "

Charisma and the adulation of the masses. "Haya does everything dramatically. He has the girth of a truck driver, the bounce of a ballet dancer, and the tallow-skinned round face of a Chinese mandarin. To 8,000,000 Peruvians, he is almost a Messiah—*el Jefe Supremo*.... Haya's Indian and mestizo followers call him Pachacutec—'he who moves the earth'—after the greatest Emperor of the Incas who confederated their empire.... They contribute 10 to 15 percent of their earnings to his smoothly organized APRA organization... and go to him for guidance on everything from what to eat to how to woo a favorite señorita. Haya himself, while he does little to discourage this intense personal loyalty—or APRA's mystic salutes, totems and Inca-borrowed Condor symbols—rationalizes by saying, 'It's necessary to put the point across.' ...With an energy and magnetism likely to bowl over anyone not expressly hardened to hero worship, Haya expresses his viewpoint well.... APRA numbers over 1,000,000 dues payers in Peru alone."

Persecution by the privileged classes. "Víctor Raúl Haya de la Torre is no longer officially a fugitive. [Ironically, he became a fugitive once again just before Joseph's article appeared.] He was, however, for 15 years the most desperately hunted man in the hemisphere, the hero of more hairbreadth escapes than a Hitchcock movie character.... [The reason is] that he was ... upsetting the order of 500 years by organizing and fighting for the millions of Latin America's inarticulate underdogs.... Many of the concepts he stressed were first worked out in jail cells.... He jokes about his jail record with a lusty, roaring sense of humor, explaining, 'At least all that exercise, running from the police, kept me thinner.' "

Valor in confronting continual danger. "Haya's first big fight came in 1919, when as president of the Peruvian University Students Federation, he was called on to aid a strike for the then unprecedented idea of an eight-hour day.... Behind the scenes, the young Haya turned his persuasive powers on the Labor Minister. He got a promise—the minister would fight alongside the workers. For the next 36 hours the city got more and more tense—for the Army refused to go along. Machine guns

were finally turned on the library where the strikers were meeting. . . .
Eyes ablaze with Latin melodrama, Haya dashed out, ripped open his
coat and demanded: 'Shoot me first!' He kept talking. A half hour later
the officer was awash with tears. 'I am a soldier, not a murderer,' he re-
portedly announced, and joined with the dissidents. . . . [1] 'If I am assassinated,' he told me not long ago, 'I want it to be in a place where
thousands will see and be galvanized into the kind of action that will forward my program. I insist upon it.' It is not unlikely that he will get his
wish."

Self-discipline and asceticism. "His day at his hideaway in the Andes
starts at 6:00 A.M. with a dip in an icy mountain stream. . . . Writing is
his only source of income. He owns four suits, none of which has ever
seen pressing. His one expensive taste is tomato juice. . . . With one suit-
case, two pairs of baggy plus fours and a battered typewriter, he hitch-
hiked across the United States. . . . His household is simple. There are
no women in his life—an unfortunate love affair at eighteen, he confesses,
killed off his interest."

Boundless energy. "Haya is on the move at least 70 per cent of the
time. Behind his ceaseless energy is fear. . .he may not survive to see his
ambitious program through. . . . So he keeps on the go."

An intellectual of international repute. "Books and magazines overflow the house; Haya reads for two hours every day even if it means get-
ting to bed at 4:00 A.M. . . . Haya expresses his viewpoint well—in
faultless English or in seven other languages including the Indian
tongues of Aymara and Quechua. . . . Haya's thinking, methods and
words have drawn to him a powerful corps of Latin America's top intellectuals, statesmen and students. They know that Einstein has called
Haya one of the twelve men in the world who really understands the
theory of relativity. And they tell you with pride that Toynbee, a world-
famous historian, credits Haya with evolving many of the concepts of
the interlocking of time and space which are currently knocking conventional thinking into tail spins."

The influence throughout Latin America. "At gigantic meetings in
his native Peru, at sessions in both capitals and removed villages of Mexico, Venezuela, Colombia and elsewhere below the border, the black-
haired, flat-nosed Haya de la Torre has been stressing the need to unite
the Americas. . . . And few of the 84,000,000 in the other Latin Americas [outside Peru] are indifferent to him or his current battles. . . .

When Haya de la Torre speaks, Latin America pays heed."

Only Haya and APRA can save Latin America from communism and fascism. "Chin jutting, arms flailing. . . he explains, argues and tries to convince his listeners that: 'The United States is ready to help, realizing there can be no peaceful world, only Fascism or Communism, where other nations starve or are slaves. . . . Together we can succeed. But if we don't—look out! The hemisphere will go down with us. . . . The U.S. needs us if your southern flank is to be protected.'. . . His current battle, climaxing 30 years of fighting,. . . may determine whether his pivotal country will go right, or left or get onto the path of democracy and real union with the United States."

In preparing his article, Josephs listened only to Haya de la Torre and his partisans, taking their statements at face value. Filled with exaggerated, partially true and blatantly false statements, his piece has value only insofar as it reflects the legend that Haya consciously sought to create about himself. Along with these flaws, the article suffers from omission; there was more to the legend than Haya chose to reveal to his North American interviewer. Missing altogether from the article is any allusion to Haya the spiritualist.

To respond to the full dimensions of the legendary Haya de la Torre, one must perceive him as he saw himself and as many followers saw him: as a man of supernormal powers, able to utilize spiritual and extrarational forces in fulfilling his visions of the rebirth of humanity into a new era of cosmic wholeness. It is precisely this aspect of the legendary Haya de la Torre, missing not only in Joseph's propaganda of 1948 but in most serious studies, that I chose to investigate, beginning several years ago. In the process, I have incurred a number of debts.

First of all, I am indebted to my son, Fredrick B. Pike II. Aware of my awakening interest in past and current uses of mythology, he insisted that I dip into the works of Carl G. Jung, which he had encountered in some of his University of Notre Dame courses. Reading Jung, who became my favorite author for about two years, I acquired new insights into Haya de la Torre, who had intrigued me for years. Soon it became clear that I had to reread Haya's works, focusing this time on the substantial mystical and occult passages in his writing. Previously I had skimmed over these sections, dismissing them as gibberish. Now with the help of Jung and of an ever-expanding number of writers concerned with spiritualism, millennialism, and the occult, the gibberish began to emerge as the most revealing and in some ways the most important aspect of Haya's published works.

Increasingly persuaded that a study based on Haya's connection to the spiritualist tradition would reveal a great deal not only about him but about the times and the places that helped shape his thought, I tried to put aside my previous distaste for anything smacking of the occult and the extrarational. Little by little, especially after immersing myself in a bit of the literature on the world view of American Indians and other "primitives," it became possible to approach with empathy, even if not as a true believer, the sort of cosmic quest in which Haya engaged throughout his life.

At various points in my research I benefited from the suggestions of academic colleagues, including Robert J. Alexander, John Britton, Leon G. Campbell, Ronald C. Newton, and Michael Ogorzaly. Especially to Thomas M. Davies, Jr., who has educated me through the years in so many aspects of Peruvian history, am I indebted for the initial insight that Haya's complex personality included a spiritualist facet—although it remained unclear as to how much Haya was a genuine believer and how much a charlatan. Along the course of my study, Davies kept tips and books from his personal library, as well as archival microfilms, coming my way. From Lima, Juan Mejía Baca, book dealer and publisher *extraordinaire*, passed along valuable information and generously granted permission to quote from Haya de la Torre's seven-volume set of *Obras completas*. Also from Lima, Paul A. Dolmage-Heath provided valuable information as well as an extensive and rich collection of clippings.

Along with the *Obras completas*, which the editors concede are far from complete, the published correspondence between Haya de la Torre and Luis Alberto Sánchez proved a valuable source. Undoubtedly, as the years go by additional correspondence of Haya's will surface in private archives and, hopefully, be published. · Already Davies and Víctor Villanueva have begun this type of publication, as any reader of my endnotes will discover.

Often more valuable for my research then specialized sources on Peruvian history were books dealing with spiritualism in general and with the timeless quest for the perfect society in particular. Since H. Richard Niebuhr concluded in his 1927 classic, *The Social Sources of Denominationalism*, that "apocalypticism" had always found a welcome among the disinherited, scholars have arrived at a deeper understanding of the phenomenon. In her 1983 book, *A New Jerusalem*, Mary Ann Myers summarizes recent findings and adds valuable ones of her own as she explains that the millennialist fever grips not only the disinherited, the geographically uprooted, and the psychologically disturbed, but also "normal" beings who by education, occupation, and even income stand well above the social norm. Once this fact is grasped, Haya de la Torre emerges not as a visionary freak in an age of rationalism but simply as another example among a host of archetypal seekers, contemporary as well as past, of the new human and the new earth.

A National Endowment for the Humanities fellowship facilitated research on this book. As with several previous projects, various friends at the University of Texas at Austin made my work in the superb Benson Latin American Collection an unalloyed pleasure. I am awed by Patricia A. Andrews, who, as copyeditor, corrected an embarrassing number of mistakes in a manuscript that I had thought virtually without blemish. Above all, I am grateful to my wife, Helene, whose unflagging cheerfulness and apparent inability to complain about the inconveniences occasioned by my research and writing, are appreciated more than words can express.

With so many having helped me, I shall feel all the more distressed upon becoming aware of the errors and lapses of judgment that undoubtedly abound in the following pages, for which I assume sole responsibility. For all its shortcomings, this book has at least provided an opportunity to atone for the injustice of some of the harsh appraisals of Haya in my publications of the mid-1960s. At that time, I simply did not understand Haya and could not appreciate that he merited at least a bit of the legend that accumulated around him, often under his careful cultivation. Certainly I do not pretend really to know him now. Perhaps, though, I have managed to come a bit closer. In the long process of trying to understand him better, I have come to regard Haya as one of my favorite friends among historical personages—I never knew him personally. But the friendship is by no means uncritical. In particular, I find it easy still to criticize Haya in the early and middle stages of his career. In these stages of his life, Haya found it difficult to accept a friendship that was not uncritical. Toward the end, though, he grew more tolerant and less psychologically hungry for adulation. Toward the end, he might have accepted my friendship. I would like to think so.

The Politics of the Miraculous in Peru

One: Introduction

> "If we dismiss. . . ideas because they seem irrational to us, we may be depriving ourselves of valuable insights into the society."
>
> Christopher Hill, *The World Turned Upside Down* (New York, 1972), p. 14.

Nowadays, in their pursuit of scientific methodology, historians of Latin America tend to ignore the vogue that spiritualism enjoyed not only in the lands to the south of the Rio Grande but in most parts of the Western world from the late nineteenth century to the 1940s, before peaking anew as one ingredient of an international counterculture in the 1960s. By spiritualism I do not have in mind just people assembled in darkened rooms attempting to make tables rise or to commune with the shades of departed friends, relatives, pet cats, dogs, and canaries. Rather, I am thinking of such matters as the quest for "wholeness" between "microcosm" and "macrocosm" and the rediscovery of an "ancient wisdom" that reveals, purportedly, how to assert the powers of mind and spirit over matter. In its Latin American guise, spiritualism's avowal of a connection between inward states and the outer world, along with its faith that the second is shaped and controlled by the first, often places a premium on uniformity of belief. To transform the physical milieu, people must think and "vibrate" harmoniously together; otherwise, their spiritual energies will lack focus and remain ineffectual. In some ways, then, spiritualism added another element to the kind of exclusionary thought that had originated with Hispanic Catholicism and the tradition of the Inquisition. But the tale I hope to tell is not a simple one, and often Latin American spiritualism contributed to democratic pluralism, as I indicate later in this chapter.

In their approach to what for lack of a better term I call spiritualism, Latin Americans picked up on new perceptions of the world that became common in England, Europe, and the United States around the turn of the twentieth century. Various thinkers interested in parapsychological phenomena abandoned the belief in spirits "out there" as the cause of supernormal effects in the observable world. They turned instead to the possibility of a noncorporeal presence *within* all persons—although more readily accessible to a few especially sensitive beings than to the commonality of humans—that constituted a source of potential consciousness and cognition not altogether at the mercy of physical, neural, sensory, and mechanistic determinants. Some who speculated on the parapsychological went on to hypothesize that the spiritual presence or power in all humans, which differed from standard Christian concepts of the soul, could interact with and to some degree influence the material world. It could also transmit extrasensory messages perceptible to properly attuned individuals. A new spiritualism, without the ghosts or spirits of conventional superstitions, had appeared. For a time, it found an altogether respectable place among the variety of intellectual currents that challenged positivism and the materialism of what then passed for "normal science" (to borrow Thomas Kuhn's term).

In certain respects, what I shall generally refer to in this book as spiritualism might also be termed esotericism. Purportedly, esotericism traces back to Hermes Trismegistus, who is often identified with Thoth, the Egyptian god of wisdom. Especially during the Renaissance the Hermetic tradition was synthesized with elements of alchemy, the Cabala, a smattering of Gnosticism, and other heterodox beliefs by men such as Giovanni Pico della Mirandola and Giordano Bruno. Complex, eclectic, and varying from one believer to another, esotericism often rests ultimately upon a cosmology of holism according to which all in the universe, whether human, animal, vegetable, or mineral, shares in the same essence. Seen in the light of this belief, esotericism denies reductionism, as popularized in the seventeenth century by René Descartes and taken to heart by the Enlightenment. Reductionism stresses individuality and discreteness and analyzes wholes in terms of the underlying properties of their parts. In contrast, esotericism denies a fundamental and total distinction between what is human and nonhuman; it affirms that even matter and spirit are copenetrating opposites within one complete system.

Manifesting what may be the influence of Heraclitus (the fourth-century disciple of Plato), esotericism envisages a constant process of change arising out of a dialectical interaction between interpenetrating elements that are noncorporeal and at the same time corporeal (or at least appear to be corporeal), between spirit and what is, or appears to be, material. Thus when spirit influences or alters matter, the alteration is not the result of the intervention of transcendent, "supernatural" forces outside the ordinary cosmic system; rather, change derives from the interaction between interpenetrating elements within a system that is whole, complete, and indivisible. What for Christians would appear to be supernatural or miraculous, resulting from the intervention of a transcendent God, for the esotericist results from the altogether natural interaction between the elements of a single holistic cosmic system. If divinity there be, for the esotericist it is immanent in and not transcendent to the stuff of the cosmos.

The widespread, early twentieth century revival of interest in an esoteric tradition that challenged "common sense," Newtonian, or billiard-ball concepts of matter occurred simultaneously with a surge of interest in communicating with spirits of the departed through séances and in other phenomena commonly associated with spiritualism. At this time, spiritualism—whether justifiably or not—tended to become an inclusive term referring to whatever might be deemed extrarational and beyond verification by the tools of nineteenth-century science. Thus, in popular usage at least, the rubric spiritualism began to embrace not only what was associated with the holism of an esoteric tradition but also such things as the intervention in the "real" world of spirits somehow different from the tangible building blocks of the cosmos.

Because of the connotation of inclusiveness associated with the word spiritualism, I have chosen to use this designation rather than esotericism in dealing with the beliefs of Víctor Raúl Haya de la Torre. The inclusive term is necessary because Haya placed his faith not only in the esoteric conventions of wisdom. In addition, he seemed, now and then at least, to perceive a cosmos with both transcendent supreme being and finite spirits—spirits that were not a part of a holistic cosmos but instead participated in a different sort of reality than that of flesh-and-blood individuals and that might be contacted through mediums.

In his approach, Haya de la Torre was shaped by the turn-of-the-century Latin America milieu. In this milieu, a spiritualism of ghosts and other supernatural beings mingled with traditional Hispanic Catholicism and at the same time shared an ill-defined zone with esoteric beliefs. Like many other Latin Americans (and also many Europeans and North Americans), Haya found it difficult to draw the line between spiritualism of the séance-holding variety, various popular-religion superstitions, and the esotericism of serious pursuers of unconventional wisdom, who were convinced that new scientific discoveries had begun to verify the Hermetic vision of a holistic cosmos in which the interpenetrating opposites of spirit and matter were in constant, rhythmic, dialectical, and mutually transforming communion.

Using it as an inclusive term, I intend spiritualism to encompass still other elements often associated with the esoteric tradition, specifically with elements of nonlinear time. Prevalent in the purview of esotericism (or humanistic occultism, as it was sometimes called) are assumptions about the nonlinearity of time: assumptions, in short, about the mutual encompassing of past, present, and future, about the circularity of time, and about the ascent of humanity through cycles of death and rebirth.

As the twentieth century began, cyclical ascent theories surfaced in various parts of the developed and underdeveloped worlds and caused many a person to believe that a new Renaissance was at hand. A plethora of painters and composers, poets and novelists, architects and choreographers came to believe that through their art they could personally attain a "cosmic consciousness." From their exalted heights of awareness they could deliver a coup de grâce to the moribund bourgeois order and then, by awakening among others what had previously been only a subliminal part of their psyches, usher in a cycle of enhanced life. Mirroring the pretensions and delusions of artists, political leaders appeared who fancied themselves the creators of a new order. By exercising the art of politics they would summon their people to a great awakening. Reintroducing myth, symbolism, and ritual into the spiritually barren lives of their followers, the politicians-artists-gurus would teach the masses to cast aside the blinders of materialism and positivism so that they might have recourse to what lay both beneath and above reason. Responsive to their full capacities, new men and women could proceed, following the example of predestined leaders, to synthesize the rational and the pararational, the corporeal and the spiritual, the conscious and the unconscious, the finite and the infinite. Thus would be achieved the archetypal objective of the esoteric quest: the reconciliation of opposites in harmony and the banishing of reductionism in comprehending the cosmos.

By promising to assuage the hunger of the masses for wholeness, a new breed of populist leaders hoped to eclipse the appeal of the traditional churches that, in their estimation, had so fully lost credibility in their old pronouncements about ushering in the heavenly kingdom on earth that they had long since abandoned such pronouncements. Moreover, by dealing in new promises of wholeness and a higher stage of existence, politicians and self-styled creators of a new and unalienated humanity thought to restore the sort of charisma that rulers in bygone times had claimed as the basis of the divine right of kings. In Latin America, so acutely plagued by problems of governmental legitimacy since discarding the Spanish royalty, the recapture of charisma proved an especially enticing dream for politically ambitious people beguiled by spiritualism's dazzling illusions. Max Weber may have thought that throughout the world the case for legitimacy was coming to rest more and more on rationality, empiricism, and reductionism. Many Latin American political leaders, however, disproved Weber's assumptions as they reincorporated the magical and the esoteric into their claims to legitimacy. Like characters in a Carlos Fuentes novel, they were "alchemists at heart, revolutionaries who attempt to usurp the divine monopoly on magic and creation."[1]

Without some attention to spiritualism in its inclusive sense and broadest implications, it is impossible to recreate the lives and times of, among many others, the following figures: Mexico's visionary leader Francisco I. Madero, who believed that a mystical community of prescient beings, living and dead, could guide humanity toward new heights; El Salvador's theosophist president, Maximiliano Hernández Martínez, who, like kings in times long past, imagined himself endowed with supernatural healing powers as well as supernormal political vision; Guatemala's spiritualist socialist chief executive Juan José Arévalo, many of whose ideas seem traceable to an esoteric, heterodox stream of Christianity that mingles with occult humanism; Ecuador's mystical populist José María Velasco Ibarra, whose political symbolism seemed sometimes to derive more from alchemy than from any realistic system of thought; Argentina's horoscope-infatuated president, Hipólito Yrigoyen, who anticipated the reintegration of man with the cosmos; and Juan and Evita (and later Isabel) Perón, whose political mythology, dubbed *justicialismo*, should be seen in terms of the spiritualist quest of utopia through reconciling such opposites as individualism and collectivism, capitalism and socialism. Nor can Ernesto "Che" Guevara's mystical, moral-rewards type of Marxism, with its stress on the powers of *conciencia* (consciousness) over matter, be fully comprehended in isolation from the spiritualist element that has infused a good deal of what passes for Marxist-Leninist thought in Latin America. Peru's renowned political philosopher José Carlos Mariátegui, moreover, with his Crocean and Sorelian brand of Marxism that was never fully removed from mystical Christianity, stands alongside many other Latin American *pensadores* (thinkers or intellectuals) as an intellectual—or spiritualist—forebear of Che Guevara.

These figures represent but a sprinkling of the host of important Latin Americans attesting to a vast spiritualist current extending even to the highest levels of society.[2] In one of her finest short stories, Katherine Anne Porter, an enormously perceptive observer of Mexico in the 1920s, draws the portrait of a typical embodiment of the spiritualist current:

Betancourt had spent his youth unlocking the stubborn secrets of Universal Harmony by means of numerology, astronomy, astrology, a formula of thought-transference and deep-breathing, the practice of will-to-power combined with the latest American theories of personality development; certain complicated magical ceremonies; and a careful choice of doctrines from several schools of Oriental philosophies which are, from time to time, so successfully introduced into California. From this material he had constructed a Way of Life which could be taught to anyone, and once learned led the initiate quietly and surely towards Success: success without pain, almost without effort except of a pleasurable kind, success accompanied by moral and esthetic beauty, as well as by most desirable material rewards. Wealth, naturally, could not be an end in itself: alone it was not Success. But it was the unobtrusive companion of all true Success.[3]

The Betancourts flourished not only in California and Mexico, but throughout Latin America as the twentieth century began, and there are many historical reasons for this. Latin American interest in the extrarational arises in part out of indigenous sources extending back through the centuries. Among these sources one can point to the animism and shamanism of Native and Afro-Americans,[4] as well as to Catholic mysticism, which by the time it crossed the seas had absorbed Jewish and Islamic ingredients. Moreover, especially in the twentieth century, spiritualism had been nourished by new forces from outside the continent. With particular abandon, Latin Americans responded to the virtual explosion of interest in esoteric wisdom that occurred in turn-of-the-century England, western Europe, Russia, and also the United States and Canada. This was a period when, even in "advanced" societies, occult thought—old and new—gained acceptance in many quarters as the common intellectual coin.

One of the most formidable of Latin American's public figures whose life and political significance cannot be understood without inclusion of the spiritualist facet is Peru's Víctor Raúl Haya de la Torre (1895–1979). A visionary, obsessed by dreams of a Peru and even of a world reborn,[5] Haya was at home in a *mundus imaginalis*, where images were as real as matter in the outside world. Those who responded to Haya's visionary writings and oratory often did so on an emotional and subliminal rather than an intellectual basis. Like Haya, they tended to be in quest of a religious experience of oneness with the ineffable. The political movement that Haya founded, the Alianza Popular Revolucionaria Americana, or APRA, was in a way more like a religious cult than a party. Presiding over the APRA, Haya was not just a politician: he was in many ways a revivalist, neither more attractive nor repulsive, neither more sincere nor hypocritical, than that group as a whole.

Like Michael Bakunin, another man who believed in the possibility of transforming reality by an effort of the will, Haya de la Torre pursued a vision of the unified, unalienated human personality and also of social integration in which the individual would merge with the whole. Like Bakunin and others who have shown symptoms of the utopian psychology, Haya often praised liberty as a precondition of the new society, while at the same time exhibiting a fascination with totalitarianism. According to Aileen Kelly in her probing biography of Bakunin, this sort of inconsistency is the mark of persons seeking to resolve the tension between the individual and the whole. Invariably, such persons are drawn toward dictatorial measures that will submerge the individual, clinging tenaciously to the right to be distinct, into the whole, thereby achieving, supposedly, the ideal society.[6]

Because of the importance to him, and to many of his followers, of utopian dreams, Haya de la Torre must be approached in terms of his visionary spiritualism. The biographer of figures like Haya must deal with the visions they aspired to make happen, not just with what actually occurred. With such men, the biographer needs to remember that, as Frances Yates has put it, "history as it actually occurs is not quite the whole of history, for it leaves out of account the hopes which never materialized."[7] These hopes are as important as the events that frustrated their realization.

In the present book I have chosen to concentrate on Haya as a spiritualist—using the term in the broad meaning I have ascribed to it in this introduction. In particular, I am concerned with how a vision of wholeness—inward oneness and organic social unity—led Haya to seek rebirth of Peru and the entire American hemisphere. Admittedly, my approach to Haya leaves out a great deal. Haya was far more than a visionary, and spiritualism does not explain everything or even necessarily the most important things about Haya de la Torre. Spiritualism, in fact, provides only one perspective of a remarkably complex individual who was also a pragmatist and shrewd opportunist, keenly alive to the possibility of influencing the material world through material means. Furthermore, as a practical politician, Haya often responded not so much to the idealist realm of a "superstructure" as to the reality of a Peruvian "base" shaped by demography, regionalism, imperialism, and urbanization, among many other determinants.

Although tempted by philosophical idealism, Haya stopped short of its full implication. By and large, he did not regard whatever was of value in the world as the by-product of the mind. For him, the two realms had equal claims to reality; what was important in human existence was the interaction of the realms of mind and outer world.[8] Previous biographies have focused on Haya as the politician at home in the outer world. It is my hope simply to add a further perspective by discussing Haya's life of the mind or spirit and how he sought to control the way that noncorporeal life interacted with, and occasionally changed, the material world.[9] Readers, therefore, should not expect to find the full, the complete Haya de la Torre in these pages. I hope, though, that they will encounter the visionary Haya. In the process, they may discover how his visionary streak resulted not just from his inherited nature but from the spirit of his times, both in Peru and in the capitals of the developed world where Haya spent much of his time during his most formative years.

Many visionaries who have believed it possible to create a new humanity through the power of thought or of conciencia have ended as repulsive totalitarians, for they have been obsessed with controlling thought processes in order to transform what passes for the outer world. Because of his practical and empirical streak and his recognition that only so much could be accomplished in the world through "mentalism,"

Haya stopped short of the totalitarianism that did, at some moments (along with philosophical idealism), tempt him. Furthermore, in quantum physics Haya found a cosmic view that militated against his totalitarian temptation. He was fascinated by the apparent indeterminacy of subatomic particles discovered by quantum physicists. Unlike his idol Albert Einstein, Haya could believe that God might indeed play dice.[10] If out of the indeterminacy of the basic ingredients of the cosmos emerged an awe-inspiring order, might not a dazzling new political order result from the free interplay of the greatest possible diversity of elements? This was a possibility that intrigued Haya, along with a good number of comtemporary mystics, in the middle and late years of his life. In the end, the implications of indeterminacy led him away from his totalitarian leanings and helped transform him into a believer in untrammeled pluralism. In this laudable intellectual journey, Haya was aided by one aspect of the spiritualist, esoteric, and millennialist tradition that has fascinated thinkers through the centuries: the belief that human and social perfection lies in the harmonious mingling of all opposites.

Understandably, most observers have concentrated on the outward drama of Haya's life as he helped introduce the populist style of mass politics into Peru, triggering a decade of virtual civil war and sparking passions that continued to flame for thirty years and more. For me, the compelling interest in Haya's life arises out of its drama of inward change. In the pages that follow, I explore many facets of this change, including the one from totalitarian leanings to acceptance of pluralism. One additional aspect of change should be mentioned now.

During a good part of his life Haya seemed to believe that only the exercise of power as the president of Peru could bestow on him the sense of reintegration and completeness that his divided and unfulfilled personality craved. Late in life, however, he discovered that even though denied political power he had stumbled onto a fair approximation of wholeness and that he might lose this prize were he to have to assume the burdens of the presidency. Almost to the very end, though, Haya could not admit this discovery, for many of his followers believed that fulfillment of their own wholeness quests required that the man on whom they had grown emotionally dependent become the president of Peru.

Because of the complexity and the changing and even contradictory features of his nature and still more because of the intensity and also unscrupulousness with which he practiced politics, Hay de la Torre remained throughout his life a figure of controversy. Some countrymen hailed him as "the most important politician of the past half century" and as a "colossus of politics."[11] And a level-headed United States scholar asserted in 1973: "Víctor Raúl Haya de la Torre is certainly the most important political philosopher and ideologist of the democratic left that Latin America has had in the present century."[12] On the other hand, the Mexican intellectual José Vasconcelos, for whom Haya briefly worked as secretary during a period of exile in the 1920s, rendered this assessment: "Probably there is not another case in Hispanic American history in which a subject of such mediocre dimensions has managed to create and maintain during various decades such a powerful political movement."[13] Through the years, a great number of people, both within and outside Peru, have agreed with Vasconcelos.

Indeed, the Vasconcelos criticism was mild in comparison with the charges often leveled against Haya de la Torre. To a 1951 book detailing the allegedly moral and political shortcomings of Haya and his Party, Luis Eduardo Enríquez (who for a time had been under Haya's spell) gave the title *Haya de la Torre: The Greatest Political Swindle of America* (the book appeared in Spanish as *Haya de la Torre: La estafa política más grande de América*). And Alberto Hidalgo, like Enríquez a one-time member of the APRA, rendered Haya what in the *macho*-venerating lands of Latin America is generally intended as the supreme insult among males by accusing him of being a lifelong homosexual.[14] What is more, many of Haya's enduringly loyal partisans assumed his homosexuality.

Those with greater faith than mine in psychohistory may assume that Haya's probable homosexuality contributed to his perennial questing after the union of ideas and also political and social factions that others found altogether incompatible. Conceivably, also, homosexuality—abetted by an uncommon devotion to animals—could help explain a part of Haya's readiness to champion the vulnerable and the exploited. Finally, devotion to animals might be connected to Haya's vitalist, antimechanistic beliefs according to which nature is indivisible and all its components, from humans to animals and rocks, share in one great animating principle or—to use the term Haya and many spiritualists would prefer—rhythm. These are matters, though, on which one can only speculate.

Readers who approach this book without already having made up their minds about its subject will, I should imagine, find themselves as puzzled and ambivalent as I have often been in trying to assess Víctor Raúl Haya de la Torre. Perhaps they will be indulgent when I experiment with interpretations that have had to be based partially on guesswork and on that highly suspect art, psychohistory. I hope that some at least will come to share with me a judgment that ultimately is not only favorable to Haya but actually admiring.

It is possible, though, ultimately to admire Haya personally and even to admire his ideas in the abstract, yet to remain uneasy over the practical consequences of the spiritualist politics that he practiced with consummate skill for over fifty years. For Haya's proposed solutions to Peru's national and international problems to have yielded optimal results, it would have been necessary for the European and American avant-garde in the early twentieth century to have succeeded in undermining faith in conventional bourgeois values while persuading vast majorities in the Old World and the New to seek exalted states of being and nonmaterial treasure. In fact, for better or for worse, throughout the Western world the bourgeois consensus seemed more universal and more secure at the end than at the beginning of Haya de la Torre's life. The legacy of an antimodern politics of the miraculous that he helped to strengthen among Peruvians left them ill-prepared to earn their share of whatever benefits bourgeois capitalism can be made to yield.

Two

Modernization and the Emergence of Millenarian Hopes: Peru from the 1890s to World War 1

The Fruits and Costs of Peruvian Modernization

In the first half of the twentieth century, the clearest symbol of Peru's entry into the international capitalist system was Casa Grace. Developing by the time of World War 1 into a huge conglomerate with interests in the production of textiles, sugar, rum, paper, industrial chemicals, paints, and food, in the processing of ores, and in commodity distribution and transportation, Casa Grace stood preeminent among the many economic forces, native and foreign, that were propelling Peru out of the nineteenth century toward a desired but also feared rendez-vous with development.[1] The enterprise maintained a position in the forefront of development between the two world wars, and by midcentury there was "hardly a Peruvian participating in the money economy of the country who does not eat, wear, or use something processed, manufactured, or imported by Casa Grace."[2] By this time many Peruvians had come to regard this foreign-controlled enterprise as a mixed blessing, as the symbol both of the promise and the curse of progress.

The saga of Casa Grace had begun in 1871, when a thirty-nine-year-old Irishman named William R. Grace, who had been active in Peruvian commerce since 1854 and had married the daughter of an American sea captain, organized with Michael P. Grace in Lima the firm of Grace Brothers. By the 1880s Grace Brothers had branches in Valparaíso (Chile), San Francisco, New York, and London and had assumed an American-Anglo-Peruvian character. W. R. Grace had become an American citizen, making New York his headquarters and serving two terms as mayor of that city; but Michael Grace maintained his closest ties, personal and financial, with England. In 1884 Casa Grace acquired through the settlement of a private debt the huge Cartavio sugar plantation in northern Peru. Subsequently the firm took an important role in financing Peru's railroads and in handling the country's foreign debt; it also undertook the operation of nine Bolivian railroads and helped build two new ones. In 1894 it consolidated its various enterprises in the American corporation W. R. Grace and Company. The new corporation, however, remained closely linked with British interests, and not until World War 1 "did W. R. Grace and Company take on a character that was clearly North American."[3] Even by 1900, however, the company had gained control over most of the commerce between the United States and Peru.

By 1902 North American capital had begun its entry into Peruvian mining. Established in that year, the Cerro de Pasco Mining Company staked out for its field of operations the rich copper, silver, lead, and gold deposits that lay at a height of some fourteen thousand feet in the Andean ranges northeast of Lima. After gaining the upper hand in a dispute with a Peruvian firm, the North American-controlled Cerro de Pasco Company acquired nearly six thousand acres of land, laid about eighty-three miles of railroad track to link its plant to the national line, and established a refining operation eight miles south of the town of Cerro de Pasco. As of 1912 the North American owners has already invested some $25 million in their Cerro de Pasco holdings. They had also begun to antagonize various Peruvians. According to one critic, the company had created a vast latifundium where before there had been a thousand small proprietors, and it had ruined the vegetation and the fauna of the whole region with smoke from its ovens. Its estates allegedly had become "new Californias," where gambling, drunken fights, assassinations, and assaults on Indians abounded.[4] Whatever the drawbacks, North American capital had helped initiate the age of copper. On the verge of World War 1, Cerro de Pasco was Peru's largest producer of the commodity, and a firm recently formed by the North Americans J. H. Johnston and Jacob Backus was in second place.

In 1910 combined United States–British capital invested in Peru was estimated at $84 million. Five years later, United States investments stood at $40 million,[5] well below the British total of approximately $120 million[6] but climbing much more rapidly. In 1919 combined United States and British investments stood at $209 million.[7] Thanks to British and American investments in mining, sugar production, railroads, commerce, and utilities, Peru had been integrated into the world economy, a process accelerated by the opening of the Panama Canal in 1914.[8]

The two presidential terms served by José Pardo (1904–8, 1915–19) seemed to herald the arrival at last of good times. All the frustrations and disappointments following attainment of independence in 1824, including political chaos, economic instability, and military defeat on two occasions at the hands of neighboring Chile, seemed now only a bad dream. More and more a dynamic coastal export sector was being linked, by road and railway, to the mountainous interior, or sierra. Burgeoning coastal markets for food products stimulated agricultural production in the sierra, adding to the prosperity of numerous landowners and encouraging the rise of a new class of middlemen who bought the products of highland estates and shipped them to coastal urban centers.

On the coast, Peruvians as well as Yankees and Britishers contributed to the startling increase of cotton and sugar production that characterized the first two decades of the twentieth century. This was the period when foreign and local capital combined in creating a technically advanced agricultural export economy.[9] Mining and agricultural wealth in turn led to the rise of new export-import firms (some of them in the hands of the steadily mounting number of Italian and Spanish immigrants), to the founding of textile mills, and to the birth of a modern system of finance capitalism. Between 1897 and 1908, the number of banks in Lima rose from four to ten, and their paid-in capital more than quintupled.[10] Peru's directing classes, provided they glanced only superficially at their county, could congratulate themselves on the success of the new mercantilism as they boasted of an uninterrupted favorable balance of trade between 1900 and 1913.[11] And, if they avoided probing beneath the surface, observers could hail an emerging amalgam of the old aristocracy with a new bourgeoisie, an indication of upward mobility and social cohesiveness that seemed to augur well for the attainment at last of social and political stability.

Claiming credit for much of the mushrooming economic progress were a group of well-to-do intellectuals, often linked to or personally active in Peru's awakening business world. Generally designated positivists, although in truth they lacked the unity to be considered a school, they looked with fascination on United States models of growth and development and speculated on how to adapt those models to Peruvian circumstances. By and large, the positivists hoped to inculcate a bourgeois, capitalist ethic among their compatriots. Indeed, the entry of United States and British capital into Peru at this time was enormously facilitated by the attitudes of the positivists. By the time of World War I they pointed especially to North American businessmen as a new class of beings uniquely endowed with the talents and virtues needed to banish want and poverty.[12]

Heartened by the signs of economic development that Peru presented in the early twentieth century, the positivists believed that their gospel of individual enterprise and self-reliance, with its suspicion of centralizing bureaucracies and state capitalism, deserved much of the credit. If only Peru would persevere and become more consistent in living by the newly introduced ethic of free enterprise, the rewards of modernity were assured. But a number of difficulties had appeared. Because of these, Peruvians would not, as it turned out, sustain the march toward the values of bourgeois capitalism. Already by World War I it was becoming apparent that as far as many in, or on the fringes of, the power elite were concerned, the message of sacrifice and self-control in the interest of *becoming* (in short, sublimation) was not nearly so attractive a lifestyle as the unrepressed enjoyment of *being*. And, if privileged members of society showed themselves unwilling to assume some of the costs of modernization, less privileged individuals grew bolder about rejecting the costs that they were expected to bear. Caught on the edges of modernization, they resented the shift from a corporate, organic social structure toward an individualistic, contractual, atomistic political culture.

In its middle ranks, Peruvian society was turning restive. Some persons grumbled that they were being left behind as the spoils of new material success were distributed. Others suffered the sense of unease that is symptomatic of "structural binds."[13] In a changing society, they had become aware of amazing new possibilities; but when it came to realizing these opportunities, impersonal forces were at work to hold them back. Life had become bewildering and unpredictable.[14] Under circumstances similar to those that had precipitated the rise of fascism in Europe and of populism in the southern United States, Peruvians, apprehensive about diminishing status and perquisites, cast about for a new ordering myth that would reestablish justice, security, predictability, and community.

From the bottom of the social scale, other Peruvians began to register their objections to the transformations underway. Frequently, they resembled the revolutionaries-in-the-making among the peasants and dispossessed of nineteenth-century Italy and Spain about whom E. J. Hobsbawm has written. Not born into the world of capitalism, they were experiencing capitalism's consequences for the first time; and nothing in their backgrounds prepared them to cope with the consequences that assaulted them from an outside, alien world.[15]

Since the 1890s, landowners in the Peruvian sierra had intensified the despoiling of Indian communities as they sought new land to increase the output of products for which coastal urbanization, the creation of highland mining centers, and the availability of transportation had created markets. In the sierra, some Indians became agricultural laborers, generally with semifeudal obligations to the latifundistas, while others found work in mining centers. Still others migrated to the coast, lured sometimes by the fraudulent promises of recruiters but just as often responding on their own to fantasies of a better life. On the coast, they sought employment in small-scale urban industry or on sugar and cotton estates. Whatever the precise circumstances of change, migrating *serranos* (people of the sierra), whether Indian or of mixed blood, experienced the disruption of the old extended kinship groups. Increasingly, Peru was accumulating an undermass made up of people partially adrift, no longer fully integrated into community or manorial life. Nor could they be incorporated into the old structure of artisan guilds, for these were falling victim to the import trade and to urban manufacturing.

Many workers, hungering for some sense of security and connectedness, turned to the anarcho-syndicalist organizations that appeared throughout Latin America at the turn of the century, often under the aegis of "agitators" exiled from Italy and Spain. From anarcho-syndicalism came the main ideological thrust behind the series of strikes that gripped Peru in 1918 as coastal workers, agrarian and industrial, protested the inflation and rising food costs resulting in part from the trade imbalances that accompanied World War I.[16] These strikes, the culmination of labor unrest and violence going back to the turn of the century,[17] did win the eight-hour day for many workers in 1919. But they did not precipitate the sort of social revolution to which many labor organizers aspired. Still, upper-class Peruvians were alarmed, as well they might have been. They noted, after all, the frightening examples of Spain and of Italy in 1918 and 1920. In both countries, syndicalist revolutions had come to the very threshold of success. Even more perturbing were the events of November 1917 in Russia. Not only in Peru but along the entire periphery of the Western world the emerging lessons of history seemed to teach that the spread of the capitalist spirit in underdeveloped lands resulted not, as the positivists maintained, in linear progress, but rather in social upheaval.

Peru was approaching a watershed in its history. The freewheeling enterprise and unchecked capitalist spirit urged by the positivists had resulted in many signs of progress. By the end of World War 1, however, the positivist faith was in decline among the ruling classes. If they had persisted a bit longer in pursuing its tenets and had not shirked from the brutal and sustained assaults against the middle sectors and laboring classes that accompanied the coming of modernity to Great Britain and the United States, then positivism *might* after all have brought self-sustaining development to Peru. No one can know for sure, for the ruling classes lost their nerve.

Contributing to the repudiation of positivism, beyond the fear of social upheaval, was a new awakening of upper-class social consciousness influenced both by the rash of European social legislation and by the residue of scholasticism's just wage and price concepts. At work also were forces of inertia that buttressed traditional aristocratic prejudices against bourgeois values. Undoubtedly, numerous other factors intervened also to persuade Peruvian leaders to move from positivist formulas toward those of the welfare state in the attempt to restore social harmony. Peru's initial steps toward the interventionist state were timid. Nevertheless, as World War 1 ended, the process of seeking social peace through the bureaucratic conferring of benefits on the undermass had begun. The difficulty was that benefits programs were conceived before Peru had achieved anything beyond the most rudimentary stages of economic development; and the steadily mounting demands for social capital decreased funds available for economic development. In consequence, Peru grew ever more dependent on the presence of foreign enterprise that could provide a tax base to facilitate the financing of social projects. Through dependence Peru's leaders hoped to achieve some of the results of modernization without paying the costs that independent capitalist development seemed inevitably to demand. As initially conceived, this approach had much to recommend it, even if many of the unforeseen consequences were regrettable.

As the 1920s began, Peru's leaders had formidable difficulties to surmount if they hoped to obtain social stability within a framework of dependent development. They had somehow to expand economically to allow for the painless cooptation by the privileged of the discontented aspiring elites. Beyond this, they had to deal with those elements among the laboring classes who yearned for far more than timid, halfway measures intended only to remove a few of the roughest edges of poverty. Beset by fears of "impending annihilation," some of Peru's marginal elements sought total escape from the afflictions that had come to them in consequence of what they were told was individual freedom.[18] Desperate to escape from atomistic freedom, they were ready to surrender to any mythmaker persuasive enough to convince them that he had a total solution for their ills. They were, in short, ripe recruits for a millenarian movement.

It so happened that millenarian visions had begun to grip a new generation of Peruvian intellectuals. These men spurned the sort of world the positivists sought to make as coarsely materialistic and unheroic. At the same time they rejected the timid reformism of the ruling elites who sought to resolve social ills only by economic and material means. Such an approach would, the millenarians feared, shunt aside men of dreams, imagination, and spiritual vision who possessed holistic solutions to the ills of humanity and who understood how to minister not just to the material wants of creatures but—and this was far more important—to their spiritual aspirations. The visionaries soon discovered they could enlist not only the lowest-sector victims of socioeconomic transition. Perhaps even more readily available were middle groups, perplexed by cultural binds and resentful that they were being outstripped by men superior to them only, so they believed, in greed and unscrupulousness. Whereas the established elites hoped to coopt victims of status anxiety by offering greater material well-being, a new breed of prophets would offer them instead the chance to play a decisive role in an apocalyptic movement that would usher in a new stage of human existence: alive, vibrant, and whole, such as no previous stage had been.

The prophetic dreams of a veritable human rebirth delivered the coup de grâce to positivism's prescriptions for steady, evolutionary, linear progress. A new generation of Peruvians, coming of age in the era of the Mexican and Russian revolutions, of the near misses scored by various followers of the anarchist credo in Spain and Italy, and of the rise of Italian fascism, turned their backs on models of gradualist capitalism that promised in the end to produce what might be no better than more efficient human machines, cut off from passion, instinct, and myth and from access to "mind-energy." Peru, the millenarians believed, must be awakened to its full human potential, which included a large element of the extrarational. In all awakenings, William G. McLoughlin writes, "the line between science and magic, the real and the unreal, has temporarily disappeared. People are ready to believe almost anything."[19] For the positivists, believing only in what was scientifically verifiable and logically possible, Peru's new seekers of the millenium had nothing save contempt.

Millennialist expectations surface during what Victor W. Turner designates a liminal moment.[20] The societywide counterpart of individual rites-of-passage interludes, the liminal moment occurs when traditional prescriptive demands lose their authority, when the old faiths and value systems no longer seem compelling or even meaningful, or when a people comes to believe that all is possible as it sets out to forge a new identity. During liminal moments, thoughts that would ordinarily be dismissed as bizarre and absurd become common coin. These are moments when people can be tempted by "the politics of the miraculous."[21] Having succumbed to the temptation, they seek amelioration of the natural world through magical shortcuts and supernatural means. The true powers of transformation are seen to reside in the souls or minds of men and women; dreams now assume the authority of reality;[22] spirit, it is assumed, can overcome matter.[23]

In Peru's liminal moment when mystics and dreamers arose to challenge capitalism's road to modernity, spiritualism came to play an important role. It became a way of confronting—or perhaps of not confronting—the pressures of contemporary life arising out of a transformed country in which specialization, mechanization, and large-scale production were replacing a sense of belonging with one of alienation.[24] Just as much as Marxism on one hand and a revival of Catholic traditionalism on the other, spiritualism in Peru was in the vanguard of the reaction against the sort of capitalist modernization that positivists had urged on their countrymen. The spiritualists offered a shortcut—one that would, among other things, restore secular power and prestige to those select beings endowed with superior spiritual powers.

That Peruvians would in times of anxiety turn to spiritualism and even to magic is not really cause for surprise. In the early 1930s Carleton Beals, the most perceptive North American observer of the contemporary Peruvian scene, noted: "Any extended conversation in any Lima home soon turns to tales of ghosts, enchantments, fortune-telling, black magic, bedevilment, witchcraft, and in a few bolder instances to spiritualism, telepathy, spirit-rapping, and astrology—all passionately believed. Lima lacks an Indian tradition, but pagan superstitions have oozed up through faith in miracles and direct saintly interventions in petty affairs to color the Lima mind with a muddy tinge of supernaturalism."[25] About the same time that Beals recorded his impressions of the capital, the German writer Alma Karlin traveled widely in provincial Peru and marveled at the surviving practices of "witchcraft" and the esoteric among small-town dwellers, especially those of Indian and African background.[26]

Peruvian "witchcraft" and shamanism, shaped by the Indian and African contributions to national culture and also by local religious beliefs implanted by sixteenth-century Spaniards, may have been too "far out" for the tastes of observers from materially advanced countries. Nevertheless, in the first third or so of the twentieth-century spiritualism, in both its table-raising and more grandiose world-renewing aspects, had become an ingredient of mainstream culture in the developed world. This is a topic taken up at some length in chapter 4. For the moment, it will suffice to call attention to the widespread affirmation in post-World War I Europe of the "superiority of spirit over matter, of...instinct over thought."[27] Moreover, a veritable Nietzschean cult lingered on from the turn of the century, its members convinced that a people could become what they willed to become and infatuated by the myth of the "eternal return" that promised the possibility of rebirth into a utopia that had been presaged in a distant past.[28]

Even more influential in spearheading a turn-of-the-century European reaction against materialism and bourgeois culture was the influence of Henri Bergson's neo-Platonic thought. Through Bergson's "mind energy" (the title of one of his most widely read books), not a few disciples believed they had been introduced to an alternate route to development, one altogether different from the mechanistic-utilitarian-pragmatic-positivist approach.[29] Together with avant-garde artists and Eastern mystics, Bergson led a revolt against the old view of the world based on sensory perception and issued a "declaration of war against positivism, the philosophical system of bourgeois society," whose view of reality was limited to observation and rational analysis.[30] Thanks to Nietzsche and Bergson and to modern art, architecture, and music, Europeans were acquiring a new way of looking at the world, one that in some ways harked back to the medieval vision that included in the realm of the real all kinds of spiritual emanations altogether beyond the apprehension of science. In the new, yet in some respects very old, way of perceiving reality, it lay within the realm of the possible to fashion a different world out of the power of the artistic, creative imagination.

In the belief that a new social order awaited its making and that it would not be made the way superannuated materialists assumed, Peruvians fell into line, a generation or so later, with Europe's reaction against positivism and materialism. As the 1920s began, an articulate Peruvian avant-garde admired Nietzsche[31] and lionized Bergson.[32] New currents in art, music, literature, and science were, it is true, slow to penetrate. But intellectually restless and adventurous Peruvians could find ample sources—whether newly imported from Europe or rooted in national culture—to persuade them that a new humanity could be created by harnessing long-untapped spiritual energies and that in this process scientific-technological expertise was largely irrelevant.

Europe's reaction against positivism and materialism, resonating with various elements of romanticism, had created a huge cultural wave that crested around the turn of the century and then again in the interwar years. However, the old bourgeois order had acquired the strength and resilience needed to strike back against those denouncing it and to limit the extent of their influence. In Peru, however, where material progress had gained no more than a foothold, the antipositivist reaction, resonating with the other-worldy approach of traditional Catholicism, was far more consequential. Indeed, its contributions to continued underdevelopment in the years ahead would be crucial.

Modernization in Peru: A Perspective from Trujillo

Infatuation with the politics of the miraculous is most likely to beset a people, according to Michael Adas, in circumstances that pro-

duce widespread feelings of "relative deprivation." When new groups,
ideas, and organizational patterns appear from outside or begin to
emerge within a settled society, old groups become—or believe themselves to have become—victims of relative deprivation. They detect a decline in their standard of living and status when contrasted with the
wealth and power accruing to persons who are newly arrived in their
midst or who only recently have become conspicuous. In particular, the
old groups perceive a growing gap in material rewards and status between what they feel is due them, because of their presumed superior
moral qualities, and what they are actually capable of achieving.[33] Feeling
insecure and vulnerable, they fret over the disappearance of the old community, which served and succored them because of their ability to dominate it, and they complain about the emergence of an impersonal and
fractured society that appears hostile because of their inability to manipulate it.

By the time of World War I, Peru's entry into a world capitalist system
had begun, as I have already suggested, to foster conditions conducive to
relative deprivation feelings. In the northern coastal community of Trujillo these conditions had taken on a singular intensity. It is not surprising, then, that Peru's most notable movement inspired by millennialist
expectations and committed to the politics of the miraculous issued out
of Trujillo.

As the twentieth century began, the land around Trujillo was "becoming monopolized,"[34] much of it falling into the hands of new arrivals
such as the German Gildemeisters and Albrechts and the Italian Larcos,
while not far away the Anglo-North American Grace enterprise gradually expanded its holdings. Sugar had become the king of north coast exports, and the introduction of high-intensity production changed the
style of life. In the Chicama Valley, one of the largest new sugar estates
bore the name Roma. Owned by the Larco Herreras, Roma was in the
forefront of a movement that was driving many of the old landowning
families out of business, replacing a relaxed manorial style of production
with a technology that was wedded to a proletariat labor force. One sign
of the new times was the labor agitation on the Gildemeister estate, not
far from Roma, that led in 1912 to burning and looting by angry workers
and, in short order, to their suppression by government troops. Railroad
track was laid between the sugar estates and nearby ports, where wharves
were constructed to handle the rapidly expanding exports and facilitate

the imports of finished goods and foodstuffs, many of which had previously been made by local artisans or raised on local estates. Finding their hideaways along the beach converted into bustling ports, many old-line families had to seek new vacation havens. Huanchaco was one of the towns transformed from a tranquil escape into a noisy, burgeoning commercial center. Among the families abandoning Huanchaco as a summer retreat in favor of Moche, founded by the pre-Inca Mochica civilization and located a few miles inland, was one headed by Raúl Edmundo Haya y Cárdenas.[35] Except for the summer season, the family resided in Trujillo. There, too, changes were underway, but of a different sort from those in Huanchaco.

In the midst of quickening economic activity along the northern coast, Trujillo was slowly decaying as its economic roots atrophied. Coastal estates, increasingly foreign owned, had their ties with the outside world, not with the towns of old Peru. Here is the way Carleton Beals describes the situation: "Products are brought in to Casa Grande [the Gildemeister estate] from Germany in company bottoms; Grace also uses its own steamship lines, thus . . . nearly all commerce with adjacent towns and cities is cut off. . . . [In consequence] the great Chicama Valley estates have well-nigh ruined not only Trujillo but Chicama, Santiago de Cao, Magdalena de Cao, Paiján and other centers. The haciendas creep closer and closer to near-by communities, blocking their expansion, destroying their business and trade."

As a new world encroached upon the old, traditional communities faced a loss of local revenues and thus were unable to maintain adequately schools, streets, and sanitation. Important businesses went bankrupt, wholesale houses withdrew their representatives, and unemployment rose along with crime and violence. Thus Trujillo, Peru's third-largest city "founded before Lima and once the flourishing center of two large valleys and an important outlet for much of the Sierra," gradually withered away.[36] Amidst economic decline, the children of families that still enjoyed relative well-being found little incentive to prepare themselves for business or professional careers. They frittered away their time in hunting, card playing, and watching cock fights, and the rest of their lives they passed in boring monotony "behind the closed doors and barred windows of the silent city."[37] Trujillo was at the same time a den of decadence and a monastery.

In Trujillo on April 28, 1894, Raúl Edmundo Haya y Cárdenas married his third cousin, Zoila Victoria de la Torre. According to most accounts, both descended from the colonial aristocracy. Whatever the distinction of his heritage, Raúl Edmundo, born in the northern sierra city of Cajamarca and recently moved to Trujillo, was an aristocrat down on his luck, and because of that Zoila's family had for a time objected to the marriage.[38] While close relatives were still well enough off to live in style, Raúl Edmundo had to support himself as a schoolmaster and journalist—the year after his marriage he founded the daily *La Industria*. It was not a bad life, for the Haya family occupied a twenty-two-room house, spent the summer months at a retreat on or near the shore, and employed a nurse for each of their children. But the family's economic basis was never robust or entirely secure. Moreover, compared with many of their relatives and friends they were embarrassingly wanting in signs of prosperity. In turn, even the better-off members of their family and social circles had reason to complain about their diminishing prospects as Trujillo and its environs endured economic decline. Perhaps the straitened circumstances that beset him throughout his life account for the dour and severe countenance that Raúl Edmundo displays in most surviving photographs. Doña Zoila's photographs suggest a more outgoing personality. Moreover, she remained slim and attractive throughout most of her life. The first child that Zoila bore Raúl Edmundo was Víctor Raúl Haya de la Torre. Born February 22, 1895, he was in fairly quick succession joined by four siblings: two girls and two boys. Only Víctor Raúl and the last-born Edmundo survived beyond middle age.

While the evidence is sketchy, it seems that Víctor Raúl's relations with his father and mother were not especially intimate. Accounts indicate that he was closer to a paternal uncle and a maternal aunt than to either of his parents. Through the uncle he acquired his initial interest in astronomy[39]—an interest that later transferred into a fascination with astrology—as well as a small inheritance that would permit him to set forth in 1917 to study at Lima's San Marcos university. When he was about twelve Víctor Raúl's beloved "aunt-mother," perhaps consoling him for the fact that most of his playmates in his extended family were economically better off then he, told him: "Don't worry about anything; you will be a millionaire."[40] But the aunt-mother misread the young Víctor Raúl. Out of his circumstances of relative deprivation came a passion to possess not more wealth, but more power, than others. As a preadolescent his favorite game was to preside over a republic inhabited by empty spools of thread out of which figures were fashioned. These represented a complex political hierarchy. Describing the republic of spools with which he and his siblings used to play, Haya told the North American researcher Steve Jay Stein in a 1971 interview: "We had a president, we had cabinet ministers, deputies. We had politics. And there we practiced. And we were twelve-year-old kids. And we practiced at reproducing the life of the country with spools of thread. . . . I used to receive very nice toys. . . . But I was not interested in these things. What interested me was to have an organized setup, like a country. . . . Now I tell myself, how I've always had this thing about organizing."[41]

Study of the piano and violin also occupied Haya de la Torre as he grew up. Though he quite early abandoned formal musical study, feeling he lacked talent, he retained throughout his life a passionate interest in classical, semiclassical, and folk music as well as some considerable competence for accompanying singing sessions at the piano. In addition to music and games, lengthy conversations around the dinner table, where frequently the immediate family was joined by guests, provided distraction for Víctor Raúl as he entered adolescence. His attention perked up especially on those occasions when his father or perhaps an uncle would comment on the rising power of foreign landowners around Trujillo and complain about their treatment of workers. The foreigners in the Chicama Valley, Edmundo Raúl often complained, dealt very differently with their workers than the Peruvian landlords they replaced. From the foreigners came a harsh, inhuman, "anti-Christian" regimen that represented a reversion to the era of Spanish conquest.[42]

Víctor Raúl's background reveals itself in one of his early political pronouncements. In it he denounces the treatment of labor and laments that much of the wealth of the coast has fallen into foreign hands. At the same time he notes that the properties still remaining under local ownership are in imminent danger of passing to the foreigners and their favorite Peruvian collaborators. This is the well-advanced process, he concludes, that has brought ruin to the province of Trujillo through foreign monopolization of trade that suffocates national commerce.[43]

Later in life, Haya de la Torre would object strenuously to an interpretation that United States historian Peter F. Klarén developed. According to Klarén, the motivating inspiration for the mass-based populist movement that Haya founded in the 1920s, and the reasons for the solid support it commanded in the Trujillo area, arose out of status insecurity occasioned by the decline of the old and the rise of a new oligarchy along the northern coast.[44] Haya protested this interpretation heatedly but not very convincingly. The fact is that Haya, with some fair degree of consistency, identified throughout his life with Peru's middle sectors, in which he included a beleaguered aristocracy, reeling under the onslaught of a new plutocracy. Undoubtedly, it was the experiences of his Trujillo upbringing that nurtured this identification and led him to write in 1930: "The disequilibrium which the initiation of the capitalist epoch produced in America...as a result of the expansion of the great capitalist centers of the world...caused an enormous weakening of the middle classes [in Peru].... Imperialism, which brought large industry, large-scale commerce, and agriculture, destroyed through absorption the greater part of small industry, small commerce, and small agriculture." In consequence of this development, Haya concluded, the state became the instrument of oppression of the national classes; this produced the resistance of the middle classes, "born of the desire for self-preservation."[45]

The beginning of Haya's social, economic, and political analyses seeped into his consciousness through his family circumstances. But, although his father played some part in the formulation of these analyses, the relationship between father and son continued to lack warmth and if anything grew more formal. In delivering reprimands to his children, the father took to the habit of communicating through typed letters; the children were required to type letters in reply, providing explanations concerning the censored conduct and proffering promises of amendment. Any lapse in grammar or spelling led to a fresh reprimand, requiring the writing of a new, letter-perfect missive.[46]

Never a warm or ingratiating type, Don Raúl Edmundo seemed to epitomize the harsh disciplinarian aspects of the new capitalist ethic that positivist intellectuals exhorted Peruvians to take up in the quest of progress. Even though he might grumble about the consequences of capitalism in the Trujillo region, Raúl Edmundo stood, in the eyes of his first-born son, as the living symbol of the type of austere sublimation that resulted in the destruction of warm interpersonal ties and, beyond that, in alienation of the self from the spontaneous realm of nature within. If Haya were to join—and eventually lead—his generation's revolt against positivism, he would have to begin by repudiating the example set by his own father. When as a youth of eighteen he helped organize a group known as the Trujillo Bohemians, he was issuing a challenge not only to his father but to the whole positivist approach to life as it was interpreted in Peru.

Despite his cultivation of the bourgeois virtues that the positivists extolled, Don Raúl Edmundo remained by all economic criteria a failure. In 1910, in fact, his affairs took a turn for the worse when he sustained a setback that virtually wiped out his small savings and seemed to doom the fifteen-year-old Víctor Raúl to attending, when the time came, the local university rather than the more prestigious San Marcos. No additional proof was needed for Víctor Raúl that the positivist approach not only removed grace, charm, conviviality, and community from life but also failed to produce the promised material compensations.[47]

Denied a close bond with his own parents, Víctor Raúl felt like little more than a hanger-on in the extended family circles in which he could never be more than a poor relative. Even in the outside world of the large estates, community was disappearing as labor strife and violence became more and more the order of the day. The only community left to the young Víctor Raúl, where he could feel secure and in charge, was the one of the spools. Out of these circumstances came Víctor Raúl's obsession with the restoration of community, first to his personal life, then to the nation. In a way the political movement he founded in the 1920s arose out of his endeavor to duplicate, in real life, the community of the spools.

As late as 1970, Haya de la Torre continued to be obsessed by a vision of a golden community in the past that had fallen victim to a harsh new order that imposed isolation on its subjects. In an interview in December of that year he confided to Stein:

Aristocratic ties were conserved in Trujillo. . . . I was nurtured in this aristocratic tradition. . . . One inherited this like a kind of code of conduct. This aristocracy was closer to the people. . . . They treated the people very well. In Trujillo the good treatment of the servants is traditional. . . . It's a different spirit. And we who come from the north, for example, with blacks, very affectionate and everything. At the same time, there was always something very cordial with the people. . . . We were educated in that school. . . . We were born of this stock. . . . In a country which was not an industrialized or bourgeois country, still a patriarchal country, and these ties mean much.[48]

There is something wrong, though, with Haya's reminiscences. He described in 1970 a world that was disappearing even during his child-hood, a world to the remnants of which he had gained only partial admittance. In his interview he described not so much the Trujillo in which he had grown up as the Trujillo, aglow in nostalgia, of a previous generation or even of a past century. This Trujillo, this community of a bygone era, was the one he hoped throughout his life to restore. In the restored community—and its dimensions gradually grew in Haya's rich imagination to encompass not only Peru but all of Latin America and even the entire hemisphere—he would be at the center of something that was alive and vital, no longer on the fringes of what was dying.

All of this was for the future. During his youth, however, Haya did derive satisfaction from a growing sense of belonging to a community of the dead—but one with potential for rebirth. Present at Moche during many an excavation conducted by his relatives, Haya became fascinated by the pre-Inca weavings and ceramics that were turned up. Moreover, an uncle was an archaeologist with a rich collection of preconquest artifacts, and from him Haya learned much about Peru's original inhabitants. Then too there were moonlight picnics at the great pre-Inca Chimú ruins of Chan-Chan, near Trujillo, that Haya enjoyed in the company of close friends. Although his family assured him of its pure Spanish antecedents, "Haya was struck with the similarity of some of the sculptured heads at Chan-Chan with his own physiognomy."[49] Puzzling over this resemblance, for which his family could provide no satisfactory explanation, Haya began to feel spiritually a part of the great Indian community of the past. To it, and not just to the Trujillo background in its halcyon days of aristocratic splendor, Haya now began to look for guideposts toward the golden society of the future.

The sense of lost community and the hope of forging a new one appeared in the anarchist writings that Víctor Raúl turned to at an early age. His father opened his private library to his oldest son not long after he turned thirteen. Among the books that most intrigued Víctor Raúl was the *Páginas libres* of Peru's home-grown anarchist Manuel González Prada. And, close to the family house in Trujillo stood the library of the League of Workers and Artisans of Peru, an anarcho-syndicalist organization. By the time he was fourteen, Víctor Raúl began to pour over its collection of anticlerical and radical books and periodicals, paying especial attention to the works of Peter Kropotkin.[50] From anarchist ideology Haya derived some of his earliest ideas on how it might be possible to destroy the increasingly atomized existing order and to build on its ruins the new, humane community. By the time he entered the University of Trujillo in 1913, Haya had begun to surround himself with a group of like-minded seekers in whose companionship he found a harbinger of the community of the future.

In addition to Haya and his year-younger brother Agustín ("Cucho"), the Trujillo Bohemians included the poets César Vallejo and Alcides Spelucín and the philosopher-journalist Antenor Orrego. Vallejo and Orrego were three years older than Víctor Raúl; Spelucín was the same age. Uniting the bohemians were a spirit of rebellion against what they perceived as a new plutocratic order in which money had become the sole basis of social and political distinction and a mystical faith that poets, visionaries, and men of moral superiority had the power to create a new world. According to Orrego, the bohemians found cohesion also in their shared neo-Platonic outlook. Rejecting positivism, which accepted only sensory evidence, they believed that spirit was more important than matter; in fact, they understood that "concrete reality" might be nothing more than a "metaphor."[51]

The favorite pastime of the bohemians seems to have been gathering together, sometimes by moonlight amidst Indian ruins, to read their latest poetry or prose, discuss their visions of the future, and, above all, render homage to the exalted genius of each member of the group. Already it was becoming clear that Haya de la Torre, as Spelucín put it, craved to play the role of hero to his peers.[52] It was also clear that Haya, in spite of the later myth he fostered of delighting in the loneliness of study and meditation,[53] functioned most happily when surrounded by a circle of admirers.

The only member of this coterie with genuine world-class literary talent, César Vallejo arrived in Trujillo in 1913 from his native sierra town of Santiago de Chuco. Although his family considered themselves aristocrats in this town of some fourteen thousand inhabitants, César upon reaching Trujillo was dismissed as a "humble mountain boy."[54] He brought with him, nonetheless, a background of richer experience than his fellow bohemians could boast. He had served as tutor for the son of a wealthy mine owner in the province of Pasco in central Peru and in 1912 had worked in the accounts department of the Roma sugar estate in the Chicama Valley. Undoubtedly, he had been impressed by the violent suppression of labor unrest that year by government troops on the nearby

Gildemeister estate. Registering in 1913 at the University of Trujillo, he had to find work as a school teacher to cover expenses. In his early poems, Vallejo mixed attacks against Trujillo's bourgeois society, in which he reveals a sense of self-pity that becomes "quickly sublimated into the myth of the poet's superiority,"[55] with expressions of a longing for wholeness in which mankind would surmount the divisions that had torn it asunder. Confident that "there will be a new dawn tomorrow,"[56] Vallejo was still dreaming of the creation of a new era, a new world, and a new man and woman when he joined the Communist Party in 1927. But he saw life as a constant process of death and regeneration, and did not believe that revolutions made by Communists would by any means be the last ones.[57] A year after joining the Communist Party, Vallejo broke with Haya de la Torre. But Víctor Raúl never lost his youthful admiration for the great poet. Throughout his life he continued to recite Vallejo's verses in a way that seldom failed to move his listeners.

Attracted by many of the same themes on which the more talented Vallejo wrote, Spelucín reviled the crass materialism that he saw suffocating his native Trujillo. These sentiments gained intensity during the 1920s when Spelucín spent some time in Cuba and had the chance to witness the alleged destruction of a culture by the all-engulfing invasion of Yankee capital.[58] By the time of his university studies, his poems had begun to focus on the sea, the classical symbol of the promise of rebirth.[59] He also dealt in mystical imagery as he envisaged a resolving of contradictions that would restore human existence to wholeness.[60]

As a journaiist, Antenor Orrego published a Trujillo newspaper that "flew the banner of anti-imperialism" and Latin American unity.[61] As a philosopher he cultivated an obscurantist style in which he presented mystical, utopian visions that owed more to sources of occult enlightenment than to conventional metaphysics. His best-known work, *Pueblo continente*, published in 1939, was the distillation of ideas he had been developing since his association with the Trujillo Bohemians. In it he envisioned Peru as the womb of a new humanity that would inhabit a sacred center in which East and West would fuse in harmony. In addition to being the leader among his Trujillo companions in conjuring up millenarian fantasies, Orrego encouraged their rebelliousness of spirit. "We are not," he explains "and could not be conformists...." Therefore, "we had to come into conflict with everything and everybody—with institutions, political power, social conventions, the university, an exploiting and insolent plutocracy, its sacred falsehoods, class etiquette, its lack of honesty and honor, its base servility, its exploitation of the worker, its bureaucracy, professional politics, presumptuous ignorance . . . . all these had to endure our attacks.''[62]

Resentment against the plutocrats and philistines of Trujillo was by this time a guiding principle of Haya de la Torre's thought. And in the play *Vanity Triumphant*, which he wrote and had produced in Trujillo shortly before his departure for Lima in 1917, he heaped scorn on the bourgeois values of his native city while celebrating the superiority of the poet. Here was Haya's first public cry of rebellion. Orrego and the other bohemians were ecstatic over the work. From this time onward Haya was perceived as a rebel; perhaps in order to sharpen his own sense of identity be began to act more and more like a rebel.[63]

As he departed Trujillo to continue his studies at San Marcos, the way paved by the small inheritance from his favorite uncle, Haya's intellectual and psychic baggage included considerably more than rebelliousness. It included a thirst for power and recognition and for community. In addition, it included anarchist ideals, a fascination with preconquest civilizations, utopian expectations concerning Peru's future, and certain mystical-spiritualist predilections nourished, in part, by his fellow Trujillo Bohemians.

Even without these friends, Haya could scarcely have avoided awareness of the extrarational. Trujillo, after all, enjoyed a reputation for producing the best *hechiceros* (magicians) and shamans in all Peru. Among its citizens—and not just those of the lower classes—widespread belief prevailed in white and black magic and the power of amulets, whether deriving from alleged connections to Christian saints or from the incantations of hechiceros.[64] Given his Trujillo background and his visionary friends, Haya could scarcely have failed to ponder the ways of incorporating the extrarational into his rebellion against the reviled bourgeois-capitalist life-style with its insistence on the rational and the empirical and its smug disdain for all extrasensory sources of cognition.

The seed of another intellectual predisposition Haya took with him to Lima: a predisposition toward envisioning an ideal future in terms of the reconciliation of opposites. This was the way in which Vallejo, Spelucín, and Orrego looked toward the future. Beyond their influence, Haya once again was shaped, I believe, by his native Trujillo. Consider the impression this city left on Beals at the beginning of the 1930s: ''Trujillo has a population more mestizian, mulatto, and zambo [a mixture of Indian and African] than that of Lima. Here . . . in Chimú and Inca Perú [is a populace] thinned by scornful Spanish blood, blackened by Africa, yellowed by Chinese. It is the melting-pot of the coast."[65] Haya's convictions about the potential of the mixed or cosmic race helped him resist, if not with absolute consistency, the fascist temptation when he encountered it during the 1920s while in Europe. Preference for purity of race and disparagement of dark skin were attitudes that he found genuinely abhorrent.[66]

To be white of skin and relatively free from racial prejudice was a stunning attribute for this time in Peru—or for most other places in the world, for that matter. And, as will become apparent in subsequent chapters, the sort of spiritualism that influenced Haya de la Torre and his colleagues, with its stress on synthesis, contributed to weakening the prejudices against Peru's non-white populace that was as prevalent in pious Catholic circles as among radical anticlericals and freethinkers. Here was a decided plus in the role that spiritualism, often intermingled with Symbolical Masonry, played in the antipositivist movement. Although positivists had recognized the potential of Indians to become efficient producers and large-scale consumers, most of them had tended to minimize the spiritual, mental, and psychic capacity of the native Peruvians and of the dark-skinned mixed races. However zany some of its concepts, the kind of spiritualism that came to thrive in Peru, with Haya de la Torre as a leading exponent, had the distinction of helping challenge the racial connotations of Spencerian positivism.

Three

Peruvian Opposition to Modernity in the 1920s
(I): Hispanism on the Right, University Reform
on the Left

*The "Oncenio," 1919–30: The Triumphs and Strains of
Accelerated Modernization*

Not wishing to be unduly encumbered by constitutional
processes, Augusto B. Leguía, who had been elected to the Peruvian
presidency in 1919, did not wait for the ordinary procedures leading to inauguration to run their course. Instead, he prematurely seized power
through a coup d'état (in Spanish, a *golpe*). Thus began an eleven-year
period of moderately dictatorial rule known as the *oncenio*.

"I have come not only to liquidate the old state of affairs," Leguía is
reported to have said after installing himself in office, "but also to detain
the advance of communism."[1] In his mind, the best way to prevent communism was to develop a dual society. At the top, positivist-style competition, abetted by favors from the central government to its friends,
would spearhead the advance of capitalism. For those at the bottom, an
interventionist state would succor the many discomfited by the progress
of the few. The envisaged paternalism would, of course, inculcate dependence rather than competitive individualism among the masses. Competitive individualism might, as the positivists argued, produce the most
dramatic strides toward progress. But, unless confined to a relatively
privileged minority, it threatened to destroy the vertical order on which
social stability had traditionally rested. That order depended on asym-
metrical relationships of domination and dependence. And, to Leguía
and the majority of accommodated Peruvians, preservation of the tradi-

tional order took precedence over optimum rates of economic development.

A new constitution, promulgated in January 1920, committed the state to improving the working conditions of laboring classes and to constructing hospitals, asylums, clinics, and primary schools for all of the country's needy.[2] About the same time a new labor section was created in the Ministry of Development, and it became the basis of a future independent ministry. Through these and related measures, such as the founding of a labor arbitration commission, the state moved to end the isolation of labor that had resulted from the Spencerian-positivist approach and to forge a relationship in which workers would depend upon government rather than their own pursuit of wealth for protection and security. Independent labor organizations, of course, were not to be tolerated. The new approach was described by Leguiístas as a concession to socialist theories. The mask of socialism, however, did not furnish a convincing disguise for a system basically intended to wed traditionalism to a measure of capitalist development.

During the early oncenio, money seemed readily available to finance new social projects as well as huge government-sponsored public works projects, for Peru at this time was caught up in a frenzied "dance of the millions." One source of money was foreign borrowing, and during the oncenio the foreign debt rose from approximately $10 million to $100 million. Largely thanks to loans from abroad and deficit financing, the Peruvian budget by 1929 called for an expenditure of approximately $80 million, a figure that exceeded income by a considerable margin and represented nearly a fourfold increase over government outlays in 1920.[3] As a result of what seemed an endless supply of money, government was in a position to become the benefactor, and often the employer, of an ever-increasing percentage of the urban labor force.

Government paternalism and employment, however, could scarcely keep pace with the expectations of a hugely increased urban lower mass, its numbers swelled by the steady arrival from the sierra of Indians who had been victimized by the steady encroachment of latifundistas upon native comunídades (semicommunal entities based on kinship ties that in many instances had occupied the same land for centuries) and by demands of forced labor for the building of roads. "Between 1919 and 1931," as Stein points out, "some 65,000 provincianos came to live in the capital. By 1931 over 19 percent of the city's inhabitants had moved from the countryside in the preceding eleven years." Whereas in 1920 some 66,000 *limeños* (residents of Lima) held working-class jobs, the number by 1931 had risen to 110,000. "In sum, during the decade of the 1920s Lima had undergone a process of massification." The working classes had grown from their position as a mere component in the urban scene to one of demographic domination.[4] Regardless of how rapidly Peruvian prosperity advanced at the top, it did not advance enough, nor were charitable inclinations among the new rich adequate, to purchase the quiescence of the masses.

Those at the top, in what Leguía termed the New Fatherland (*Patria Nueva*), were to a considerable degree "new men," catapulted upwards by their access to government and, through it, to the foreign capital that poured into the country as never before. By 1930 United States direct investment had reached the $200 million mark, more than a thirtyfold increase over the modest $6 million figure for 1897;[5] British capital in 1930 stood at just under $125 million but had been slowly falling for about five years. Clearly, Peru's horn of plenty originated in the United States, and Leguía did all in his power to increase the treasure it poured onto his country. He appointed North Americans to high posts in the customs service, tax bureau, and department of education, as well as the Central Reserve Bank. On one occasion he even affirmed, "My hope is to put an American in charge of every branch of our Government's activities."[6] He took another step toward the North Americanization of Peru when, in 1920, he proclaimed the Fourth of July a national holiday. Waldo Frank, a North American writer who lectured in Peru toward the end of the oncenio (and is discussed at some length in chapter 9), accurately summed up the nature of the administration. Leguía, he observed, "belonged to a new class of dictator, whose strength lies not in an instinctive contact with his people but in business contact with what may be symbolized as either Washington or Wall Street. . . . This contact abroad implies of course detachment from the ethos of the dictator's people."[7]

Many Peruvians prospered under the new dispensation, relying on their own enterprise and their contacts with the government—not necessarily in that order—to carve out for themselves a place among the old-line ruling families. Peru's oligarchy became increasingly an amalgam of traditional aristocracy and new plutocracy. And, just like the dictator himself, the new oligarchy seemed to distance themselves from the Peruvian people *(el pueblo)*. Moving out into the suburbs to build lavish residences, they created their own version of the Ringstrasse that had risen in late nineteenth-century Vienna: an enclave where a new bourgeoisie mingled with the old nobility in splendid isolation from the urban masses with whom they had once lived in close proximity within the city proper.[8] Those not fortunate enough to transfer from Lima's center lamented that the capital had ceased to be an organic community. In nostalgia, they looked back to the old days; and, often in revolutionary anger, they looked forward to forging a new community with, so they said, the people.

Life was not without its blows even for those who seemed the beneficiaries of the New Fatherland. Many who had thought themselves secure within the new order were likely to echo the complaints of the most radicalized intellectuals, students, and struggling middle sectors when industrialization and modernization took expected turns and left them in the lurch or when upstarts eclipsed them.[9] All the while the growing corps of bureaucrats began to muse on how much better, how much more scientifically they could manage the march toward progress than the motley assortment of men on the make and aristocrats of rentier mentality presently guiding the way. Even before the Great Depression of 1929 toppled Leguía's economic house of cards, the potential was at hand for a multiclass movement of protest against the costs and even some of the fruits of modernization.

Hispanism: A Traditionalist Challenge to Modernization

From traditional Catholicism issued early twentieth-century rumblings against the positivist-spearheaded materialism that threatened to undermine spiritual values. As World War I began, a group of intellectuals under the leadership of Carlos Arenas y Loayza decided that Peru needed a Catholic university to counter the secular influences at San Marcos.[10] With the French priest Georges Dintilhac as its first rector, the Catholic University opened its doors in Lima in 1917. More like a seminary than a university in its early years, it sought to prepare a new elite "to conquer the sensual epoch, to banish the dominance of science in the modern generation, and to overcome its laziness and love of pleasure," an elite that would also give precedence to spiritual over material values and arrest the spread of class antagonism. Urging the solution of social problems through charity and the shaping of social consciousness among the elite, the founders of the Catholic University regarded themselves as the only group that understood the meaning of "true social reform."[11]

In the early 1920s the eminent intellectual and statesman Víctor Andrés Belaúnde, who for some time had been complaining that Peru's new directing classes were obsessed only with accumulating personal fortunes and had abandoned moral and cultural values,[12] returned to the Catholic fold that he had abandoned in youth—in line with the fashion established by many positivists. Belaúnde was but one among many members of what Peruvians came to call the "Generation of 1905" who returned to the Roman Catholic Church in the 1920s, seeing in it the defender of tradition and the true fountainhead of national identity, as well as the ultimate foundation for a way of life that stressed spiritual refinement rather than material accumulation. Undoubtedly, too, those members of the Generation of 1905 who rediscovered religion recognized that among the masses anticipation of rewards in the world beyond could contribute as much as paternalism to social tranquility. Thus, they resolved to counter the secularization trend that had accompanied the triumphs of Peruvian positivism.

The revival of Catholicism ties in with the reaction against positivism that a movement known as Hispanism *(hispanismo)* had begun to spearhead in much of the Spanish-speaking world around the turn of the century. Originating in Spain in the early nineteenth century[13] but beginning to flourish there only in the 1890s, Hispanism taught that the Hispanic *raza* (meaning race as defined in a cultural rather than a biological sense), ostensibly comprising Spanish-speaking peoples throughout the world, had its own unique *ser* (essence or identity), setting it apart from all other peoples and cultures. Distinguishing those who shared in the Hispanic ser was an indifference to material considerations, a paramount concern with cultural, spiritual, and intellectual values, and a devotion to the organically (corporatively) structured, stratified society. Any attempt to alter the vital elements of Spanishness, said Hispanists *(hispanistas)*, would lead to the gradual disappearance of the Hispanic raza.

Especially after the defeat of Spain by the United States in 1898, Hispanists feared that the survival of the Hispanic raza was in jeopardy. The danger was thought to be greatest in Spanish America, where the republics were most exposed to and most apt to be seduced by the United States life-style. Allegedly, the basic flaw in that life-style was its exclusive concern with material development and progress. In a society characterized by a lack of appreciation of higher values, the masses could only be expected to acquire an insatiable appetite for multiplying their creature comforts. Incapable of experiencing satisfaction and fulfillment regardless of how much they might obtain in the way of material goods, they would eventually in their frustration strike out against the prevailing social order.[14]

Hispanists urged the unification of Spanish America to present a common front against the further penetration of Yankee imperialism. And this particular message of the Hispanists found approval among Spanish Americans of wide ideological diversity. Regarding Hispanism as a whole, however, Peruvians and their counterparts throughout Latin America tended to resent Spain's presumption in claiming the status of moral leader in the crusade against materialism. Moreover, most— though certainly not all—of the more vociferous Hispanists associated their cause with Catholicism, and this proved a serious drawback among the university youth of Peru in the 1920s. Just as many of their fathers were reentering the Church, Peru's youth turned increasingly from the old religion, persuaded that their continent required the animation of a new spiritual drive deriving from the dream of forging a new society, unique from all that had preceded it.

Even if not guided by such lofty and mystical hopes, young Peruvian intellectuals in the 1920s were outraged by the apparent success Leguía enjoyed in coopting the Catholic Church and making it an instrument of the New Fatherland. The dictator collaborated closely with Catholic Action programs, the aims of which were twofold: to stimulate the well-to-do to take up anew the Christian obligations of charity and to provide the clergy with broadened access to the masses in the attempt to persuade them of the priority of spiritual rewards over material gratifications. When Juan Benlloch y Vivó, a distinguished Spanish prelate and cardinal, reached Peru in 1923 in the course of a short South American tour to popularize the tenets of Hispanism as equated with Catholicism, Leguía provided a lavish welcome. Benlloch returned to Spain highly enthused by the favorable reception he had received not only in Peru but elsewhere in the former colonies as he promulgated his message that Spain and Spanish America must unite around the eternal truths of Catholicism to abort a massive social upheaval.[15] The favorable response to Benlloch, however, came mainly from those of mature age. Among university students and young intellectuals, neither the Spanish motherland nor the traditional religion had much to do with the utopian future on which they had set their hopes.

Not surprisingly, Haya de la Torre spurned the message of conservative Hispanism as the siren song of a dying culture. His antimaterialism was of an altogether different variety. It grew out of the university reform movement that coincided with his arrival in Lima. In this movement Haya found his metier, and through it the Trujillo provincial made his first mark on Peruvian society outside his native city.

The University Reform Movement:
A Utopianist Challenge to Modernization

The shared experience that molded the disparate elements of Peru's university population into a purportedly integrated generation, the "Generation of 1919," was the university reform movement. Filled with heady and mystical concepts of presiding over the birth of a new humanity whose spiritual and intellectual accomplishments would eclipse those inspired in earlier centuries by Christianity, Peruvian youth strove to remake the university as a preliminary step to remaking the world. Strikingly similar in one respect to their Chinese counterparts who initiated the May Fourth Movement (1915–27), Peru's activist youth embraced the notion that "a change of basic ideas qua ideas was the most fundamental change, the source of other changes." Out of a change in ideas, originating in the university, would come the power to transform the whole of society.[16]

The rumblings of a university reform movement had been audible for quite some time in Latin America. But it took the disillusionment with the old capitalist order of the advanced Western world produced by World War I, plus the hopes for a new order arising from the Bolshevik Revolution, to transform university reform into a powerful, continentwide movement.

Generally, if not altogether accurately, said to have originated in 1918 at Argentina's University of Córdoba,[17] where students compared their initial success to the taking of the Bastille in 1789,[18] the university reform movement proclaimed the need to surmount the sordid materialism and capitalism that had allegedly spawned the Great War.[19] For Latin America, the first need was to launch a crusade against the economic imperialism from abroad, especially from the United States, that was inundating the southern continent not only with its exploitative firms but also with its dehumanizing culture.[20] The struggle against imperialism had to begin in the universities, which had come to be dominated, the reformers charged, by professors who were lackies of a new plutocracy tied to foreign capital. Agents of an insidious, antinational set of values, the professors were systematically corrupting Latin American youth and severing it from its cultural moorings. In the university classrooms, therefore, Latin Americans must begin the struggle to liberate themselves from alien oppressors.

According to Gabriel del Mazo, elected president of the Argentine Confederation of University Students in 1919 and destined shortly to become one of Haya de la Torre's most steadfast friends, Latin Americans were not by nature "commercially oriented; they do not possess the passion for money; they prefer the spirit to calculation, hospitality to economic conquest. They constitute an emotional order." By predilection more interested in ethics than technology, they were being subjected in their own classrooms to an "illicit" attempt to transform them into single-minded pursuers of material and economic goals.[21] By ridding the universities of the control of a foreign culture, Latin Americans would free themselves to return to authenticity.[22] As the initial step toward this goal, university students, perceived as select souls, a chosen people of idealism, abnegation, and moral purity,[23] must gain the right to share in university administration (co-gobierno) so they could remove all professors who had become agents of cultural imperialism. In Mazo's view, which was representative of the reform movement, the university was the cell, the focal point for effecting the change of society: first rid the university of the "teaching oligarchy," and then youth would be in a position to carry out the next step of wresting control over the state from the political and economic oligarchy whose members collaborated with imperialism.[24]

Throughout Latin America, the mythology and rhetoric of rebirth accompanied the university reform movement. Mazo referred to it as a "mother movement," while another spokesman stressed the rebirth of spirit that would uplift the races "that inhabit our mountains and forests, which in their voyage toward the mysterious future carry the secret of the submerged Atlantis."[25] In one of their manifestos the Student Federation of the University of Córdoba announced: "The new generations believe that a new cycle of civilization is being initiated and that its seat is located in America, with its distinct orientation toward spiritual forces. The goal should be to realize the great collective aspirations bequeathed by our historical factors and to mark clearly the route that, in consequence, these countries should follow."[26] In order to put themselves in contact with the great collective aspirations bequeathed by history, Latin American youth were advised to return to the soil of their own countries, for this was the way to be reborn.[27]

The university reform movement gave rise to a vision, common to millenarian expectations, of a new and more humane order that would issue from the harmonious union of opposites. One of its advocates saw its ultimate result as the "synthesis of European technology and the Oriental mystique."[28] Another saw the reform as leading to a "perfect synthesis between spirit within and matter without."[29] And Mazo turned to the cross, that classic symbol of redemption through the merging of opposites, to express his view of the new humanity that would arise out of the reforms originating in the university. The new race that he foresaw had "its arms on the cross of redemption of which there were already presentiments."[30] Significantly, the essay from which this quotation comes, containing Mazo's most mystical writing on the ultimate meaning of university reform, was dedicated to Haya de la Torre. While Haya's hopes of forging a new religion and a new humanity may have had their dim origins in Trujillo, they blossomed into full life only under the influence of the university reform movement.

Throughout his life, Haya de la Torre attested that along with the Mexican Revolution of 1910 the university reform movement exercised the dominant influence in shaping his political faith.[31] Undoubtedly, it was the mystical, regenerationist, millenarian aspects of the reform, together with the possibilities it offered for the immediate acquisition of power, that aroused Haya's enthusiasm. University reform, in its full intensity, arrived in Lima in 1919, just as Haya was establishing himself in the city. After reaching the Peruvian capital in 1917, Haya had shortly gone to Cuzco, where for a time he enrolled in that city's university. By 1919, however, he was haphazardly pursuing his studies at San Marcos and was looking for a way to make his mark. Through the university reform movement, he would soon attract attention well beyond provincial Trujillo for the public cry of rebellion he had first issued in his play *Vanity Triumphant*.

In 1919 Argentina's distinguished socialist statesman Alfredo Palacios appeared in Lima to explain the background and ideology of university reform; it was then that Haya first began to enthuse over the movement's possibilities.[32] Translating into action some of the reform's ideological tenets, a group of San Marcos students joined in the general strike then being waged by workers to obtain the eight-hour day[33] and demanded the removal of sixteen professors singled out as the most conspicuous examples of propagandists for cultural values alien to the authentic Peru. Demands also included student exercise of co-gobierno—the right to participate in administrative councils and to have a voice in faculty selection—as well as suppression of class attendance lists. At this point a majority of delegates serving in the Federation of Students, the national organization with its headquarters at San Marcos, resigned in protest against Leguía's alleged assaults upon university autonomy. Among those resigning was federation president Hernando de Lavalle. With federation ranks depleted by resignations and ordinary procedural processes brought to a standstill, a mere shell of members met to elect a new president, despite widely voiced protests against holding elections under these circumstances. Bargaining and manipulating in masterful style, Haya garnered forty-six of the sixty-one votes cast for federation president. Thus a mere forty-six votes sufficed to make a twenty-four-year-old provincial president of the Federation of Students.[34] However unusual the circumstances that had brought about his election, Haya now felt he had received a call to embark upon a mission of destroying "the viceroyalties of the spirit."[35] In short, he saw his goal as the destruction of his country's bastions of cultural imperialism.

As federation president, Víctor Raúl helped cement the student ties with organized labor that had originated in the general strike.[36] And he campaigned indefatigably for the convoking of a special National Congress of Students in Cuzco.[37] Although most San Marcos students remained indifferent or hostile to the Cuzco congress, dismissing it as a tourist outing,[38] a small number of representatives from the four national universities turned up when sessions convened in March 1920. As his last official act in his expiring term as federation president, Víctor Raúl presided over many of the sessions and also delivered an impassioned harangue against a motion proclaiming student endorsement of "private property and social order." Notwithstanding his efforts, the motion carried by a vote of twenty-three to twenty-two.[39] In the endeavor closest to his heart at the Cuzco conference, however, Haya prevailed, for the congress voted in favor of having university students establish worker or "popular" universities.[40] Based on the concept that young and idealistic students should form a permanent alliance with manual laborers to awaken the social awareness of the "popular classes," the worker universities would shortly be named in honor of Peru's renowned socialist and anarchist precursor, Manuel González Prada—for whom Haya de la Torre had briefly worked in Lima's National Library.[41]

To some degree at least, the popular university concept in Peru grew out of the idealization of the workers by middle- and upper-class youth that characterized most radical movements in the early twentieth century. Glorification of the working poor, which also figured prominently in the Social Gospel movement in the United States, reflected the universal objective of regeneration ideology to turn the existing order on its head. More specifically, Peru's popular universities may be seen as intellectually linked to similar institutions sired by the Free Institution of Instruction (Institución Libre de Enseñanza), founded in Spain in 1876 by Francisco Giner de los Ríos, a man venerated in reform-minded anticlerical circles throughout the Spanish-speaking world. With the institution's spirit of non-Marxian socialism reform in mind, Haya in 1920 hailed "the ample and effective spiritual unity of the peoples of the Columbian continent with the glorious Spain that lives in our blood."[42] Thus, although implacably opposed to the spirit of conservative, clerical Hispanism, Haya could respond—but only for a brief moment in 1920, as it turned out—to a regenerationist vision of solidarity among spiritually enlightened Spanish-speaking peoples of the Old and New Worlds.

Instrumental in founding Peru's González Prada popular universities in 1921, Haya de la Torre served as their rector from then until his exile two years later. The most significant practical consequence of this experience was the forging of working-class ties that would stand Haya in good stead throughout a long career in politics.[43] In a way, though, the symbolic importance was even greater. Be descending into the very bowels of national reality, the sun people of superior consciousness were bringing about the sort of sacred marriage of opposites that would produce a new race as its progeny. While I cannot pretend to know exactly what Haya meant when he referred to the popular universities as a "Zarathustra-like daughter [of the reformed national universities]" that would in turn "conquer its own mother," some element of regeneration lurked in his opaque prose.[44]

Considerably clearer in his use of regeneration mythology (at least in this instance), Haya's Trujillo companion Antenor Orrego hailed the popular universities as representing the descent of intellectuals, Orpheus-like, into what Miguel de Unamuno termed intrahistory *(infrahistoria)*: the level beneath political consciousness inhabited by marginal elements who remained virtually invisible to observers of their society. As students, who were "the most generous, the most sacrificing, the most perceptive, and the most enlightened" of their society, penetrated into the masses, they would initiate the task of bringing salvation to their people. Setting free the spark that inhered in intrahistory was, Orrego believed, a step that had to be taken *before* Latin Americans embarked upon the task of making their countries learned and wise. Only students, Orrego affirmed, because they alone understood how to create out of primordial chaos,[45] could undertake this task of liberation.

A cynic might look upon the popular universities as representing little more than the attempt of self-proclaimed intellectual-spiritual elites to liberate the masses from the domination of alleged cultural barbarians in order that the elites could then establish their hegemony. And a cynic would not be entirely wrong to apply this analysis to Haya de la Torre, Orrego, and other Peruvians who acclaimed the prospects of the popular universities. Nevertheless, those who disregard altogether the presence of regenerationist, millenarian hopes in the popular university movement simply fail to appreciate the full intensity of the extrarational visions that dazzled many a Peruvian in the 1920s. In the final analysis, though, it is simply impossible to determine exactly just how much motivation originated from these visions and how much the visions served as a rationalization for the urge to dominate.

Whatever the mix of inducements that inspired them, the popular universities helped bring about in Peru the same sort of powerful turning point that appeared in Russia, Italy, Spain, and other countries on the periphery of modernity when intellectuals and students came together with the urban laboring classes. In all instances, "the great divide between intellectual and workers was bridged in rituals that had some of the qualities of baptism into a new life."[46]

Subsidized by student federation funds, Haya undertook in 1922 a tour of Argentina, Uruguay, and Chile, exchanging ideas in each country with other university leaders. In Argentina he was received by the mystical and extremely shrewd president of the republic, Hipólito Yrigoyen, whose Radical Party was closely affiliated with the university reform movement. Haya developed a strong admiration for Yrigoyen. And, in Buenos Aires, he formed a fast and what was to prove an enduring friendship with Gabriel del Mazo. Perhaps the leading spokesman for the visionary, regenerationist component of Argentina's radicalism and university reform, Mazo, like Haya, seemed to have come to his millenarian ideas in part by way of a lost-community mythology. In reminiscences that bear striking similarity to Haya's nostalgic recollections of the manorial, aristocratic style of life in Trujillo, Mazo lamented that the intrusion of capitalism had disrupted an idyllic existence. In the households of the well-to-do in and around Buenos Aires in a bygone era, patriarchs had presided through "tenderness" over extended clans that spanned a range from close relatives to Negro servants. A community of the mighty and the humble had prevailed, resting upon the foundation of paternalism.[47] In short, life had once been whole and connected. Haya and Mazo were kindred souls in turning to the university as the source of a new community, one that would eventually spread beyond the classrooms to take in whole nations and clusters of nations.

While in Chile, Haya visited with Arturo Alessandri, chosen president in 1920 in a bitterly contested election. Insistent, at least verbally, on sweeping social and economic reforms, Alessandri found accord with Haya in opposition to the then-prevailing war spirit that threatened to plunge their respective countries into combat over the Tacna-Arica boundary dispute that had festered since the end of the War of the Pacific in 1883. Through the years, many Peruvian chauvinists found in Haya's 1922 stance the first indication of an allegedly dangerous internationalism that led him to disregard national interests.

Even as he was building a labor constituency in Peru and establishing contacts abroad, Haya de la Torre was incurring the enmity of many fellow students at San Marcos who bitterly resented the consequences of the politicization of the university. A witness to some of the early fruits of university reform, Jorge Basadre—who went on to become the finest historian his country has produced—provides a graphic account of the disruption of classes, the constant rallies, meetings, manifestations, and public acts to which some students devoted nearly all their time, with the exception of those in the school of medicine. It seemed that the more authorities acceded to student demands, the more politicized the students became. Instead of concerning themselves with improving standards of study so that the university might produce better-qualified professionals, the students turned, under the delusion of "the omniscience of youth," to political issues and sought to purge the university of all conservative professors, regardless of their competence. To make sure they had their way, they resorted to "Mafia tactics." Controlled and manipulated by students who wanted not so much to study as to hasten the day when they might wield power in national government, university reform provided above all—according to Basadre—a rationalization for those who chose not to be serious about their studies. From this time on, no one flunked out of San Marcos who did not want to.[48]

As the university took on the characteristics of a political zoo, many students turned bitterly against Haya de la Torre.[49] Enrolled in one anti-Hayista group was Pedro Ugarteche, who in a 1971 interview with Stein expressed sentiments quite widespread among San Marcos students at the beginning of the 1920s: "Haya had become a kind of professional politician within the university.... He remained a first-year student. He did not study. For him the idea was to make himself known, to make himself known in proletarian and student circles.... Therefore, all of this awakened a certain resentment, a certain hatred toward Haya de la Torre."[50] Many of those who came to resent and dislike Haya during their time at San Marcos never abandoned their distaste for the extroverted, self-advertising student-politico. By the same token, many who had been attracted to Haya and who apparently believed that diligent pursuit of professional competence made no sense before the apocalyptic creation of a new society remained faithful followers for years to come.[51]

The attempt to remold the university by powers of enthusiasm and consciousness, in the conviction that (as China's May Fourth movement contended) "a change of basic ideas qua ideas was the most fundamental change" out of which all other changes would flow, left the university a disaster area. Although it could not be known at the time, the results of university reform provided a revealing harbinger of the effect on overall national development that would accrue from frenzied efforts to think, to will, to dream, to imagine a new world into being through the politics of the miraculous.

Meantime, to relieve the poverty and even hunger that he claimed had become his lot after the term as federation president ended in 1920,[52] Haya had taken employment as a teacher in the Colegio Anglo Peruano de Lima. A boys' school, the Colegio was supported by the Scotch Presbyterian Mission and run by its founder, John A. Mackay. To the young Haya this Presbyterian minister, destined for a distinguished career as president of the Princeton Theological Seminary,[53] soon became a warm friend and counselor. Under his influence, Haya began to read the Bible and thus to familiarize himself with one of the greatest sources in all literature of regeneration myth and symbol. To judge from some of his future rhetoric, Haya took particularly to heart the Book of Revelation. Under Mackay's influence, moreover, Haya began to look upon Christ as a revolutionary and to see in religion a means for basically altering the world. Here was a sharp contrast indeed to the traditional Catholicism of Peru that depicted Christ as a model of suffering and resignation and that preached, among the poor at least, the virtue of the fatalistic acceptance of poverty and adversity on this earth as a means of guaranteeing eternal happiness in the next world.

The view of religion that Mackay brought to Haya was, of course, one that had become commonplace in late nineteenth century Europe as part of the reaction against positivism; and about the time Haya met Mackay a similar view had surfaced in the United States as part of the Social Gospel movement. But, it was a new concept to Haya de la Torre, and he enthused over Mackay's contention that at times the principal task of the educator was "to attack everything in society that seems responsible for the suffering and backwardness of men."[54] However, Mackay most decidedly did not advocate social revolution. Instead, he urged the inward revolution that came from redemption. Out of the inward redemption would issue, later, the transformation of the outer world. Men must seek greater perfection and austerity of life to put themselves in touch with the spirit of God. Thereby the will of God, who did not want men to suffer and would end their sorrows if they put aside the ways of the devil, would be realized, and the world of suffering would give way to one of rejoicing. Once he put himself in touch with the divine spirit, beginning by reading the Bible, man would undergo transformation; his life, according to Mackay, would begin to "give out music as sweet and harmonious as the legendary music of the spheres."[55]

Through Mackay, Haya acquired a new perspective on religion and a

renewed conviction that it was possible to change the world through recourse to supernatural power. When Haya came a few years later to
shape a political movement that he and his followers actually saw as a religion, he would not forget what he had learned from his employer and
confidant at the Colegio Anglo Peruano. Meanwhile, in 1923, Haya's
new religious views resulted in his issuing a challenge to the traditional
uses of religion in Peru, as currently abetted by President Leguía.

Hoping to cement his ties with the Catholic Church and avail himself
more effectively of its powers, whether real or imagined, to pacify the
masses through otherworldly expectations, Leguía resolved, with the
approval of Lima's Archbishop Emilio Lissón, to consecrate the republic
of Peru to the Sacred Heart of Jesus. Soon rumors began to circulate that
this act, scheduled for May, would be followed by a concordat with the
Vatican ending religious toleration and facilitating an influx of foreign
clergy, particularly from the United States.[56] Already the archbishop was
perceived in some circles as having sold out to the United States. According to various critics, he made more trips to New York than to Rome.
Critics also railed against the prelate for contracting with a Yankee firm
to administer the church's property holdings.[57] Whatever the truth of
these allegations, Haya held the archbishop in low esteem and had even
clashed openly with him.

Unexpectedly one day Lissón, who had taught Haya natural history
and geography at the University of Trujillo, appeared as the young rector
of the González Prada popular universities began a discourse to workers.
Following Haya's talk, the archbishop asked for and was granted permission to add a few words. After his remarks, there ensued a lengthy debate over whether the Christian faith demanded suffering and humility
in this life in preparation for rewards in the next, as Lissón insisted, or
whether, as Haya contended, its message was that people should redeem
themselves from ignorance to be better able to attain social justice on
their own initiative.[58]

From this time on, Haya de la Torre, undoubtedly encouraged by
Mackay as well as by his anarchist connections in the labor movement
and perhaps also by Freemasonry lodges[59] and certainly egged on by a variety of Leguía's political foes, mobilized students and labor groups to
demonstrate against the proposed dedication to the Sacred Heart. An
estimated twenty thousand turned out on May 23, 1923, to vent their dis-
pleasure with the upcoming consecration and also to manifest their gen-

eral opposition to the president, the archbishop, clericalism, and the close traditional bonds between church and state. If his own accounts and those of his admirers are to be trusted, Haya assumed the most conspicuous role on this occasion. Despite police harassment that resulted in the death of one worker and one student—thus uniting in blood the manual and the intellectual worker, the soil and the sun—Haya delivered a notable address from the cathedral steps and another in the Lima cemetery. Two days later, with Haya in hiding in Mackay's home and a general strike in effect to protest the two deaths, the archbishop announced cancellation of plans for the consecration.[60]

Scarcely a literate Peruvian was now unaware of a man who a few years ago had been only a Trujillo bohemian. Haya de la Torre's friends and admirers, and also his enemies, now swelled in number. For the moment the enemies had the upper hand, for they included the president of the republic. Earlier, Leguía had tried and failed to co-opt Haya by offering him government employment. Now, he resolved to exile the rebel. Before his enforced departure, Haya issued a dramatic "I shall return" proclamation: "I do not know what will happen to me, and I am not interested in thinking about it. . . . If I have to go into exile, some day I shall return. I shall return in my own time, when the hour of the great transformation has arrived."[61]

Expelled from his native land, the twenty-eight-year-old "student" proceeded by ship toward Cuba, stopping first at Panama. There, among the persons he met was Dr. Harmodio Arias. "Listening to Haya de la Torre," Arias reported, "it seems to me at times that he's a demagogue; but later, seeing him so sincere and convinced, I am filled with uncertainty."[62] Throughout his life, Haya would create similar uncertainty among a great number of people, including the present writer.

Arriving in Cuba in November 1923 Haya de la Torre, as a fervent apostle of university reform and fearless foe of reactionary archbishops and dictators, received a warm welcome in leftist quarters. Even more appealing to many Cuban radicals, outraged by the Yankee presence on their island, was Haya's anti-imperialist stance: "I have been exiled," he announced on arrival, "by the government of Leguía, which is an agency of Yankee imperialism, to which it is selling all the riches of Peru."[63]

Haya remained only briefly in Cuba before proceeding on to Mexico, where before long he was employed by the minister of education, José

Vasconcelos, a pensador with dreams of a new humanity that he chris- tened the "cosmic race." Indeed, millenarian dreamers abounded at the time in Mexico, still caught up in the starry-eyed frenzy that had con- tributed to the Revolution of 1910. In Mexico on May 7, 1924, before an assembly of the National Federation of Students, Haya announced the founding of a continentwide movement of political redemption, the Alianza Popular Revolucionaria Americana, or APRA. Its goal was to spread throughout the countries to the south the regeneration move- ment that Mexicans, through their revolution, had inaugurated. Before the assembled student leaders, Haya unfurled the APRA flag; "the flag of a new Hispano-American generation." The banner was red, and in its center was a golden map of Latin, or, as Haya now preferred to call it, Indo-America. The red field, he explained, "represents the palpitating aspirations for justice which in this admirable hour of the world inflame the consciousness of the people; red reminds us also of love, united to justice. On the wide field, the depiction in gold of the Indo-American nations indicates the vast lands which, united and strong, salute the fu- ture home, without inequalities, of all the children of the human race." Haya concluded by asking the Mexican students to accept the APRA flag because "you are the youth of the people who most gallantly have defended the liberty of the race; because from your own blood has surged the example of a new egalitarian society that now advances."[64]

Why the insistence by the founder of APRA on Indo, rather than Latin, America? In his native Peru Haya had been caught up in the cause of Indianism *(indigenismo)*, or glorification of the Indian. And, in revo- lutionary Mexico, far more than in Peru, Indianism was well on the way to becoming an official cult. In stressing the Indian above the Latin ori- gins of Spanish- and Portuguese-speaking America, Haya manifested his agreement with the widespread conviction that Europe, especially Latin Europe, was in decline. For Haya, Latin America was, in fact, dying; but regeneration was already at hand in Indo-America.

By insisting on the Indo-American denomination, Haya also indi- cated his total repudiation of Hispanism (whether of the conservative, clerical stripe or the liberal, regenerationist variety), with its claims on Spain's parental right to exercise cultural and spiritual leadership over the former colonies. Because Spain purportedly had created the ser of all those in the New World who spoke her tongue, Hispanists insisted that the lands to the south of the Rio Grande, including even Portuguese-speaking Brazil, be called Hispanic America. In rejecting Hispanists on the name issue Haya was, in effect, reasserting his own personal break with parental authority.

In many ways Haya's personal drama reflected one in which much of upper- and middle-sector Peru was involved. As an older generation reacted against positivism by returning to the Catholic faith with its promise to buttress an idealized ancien régime, the children of that generation repudiated the positivist spirit by discarding the traditional religious establishment and turning to new beliefs that supposedly derived in part from the indigenous cultures that had flourished before Spain had established parental tutelage.

Through his preference for the name Indo-America Haya (as the following chapter shows) revealed the conviction that his America could find redemption only by returning to the authenticity of its Indian "rhythm." His association of the Indian with redemption was by no means unique for this period. At about the same time the North American writer and mystic Mary Austin voiced a feeling in which many of her country's alienated intellectuals concurred. The United States, she maintained, had become alienated from the "American rhythm" because of the excesses of its modern, materialistic, capitalist culture. On the other hand the Indian, by remaining close to the land, maintained the perfect life rhythm. From the Indian would come guidance for restoring the authentic American rhythm.[65]

Four

Opposition to Modernity (II): Indianism, Marxism, and Regeneration Mythology

Indianism and Regeneration Mythology

Like university reform, Indianism in Latin America was a movement of reaction against positivist materialism and capitalism, resting on millenarian hopes of a new society.[1] Indianism had other aspects as well. Some, for example, professed an interest in the natives only because of the hope that they could be uplifted, Westernized, and turned into consumers of manufactured goods. But, to youth in rebellion against modernity, it was more likely to be the mystical element of Indianism that appealed. Just as Europeans, lamenting the decadence of their societies and longing for a new awakening, looked with fascination toward the Orient,[2] so Peruvians and Latin Americans in general looked toward Indians. What Goethe had once written about the Orient, a youthful generation of Latin Americans was coming to feel about Indians: "There in purity and righteousness will I go back to the profound origins of the human race."[3] For Europeans regarding the East and for Indianists contemplating Indians, there was "an almost phallic rivalry"[4] over who should lead the procession back to origins and awaken slumbering femininity.

There are, it has been suggested, two great myths to which humans respond. One of these is the myth of the long march, which posits the steady, gradual, linear advance through which men and women achieve progress as they come more and more to dominate nature. The progress associated with this myth may be seen not only in terms of gaining mastery over the outer world but over the inward domain of nature as well. In its inward connotation it represents the steady expansion of the world of consciousness and the accompanying diminution of the realm of unconsciousness or darkness. In Freudian terms, it can be described as the progressive mastery of superego and ego over the instinctual drives of the id.

The second myth is that of the lost community.[5] It suggests a circular, rather than a linear, view of human existence and might just as well be designated the myth of the eternal return. According to the basic tenets of circular mythology, humans originated in a community of wholeness but are doomed to depart and thus to suffer alienation. Renewal can be accomplished only through a return to nature—both to nature within and to a mythical, stereotyped people of nature living someplace in the outside world who are still complete and not severed or uprooted from the great primordial earth mother.[6] Thus renewal has a psychic and a social component. Psychically, it is accomplished by returning, through dreams, meditation, introspection, fantasy, and vision quests, to the unconscious, the great womb whence sprang consciousness. Socially, renewal is accomplished by returning to natural people of the earth—a process associated with Anteus mythology.

Out of the opposing tenets of two great myths emerges the terrible ambivalence associated with the great mother archetype.[7] As the starting point, the womb from which we set out, the great mother can have a fearsome, threatening, devouring, enveloping, suffocating aspect for those who subscribe to the long march myth: to succumb to her would be to end progress and surrender to nature. The great mother can also have an inviting, kindly, nourishing demeanor as she beckons us to her to be recreated. This is how she is perceived by believers in lost community mythology.

Modernity, positivism, capitalism, and the whole rational-technological approach to life rest, of course, on the long march myth: they demand the increasing subjection of nature, whether within us or in the outer world, to the "iron cages" of civilization.[8] In moments when psychic sublimation and stringent superego controls result in personality formation that we find endurable and conducive to personal progress, we feel we are on the right track and try to stifle any back-to-nature, back-to-mother temptations. Similarly, when increasing technological domination over and exploitation of nature seem to result in steady progress for society, nature is perceived as having no rights of her own and as representing only wild forces to be enslaved and raped by the forces of technological calculation. At such times, people remaining close to nature must, it is assumed, be uplifted, kept safely under control, or exterminated. In psychic and social moments when all seems well with the functioning of the long march myth, nature, whether associated with the id or with "id people" living in the outer world, is depicted in pejorative terms. It seems not to matter that often the terms are wildly contradictory: inconstant, unreliable, devious, subrational, intuitive, lascivious, libidinous, yielding, effeminate, passive, innocent, indolent, ferocious, savage, rebellious, stubborn, intractible, inflexible, and the like.

In times when the myth of linear progress seems credible, individuality becomes an end-all, be-all; people resolve to be masterless. Even the word community is apt to assume pejorative connotations: for community entails surrender of individual to common interests. Accordingly, "primitives" living in a tribal or communal ambience are dismissed as refractory to civilization. In the realm of psychic values, the individuality of ego consciousness is exalted above the collectivity of the unconscious; the first must dominate the second. To be modern, humans must advance steadily toward autonomy, both social and psychic.

Inevitably, though, times come when the linear progress needed to legitimize the long march myth encounters difficulties, slows down, stops, or even reverses itself. Or, and this is just as important, times come when progress is perceived by some people in the society to be slowing down, stopping, or reversing itself—for them. And it is now that millenarian, regeneration movements are likely to appear, based on lost community myths. When people feel threatened and when a romanticized old way of life seems doomed, they long for rebirth by a return to nature that is now shorn of its threatening aspects. Whether within themselves, in the unconscious, or in the outer world, in the form of natural people, the great mother begins to beckon. There now arises a desire to recapture those halcyon days of innocence when there was no contention, but instead community, between consciousness and the unconscious, between civilization and nature.

All of this has a good deal to do not only with the rise of Indianism in Peru among a group of thinkers for whom the long march myth had gone sour, but also with the appearance of primitivism as an essential ingredient among European questers after lost utopias.⁹ Since at least the middle ages, with the frequently surfacing mystique of the wild man, primitivism and millenarianism have tended to go hand-in-hand. The "facts" that primitives knew intuitively, not by rational processes of thought; that they enjoyed a community—rather than an adversary relationship—both among themselves and with nature; that they could be depicted in terms of sheer energy and raw vitality; that they believed in sharing rather than capitalist-style competition—all of these "facts" rendered primitivism well-nigh essential to Europe's turn-of-the-century avant-garde intellectuals and artists. The same "facts" led to the cult of the Indian among those Latin American thinkers who grasped at regeneration mythology. For them Indians ceased to be a projection of the Freudian id and became instead a projection of the Jungian anima, promising to redeem and fulfill modern man by joining to his overdeveloped capacities for calculation and becoming the mystical, "feminine" ways of understanding intuitively and of enjoying the tranquil repose of being.¹⁰

In Fellini's movie *La Dolce Vita*, one of the characters observes, "We really have a great deal to learn from these magnificent Oriental women, because, you see, they have kept close to nature." Another character declares his admiration for someone who "still has the freshness of a child." In Peru, and indeed virtually throughout the world, the stereotyped Indian was like those magnificent Oriental women, "close to nature." The prototype Indian has been described in these terms: "When the Indian speaks of nature, it is like one of the elements speaking of another element. The Indian lived in nature so long that he became part of it."¹¹ The stereotyped Indian was also childlike. For the positivists intent upon the spread of capitalist modernity, these were negative qualities. But, for those wishing to escape the burdens of modernity and to find in uncontaminated sources the opportunity to start life anew, the stereotyped Indian qualities held forth the promise of regeneration.

Peru's preeminent Marxist Indianist, José Carlos Mariátegui, may well have been more influenced by the myth of the lost community than by the Marxist myth—Marx himself, of course, appreciated the influence of the first, observing once that when men are about to make a revolution they fortify themselves by acting as though they are restoring a vanished past.¹² Mariátegui, it has been said, believed profoundly that the Indian, because of his contact with the earth and "his consonance both

56

practical and mystic with the Nature whence man must draw his food and the metal of his machines," constituted the essential ingredient "without which no revolution could survive in American soil."[13]

The stereotyped "natural preference" of the Indian for communalist existence also rendered him useful to those in rebellion against the consequences of capitalism in Peru.[14] Thus antipositivist Peruvians fell into line with the fashionable theories of the 1920s associated with Lucien Lévy-Bruhl. According to him, primitive nature was antithetical to individualism.[15] In Peru, the glorification of Indian peasants because of their purported freedom from acquisitiveness can be traced back to millennialist sixteenth-century Spanish missionaries. In the alleged natural antipathy of Indians for anything having to do with the capitalist way of life, we are back once again to some of the stereotyped qualities that Orientals share with Indians. Gaius Glenn Atkins writes; "The East at its best has been strong in a type of life wanting in the West; the East has been rich in patience and gentleness and in consideration for every kind of life, even the ant in the dust or the beast in the jungle. . . . It has had little of the hard driving quality of the West. Not a little of the teaching of Jesus fits in better with the temper and devotion of the Orient than the competitive materialism of the Occident."[16] Often, the same contrast is made between Africa and the West. Indeed, the white skin seems to have become associated with capitalism; the black, the yellow, and the red with the collectivist, integral, organic way of life. Understandably, then, the Indian became for Peru's regenerationists the symbol of their defiance of the capitalist West.

Except for a few genuine extremists among them, Peru's Indianists did not urge a reversion of Peru's coastal, modernized culture to the lifestyle of the sierra's Indian *comunidades*. What they had in mind, apparently, was a merging of modern with premodern cultures. The exact details of this merger were never spelled out, and it existed more as a vague myth and symbol than as a concrete blueprint for action. The underlying hope was that somehow coastal culture could penetrate into the sierra. The first would in consequence undergo attenuation of its striving, aggressive, individualistic, "masculine" lust to dominate, while the second would awaken to some degree from its quiescent, submissive, collectivist, "feminine" traits. In the envisioned fusion, however, neither element would altogether abandon its distinguishing qualities.

All great myths, of course, are vague and ambiguous. Precisely because of this they exercise an enduring fascination. And the Indianist myth of the natural person who constitutes a worthy element in a process of *mestizaje* that blends two diverse cultures in some unspecified way has appealed to Peruvians, off and on, through the ages—beginning, most notably, with Garcilaso de la Vega, called "el Inca" to distinguish him from the identically named Spanish poet and soldier of the sixteenth century. At the turn of the seventeenth century, Garcilaso, who with his aristocratic Spanish father and royal-blooded Inca mother emerged as the preeminent symbol of the Peruvian mestizo, idealized the Indian background. This was his first step in positing the eventual emergence of a new and exalted mestizo race. A similar vision of the ideal fusing of opposites fired the imagination of Haya de la Torre, who within a short span of time in 1917 read twice Garcilaso's lengthy *Royal Commentaries*.[17]

As already noted, Haya came initially to Indianist leanings during his youth in Trujillo as he admired the nearby ruins of Chan-Chan and puzzled over the physical resemblance that seemed but an outer manifestation of the spiritual community he felt with the native Peruvians. When he came to Lima, he discovered an intellectual environment coming alive with a literature and a school of art that drew on Indian themes for inspiration. He discovered, also, an ambience alive with interest in archaeology and anthropology, an ambience in which increasing numbers of trained professionals were turning to the Indian past, partially because of misgivings about the modern world system.[18] Appropriately enough, though, Haya's real conversion to Indianism came not in coastal Lima but in highland Cuzco, the old Inca capital of the Empire of Tahuantinsuyo, or the Four Corners.

Departing Lima very shortly after his arrival there in 1917, Haya had made his way to Cuzco in the service of a family friend who had just been appointed to a political post in the old Inca capital. Cuzco transformed Haya, as he attests in a 1928 essay virtually unique in his oeuvre for its autobiographical frankness. Of his transforming experience Haya wrote: "I would not have felt devotion for the indigenous race, nor love for the Peruvian sierra, nor sorrow for social injustice, nor rebelliousness before the barbarity of the political system if I had not lived at close hand the life of Cuzco. Son of a *serrano*, I had not seen the sierra except for the roads that lead to Cajamarca. But in a good hour I went to Cuzco. . . . Then and only then did I understand the great problem, and I decided to make myself a soldier of the cause who would struggle for the solution." Haya now felt himself a prophet who had ascended the mountain, had his vision, and awaited only the moment of return that, as he expressed it, "has to come soon. . . ."[19]

While living in Cuzco and observing those natural people, the Indians, increasingly threatened but still relatively free from the repressions that materialistic civilization had imposed, Haya encountered circumstances conducive to plumbing his own interior natural resources. In Cuzco, Haya attests in the 1928 essay, "the new man I bear within me" first revealed himself. In a subsequent essay (written in Berlin in 1930), Haya asserted: "The subconscious Indian lives in all of us."[20] What this suggests is that Haya's Indianism was complementary to a psychic experience in which Indians came to represent his own unconscious. For Haya, Indians had become a symbol, a metaphor for the infinite potential of one's own unconscious that awaits rebirth through liberation from repression. Furthermore, when Haya declared, " The new revolution of our America will be the revolution of the Indian foundation,"[21] he was, I believe, equating the psychic with social revolution, both of which have to emanate from the foundation, from the unconscious or nonaware elements.

In an essay written in 1924,[22] Haya resorted to the same terminology deriving from Miguel de Unamuno that Antenor Orrego employed in connection with the popular universities in the preceding chapter.[23] The Indians, Haya averred, lived still on the level of intrahistory (infrahistoria): the level inhabited by the politically nonparticipating and socially unaware components of society. Unamuno, whom Haya met and admired in Paris in the mid-1920s, wrote of the need for societies to elevate intrahistory to the level of conscious participation, thereby accomplishing social regeneration. For Peru and her sister republics, in Haya's analysis, such a process seemed to mean raising the Indians' level of social consciousness so they might be included in the wholeness of a new order. Actually, though, it is difficult to know how much social action Haya had in mind. His main concern could very well have been simply with individual, psychic rebirth, to be accomplished by raising "the subconscious Indian" who "lives in all of us" to the level of awareness.

By this time, although as yet unbeknownst to Haya, Carl G. Jung had attached the name "individuation" to the process of psychic rebirth, as accomplished by making contact with the infinite resources of nature within oneself, thereby expanding consciousness not through sensory

perception and thinking but through intuition and feeling.[24] When
Haya came upon Jungian concepts through Romain Rolland and Count
Hermann Keyserling,[25] whom we shall encounter in the next chapter, he
found an explanation for some of his own vaguely defined longings.[26]

As is so often the case when non-Indians view Indians, Haya's assessment was on the level of the "cosmically mythic." He saw an Indian of
"inflated stereotypes," rather than flesh-and-blood individual Indians.[27]
In line also with the white man's customary use of Indianism, Haya's
primary concern lay with his own rebirth and that of his non-Indian social peers through the awakening of the Indian within rather than the
awakening of Indians in the outer world. As often as not the Indianist's
belief that his concern lies with awakening "real world" Indians is little
more than self-delusion. Still, self-delusion is frequently the paramount
inspirer of action, and for a time Haya in fact propounded an Indian
awakening in the external world. This he did, though, mainly while
writing in exile. Once back in Peru by 1931, his call for an uprising of
flesh-and-blood Indians became muted. But the political damage had already been done, and for many years Haya's foes accused him of advocat-
ing a social revolution with racial overtones. In the heat of politics it is
difficult to distinguish Indians inhering in the psyche from those inhab-
iting the valleys of the sierra.

In dealing with Haya de la Torre, it is not necessarily useful to distinguish inner from outer worlds. The two worlds fused with one another,
and what went on in the interior, spiritual world could actually
influence—so Haya believed—what transpired in the outer, material
world. Conceivably, then, Haya could have thought that if Peru's non-
Indians managed to achieve psychic regeneration by liberating the Indian within, then the outward, social regeneration resulting from liberation of real-life Indians would ensue, accomplished through the powers
of sympathetic magic. Preposterous though this sounds, it could have
seemed within the realm of the possible to Haya and his associates who
shared in the cresting spiritualist belief of the times that inward energies
and rhythms and states of being could exercise considerable control over
the outer world. Even if Indianists believed at best only halfway in concepts of sympathetic magic, they could nonetheless find rationalization
in these concepts for doing nothing concrete to translate their professed
Indianist faith into direct social action. Like prayer for members of conventional churches, what smacks of primitivism's sympathetic magic can

be deemed a conscionable substitute for action for a spiritualist.

Whatever the true inspiration and purposes of his Indianism, Haya de la Torre did insist, as already mentioned, that the name Indo-America be substituted for Latin America. Indians, in his view, composed the continent's basic intrahistory. Even where they had disappeared, the Indians' spiritual presence lived on, constituting a psychic bedrock, a racial collective unconscious as it were, that underlay the entire area from the Río Grande to Tierra del Fuego. "I sustain," Haya wrote, "that the force of American unity lies not in the European elements that envelop us but in the Indian elements in which we are rooted."[28]

The Indian, according to Haya, had determined the rhythm of Indo-America; and always, in his view, it was rhythm that imposed identity on an individual and a culture. In part, Indians set the Indo-American rhythm by determining the phonetic style: in Indo-America, everyone speaks or "sings" according "to the Indian phonetical rhythm."[29] Recent research in phonetics may conceivably imply that Haya's speculations are not totally devoid of plausibility, for it is being suggested nowadays that different languages are based on different rhythms, which may be to some extent innate. According to one writer, language helps shape the identity of a culture because "a culture is a rhythm." Consequently, "different cultures speak and move in different specific rhythms."[30] In any event, Indo-America's reencounter with herself, from which would come regeneration, depended upon what I think can best be described as a communal ritual of Jungian individuation. In the ritual, Peru's non-Indians would participate in a collective psychic descent (perhaps abetted by living for a time among Indians and steeping themselves in Indian lore) into their own and the continent's collective unconscious, where the authentic, identity-giving rhythms were still perceptible.

From 1917 onward, Cuzco assumed for Haya a mystical importance. He insisted on holding the student congress there in 1920, convinced that otherwise his university associates would be incapable of sharing his visions for the future of Peru. Once the students assembled in Cuzco, contact with the light and open air brought understanding to their minds, Haya wrote. "The altitude broke the germs of poison carried from the dark bedrooms of Lima. The rain cleansed the stains, the thunder and lightning washed the eyes and ears of the myopic and the deaf."

In Cuzco, "our blood, purged and active, gave all, even the most sordid, purity and happiness." Limeños in particular, Haya attested, were overwhelmed by the effects of Cuzco, and from the mountain they returned "more worthy to Lima."[31] "Out of Cuzco," Haya asserted, "will come the new world, and out of Cuzco will come the new action."[32] At another time Haya stated: "In Latin America, the mountains save us."[33] On still another occasion came the observation, "only from the Andes could come renovation."[34]

Mountains, of course, along with ziggurats play an essential role in regeneration symbolism and mythology. Nazi millenarian imagery, for example, is infused with expressions of longing to march from the abyss toward a sun-drenched summit, a "sunny peak" where true believers could live happily ever after.[35] In a study on the metaphors of utopia, Melvin J. Lasky notes how often the sacred mountain theme appears in revolutionary thought. The mountain is the peak of consciousness, the place where opposites meet. Mountains "kiss the Heaven," as Shelly put it, while Blake found "Great things are done when men and mountains meet." In the mountains, Lasky adds, men are though to "become strong, at once resolute and responsible," worthy and capable of waging redeeming revolution and national liberation.[36] The great American painter Marsden Hartley was by no means unusual when he extolled mountains as "the pure, virginal, unalienated source to which we return for regeneration: serene, standing above the strife of the plain.[37] Much of the subliminal appeal of the Mountain Man in United States lore stems from the archetypal mythology of mountains as a source of renewal.

Haya's dislike of Lima originated not just in the provincial's resentment of the seat of a centralizing government, though this certainly was a factor. Beyond this, his anti-Lima sentiments were tinged by the symbolism of his regeneration-from-the-mountain mythology. To his mind Lima was cut off from the country's true essence because, unlike Mexico City, it was not constructed on an Indian base.[38] From Lima spread the suffocating spirit of capitalism and epidemic sickness, especially tuberculosis.[39] Perhaps Haya, even as Susan Sontag in her writings on illness as metaphor, associated tuberculosis ("consumption") with capitalism.[40] This we cannot know, but it is certain that Haya often railed against the debilitating sensuality, the dissipation, decadence, and degeneration of Peru's coastal capital.[41] Haya's North American admirer Waldo Frank caught the Aprista anti-Lima spirit when he wrote that in the Peruvian capital there "is no exaltation, no surplus energy for flight into transcendental heavens."[42]

As Peru's city on a hill, Cuzco had ample symbolical claims to numinous qualities, dating back to preconquest times. Like almost all sacred cities of world mythology it was a quaternity or mandala, that classic symbol of wholeness. Into its four quarters entered four roads, comparable to the four rivers that flowed into paradise. And in its center, corresponding to the lamb in the center of the heavenly Jerusalem as depicted in the Book of Revelation, was the cosmological *axis mundi*—reminiscent also of the sacred center around which the Aztecs, Zuñis, Hopis, and ever so many other civilizations of the New and Old Worlds, including the Romans and Chinese, built their societies.

In the Incas' Cuzco, as described by Burr Cartwright Brundage, the four regions of the whole world joined at the city's corners. The rightful occupants of the city dwelt within its walls in a state of blessedness, while immediately without, assembled in an area extending some twenty-five miles beyond the walls, resided a representative sampling of persons drawn from the entire area conquered by the chosen people and deployed according to their geographic location in the larger imperial world. Thus greater Cuzco was a microcosm of the empire. Persons from the conquered areas, whether living in the area of the imperial microcosm or in the farther-removed sections of the empire, were designated *yanca ayllu*, "the worthless people."[43] Gradually, though, the chosen people thought to uplift the worthless ones. Such as least was one of the early justifying myths of Inca imperialism. And, as he assumed the role of Peruvian regenerator, Haya de la Torre laid symbolic claims to taking up anew the cause of redeeming the unenlightened ones who inhabited the plains and coast.

Significantly, Haya soon adopted the name Pachacútec as his pseudonym: the name may roughly be translated as "cataclysm." The ninth ruler of Tahuantinsuyo, Pachacútec reformed and revitalized the empire and even moved toward the adoption of a new religion—as Haya did in the 1930s. As the cataclysm who first destroyed the old to create his new order, Pachacútec stands out as supremely great among all Inca rulers. "No person in all pre-Columbian history," Brundage writes, "ever created such a large structure as he, and none so judiciously orchestrated the harmonies of both heaven and earth."[44] Haya de la Torre actually believed, according to a detractor, that he was the reincarnation of Pacha-cútec.[45] About this, one cannot be sure; but some of the writings already cited and a good deal more that we shall examine in later chapters do suggest that Haya de la Torre aspired to orchestrate the harmonies of heaven and earth, of consciousness and the unconscious, of spiritual elites and natural persons, of intellectuals and manual workers, and of capitalism and collectivism. Indeed, out of the desire to orchestrate the rhythms and harmonies of capitalism and collectivism Haya eventually developed his very personal approach to Marxism. From the very beginning, Haya came to his Marxism through the mythological and even spiritualist elements that many have professed to find in this ideology or faith.

"Soft" Marxism as Regeneration Mythology

What is true of Sigmund Freud—and I suppose of all pro-phetic figures—is eminently true of Karl Marx: what each meant to say is not so important as what he has been perceived as saying by people in search of beliefs that will make their lives more comprehensible and en-durable. It is not surprising, then, that Marxism has from the outset been seen differently by different people, according to the sort of needs they find most pressing in the quest for meaning in their lives. In partic-ular, Marxism has been perceived by some as a "hard" ideology or sci-ence, and by others as a "soft" metaphysics. Those who take the hard view see in Marxism a scientific belief system based on empirical evidence gleaned from the material world. Opposing them are those who opt for a soft version of Marxism, finding in it elements of Neoplatonism and even Gnosticism. Max Eastman, among many others, has referred to Marxism's split personality. The split arose, in his view, out of Marxism's practical, scientific realism, which is counterbalanced by a mystical He-gelianism.[46] More recently Alvin W. Gouldner has found Marxist thought to be a downright muddle, torn between its claims, on one hand, to scientific accuracy and its insistence that the economic base de-termines human response to social conditions and, on the other hand, its stress on conscious agency and voluntarism that can carry to the ex-treme of assigning causality in human affairs to an ideological, even spir-itual, superstructure.[47]

64

In the Peruvian reaction against positivism and capitalism, soft Marxism exercised the most widespread appeal. Along with Indianism, Marxism came to provide a mystical, mythological vision of regeneration. To understand the Peruvian response to and uses of Marxism, it is necessary to consider for a moment the broader context in which Marxism made its early twentieth-century impact.

Following the failure of the 1903 Dutch general strike and the 1905 revolution in Russia, "a left wing of European socialism began to emphasize the myth-making, ideological, and even religious dimension of Marxism as a belief-system capable of inspiring mass action, even if the doctrine had proven unreliable as a description of historical reality or inevitable revolution."[48] The dimensions of this approach were European-wide and, as Robert C. Williams has shown, its popularity stemmed in part from the rediscovery of the nineteenth-century philosopher and friend of Marx, Joseph Dietzgen. "Dietzgenism," like the theories of Georges Sorel, stressed the need for a myth that would appeal to the unconscious of the masses and would inspire them to act as if the myth were true.[49] By inspiring action, then, the myth could acquire truth, whether or not truth initially inhered in it. Above all, then, belief was stressed as the paramount factor in inducing individuals to act.

Belief in Marxism as an energizing myth found its way into Russia in the early twentieth century in part through Alexander A. Bogdanov. For Bogdanov, Marxism had to be understood not as a scientific description of reality, but as a myth, almost as a religion. Thus, he made Marxism accord with his conviction that "the driving forces in life were biological and psychological, not economic...."[50] About the same time in Russia, the Marxist Anatoly Lunacharsky anticipated by approximately a decade the interpretations of George Lukács and Antonio Gramsci in stressing the role of consciousness and of intellectuals in fomenting revolution.[51] Even with the Bolsheviks in power, it was some time before these concepts called forth official censure. Between 1917 and 1920 "suprematist" artists were not muzzled as they preached that the energies of the unconscious, to be unleashed by abstract art, would play the leading role in bringing a "new face to this globe" and reshaping it so thoroughly that "the sun will not recognize its satellite."[52]

In Germany, the celebrated Frankfurt school enlisted not only Georg Friedrich Hegel but Friedrich Nietzsche, Martin Heidegger, Oswald Spengler, Freud, and Jürgen Habermas in the interpretation of Marxism. In stressing the importance of visions of redemption in the midst of an unredeemed society, they tended to clothe the dialectic with the aura of religious myth. Even as the Frankfurt school flourished in Germany, André Malraux expressed the conviction of many French Marxists as he emphasized the power of the communist myth "to give creative energy to the heroic soul."[53]

The very term communism, James Billington notes,[54] was coined by a "fetishist and nocturnal streetwalker in prerevolutionary Paris, Restif de la Bretonne," whose main interest lay in spiritualism and mystical utopianism. In England, Goodwyn Barmby first popularized this term, linking it with "inventive fantasies that were bizarre even for this period of florid social theory."[55] Through his short-lived Communist Church of the early 1840s, Barmby described the struggle for communism in "apocolyptical terms."[56] Even after it acquired its Marxist structure, communism never altogether shed its spiritualist or its soft aspects. Indeed, from the moment Marxists "had admitted the Dialectic into their semimaterialist system, they had admitted an element of mysticism."[57] From that time onward, "esoteric and mystical sources have been identified as part of the intellectual background for Hegelian and Marxist thought."[58]

Central to the thought of an imposing number of early twentieth-century Western thinkers, ranging from mystics to scientists, lay an emergent "paradigm shift," leading away from the Cartesian concept of duality between matter and spirit and toward faith in the ultimate interpenetration and unity of elements deemed unconnected and unconnectable by the world of the Enlightenment. In consequence of the paradigm shift, which resulted in part from new discoveries in physics to which I shall turn shortly, many a European thinker accepted a form of Marxism that was simultaneously materialistic and nonmaterialistic. And, to Marxists caught up in the paradigm shift, any attempt to distinguish between the two kinds of reality was altogether irrelevant. From a large number of European Marxists, then, a new generation of Peruvian leftists imbibed a Marxism that was simultaneously scientific materialism and eschatological mysticism.

Next to Haya de la Torre, José Carlos Mariátegui (1894–1930), whom we have met in his guise as an Indianist, was the most important Peruvian thinker to fall under the influence of the scientific-mystical Marxism. Like Haya, Mariátegui acquired his perspectives on Marxism while in Europe in the years after World War 1—though José Carlos returned to his country in the very year that Víctor Raúl was exiled from it. Like Haya, and in manner typical of many of Latin America's most influential thinkers in the post–World War I era, Mariátegui stressed superstructure rather than base and utilized Marxism in a crusade against materialism.[59]

Increasingly in bad health after his return to Peru and forced to undergo the amputation of a leg some months before his death, Mariátegui seemed in many of his views to follow communism's party line. Capitalism, he confidently predicted, was doomed to an imminent death and there was no possibility of cooperation between Peru's incipient proletariat and its inchoate bourgeoisie.[60] Still, he fully appreciated that in Peru the proletariat had barely begun to exist, and this is one reason that he accepted the opinion of Haya de la Torre that the continent stretching below the Rio Grande should be called Indo-America. To him, Indians had for Peru the same symbolical, metaphorical significance that, within the context of the Marxist myth, the proletariat had for developed countries: the Indians were the dispossessed who must become exalted so as to bring forth a new order.[61]

Mariátegui deviated from commonly accepted communist orthodoxy—and the Comintern condemned many of his ideas in 1929—in asserting that the mystique needed to inspire Peruvians to undertake the socialist revolution would be provided not by Marxism-Leninism but rather by pride in the past accomplishments of the Inca empire. Believing that a socialist, classless society had existed in Peru before the arrival of the Spaniards, Mariátegui accepted the lost-community myth and dreamed of reanimating preconquest social structures and values. In arriving at communism, Peru would not have to pass through the intermediary stage of full-fledged captialist industrialization with the attendant formation of a mature proletariat and bourgeoisie.[62] While not in line with those of Marx and Engels at the time of their *Communist Manifesto*, these views are not altogether contrary to their later theories. Learning from the works of anthropologists such as Lewis H. Morgan, Marx and Engels became convinced that a communist *gens* had been the actual form of social organization in primitive societies. "As a result, [they] looked back—and thereby nourished their faith in the future—to something in the nature of a Golden Age of communist ownership and brotherly love."[63]

Unabashedly, Mariátegui questioned the materialistic interpretation of history advanced by many communists. At heart something of a mystic and apparently never able to discard totally the deep Catholic faith of his youth (shaped, I believe, more by popular religious beliefs than by official Church doctrine), Mariátegui insisted that communist materialism was much less materialistic than commonly assumed.[64] He argued, in fact, that communism was essentially a spiritual movement. For communists, he wrote, the force of revolution "does not lie in their science; it lies in their faith, in their passion, in their will; revolutionary movements embody a mystical, religious, spiritual force."[65] In seeking converts to his school of regenerationist socialism, he often employed arguments that were primarily spiritual and aesthetic. He praised the "prodigious impulse" to art, religion, and philosophy that would ensue from the new society, transporting "the workers to new heights. . . . The materialist who professes and religiously serves his faith can be distinguished from the idealist only by a convention of language. . . . There is a mysticism in Marxism, and those who adhere to it come very close to the spirit of the Christianity of the catacombs."[66]

By his infusion of Christian terms and ideals, Mariátegui seemed intent on harnessing religious enthusiasm to politics. He has, in fact, been seen as a precursor of the Catholic social justice movement that assumed a revolutionary stance of its own in the 1960s.[67] Undoubtedly, though, it was the mystique not of the old but of a new religion that most concerned Mariátegui, just as it did Haya de la Torre. To the degree that he drew upon old religion, Mariátegui—again like Haya—descended from the popular religious movements going back to the third-century Christian tradition that had stripped transcendence from their interpretation of the Book of Revelation, seeing in it a prophesy of a paradise on earth.[68]

The general milieu that shaped Mariátegui's soft Marxism operated also on Haya de la Torre, who had his first direct exposure to Marxism-Leninism in the Soviet Union itself. Not long after founding APRA in Mexico, Haya made his way to the United States and from there embarked by ship for the USSR, bearing credentials of Peru's anarcho-syndicalist Local Worker Federation (Federación Obrera Local). The immediate purpose of his trip was to attend the World Congress of Communist Youth being held in the Soviet Union in conjunction with the Fifth World Congress of the Third International. His travel expenses were provided by Anna Melina Graves, with whom Haya had worked at the Colegio Anglo Peruano in Lima. Miss Graves belonged to that "peculiar family of philanthropical but independent Christians, who are open to all kinds of novelties and are disposed to give their life and, what is the most difficult, their money, in the service of a cause they consider just."[69] For many years, Miss Graves continued to be a generous benefactor to Haya de la Torre.

Among those who most impressed Haya in Moscow was Leon Trotsky. In Trotsky, Haya found "a man of action, a deep thinker, and a finished artist." Here was a "good combination." All the more after hearing him address a large audience did the twenty-nine-year-old Peruvian find a model in Trotsky. "The art and technique of the orator attract me," Haya observed, as he noted in awe that all in Trotsky's audience had been "consumed by emotion."[70] Haya marveled also at the degree to which communist youths surrendered themselves and their entire personalities, without reservation, to the party. Here in Russia he found "the conscious discipline of integral cooperation toward a common objective," and he was enormously impressed.[71] Like many other foreign witnesses of the early Russian Revolution, Haya was also influenced by the promise that communism held for attaining modernization without unleashing individualistic egos. In admiring wonderment, he noted that socialism in Russia had wrought a revolutionary change in the nature of youth by suppressing egotism.

Further amazement came as Haya observed the fervor with which Russian youth served their new faith. Inspired by their vision of fashioning a new world, youth had acquired "a truly admirable revolutionary morality." The new Russian, he found, had discarded dissipation and given up drinking. The old generation might overindulge to the point of intoxication, but not youth. There was a song, Haya noted, that summed up the change: "Youth doesn't drink," went the words of one stanza, "because it has attained consciousness." Accounting for the transformation of youth, Haya believed, was the emergence of what amounted to a new form of religion.[72] Ascetic mysticism, he observed, together with liturgical rites, was appearing in new guises. Above all, belief and spiritual energy were propelling the country ahead. The Revolution sprang from spiritual impulse; "the Bolsheviks only took advantage of this and directed it." Before the revolution, a Russian graduate student told Haya, the people lacked optimism as well as discipline and direction when it came to applying their creative impetus. But the revolution had provided them with all that was previously missing. Consequently, the student claimed, the great vitality of the people and their "stupendous racial energy, have become the decisive contribution to the transformation of Europe and of the world that the Russians want to achieve." He concluded: "Our people is pure, it is strong, it is young. And it has a religious sentiment so profound that even though the icons and prayers are repressed, it lives and is channeled into community fervor."[73]

In Russia, Haya learned a great deal that would guide him later as he struggled to turn the fledgling APRA into a Peruvian-based mass movement of Indo-American regeneration. And one of the things he learned was that Marx, as Waldo Frank put it in a 1933 book, "attacks the church because he wishes to gain for his cause the impulses which move men to go to church. Marx attacks theology because he wants to channel into the social revolution the energy controlled by theology: the religious energy."[74] In moving to establish the new religion of Aprismo, Haya de la Torre would also set out to channel and control the energies of the religious spirit.

Summarizing the impressions acquired during his three months in the Soviet Union, Haya wrote, "Russia is not a paradise, where all is made and the men live as in heaven. In Russia one labors and struggles still, and even suffers; but at the same time one constructs, creates, and progresses. There is a vast and profound national enthusiasm. Especially the youth, which neither drinks nor dances and is happy, had a strong spirit, a marvelous energy and a vivid faith in the future."[75]

Clearly, Haya had been impressed; but he was not altogether swept off his feet by the Russian experience. Like his friend Mariátegui, with whom he remained in contact through an occasional letter, he resisted conforming to rigid Marxist-Leninist ideological restraints. Mariátegui had averred: "True disciples of Marx are not those pedantic professors who can only repeat his words, those incapable of adding to the doctrine but rather limited by it; the real disciples of Marx have been the revolutionaries stained with heresy."[76] This also was the approach of Haya's friend from Trujillo days, the poet César Vallejo. Although joining the Communist Party while in Europe in 1927, he praised above all else Marxism's "new spirit" and insisted that those who sought to dogmatize that spirit were the scribes and scholastics of Marxism.[77] Along with Mariátegui and Vallejo, Haya de la Torre stood with Georges Sorel in regarding Marx as a writer of "social poetry" whose doctrines were not to be taken as literal statements of historical fact. Instead, Marx's value and originality lay in his "happy intuition of the psychic needs of the proletarian movement."[78]

A sense of inflated self-importance may have contributed to Haya's definitive break with Marxism-Leninism. Aspiring to see APRA grow into an Indo-American movement that he would dominate, alone and absolutely, Haya could hardly countenance the right that international communism claimed to guide other parts of the world toward their secular redemption. But, ideological convictions contributed just as much to Haya's rejection of Marxism. The public proclamation of this rejection took place in 1927 at the Brussels Anti-Imperialist Congress. Here Haya clashed with many of his former friends and associates as he refused to join in a blanket condemnation of imperialism.[79] In part, his justification came from his thesis that imperialism was the last stage of capitalism for developed countries but the first stage of capitalism for underdeveloped countries—a stage the latter must undergo in acquiring the skills and technology necessary to produce the abundance that in a later period could be distributed equitably.[80] In the following year came a rupture between Haya and Mariátegui. In addition to doctrinal disputes, personal considerations entered into the matter. Mariátegui, for example, distrusted Haya's personal ambitions and condemned his adventurism as manifested in a far-fetched 1928–29 plot to install the APRA in power by means of a revolution against Leguía.[81]

Haya de la Torre's increasingly outspoken rejection of Marxism-Leninism,[82] even as defined loosely by many of Peru's and Latin America's soft Marxists, springs, I believe, from deep personal convictions that go beyond the quest for power and ideological considerations. His 1924 response in Moscow to an inquiry from Lenin's widow as to why he had not become a communist is revealing. Haya replied, in effect, that he identified communism with the Russian world; and by circumstances of birth his anti-imperialism belonged to the Indo-American world.[83] Haya returned to the same theme in 1928 as he referred to his mystical experience more than a decade earlier in Cuzco. Since that experience, he averred, he had felt himself a son of the sierra and thus could not lose himself "in a simplistic and foolish internationalism" that arose out of the European reality.[84]

In still other ways Haya, as the product of his continent in a particular moment of its development, found Marxism uncongenial. The generation of the university reform had virtually no knowledge of Marxism beyond the *Communist Manifesto*. But ideas of Pierre Proudhon and Bakunin were known to some degree and admired, owing to the prose-lytizing efforts of Spanish anarchists. Among university students, the tendency was to equate Marxism with dictatorship and anarchism with liberty.[85] Furthermore, virtually all university youth during the first quarter of the twentieth century fell under the influence of Arielism. Rife with Neoplatonism and Bergsonian influences, Arielism excoriated base materialism and extolled uplifting idealism. An outgrowth of a book entitled *Ariel*, written by the Uruguayan pensador José Enrique Rodó and published in the first of many editions in 1900, Arielism had flourished as an intellectuals' elitist movement in Peru during the years just preceding World War I. In manner typical of his cohort and the pre-ceding one, Haya came to Marxism from an Arielist background;[86] and he saw no reason not to combine the two approaches in his rejection of positivist modernization. In seeking to join Marxism and the Hellenistic Arielism, Haya strayed a good distance from conventional Marxism. In his attempt to make Marxist materialism just one element in a fusion of opposites he drew not only on his Arielist background but on ideas ac-quired in England. According to the English intellectual and Fabian So-cialist G. D. H. Cole, with whom Haya studied while in England during the second half of the 1920s, Marx himself had sought an amalgam of op-posites.

Cole's book *What Marx Really Meant* appeared in London in 1934. Well before this, through classroom contact, Haya had become familiar with Cole's principal thesis, and it influenced him deeply by way of rein-forcing and formalizing inchoate intellectual predispositions.[87] According to Cole, Marx, despite the stress he had attached to economic determi-nism and the scientific analysis of social problems, had never really es-caped the influence of Hegelian idealism. In consequence, he was neither purely a philosophical idealist nor purely a materialist. Instead, he merged these opposites in his world view. At the heart of Marx's per-ceptions lay, according to Cole, a belief that "in the world of men and external things, mind and matter are so interpenetrated and at one" that it is "futile to ask which counts for more."[88] Whether or not Marx be-lieved this, there is no question that Haya de la Torre placed his faith in the interpenetration of mind and matter.[89]

Ultimately, Haya came to think it impossible that Marx could really have believed what Cole attributed to him. Marx, after all, had lived at a time when Newtonian physics still held sway. He did not have the advantage of the breakthroughs in particle physics and quantum mechanics, and thus his system, despite all the overtones of Hegelian idealism, had rested on a scientific view that accepted material determinism of the sort that results when solid billiard balls act upon other solid billiard balls.[90] Only in the age of the new physics, whose discoveries Haya maintained he had incorporated into Aprista ideology, was it possible to understand that matter consisted simultaneously of waves and particles. This meant, for Haya, that there was no contradiction, in fact no true distinction, between materialism and idealism. It meant, further, that any social ideology posited on duality was bound to be basically flawed and unscientific.[91] The only ideology that could truly point the way toward the new earth and the new humans, the latter shaping the former because they understood the power of mental waves, energy, and vibrations to control the matter with which they were one in the same, was Aprismo. In effect, Haya advanced the claim, derived allegedly from science, that APRA could apply faith healing methods to social ailments.[92]

Like spiritualists and philosophical idealists through the ages, beginning with Pythagoras and Plato, Haya de la Torre seems to have rejected Aristotle's "law of the excluded middle" and subscribed instead to the belief that a thing can be two things at the same time.[93] Above all, his grounding in "esoteric wisdom" caused Haya to reject the materialist interpretation of Marxism as a totally inadequate approach to the new order.

Other considerations, both of a down-to-earth and esoteric nature, inspired Haya's rejection of Marxism. Whereas Marxism casts the proletariat in the role of redeemer,[94] Haya always reserved this role for the middle classes. These constituted the social sector he envisaged as providing the core constituency of APRA. With steadfast consistency, he insisted it was Peru's middle sectors, united in their common victimization by foreign imperialism in league with a collaborationist oligarchy,[95] that must transform their country. Part of this analysis emerges in an essay of the late 1920s:

There is a middle class, made up of artisans and peasants who own means of production, of mining and industrial workers, small capitalists, landowners, and merchants. To this class belong also the intellectual workers, the professionals, the technicians, as well as private and state employees. It is this middle group that is being pushed toward ruination by the process of imperialism.... The great foreign firms extract our wealth and then sell it outside our country. Consequently, there is no opportunity for our middle class. This, then, is the abused class that will lead the revolution.[96]

Haya's concern for the vaguely defined middle class was associated with the fact that for all his unease about capitalism, he did not wish it banished from Peru. Thus arose his insistence—voiced in the last-stage first-stage hypothesis first presented at the Anti-Imperialist Congress in Brussels—that a retarded country had to permit the development of capitalism through the agency of economic imperialism. But Peruvian middle classes, buttressed by a friendly and *dirigiste* state, had to make certain that the potential benefits of penetration by foreign capitalism were actually realized and directed toward the common good rather than to the exclusive benefit of the outsiders and their antinational Peruvian lackeys. What Haya seems to have envisaged was a relationship in which Peruvian middle classes, under the direction of those intellectual workers who had achieved highest consciousness, extracted the necessary wherewithal from foreign-dominated capitalist beachheads to enable directing elites and middle sectors alike to remain relatively uncontaminated by materialism. Thereby Indo-America would fuse high values and creaturely pursuits, as Arielism joined symbiotically with capitalism.

Tempted toward heresy by the extreme "softness" of his initial Marxist leanings, Haya passed entirely out of the fold in his solicitous regard for middle sectors. By the late 1920s, his revolutionary ideology may have issued more from fascism than from Marxism. Specific attribution of influence, however, becomes well-nigh impossible in this instance because of the congruence, increasingly conceded by scholars, of fascism and Marxism-Leninism.[97] Indeed, fascism may be seen as the right wing and communism as the left wing of the same revolt against the capitalist variety of modernity. According to the penetrating and persuasive analysis of Alan Cassels,

Socialism began and remains quintessentially anticapitalist no matter how many maximalist and minimalist programs proliferate. Similarly, fascism everywhere in Europe between the wars constituted a reaction against the dominant materialist culture; this is why all fascisms were sworn and consistent foes of both bourgeois liberalism and dialectical materialism. How this antimaterialism was expressed—

by a flight from modernity or into new forms of modernism, for example—varied according to national circumstances, but did not change the basic thrust and identity of fascism at large.[98]

Especially in its soft variety, which stresses myth more than science, Marxism-Leninism has little to distinguish it from fascism—except that fascists reject internationalism in favor of nationalism and generally are more honest about revealing their belief in the need for permanent authoritarian, even totalitarian, rule.[99]

Although he disassociated himself from fascism's glorification of violence, sought a middle ground (as we shall see in chapter 7) between internationalism and nationalism, and offered what was tantamount to "single-party democracy" rather than unvarnished totalitarianism, Haya de la Torre shared a broad common ground with fascist millenarianism. Indeed, upon his entry into the Peruvian arena at the beginning of the 1930s, his actions would on the whole confirm A. James Gregor's contention that most utopianists of the twentieth century, however much they may profess ideological indebtedness to Marxism in one variant or another, are really firmly grounded in paradigmatic fascism.[100]

In line with the practices of paradigmatic fascism, Haya would pitch his appeal to the youth of his country.[101] Assumed to be free from the materialism that had stifled high human faculties among mature people in an increasingly bourgeois setting, youth would respond, Haya believed, to the lure of the extrarational. Youth could still believe in social and economic miracles. Haya would find in his country an ideal testing ground for his conviction, for Peru's organized labor movement was youthful. In Peru, moreover, Haya would be able to take advantage of the fact that during the 1920s university enrollment had soared, largely in response to demands of the reform movement. Thus as the Great Depression began, swollen ranks of youthful manual and intellectual workers—a distinction Haya insisted on—were dismayed by their prospects in a collapsing economy. If ever youth had to believe in miracles, now was the time—either that, or abandon hope altogether.

Haya's future political success would rest on his ability to imbue his country's youth with faith in the miraculous. Through the university reform movement he had helped plant the seeds of a mass regeneration movement spearheaded by youth. And in 1931 he would return to reap the harvest. But before that, many additional experiences in Europe contributed to his intellectual formation.

Five

The Forging of a Prophet:
Europe's Impact on a Rebel in Exile

The Spiritualist Vogue in Europe

In the Europe through which Haya de la Torre moved in the second half of the 1920s, the emphasis in many intellectual circles of highest respectability was as much on the pararational and the mystical as on the rational and the empirical. Max Weber might have believed, part of the time at least, that "one could master all things by calculation and empirical observation," safely ignoring the "mysterious incalculable forces that come into play."[1] In many ways, though, Graham Wallas in England provided a better indication of the European mindset as he stressed in his best-known book, *Human Nature*, published in 1908, the enduring importance of the nonrational in human affairs.[2] Whichever approach was uppermost at a particular moment or in a particular country, European intellectual life in the early twentieth century inherited the previous century's "furious struggle between rationalistic 'enlightenment' and mysticism...."[3] It inherited also, as part of the antipositivist purview, an interest in the esoteric extending from hypnotism, telepathy, communication with the dead, and levitation to the most ambitious, world-encompassing schemes for asserting the mastery of mental or psychic forces over matter.[4]

Writing in England in 1925, anthropologist Bronislaw Malinowski noted that interest in magic and "esoteric truth" was reaching epidemic proportions.[5] Given the perplexities and frustrations of the period, what Malinowski observed was scarcely cause for surprise, for when people become disillusioned with ordinary means to achieve what they covet and as society undergoes changes that render old processes ineffective and irrelevant, they turn to the unconventional, the bizarre, and the occult. This phenomenon has surfaced anew in every era perceived as one of profound change. When what passes for science ceases to yield the fruits people have come to expect of it, they turn to magic. They turn to magic also, and to the most primitive forms of religion, upon discovering that in consequence of transformations underway they have lost all sense of inner assurance.[6] Hungering after this inner assurance and persuaded that it must have existed in some previous age, they become unusually susceptible to gurus' claims of having rediscovered the gnosis, that secret knowledge that was the "universally diffused religion of the ancient and prehistoric world."[7] If advanced Europeans, responding to rapid social change, perplexity, and a feeling of incompleteness sought to use the esoteric and the occult to project them into the new age of Aquarius,[8] it is scarcely surprising that the young visitor from Trujillo absorbed some of their gullibility.

During those eras that produce regeneration movements, people turn to "supernatural forces" to accomplish the transformations that will introduce a new order.[9] And, as often as not, the supernatural forces are seen to inhere within persons—in line with immanence-of-god beliefs. Extreme spiritualists or idealists like P. D. Ouspensky (1878–1947), who for many years helped spread the "wisdom system" of that remarkably influential esoteric teacher Georges I. Gurdjieff,[10] may conclude that everything that exists is within and that the outer, material world is illusory.[11] According to Ouspensky, "At some future time positivism will be defined as a system by the aid of which it was possible not to think of real things and to limit oneself to the region of the unreal and illusory."[12] Many spiritualists, however, thought in terms of using their nonmaterial, inward powers to influence, shape, and control the outer material domain that they also accepted as real.

Prometheanism, the belief that man, when fully aware of his true innate powers, "is capable of totally transforming the world in which he lives," was one of the characteristics of Russia's early twentieth-century cultural mood.[13] And Prometheanism was still evident in 1924, ready to influence the erstwhile Trujillo bohemian on his visit to the Soviet Union. Also in England, the country that along with Russia and Germany was most instrumental in shaping Haya de la Torre during what may have been his most impressionable years, spiritualism's Promethean facets were much in evidence. In the years between the two great wars, according to James Webb, "quite a lot" of Englishmen were still dominated, not by the new Oxford communist poets, but by Central European mystagogues [among them Gurdjieff] with . . . eyes cocked on the mystic East. . . . In many a Garden Suburb sitting room, beside the nature cure pamphlets and the outlines of Adlerian psychology, lay a copy of [Ouspensky's] *Tertium Organum*. . . . People were bent on awakening their higher centres, emerging from the prison of mechanicalness, being at one with the One, achieving synthesis and breathing correctly."[14] If they bothered to read that book by Ouspensky that lay in the sitting room, they learned that the *tertium organum* was to succeed, in the new order of things, Aristotle's organum and Bacon's *novum organum* and also that the third organum had really existed earlier than the first.[15] In addition, they learned that as a result of the imminent breakthrough into cosmic consciousness, in which persons would see in the fourth dimension and cast aside the illusory three-dimensional world, human beings would be as much exalted over their immediate forebears as these had been over animals.[16]

Meanwhile in Germany, the lingering effects of Romanticism[17] were combining with folklore, cults of the primitive, philosophical idealism, and various streams of esoteric wisdom to prepare the way for the millenarian hysteria that National Socialism unleashed.[18] In these years immediately before Hitler's accession, when Haya de la Torre came to know Germany, a revolutionary fervor was being whipped along by mystical impulses, proto-Romanticism, and occultism. Scientific consciousness and critical rationalism were pushed to the background. Thus wherever Haya traveled in Europe, whether to Russia, England, Germany, or for that matter Switzerland, where his natural inclinations toward spiritualism received their strongest reinforcement, he found nothing to render him apologetic about some of the far-fetched regeneration visions that he and his fellow bohemians had shared on moonlight nights amidst the Indian ruins outside Trujillo.

A cardinal objective of the pursuers of esoteric wisdom was to synthesize spiritual understanding and science into one great body of knowledge.[19] As the twentieth century began, new discoveries in science seemed to indicate that this goal was actually in sight, for the great message emerging from the "second scientific revolution" was that there very well might not be any difference between what was spiritual and what was material. Spiritualists and scientists therefore were concerned with the same reality, and as they closed in on its elusive nature the differences between their approaches would disappear. Ouspensky predicted that science would soon begin to avail itself of "positive-thinking" as it struggled to formulate a new and credible view of the world,[20] and Alfred North Whitehead foresaw a reconciliation "between a deeper religion and a more subtle science."[21]

Even as the nineteenth century ended, the certitude of science was shaken by "a massive subversion of its premises; the spread of electricity and the discoveries of radium and X rays seemed to affirm that the physical appearances of the world were only deceptive veils obscuring a fundamental realm of energies more occult than rational."[22] Commenting on these and subsequent discoveries in his 1927 book *The Analysis of Matter*, Bertrand Russell wrote, "Physics must be interpreted in a way which tends toward idealism, and perception in a way which tends toward materialism. I believe that matter is less material, and mind less mental, than is commonly supposed...."[23] Toward the conclusion of this book, Russell observed that the "stuff of the world" had more affinities with idealism than with billiard-ball concepts.[24] In the light of new discoveries in physics, he maintained, the old Cartesian duality between mind and matter had broken down.[25] Some years later Sir James Jeans, to whose works Haya de la Torre occasionally referred in his essays,[26] wrote that as a result of breakthroughs in quantum mechanics and particle physics what remained of matter was "far different from the full-blooded matter and the forbidding materialism of the Victorian scientist. His objective and material universe is proved to consist of little more than constructs of the mind. In this and in other ways, modern physics has moved in the direction of mentalism."[27]

If many "realists" were perturbed by the new findings encapsulated in Werner Heisenberg's uncertainty principle that seemed (at least to some scientists and to many science popularizers) to nullify the distinction between realism and idealism,[28] spiritualists of various types felt vindicated. All the more could they claim vindication with the emergence in the 1920s of theories that appeared to prove (again, to some scientists and to many science popularizers) that something could be itself and something else at the same time. Investigators of the subatomic realm began to assert that all was corpuscle and wave, but in such a way that what seemed to be corpuscle under one set of experiments or form of perception became wave when approached through different methods of apprehension.[29] Then, in 1928, came the quantum field theory, according to which physical reality is essentially nonsubstantial and fields alone are real. Fields, not matter, are the substance of the universe. Particles, or matter, are simply the momentary manifestations of interacting fields, which although intangible and nonsubstantial are nevertheless the only real "things" in the universe. Their interactions seem particle-like only because fields interact very abruptly and in very minute regions of space. The consequences of quantum field theory are summarized by Gary Zukav, an eloquent popularizer or "spiritualizer" of science:

"Quantum field theory" is, of course, an outrageous contradiction in terms. A quantum is an indivisible whole. It is a small piece of something, while a field is a whole area of something. A 'quantum field' is the juxtaposition of two irreconcilable concepts. In other words, it is a paradox. It defies our categorical imperative that something be either *this* or *that*, but not both. . . . Quantum theory boldly states that something can be this *and* that (a wave and a particle). It makes no sense to ask which of these is really the true description. Both of them are required for a complete understanding.[30]

Because of quantum theory, the reality of matter seemed in doubt. Matter was now being identified with energy and was consequently active rather than passive, a moving pattern of electrons. And some scientists thought of electrons as waves rather than particles. "The pattern, whether of waves or particles, had no self-contained existence but was continually changing, affected both by its own rhythmical motion and its environment, including time"—and also the very manner in which it was observed.[31] In the period between 1908 and 1925 the majority of scientists, especially physicists, had ceased to espouse materialism. They were shifting to idealism or a combination of idealism and positivism. Nature they no longer saw as matter "but as mind, organism, or else some sort of 'neutral stuff' underlying both mind and matter. This tilt toward idealism, and away from materialism or mechanism, was the philosophical revolution that accompanied the scientific revolution."[32]

With Max Planck regarding consciousness "as fundamental," and matter "as derivative from consciousness," and with Jeans inclining toward idealism because of modern scientific theories and especially the principle of indeterminacy,[33] spiritualists now had company on the outer fringes, and this provided them a mounting sense of confidence. Magic, it has been said, is stuttering science. But by the late 1920s the spiritualists were coming to believe that their "magical" approach to knowledge had actually been less stuttering than that of the scientists. In a way they felt that scientists, above all Albert Einstein, who was the physicist they most revered, had caught up with them.[34]

Predictably, spiritualists turned to the East and discovered that mystics there had anticipated the discoveries of the new physics. Reading a book by Henri Poincaré on the new discoveries of science while working on a biography of the Indian mystic Vivekananda,[35] Romain Rolland was overwhelmed by the congruence of quantum field theories and the perceptions of Vivekananda. This mystic, Rolland noted, had reached the understanding that "all the various forms of cosmic energy, such as matter, thought, force, intelligence, and so forth, are simply the manifestations of the cosmic intelligence."[36] At the heart of Rolland's theories is that ever-recurring spiritualist conviction that man the microcosm is one with the cosmic macrocosm.[37] Thus as the truly gifted mystic comes by means of his singular powers of meditation to know himself and his own inward world, he comes at the same time to understand the ways of the cosmos outside him, for the two are one and the same. As Rolland put it, "That which exists in one, exists equally in the other. The laws of the inner psychic substance are of necessity themselves those of outside reality. And if you succeed in reading one properly, the chances are that you will find the confirmation and if not, the presentiment of what you have read or will read in the other."[38]

In a 1981 review of several popular and semipopular science books, Jeremy Bernstein dismissed out-of-hand as not worth the effort "*all* books that attempt to link quantum mechanics and elementary particle physics to oriental mysticism."[39] Nevertheless, works that posit this link continue to appear, to the delight of the "inveterate believers." And in the world that shaped the beliefs of Haya de la Torre, the link was coming increasingly to be accepted as established fact. West and East, rationality and mysticism, empiricism and intuition, were seen as about to join in a marriage that would lead to a new state of consciousness through which a new humanity would find peace, harmony, and completeness in its new world. This faith contributed at least as much to the revolutionary ferment in the Western world and its periphery as Marxism. Indeed, the spiritualist and Marxist faiths intermingled in strange and unfathomable ways—as they still continue to do. Haya de la Torre's revolutionary ideology to a remarkable degree was shaped by precisely this intermingling. Having encountered his Marxism firsthand in Russia, he came almost at once to his encounter with the new science, as filtered through the prism of spiritualism, when he met Rolland in Switzerland.

Even before meeting Rolland, who would influence him more profoundly than any of the other persons he met in Europe, Haya de la Torre may have had an initial introduction to the vision of the mingling of oriental mysticism and science. While still in Mexico in 1924 Haya was initiated into the Freemasonry Lodge of "Chilam Balam" in Mérida, Yucatán.[40] Like Marxism, Masonry at this time exhibited both a "hard" and a "soft" perspective, the first stressing practical, material considerations, the second emphasizing the mystical and spiritual determinants of human existence. Symbolical Masonry stands in the soft approach, and partly under the stimulus of the new discoveries in science Symbolic Masonry underwent a resurgence in the 1920s and 1930s.

Freemasonry traces its origins to the guilds of masons engaged, among other activities, in building the great medieval cathedrals. At this time Masonry, it has been claimed, accepted the primacy of spiritual energy, influenced in this by the schools of Pythagoras and Heraclitus, according to which the material world was illusory. Medieval Masonry, however, balanced its spiritualist approach with a concern for the solid blocks of its craft. Thus it achieved an ideal union of the spiritual and the material. But in its modern, eighteenth-century guise, partly because of the materialism of Newtonian science (driven to extremes by those who came after Newton and never appreciated the great scientist's respect for the esoteric), Freemasonry had begun to slight its original idealism. Then, with the discoveries of Einstein and Planck, it became clear, at least to the Masonic author of the source I am relying on, that energy inhered in what was thought to be matter and that Freemasonry must return to its pristine conceptualizations of the world.[41] Coming into Freemasonry at the time of the resurgence of its symbolical element, resting now not just on Pythagoras and Heraclitus but on Einstein and Planck as well, Haya de la Torre may have found reinforcement for his spiritualist proclivities, and at the same time a valuable preparation for the teachings he was about to receive from Rolland.[42]

The Influence of Romain Rolland and
Count Keyserling on Haya de la Torre

Exhausted and ill after his visit to Russia, Haya entered a sanatarium in Switzerland. In this country, in 1925, he met the person destined to affect his life so enormously: Romain Rolland, eminent pacifist, popularizer of Hindu philosophy, and musicologist. As author of the celebrated mystical novel *Jean-Christophe*, structured around a theme of regeneration, he had received the Nobel Prize for literature. For some years now Rolland had seen himself as "the spokesman for India, and for Asia in general, in Europe. He could find in the East, he thought, the contemplative truths that the West had sacrificed in its search for power, and for lack of which the West was committing suicide."[43] One year before meeting Haya, Rolland completed his biography of Mohandas K. Gandhi. In Rolland's mind, Gandhi, together with mystics such as Ramakrishna and Vivekananda, were, by entering anew into the spiritual depths that lie within, finding the inspiration and strength needed to transform the other world, to raise the parts enveloped by darkness to peaks that basked in the rays of the sun.[44] Thus, the East was destined for rebirth, repeating a process that had already occurred many times before in a circling process of ascent best depicted by a spiral staircase. In India, the "divine son" was ready once again to be reborn, in consequence of the fresh encounter of mystics with the divinity within. "It is always the same Man—the Son of Man, the eternal, Our Son, Our God reborn. With each return he reveals himself a little more fully, and more enriched by the Universe."[45]

Excited by Rolland's depiction of a reawakening Orient, Haya de la Torre thrilled all the more to Rolland's subsequent prediction that Latin America in its turn was destined to achieve splendid new heights through a regeneration that would result in synthesis of the contradictory essences of Asia and Europe.[46] In the following decade this idea would be taken up by Haya's bosom companion of Trujillo days, Antenor Orrego. In *El pueblo continente* (The people-continent), a work that became in a way the Cabala or Gnostic Gospels of Aprismo, Orrego would develop and lavishly ornament this theme of the fusing of opposites.[47]

As Haya responded enthusiastically to Rolland's tutelage, the Frenchman tended, as was his wont, to go overboard in his excitement about a man who appeared to possess not only the mystical powers to undergo personal rebirth but also the charisma required to lead his people toward social redemption. In a letter of March 15, 1926, to Haya, Rolland wrote:

I see the history of humanity as a perpetual combat to elevate man from the abyss of bestiality . . . into which he will fall again without supreme effort of the muscles and of the soul of the few who push him to ascend toward the sun. And you, *child of the sun,* bear heavily, in the ascent toward it, the disdain of your people, fallen into the depths of the night. . . . This is a difficult destiny. But I know that you would not exchange it for any other. For men such as ourselves, it is a joy to carry, as Christopher, on our backs, the child of humanity, and to cross the river under its weight.[48]

Well might the adulatory words of Rolland, expressed in the 1926 letter, have put Haya in mind of Abraham Valdelomar's description of how the Incas in their time had brought regeneration to a moribund Peru. Haya, settling into Lima, had come to idolize the Indianist literary figure and journalist, and after Valdelomar's death in 1919 Haya for some years carried his cane as an amulet.[49] Relating the emperor Manco Capac's transfiguration on the day he founded the Empire of Tahuantin-suyo, Valdelomar had written shortly before his death: "Above the mountains stood a being whose body threw out rays blinding to mortal eyes. The awed and frightened people threw themselves on the ground exclaiming! The Child of the Father-Sun, the Son of Light! The son of Father-Sun has come."[50] Building unwittingly on Valdelomar's influence, Rolland reinforced Haya's messiah complex, his penchant for heady visions of a new Peru and a new Indo-America, revitalized and redeemed by a person who had attained dazzlingly new heights of consciousness by becoming one with the ineffable, with the divinity principle that lay within—and who from the peaks of higher consciousness then cast salvific rays on those below.

In yet another way Rolland played a crucial role in Haya's intellectual development by introducing the exile to the works of Count Hermann Keyserling. This fascinating combination of bon vivant and mystic, with his mongolian eyes, goatee, Falstaffian figure, and penchant for nonstop talking, had published *The Travel Diary of a Philosopher* at just about the time Haya met Rolland. Much taken by the book, Rolland cited sections of it in *The Life of Vivekananda,* the work he was writing when his friendship with Haya began. Convinced like José Ortega y Gasset—who published some of the Count's material in his *Revista de Occidente*—that the world stood on the threshold of a new era, Keyserling reflected the spiritualist influence of such giants in the revival of esoteric enlightenment as Gurdjieff and Ouspensky as well as gurus he had met in India and the Far East. At Darmstadt, Germany, he established a School of Wisdom (eventually closed by Hitler) to spread the message that "intellectually and spiritually there is only one line of advance—through increasing consciousness."[51] Keyserling's works were instrumental in immersing Haya more deeply in the cresting stream of occult learning. Like Rolland, Keyserling delighted in employing musical metaphors to describe visions of the new world and the new humanity.[52] The world suffered from tensions among opposites, but these, Keyserling believed, could be resolved through emergence of a world rhythm—a rhythm that had ostensibly prevailed at one time in the ancient past, only to gradually lose its integrating power.[53] (Perhaps we discern here the origins of some of Haya's ideas on the rhythm of Indo-America, although it is impossible to be specific in singling out the origin of ideas that are part of the general patrimony of the esoteric tradition.)

In addition to rhythm, harmony was all-important to Keyserling and his fellow spiritualists. Rhythm, after all, is a matter of vibrations, and, depending on their velocity, vibrations produce tones; the important thing is to harmonize the tones into a music of the spheres. The tension within any one nation-state, the count contended, could not be completely resolved within its confines. Rather, the nation-state had to be brought into rhythm with a larger, supranational system that transcended it. Haya de la Torre and Orrego later picked up on this idea—either directly from Keyserling or from other occult sources—as they developed the need to integrate nations into people-continents, with Indo-America constituting one of the envisioned seven—that favorite number for so many mystics.[54] Resulting from the integration of nations into seven supranational people-continents, according to the two Trujillo bohemians, would be an all-embracing harmony in which previously dissonant elements would enter into a counterpoint unison[55]—similar, no doubt, to the harmony that esoteric thinkers of bygone times had ascribed to the "seven" planets.

At the moment in which he wrote, Keyserling lamented that wherever one turned his attention he observed only one-sidedness, the absence of integration, harmony, counterpoint, and regulating, integrating rhythm. Because the world had not approximated overall rhythmic unity and the full realization of harmony and counterpoint—at least not since some mythological time of blessedness in the remote past—it had remained always short of its potential for perfectibility. But this was destined to change. The materially advanced parts of the world, with their rationality and technology, contained the life-awakening spark of tension; by penetrating the slumbering, underdeveloped parts (like the spermatozoon entering the ovum), advanced civilizations would introduce a new vitality. Thereby the ovum-like parts would undergo the revitalization of their dormant spiritual, extrarational, mystical powers. Their strengthened spiritualism would then become capable of providing balance and effective counterpoint to the declining material prowess of the Western world. That world, Keyserling believed, in line with Oswald Spengler and H. G. Wells, was in decline.[56] The melody of the awakening and ascending world would before long become as audible as the declining world's refrain, producing a harmony and counterpoint that heralded the advent of a new and more perfect order. This new order Keyserling compared to a great polyphonic orchestra.[57]

Throughout the meditations on relativity and historical space-time that Haya de la Torre began to record in 1928 (and that I analyze in the following section), he harps on rhythm and harmony, on completing space by adding its time dimension, and on conciliating opposites in the new world order that will transcend narrow national emphasis without totally obliterating national distinctions. Thereby the one and the many will fuse in harmonious wholeness. Haya's space-time theorizing, I am convinced, owes more to Keyserling and to esoteric, hermetic influences in general than to Einstein, to whom Haya liked to point as the source of his inspiration.[58] In any event, both Haya and Keyserling stand in a long line of utopianist visionaries about whose assumptions Robert Lawlor has written in the following terms:

A theory of pre-established universal harmony, knowable through the mathematical sciences, moves like a wave through the history of philosophy from its mythological foundations in Egypt and India into Pythagorean Greece, and then into Hebraic and Islamic worlds, and crests again in Christian Europe as an element of Gothic architecture and Renaissance art. With the emergence of field-force theories and de Broglie wave mechanics in contemporary physics [Louis de Broglie received the Nobel Prize for physics in 1929], together with our rapidly growing understanding of the bioelectric basis of living systems, faith in a hidden universal harmony reached a new peak of intensity.[59]

A striking manifestation of the spiritualist revival of his age, Keyserling was an influential popularizer of the new Pythagoreanism; partly through the influence of his works, Haya de la Torre found his way into the cult. Subsequently, according to one of the biographers who knew him best and admired him most, Haya devoted "considerable time" to the study of Pythagoras.[60] Isaiah Berlin contends that many German and Russian thinkers in the nineteenth century looked back to Immanuel Kant, Friedrich W. J. Schelling, and Hegel for proof that "it was possible to discern eternal beauty, peace and harmony" beneath the apparent disorder and cruelty of daily life."[61] For his proof, I believe, Haya de la Torre looked first to Rolland and Keyserling, who in turn looked to the school of Gurdjieff, Ouspensky, Eastern mystics, and, more remotely, to alchemy, the Cabala, Sufism, and Gnosticism.

Once back in Peru, Haya continued to keep abreast of Keyserling's writings, notwithstanding a well-nigh total commitment to populist politics. In the mid-1930s he found in one of the count's new books confirmation of a notion Rolland had helped plant in his mind: Latin (or Indo) America's destiny to preside over regeneration by leading the world ahead—and at the same time back—to cosmic order, to an integrating rhythm. Appearing in Spanish translation in 1931, *South American Meditations* was the Keyserling work that would become most widely known in Latin America.[62] In it, Keyserling made this prediction: "It is possible and even probable that the next rebirth of that spirit which made possible in ancient times the Greek miracle and which reappeared first in Provence, later in the Italian Renaissance and later, finally, in the French culture unhappily petrified today in intellectuality; it is possible, we repeat, that the next renaissance of that spirit will arise in South America."[63] Writing in 1938, Haya de la Torre praised *South American Meditations,* although registering reservations about some of its hypotheses; most especially did he applaud Keyserling's message that "it is possible that the next rebirth of spirit will originate in Indo-America."[64]

By the time he left Europe, Haya had come to the conclusion that not only was it possible, it was altogether likely that Indo-America, under his leadership, would point the world on its way toward its rendezvous with regeneration. By now, Haya had even begun to concoct the new metaphysics of regeneration. He called his system historical space-time, and in formulating it he turned to a great number of sources in addition to Keyserling. While it is an essential key to understanding Aprismo's visionary utopianism, historical space-time is an exceedingly obscure theory; one sometimes suspects that parts of it remained sheer verbiage to most Apristas. However that may be, Haya derived enormous pride from the theory. If it is to be made at all intelligible to a contemporary audience, it must be approached from the historical context from which it emerged. Essentially, the context was one in which mysticism and science seemed to go hand in hand, as indeed they had during the birth of modern science at the time of the Renaissance and even up to—and beyond—the age of Newton.

Historical Space-Time

From the late nineteenth century, talk of a fourth dimension had been much in vogue in avant-garde and spiritualist circles. "Hyperspace philosophy," as fourth-dimension concepts were often designated, professed that the ultimate way to defeat the evils of positivism and materialism was "for man to develop his powers of intuition in order to perceive the fourth dimension of the world, the true reality."[65] Fourth dimensionality or hyperspace goes back very possibly to Pythagoras and has appeared in various guises throughout much of recorded history. In seventeenth-century England, for example, Henry More, "the most mystical of an obscure group of philosophers known as the Cambridge Platonists," proposed the fourth dimension as the realm of Platonic ideals. It was not anything altogether new, then, when allusions to a fourth dimension began to circulate with some regularity at the turn of the twentieth century.[66]

Using as his point of departure various concepts of Hindu philosophy,[67] Ouspensky "plunged into . . . researches which linked the fourth dimension to esotericism."[68] His objective was to find a means of entering the universe beyond the material universe, and for quite some time he was convinced that the methods of Gurdjieff provided access to the desired realm. The three-dimensional world, according to Ouspensky, did not exist in reality but was merely a creation of mankind's imperfect senses: "The three-dimensional world—this is the four-dimensional world observed through the narrow slits of our senses. Therefore all magnitudes which we regard as such in the three-dimensional world are not real magnitudes, but merely artificially assumed."[69] However, there was hope of escaping the confinements imposed by three-dimensional perception, described by one mystic as "the annoying bars of a cage in which the human spirit is imprisoned."[70] By developing "cosmic consciousness," the source of the sensation of infinity, mystics could begin to live in a fourth dimension. Higher consciousness perhaps had its origin within that part of the human psyche generally referred to as the unconscious and would permit at least select souls to take up their residence in hyperspace; eventually, lesser mortals might also learn how to establish residence in this higher state that existed beyond the phenomenal world.[71]

With concepts such as these in the air, it is scarcely surprising that while in Europe Haya de la Torre would begin to think about, as he put it, a "dynamic continuum" of space-time that constituted a "historical fourth dimension."[72] Historical space-times, he speculated, may be likened to electromagnetic fields and are formed and delimited by the progressive consciousness of space and time, always inseparable, that human groups acquire.[73] Again and again in his space-time speculation, which he believed achieved a synthesis between the thought of Hegel and Einstein,[74] Haya stressed the importance of consciousness. Consciousness of space-time pertains, he insisted, to consciousness of the relationship between thought and matter, spirit and telluric influences; it is this interaction that shapes the culture of distinct historical space-time entities. Furthermore, history changes, he asserted in a passage revealing his indebtedness to Hegel, through increases in consciousness.[75] Then, by mixing in Einstein, Haya could conclude that in order to understand a society's true historical space-time meaning, its members had to take the four-dimensional view of that society. Only when they attained this "higher consciousness of their four dimensionality" would they begin to acquire the power to change their history.[76]

Into his space-time musings Haya also incorporated elements of rhythm and harmony. The Indo-American historical space-time, as was the case with all old civilizations, was moving at a slower rhythm than the United States and the advanced countries of Europe. Furthermore, in Peru and all Indo-America two rhythms coexisted at the same time:

the slow one that was indigenous to the historical space-time and the more rapid one, introduced from abroad and corresponding to the North American and European historical space-times. Because its rhythm was the slow one of great age, Indo-America was ready for regeneration. And rebirth would come about through a gear mechanism, to be constructed by the leaders of an interventionist state, that would synchronize the two rhythms. The situation as it presently existed, Haya suggested in an August 23, 1931, address presented in Lima's Plaza de Acho bull ring, was like a car on one side of which the wheels turned slowly while on the other they turned at a high velocity. Such a car would go around in circles until the two velocities were coordinated. The task of political leaders was to synthesize the two rhythms in Indo-America, thereby achieving its regeneration through the harmonious blending of disparate entities, in this case the two distinct historical space-times.[77] Obviously, only leaders whose breakthrough into higher consciousness enabled them to apprehend four-dimensional reality and perceive the degree to which it differed in distinct historical space-times could accomplish this task, although Haya modestly refrained from explicitly spelling out this conclusion.

Involved in such visionary musings are a variety of obscure, esoteric concepts. To begin with, people lacking in awareness are assumed to be people of low-velocity vibrations. Perhaps this is a projection into the outer world of the notion, alluded to by Jung, that the unconscious is a low-pitched psychic realm.[78] In any event, people who have advanced to ordinary consciousness or awareness are those who have learned to dominate nature—both the nature inside, or the unconscious, and the nature that is "out there." By the very act of dominating, however, these people of relatively high velocity vibrations completely obscure (and become alienated from) the low-pitch vibrations—both inside and outside them. These people may be seen as quintessentially modern, in contrast to the premodern lowest-velocity beings. For the moderns, hope for fulfillment and completeness lies in learning to perceive anew what had become subsonic and then to harmonize their vibrations with those of lower-pitched nature. Beyond this, social redemption or rebirth into a higher stage of human existence demanded the intervention of select, postmodern souls who had attained the highest form of consciousness, who had virtually escaped creatureliness, and whose vibrations, even as those of pure light, were the fastest of all. These beings must synchronize their highest-velocity vibrations with those earth-bound creatures whose vibrations were of the lower velocity associated with varying degrees of darkness. Out of this grand synchronization would come completion, fulfillment, and self-realization for beings of sun and earth, light and darkness. The end result would be the one great cosmic harmony, of the sort that has fascinated thinkers from Pythagoras to Johannes Kepler and on up to the most recent visionaries.

Ultimately, we are dealing here with a form of incarnation mythology in which a savior or high-spirituality person is driven toward immersion in creatureliness in order to achieve fulfillment for himself and for the beings of creatureliness. But there was much more to Haya's historical space-time theory than this. To discern more of its dimensions, it is necessary to retrace our steps, to explore additional paths by which Haya came to the theory, and then to consider some of the uses that he derived from it.

As a youth in Trujillo, Haya read *The Time Machine* by H. G. Wells.[79] Published in 1895, this imaginative work drew in part on the theories of C. H. Hinton, a mystical thinker obsessed by ideas of the fourth dimension and the simultaneous existence of different space-times—discoverable by sensitive, gifted beings whereas the commonality of humanity could grasp only the one space-time reality in which they *apparently* lived.[80] In 1922 during his visit to Argentina Haya speculated, we are told, on the political and philosophical ramifications of Einstein's relativity.[81] Then, during the time he spent in Europe, Haya fell under the influence of the great metaphysical historian Oswald Spengler, taking to heart his contention that "time and space . . . are relative to a given culture."[82] And, through his stay in Switzerland, Haya came to know the uses that Rolland and Keyserling made of Einstein's Special Relativity, the very essence of which rests "in the realization that one man's 'now' is another man's 'then'; and that 'now' itself is a subjective conception, valid only for an observer within one specific frame of reference."[83] Haya would not have needed to become directly acquainted with Einstein's relativity in order to spin out historical space-time fantasies. But he did in fact happen to meet Einstein in 1929[84] and to hear a lecture that the physicist delivered in Berlin in 1930.[85] He may in addition have dipped into one of Einstein's more approachable books published in 1929.[86] In all events, he confessed that no other person then living had "so won my humble admiration."[87] And, in linking his historical space-time theories to Einstein, Haya followed the prevailing trend among seekers of esoteric wisdom to enhance intellectual respectability by associating themselves with the father of relativity.

Before encountering Einstein, Haya had already begun to envision a new world arising out "of a degree of consciousness and a social mode of being that presently we can only intuit or suspect, a new world in which human thought will expand just like Einstein's universe." When Einstein hears such suggestions, Haya wrote (implying perhaps that he had offered them personally when the two met briefly in 1929), the genius "only smiles and remains silent. His field is physics, but he knows very well that, although many still deny it, each step toward the elucidation of the new four-dimensional concept of the universe [with time as the fourth dimension of space] is an epoch gained toward a new philosophy."[88]

By the time he returned to Peru in 1931, Haya de la Torre had already developed the main outlines of his historical space-time theory. For the rest of his life, though, he added to the theory and refined it through his readings in, among other sources, Hindu and comparative mythology, philosophy, and semipopular explanations of the new physics.[89] Often it seemed that the more he refined his theory, the more opaque and mystifying it became. The fact that the preceding description of historical space-time is often well-nigh unintelligible is not, I believe, entirely my fault. The Chilean Joaquín Edwards Bello once expressed amazement over Haya's haranguing illiterates at political meetings "in frightful gibberish" that included references to the fourth dimension and space-time, and one of Haya's Peruvian detractors contended of Haya's pet theory, "no one has yet been able to penetrate its enigmas."[90] Haya himself conceded that his historical space-time concepts seemed "Cabalistic."[91] More than being simply "Cabalistic," Haya's historical space-time theory derives from the overall esoteric tradition, with its cosmological assumptions that everything (or almost everything) has proceeded from spirit and will return to spirit and that the finite world materialized from "rhythmic planetary emanations from a pristine spiritual unity...."[92]

On one level of its use, however, Haya's theory seemed simple enough. This was the refutation of Marxism that Haya derived from historical space-time. As we have already seen, Haya contended that Marxism had developed in its own, specific historical space-time and therefore was not applicable to the reality of Indo-America.[93] By means of the theory Haya could also impart a metaphysical tone to his thesis that imperialism was the last stage for developed countries, the first stage for underdeveloped lands. Beyond this, historical space-time entered murky waters. Even in its more arcane aspects, however, historical space-time, the ostensible fusion of philosophy and science,[94] of an idealism that began with Heraclitus and a science that culminated for the moment with Einstein, exhibits a few landmark peaks to guide one through the dark waters. There is, for example, the notion that Indo-America, its rhythm established by the Indians, is on the verge of regeneration. Rather than by the total domination of an intrusive rhythm from abroad, regeneration will come through the synchronization of that rhythm with the one that is natural to, indigenous to, Indo-America. Not in catastrophic obliteration of the old rhythm, but rather in its harmonization with a different rhythm will the new era begin. In the past sixty years or so, it has become commonplace for leaders of the underdeveloped world to maintain that the destiny of their lands lies in fusing traditional life-styles with modernity. When Haya first began to make this assertion, it had some element of freshness. Had it not been for his sensitivity to esoteric thought, however, he could have made his point in nonmystical language.

Beyond the more obvious messages that Haya sought to convey through the historical space-time theory lay the prophetic assurance that consciousness would be all-important in initiating the "new era in the kingdom of thinking"[95] that in turn would lead to a new era of earthly existence. Out of this conviction came Haya's 1933 declaration: "To be an Aprista is to have the instinct and the capacity for the creation of a new spiritual and physical race, a new consciousness capable in turn of creating, only by its force, its energy,...another political, social, economic, and cultural organization in the country."[96] Finally, in historical space-time inheres the notion that the new science, comprehensible only to a small band of select persons, proves the veracity of what mystics had long ago intuited: mind and body, spirit and matter were part of one continuum. Encompassing such a variety of political thoughts and such a broad panoply of spiritualism cum science, historical space-time impressed Haya as a rich metaphysical system that constituted the exalted core of the Aprista creed.[97]

While the fact may at first seem puzzling, historical space-time exercised a broad-based appeal—despite the disparaging remarks understandably directed against it. Haya knew what he was doing in making it the ideological foundation of a mass political movement. To fellow initiates in esoteric thinking, historical space-time provided a stunning rationalization for their reactions against positivist materialism, assuring them of their destiny to will, dream, imagine, or conceptualize a new world into being—a world over which they would rule.[98] Moreover, uneducated and illiterate Peruvians, all too aware as the 1930s began of the crisis confronting them and longing for some kind of miraculous, magical deliverance to be provided by exalted beings of supernatural endowment, could respond to the archetypal myths of regeneration that reached them, subliminally at least, through the verbiage of historical space-time. Anxiety-ridden masses could be both politically and religiously reassured by listening to the high priest of historical space-time.

Although writing on other matters, Robert K. Merton provides one explanation for Haya's success in waging politics on the basis of historical space-time—even though less talented disciples made an awful mess of the theory when they attempted to utilize it. Modern science, Merton observes (in a section of a book that he heads "Esoteric Science as Popular Mysticism"), is virtually unintelligible to the layman; and popularizers generally stress the aspects of new scientific theories that are most at odds with common sense. The layman has to take preposterous things on the faith that technological achievements that will benefit him spring precisely from these bizarre theories. For the general public, science and esoteric language become connected. And this connection transfers over into politics. Thus when a politician appears who promises some sort of secular redemption in terms that are a mishmash of esoteric and scientific language, some people incline to accept the claims that the speaker indeed knows how to improve their lot. "Partly as a result of scientific advance," Merton concludes, "the population at large has become ripe for a new mysticism clothed in apparently scientific jargon."[99]

Haya de la Torre returned to Peru at a time when the populace was especially ripe for an amalgam of science, mysticism, and politics because it was living in a liminal moment,[100] a moment of obvious transition. Prodigious changes had been underway for some time, and these changes seemed the product of what the common man associated with science and technological innovation. From these changes a few had benefited inordinately, even as the well-being of the masses and certain middle sectors appeared to decline. But there was no reason why, given its awesome powers, science could not be used by one who understood its mysterious ways to benefit the "popular classes." Precisely this was the promise Haya began to articulate in 1931. In effect, he assured those disadvantaged by change of his resolve and ability to benefit them. This ability he attributed to his mastery over a science that actually seemed analogous to the miraculous powers that Peruvians had always known about through popular, and for that matter the establishment's high, religion. But, before Haya returned to Peru and began to take advantage of his people's susceptibilities, he had, while living in England and Germany, acquired still more components for his politics of the miraculous.

The English and German Influences on Haya de la Torre

Leaving Switzerland after his encounter with Rolland, Haya made his way to Italy in 1925, heard a Mussolini address, and for a brief time in Florence looked into fascist ideology.[101] Before the end of the year, though, he was in England, his passage apparently paid by Anna Melina Graves, who had financed his trip to the Soviet Union.[102] For the following two years Haya spent most of his time in England, although there were occasional trips to Paris—he established an APRA cell there in 1926—and other cities on the continent. The English intellectual and political milieu had considerable impact on Haya. For one thing, the contacts he established with Fabian circles and the Labour Party helped nourish his conviction that the way of the future lay neither with Marxism nor with capitalism, but with a vital center position that incorporated elements of each.[103] If Aprista accounts are to be believed, Haya came to know Ramsay MacDonald, George Bernard Shaw, and H. G. Wells and attended classes in economics taught by Harold Laski and G. D. H. Cole.[104] Undoubtedly he also noted the close links between Theosophism and various Fabian and Labour Party circles.[105]

While in England, Haya wrote a short essay explaining the goals of Aprismo. Appearing in the magazine of the Labour Party in 1926, it was the first published description of the APRA program, and it stressed five points: (1) action against imperialism; (2) the political and economic unity of Latin America; (3) progressive nationalization of land and industry; (4) internationalization of the Panama Canal; (5) solidarity with all oppressed classes and peoples of the world.[106] Haya's development of the first point reflected the anti-imperialist ideas of J. A. Hobson that for some time had helped shape British socialism. In treating the third point he seemed also to reflect the influence of British socialism, with its stress on gradual nationalization of the means of production, distribution, and exchange, rather than a revolutionary, one-step process.[107] The importance of the fourth point, pertaining to the Panama Canal, is developed in chapter 7. The last point may well pertain to a desire to create an international pool of properly directed mental or spiritual energies to hasten the political, social, and economic transformation of the world.

Overshadowing the other influences encountered in England was the impact of the new anthropology, whose leading spokesmen in that country at the time were the Polish-born Bronislaw Malinowski (1884–1942) at the University of London (he assumed his teaching post there in 1924), and R. R. Marett (1866–1943). With both of these eminent specialists Haya claims to have studied.[108] This is not unlikely, for anyone as vitally concerned about "primitive" societies as Haya had become through his Indianist fantasizing could scarcely have ignored the school of anthropology then emerging in England. And, even superficial acquaintance would have revealed to the Peruvian the enormous affinity between his own developing beliefs and some of the central tenets of British anthropology in the pre–World War I years.

Preceding the rise of anthropology a nineteenth-century school of folklore fostered by such giants as Andrew Lang and Edward Clodd had flourished. As a representative of the positivist approach to knowledge, Clodd had tended to sneer at Lang's late works[109] because of their alleged acceptance of a form of spiritualism that was only "the old animism writ large."[110] But it was more the shadow of Lang than of Clodd that cast itself over the proponents of the new anthropology as they challenged the rationalist assumptions of a narrowly conceived positivism. Moreover, the anthropologists championed a cultural relativism that recognized the flaws of modernity while honoring the wisdom and organicism of primitive societies. The relativism of the new school could only have been taken by Haya de la Torre to confirm space-time assumptions that the political element in a culture "is neither accidental nor transmittable as a tool is to some other time or place."[111] Here was reinforcement for Haya's conviction that neither the models of Russian communism nor those of liberal, North American capitalism were suitable guideposts toward Indo-American regeneration. Most of all, though, it was the anti-empirical, antisensationalist aspects of British anthropology that seem to have appealed to the Peruvian exile.

In replacing James Frazier as Britain's "paradigmatic anthropologist,"[112] Malinowski—who has been described as given to making "apocalypic utterances" and as exhibiting a "messianic mood"[113]—helped father the anthropology of structuralism that accepts extrarational and inward sources of meaning and cognition.[114] Even if myth and magic did not have a legitimate theistic basis (Malinowski was an agnostic), Malinowski believed they did have real and genuine psychological origins and thus could not be ignored.[115]

In the essay "Magic, Science and Religion," published in 1925 (the very year that Haya began his studies in England), Malinowski argued that for primitives "all is religion," mysticism, and magic; for primitives, indeed, "religion is coextensive with life...."[116] Moreover, the ways of primitives had applicability even to the modern world, for "crises of human existence" will continue to call forth faith and cult; religion and magic in one form or another will be resorted to as mankind attempts to make his world "manageable" and "right."[117] Whether or not Malinowski intended it, Britain's advocates of indirect rule tended to find in his theories the counsel that imperialist overseers should utilize not only the manpower but the beliefs of "backward" people in maintaining control over them.

Similar thoughts on the political utility of religion occurred to Haya de la Torre as he mused over what increasingly was beginning to emerge to him as his destiny: control over the Peruvian masses. In 1925 Haya wrote that there was still need for magic as a factor of authority in the political structure: "Social anthropology teaches us this very clearly." "Modern politics demonstrates," he added, "that the force of the magical should be renewed."[118] In 1927 he observed, "The Spanish political dominion [over the American colonies] could not have succeeded except for the magical influence of the Catholic Church...."[119] After his encounter with Rolland and the writings of Keyserling, Haya was certainly inclined to agree with the 1926 pronouncement of Alfred North Whitehead, another of the passing acquaintances in England whose name he was fond of dropping, that for modern man the traditional religions "had lost their...hold upon the world."[120] As he took up his political career in 1931 Haya would move to establish a new religious mythology through which he obviously hoped to restore magic—and with it, authority—to his Peruvian world. One wonders if he would have moved quite so boldly in that direction had it not been for the exposure to British anthropology.

From the other giant of the new anthropology, Marett, Haya also heard, and probably read, highly evocative statements. In a book published in 1935 Marett gave definitive expression to ideas adumbrated in a number of earlier publications.[121] He confirmed Malinowski's findings that primitives—many of whom resided not in the bush but in pockets within modern societies—are mystics. Unlike "the modern businessman who must have 'real values' to deal with," primitives had to be approached through mystical values.[122] Furthermore, he contended, man can affirm and will into being certain values that become for him the most real things in life, "far more real than the passive [material] conditions that must be overcome and transformed before his dreams can come true." History, what is more, was to be regarded "as the progressive triumph of spirit over matter."[123] Finally, in a passage that could almost have come from Keyserling, Marett wrote: "Difference is not incompatible with unity, but, on the contrary, a diversity of elements yields the rich harmony."[124]

To a superficial student at least—and Haya at this time was too much the restless activist to become a profound student—it might well seem that Marx, as properly understood, Rolland, Keyserling, Einstein at the head of the new physics, and Malinowski and Marett at the head of the new anthropology were all saying very much the same thing. (Haya's conviction that Marx could not have escaped the materialistic science of his day came only later; for the moment he accepted the view of Cole, another of his mentors in England, that Marx was partially an idealist or spiritualist.) Truly, a new wisdom was emerging, and by mastering it an exceptional person might derive the power to transform, at least as a start, all of Indo-America.

Although direct proof is lacking, it is tempting to believe—and altogether likely—that while in England Haya de la Torre read and was influenced by the writings of Edward Carpenter (d. 1929), a man also obsessed with the quest for a new wisdom and very akin to William Blake in his vision of the cosmos. In *The Intermediate Sex* (1908) and *Intermediate Types Among Primitive Folk* (1914), Carpenter wrote of the destiny of homosexuals to lead humanity toward a millennium on earth. According to him, homosexuals were natural mediators, destined to harmonize the differences between men and women and also between the past and the present by presiding over the birth of a new and higher stage of existence. Given the prophetic role he assigned them, Carpenter assumed the moral superiority of homosexual over nondeviant men. To substantiate his view of the future, Carpenter turned to "primitive folk" of the past, discovering among them priests and shamans who had shaped the development of their societies and who were especially suited to their roles as mediators and prophets because of their homosexuality. Carpenter's prominence within a wide circle of English socialists and Labour Party members makes very favorable the odds that his works were read by Haya, whose own likely homosexuality is discussed below in connection with his appraisal of Germany's National Socialism. Even without Carpenter, though, Haya had encountered ample sources of inspiration for the grand visions with which he returned to America in 1927.

Sailing to the United States as a member of the Oxford University debate team, Haya proceeded shortly to Mexico. There, in 1928, he completed most of the writing for his book *El antimperialismo y el APRA*. Not published until 1935, this book is Haya's defense against charges raised by the Cuban Communist Julio Antonio Mella of having abandoned the anti-imperialist cause. From Mexico Haya undertook a tour of the Central American countries, where he formed Aprista cells and urged the cause of continental unity as a means of curbing the abuses of United States imperialism.[125] According to Aprista lore, Haya was expelled from Guatemala, Nicaragua, and El Salvador because of pressure applied on the governments of those countries from Washington and Lima. Apparently while in El Salvador, Haya began to plot a *golpe* against Leguía that would bring the APRA to power. Returning to Mexico, he embarked for Panama on the German ship *Phoenicia*, planning to disembark there to transfer to a ship that would take him to Peru. But, owing once again—Haya charged—to the machinations of the United States and Peruvian governments, he was refused permission to land in Panama and had to continue on board the *Phoenicia* to Bremen. A second European exile had begun, and by the end of 1928 Haya was in Berlin. Except for occasional excursions, he remained there until embarking on the voyage that returned him to Peru, by way of London and Paris, in July of 1931.[126]

During his stay in Berlin, Haya fell under the spell of Spengler's works, in which as we have seen he found inspiration for some of his space-time theorizing. He attended and was impressed by a lecture delivered by Alfred Adler[127] and was even more impressed by an Einstein lecture. In Berlin he had the opportunity to renew his friendship with John Mackay, showing the one-time director of the boys' school in Lima his worn and copiously marked Bible and predicting that the "coming social revolution in Latin America" would have to build on "the mystical spirit of the people."[128] While in Germany Haya also pondered the significance of the rise of National Socialism, observing how the Nazis integrated into their program the myth and mysticism of the *Volk*[129]— some of Haya's use of Indianist symbolism in essays written in Berlin bears a relationship to Nazi employment of *völkisch* mythology. Haya read *Mein Kampf*, attended Nazi rallies where he heard Hitler speak, and found himself quite intrigued. Unlike Mariátegui, with whom he had recently broken, Haya waited several years before publishing a sustained criticism of Hitler and Mussolini.

Haya found altogether dazzling the skill and the style with which the Nazis accomplished political mobilization. He admired their ritual, their use of salutes and uniforms, and their appeal to youth; he stood in awe of the discipline they achieved. Further, he commended the way in which Nazis mixed religion and myth in their masterful use of propaganda.[130] Also impressive was Nazi skill in absorbing medieval guild or corporative ideals into their ideology. Above all, though, leadership accounted for Nazi success, according to Haya's analysis. Because Hitler seemed to know where he was going and exuded confidence, "the masses throw themselves into his arms."[131]

Other features of National Socialism must have impressed the Peruvian during the second stage of his exile, for they found their way within a very short time into APRA ideology and practices. Thus, Aprista doctrine would soon find expression in a millennialist language promising that out of suffering, sacrifice, and martyrdom would come a miraculously resplendent new order. Moreover, while Hitler had by 1925 decided that he was a messiah,[132] Haya de la Torre by 1931 was acting as if he believed himself to be one. Weston La Barre notes that among "prophets" of revitalization movements, a great number "have identified themselves . . . with Christ." He adds, "The fact is not so much that all native messiahs derive historically from the only genuine messiah, as that Christ himself is one example of a culturally very common type."[133] Germans responded to a self-proclaimed messiah at a time when national disasters fostered actual fears of annihilation and drove them to seek security in promises of deliverance extended by a person endowed with charisma. And by 1931 Peruvians faced a situation that seemed almost as threatening as Germany's. To the dislocations and relative deprivation characterizing the decades on either side of World War 1 had been added the disasters of the Great Depression.

National Socialism's apocalyptic ideology, however, posed a difficulty for Haya. The Nazis' view of regeneration, requiring that the emergence of a superior human order be preceded by some terrible catastrophe that would destroy the forces of evil, was akin to the visions of St. John in the Book of Revelation.[134] Hitler, like St. John, accepted the need for and even glorified violent confrontation. For his part, Haya's early fascination with anarchism had brought to his attention an apocalyptic view of secular redemption. But, the appeal of this approach had been overbalanced by the nonviolent approach of the university reform movement, by Mackay's version of the Social Gospel, by Freemasonry as understood by most of its practitioners, by the Fabians and the British Labourites, and above all by Rolland and the spiritualist prescriptions for a peaceable kingdom where antagonistic elements would join in harmony. Nor could Haya have failed to be influenced by Einstein's pacifist tendencies. By and large these influences, epitomized for Haya by Rolland's and his own hero Mohandas Gandhi, prevailed over National Socialism's glorification of violence as Haya de la Torre stitched together the various patterns of his political ideology.

With National Socialism Haya de la Torre, to his credit, had other difficulties. To begin with, the Nazis, in line with their anti-semitism, assailed his hero Einstein and harassed Freemasons, whose cause Haya had taken up in 1924 and from whom he had undoubtedly derived a part of his hermetic mysticism. From the perspective of race, moreover, Haya's views on the coming utopia were precisely the opposite of those the Nazis professed. Like José Vasconcelos, for whom he had worked in Mexico, and also like Garcilaso de la Vega, whose writings he had read in Cuzco, Haya believed that fusion, mestizaje, and the harmonizing of divergent elements would produce the great race of the future; in total contrast, the Nazis of course harped obsessively on racial purity. Furthermore, Hitler's revilement of homosexuals could have weakened Haya's attraction to National Socialism. Throughout his life rumors persisted about Haya's homosexuality.[135] Not only his enemies but many a devoted Aprista had little doubt that Haya was indeed a homosexual. The degree to which Haya, in spite of widespread assumptions about his sexual preferences, forged a successful political career in a culture permeated by *machismo*, with its glorification of the heterosexual male erotic athlete, stands as one of the most remarkable facets of his life. Assuming, in any event, that Haya did have homosexual leanings, he would surely have found the tolerant climate for sexual deviance prevailing at Oxford and among other gentlemanly circles in England more to his liking than National Socialism's hysterical bigotry.

As he matured and his basic humanism and humane instincts ripened, Haya opted with increasing consistency for tolerance and inclusion over fanaticism and exclusion. As of 1931, however, many of his values had not yet crystallized. Drawn toward a politics at this time that distinguished between the chosen and the damned, he judged National Socialism to contain some useful and even attractive features. Not immune to the fascist temptation, at least he did not by any means succumb entirely to it[136]—not any more than he had succumbed to Marxism-Leninism in 1924.

By September of 1930, Leguía fell from power, the victim of the depression as much as of a military insurrection headed by Lt. Col. Luis M. Sánchez Cerro. And now old friends of Haya's from his university days as well as representatives of organized labor whom he had cultivated through the 1919 student-worker general strike and the popular universities came together to form the Peruvian Aprista Party (PAP). Persons who had supported Haya's faction during the heady days of university reform, among them Manuel Seoane, provided initial leadership for the party, which was soon joined by a stream of Peruvians returning from Leguía-imposed exiles. These included Luis Heysen, Magda Portal, Carlos Manuel Cox, and Serafín Delmar, all of them destined for important roles in the history of APRA. From the outset, there was no question in the minds of those forming the PAP that Haya de la Torre was the one man of destiny who could lead the party to victory and Peru to redemption.

The Exile Returns

Returning in 1931 to his native land after an enforced absence of eight years, Haya landed first at Talara, the northern site of the operations of the International Petroleum Company, a Standard Oil subsidiary that had come into possession of its fields in 1921. Talara was a symbol of Peru's penetration by Yankee capital, and from this city Haya announced the day would come when Peru would nationalize foreign holdings.

With the details handled in the same meticulous manner in which Jacques-Louis David organized mammoth outdoor quasi-religious rituals to celebrate auspicious occasions of the millennium-promising French Revolution, Haya de la Torre entered Lima on the fifteenth of August. The feast of the Assumption of the Virgin, August 15, was a national holiday, and a crowd estimated by an Aprista historian at one hundred thousand,[137] one-fourth of Lima's population at the time, turned out to greet the returning hero. Haya's close friend and biographer, the art historian and critic Felipe Cossío del Pomar, maintains that the welcoming masses spontaneously decided to wave palm branches and strew them in the street as they greeted the leader now restored to them;[138] but only the gullible will believe that this detail resulted from spontaneity. In any event, from the time of their leader's entry into Lima, members of the infant PAP began to refer to themselves as "the dedicated 'disciples' of a predestined, Christ-like Haya de la Torre."[139]

What sort of man was it who had returned to this adulation? Physically, Haya was of medium height. Although he had put on weight in Europe, he was still fairly trim of build, the powerful chest larger in girth than the stomach. While in exile, Haya had followed a regimen of physical exercise—admonishing all Apristas to do likewise—and the results showed. His straight black hair, cut short at this time, topped a high, slightly sloping forehead. The most notable features of a not-quite handsome face were the sometimes dreamy, sometimes intense and penetrating eyes, the full, sensuous mouth, and—above all—a prominent aquiline nose very much like the ones typically found on the visages depicted on pre-Columbian Moche effigy or portrait vessels. Through the years Haya put on weight and even acquired gross corpulence, especially in the 1950s, before trimming down to more normal proportions by the mid-1960s. Even when the features of the face receded into mountains of fat and huge

Haya de la Torre in 1931, the year of his return from exile. From the collection of Senator Edmundo Haya de la Torre, courtesy of Juan Mejía Baca.

jowls, the nose always retained its prominence. It was Haya's trademark and the delight of caricaturists.

Somehow Haya's rather coarse features seemed to suggest a certain lack of elegance. In the middle years, in fact, his appearance suggested not so much a shorter and fatter version of Mussolini—the way Haya was often described by detractors[140]—as the image many of us have of a Mafia godfather (see photograph on page 222). Yet in later years, Haya's appearance actually took on an aura of commanding dignity, mirroring in some mysterious way a change of inward character (see frontispiece).

What of the person in 1931 behind the not terribly prepossessing physical characteristics? Vain to the point of megalomania, Haya craved recognition and attention. He harped incessantly on his self-denial and poverty,[141] yet by the 1920s he had acquired a taste for expensive suits and a resolve to travel first class.[142] How he supported himself in exile is not altogether clear, although his Protestant backers in England and the United States apparently continued to assist him. In addition, Haya earned a bit of money through articles that he wrote for various Latin American newspapers and journals. Perhaps contributions came also from wealthy anti-Leguiístas, hopeful that Haya might be useful in hastening the dictator's fall.

Haya exulted in being on stage, and it scarcely mattered how large or small the audience was. A superb orator before mass assemblies, he could deliver the most intricate and lengthy discourse with a genius for timing and rhythm, and always without need of notes. With a slight tendency toward huskiness, the voice became clearer and better focused the louder it was projected. A compulsive socializer, Haya could mesmerize intimate gatherings, although he might lapse into fits of "paternal bad temper" when those around him proved insufficiently attentive.[143] Loving cats and dogs "because they symbolized faithfulness to a master"[144] (a more charitable interpretation would be that they symbolized the realm of the instinctual and the unconscious with which Haya wished to be united), he apparently was most comfortable among persons who responded with deference.

Happiest when talking (he was not always a good listener), Haya delighted small circles with his flights of fancy, his prodigious store of anecdotes, his sense of humor, his infectious and virtually unfailing optimism, and his joie de vivre. A dazzling conversationalist, Haya veritably lusted after opportunities to display his skills and exercise his social charms. Characteristically the last to leave a nocturnal gathering, he would none-

theless generally arise early the next morning. Though detractors remained skeptical about his claims to unlimited stores of energy, Haya
maintained he required only four or five hours sleep a night. Until the
1940s, when he is said to have developed an occasional taste for scotch
whiskey, Haya was abstemious in his drinking habits; and this undoubtedly contributed to his ability to arise refreshed after a few hours' sleep.
Haya both sought and was discovered by distractions that pulled him away
from solitude and study, at least until he was in his fifties. Although he
read voraciously and remembered an amazing amount of the words that
passed before his eyes, he remained capricious and desultory in his reading
habits, though ready to generalize on some of the tidbits of information
that happened to have lodged in his quick and retentive mind.

Throughout most of his life, Haya de la Torre retained traits of the bohemian, to which he increasingly added those of the discerning bon vivant
and the occasional glutton, all the while mixing in sporadic bursts of asceticism when he practiced the puritanism he preached. Not until advanced
old age did Haya attain a genuinely integrated personality. Only then
would he find, inwardly, the harmony that he aspired to bring to Indo-
America. Admiring Hitler because the Fuehrer knew where he was going,
Haya for many years lacked an internal compass. Thus he bewildered followers and foes alike by sudden changes in course. Often, the changes emerged out of rank opportunism and the pursuit of personal grandeur. Had
he died during the formative stage of his life, which with Haya extended
into his late fifties, his followers could not credibly have claimed for him
the status of greatness, to which ultimately he did acquire legitimate title.

Six

Fundamentals of Aprismo (I): Charisma
and Spiritualism

Haya de la Torre: Charisma and Narcissism

Modernity is a term that produces widespread disagreement among those who attempt to define it. Generally, however, it is agreed that one feature of the modern society is the rational-empirical basis upon which the government's legitimacy is determined. In short, citizens employ criteria that are rationally and empirically verifiable in deciding if the government is conferring on them the type of security and well-being that most of them agree they want. If on the basis of these criteria it is ascertained that the government is doing more or less what is expected of it, then it is accepted as legitimate. In contrast, the legitimacy of the ruler in premodern societies often rests on his charisma, in the sense in which Max Weber used that word: "It is the quality which attaches to men and things by virtue of their relations with the 'supernatural,' that is, with the nonempirical aspects of reality in so far as they lend theological meaning to men's acts and the events of the world."[1]

On the basis of their liberal faith in progress, North Americans generally have assumed that Latin Americans are advancing, and want overwhelmingly to advance, toward the rational-empirical sources of legitimacy, leaving behind the charismatic bases. At least through the first three-quarters of the twentieth century, this assumption has often proved wrong. When given the chance, large numbers of Latin Americans frequently have opted for the premodern, charismatic type of legitimacy, even though disagreeing whether charisma springs from traditional (largely Catholic) sources or must be sought through new links to the supernatural. In few instances of twentieth-century Latin American history has the leaning toward charisma as the font of legitimacy been so apparent as in the favorable response of about one-third of the Peruvian electorate to Haya de la Torre and his party at the beginning of the 1930s.

Whether the charismatic appeal inheres in the Latin American personality or is present only because of the area's history of chronic insecurity, if not downright crisis and emergency, is as difficult to determine as any of the myriad issues arising out of the nature-nurture dialectic. In any event, the 1930s were an era of crisis par excellence, and understandably enough in many parts of Latin America people responded to it by the longing for a charismatic leader. Such leaders are rare beings, however, and simply do not appear in response to the wishes of the people. But in the case of Peru, one was at hand.

"When old forms and customs lose their binding, their sustaining and their reassuring powers," according to Erik H. Erikson, "the people must restlessly search for new personal identities and for a new sense of collective identity."[2] In these times of anxiety, people are susceptible to the charismatic leader, a man who is perceived as having some connection to supernatural sources of wisdom that enables him to put uncertainty and fears to rout. The charismatic leader trades on fear, for this is what induces the masses to surrender their egos to "Caesaristic movements."[3] When they surrender to a Caesar who promises to lead them into a new and secure haven, people for a moment are ready to believe almost anything, for "the line between science and magic, the real and the unreal," the familiar and the new, "has temporarily disappeared."[4] Politics now becomes magic, and "he who knows how to summon the forces from the deep," from some ineffable realm existing at a different level than rationality, "him will [the masses] follow."[5]

Some psychiatrists suggest that what gives prophetic leaders their feelings of charisma, or sacredness, is their mysterious power to tap the potential of that vast reservoir of mental resources within: the unconscious. Furthermore, the charismatic leader tends often to project the unconscious onto the masses, the peasants, the Volk, the proletariat, or whatever term is chosen to designate marginal persons. As a symbol of the unconscious, such persons are assumed to operate largely on the level of preconsciousness, to know intuitively without rational calculation, to be close to the kingdom of heaven because they are as children.

If this psychiatric analysis has validity, then Haya, like Hitler and ever so many other leaders of millenarian movements, could certainly lay claim to charisma, for he did feel at one with the masses of Peru who flocked to hear his political oratory.

On many occasions Hitler expressed the idea "that there existed between himself and the German Volk a mystical tie, that he was not only their spokesman and ruler but their living incarnation."[6] Of Hitler, Jung has written: "He is the loudspeaker which magnifies the inaudible whispers of the German soul until these can be heard by the German's conscious ear. . . . Hitler's power is not political; it is magic,"[7] Haya de la Torre entertained similar feelings about his power. The words of an early political address of his, he claimed, had been "dictated" to him by his audience. And a discourse whose words were the result of what the people taught him to utter was, he maintained, "the annunciation of something permanent that could never be destroyed."[8] Haya's most notable expression of faith that he became one with the Aprista masses when addressing large assemblies came in November of 1933. He assured a responsive gathering in his native Trujillo that logical knowledge was inferior to that deriving from "what we feel in our bones." Apristas might not be able to understand all the theoretical details of what he said, but the important thing was the faith that united them and that created a means of communication that transcended words: "Our faith has the formidable force to make vibrate all our consciousness, creating authentic sentiment and marvelous intuition, of which refined consciousness can attain scarcely an inkling."[9]

Previously in his life, Haya had probably experienced feelings akin to those of mystical ecstacy when it seemed that he was one with the infinite. In Cuzco he had been overwhelmed as he experienced the Indian, the new man within waiting to be born; and in Lima he felt transformed as he energized the masses through the power of his oratory directed against the consecration of Peru to the Sacred Heart in 1923. But not until his political campaign in 1931 did he have the chance to experience exaltation on a steady basis. Regularly, now, he could become one with the many as he and the mass of Aprista believers "vibrated" together. Those of his political faith who by the hundreds and thousands listened to Haya were enormously moved; but he was even more moved by them and was convinced, I believe, that he was translating into words—words of magical power because they came from a level beyond the sphere of consciousness—the longings of the masses, who in turn responded ec-statically because part of their own psyches were being raised to con-sciousness.[10] Able to move the masses, he believed, by the magic that he felt he received from them, Haya de la Torre accepted, more than ever before, that his destiny lay in politics *and* religion. Politics had become for him a source of mystical experience. Haya claimed in a 1970 interview that had he not become a politician he would have entered the priest-hood.[11] As of 1931, he could persuade himself that he was living the two vocations simultaneously. As our story unfolds, we shall see that Haya clung to this persuasion as much in the late years of his life as in 1931.

Haya's sense of political-religious vocation did not, of course, origi-nate in 1931, but it was confirmed and strengthened then. Beginning in 1927 Haya was speaking and writing about the providential role of the heroic leader in shaping the course of history. It was the role of the larger-than-life person to "interpret, intuit, and direct the desires, vague and imprecise, of the multitude,..."[12] to create and "organize the col-lective forces that make revolutions."[13] Haya clearly had cast himself in the role of such a leader. The foreword to his first published book of es-says, *Por la emancipación de América Latina* (1927), contains Haya's as-surance that the travails he has so far endured in his struggle for justice have gone only to strengthen him as a "worker-soldier" who will strug-gle resolutely for "a cause that is and will be the only objective of his life."[14] Inspired by the sense of his mission, he wrote the following year, he was never tempted in his days of hunger and adversity to abandon the purity of purpose with which he served his cause. "I can turn my eyes today toward the past, and find it pure.... I have chosen my path delib-erately. And hunger was never so severe as to make me betray myself."[15] Already, Haya was well on the way to acquiring the sense of moral super-iority of a man out of the past, able to resist the temptations of a world that had turned decadent.

In 1931 Alberto Hidalgo, a friend of Haya's from San Marcos days who was beginning to acquire some reputation as a man of letters, published an article in which he praised Mussolini and Hitler as leaders of heroic and prophetic dimensions and then affirmed that Haya de la Torre was the "instrument that history has chosen to move the air of all Latin America.... He understands that he has been singled out for greatness, and that his actions will live forever."[16] In his letter acknowledging re-ceipt of Hidalgo's article, Haya wrote:

Very well, Alberto. For the first time, all that the sea, the mountains, and the forests have said to me, together with the mystery of a million glances that have been detained in my eyes, you have said to me with my name. For the first time I have heard the great call, coming from so high a place and in so precise a tone. Until today all the great and beautiful things of life have only stammered. Only my conscience said: greatness calls you. . . . You have said it in the words that only the great initiated ones can hear. You and I therefore have a responsibility: you, because you have spoken to me in the name of destiny; I, because I must listen to destiny. . . . After your voice I have to hear another that announces to me the hour in which I must open my arms and deliver myself to the command. Meantime, your words have accomplished a mission. Until now, no one has been able to speak like this to me. And it was necessary. I feel stronger and clearer. I will follow my road. You and I have a pact of blood. He who survives will be able to cry at death that it was fulfilled. Neither you nor I know when it is going to be fulfilled, but it will be fulfilled. . . . Do not be surprised at this religious tone. I assure you I shall not speak like this again.

Departing Peru in 1923, Haya had declared: "I maintain my creed of justice. I shall return when the moment of the great transformation has arrived."[17] That moment had come, in 1931.

As the 1930s wore on, Haya's messianic sense of mission only grew on the adversity that he and his movement encountered. In 1932, after he had been defeated in the presidential election of the previous year, he wrote that it was his destiny to serve as the *adelantado* (an official entrusted with the conquest, pacification, and rule of colonial areas by the sixteenth-century Spanish crown) and animator of his generation. This destiny belonged to him in part because of his exile, which had given him the chance to acquire a vision of the world and an ability to see the whole. This is why, he continued, "we have been followed, not only by the people—to whose marvelous instinct is united the precise understanding of their interests, who see these interests faithfully interpreted and authentically defended by us—but also by that part of youth which is most intelligent, most free or exempt from inferior passions, and most susceptible to establish with the faith of their age the sincere dedication to surpass themselves."[18] In the same year of 1932 Haya was imprisoned in the Lima penitentiary under circumstances that will be described in chapter 8. With their leader in detention, Apristas in Trujillo staged an unsuccessful uprising that resulted in the death—in most cases by execution not preceded by trial—of between one thousand and two thousand insurgents. This was the background for a letter Haya wrote to John Mackay: "If I didn't know that my life is necessary for the Party I would have preferred to die with them. Only one glory have I envied: that of our martyrs. My greatest ambition is to die as they have. If I did not know that I have to live and work, to lead and to dream, I would be now the happiest among them. But, alas, I have to live."[19]

Haya's sense of being predestined and consequently protected by supernatural powers so that he might fulfill his mission found confirmation, or so he believed, in 1937. In hiding at the time in Lima as a military regime continued to harass Apristas and fearing that his life lay in danger, Haya maintained he was visited by the shade of his dear friend and closest political associate, Manuel Arévalo (possibly the apparition was only a dream, he conceded). Just a few days before this, Arévalo had been brutally tortured and murdered by security officials. According to Haya, Arévalo's spirit brought advice that, as it turned out, saved his life. From that time on Haya (who contrived to secure the bones of Arévalo and for some time carried them about in the trunk of his car as an amulet) appeared to believe in the invulnerability of his charmed life.[20] Two years later this belief was verified anew when Haya escaped, under what he considered miraculous circumstances, an attempt on his life. He now gave renewed expression to his sense of destiny:

I can declare to the Peruvian people that I continue at my post, that nothing will make me retreat. . . . I swore to dedicate my life to the service of my people, and am fulfilling that oath. I swore to be loyal, to be pure, to be always a disinterested defender of what I believe are ideals that will redeem Peru, and I have complied with what I swore. No cajolery, no promise, no threat has dissuaded me. My struggle is and has been difficult because I am poor and I have maintained in purity the dignity of my poverty. My only aspiration, disinterested and legitimate, has been and remains to demonstrate to the Peruvian people and youth that, Yes, it is possible to save our country by the path of authentic moral renovation. . . . I am sure of my road, and on it I shall continue to entrust myself to danger, which is the best companion for one who fights for high ideals.[21]

At about this time Haya read Keyserling's *South American Meditations*, containing the prediction that the world's next great movement of regeneration might occur in Latin America.[22] Obviously drawing on the imagery that Keyserling had attached to his prediction, Haya wrote at the beginning of the 1940s, when he was still an underground fugitive, that what makes history is the concurrence of the dark movement of the masses with the illuminating and prescient idealism of precursors and leaders who synthesize the needs and desires of the masses, elevating them and guiding them into channels of heroic enthusiasm. There could be no doubt that Haya regarded himself as such a precursor and leader.[23]

The adulation accorded Haya from the 1920s through the 1930s by his followers and sympathizers would have been enough to turn the head of a normal and balanced person. In the case of the undoubtedly neurotic Haya de la Torre, this acclaim—highlighted in 1926 when Romain Rolland hailed him as a child of the sun—simply served to swell delusions of grandeur to grotesque proportions. Charisma, it has been said, arises not out of personal qualities and attributes, but rather out of a relationship: it is bestowed through "the recognition and acceptance of a leader by his followers...."[24] On grounds of acceptance, indeed of sycophancy and adulation, Haya could not doubt his charisma, for, as a North American writer observed in the early 1930s, "[The Apristas] have a fervent faith in their leadership. Haya is perhaps too much of a God to them. Apra headquarters are plastered down with pictures of Haya in entirely too Mussoliniesque poses."[25] At the time of his exile in 1923, another foreign observer had written of Haya: "His gifts of leadership, his captivating personality, his resolution and determination, his idealism have all combined to make him almost worshipped by the workmen, while his gifts of oratory and convincing speech have tended to mold public opinion in a way that was hitherto unheard of in Peru."[26] Even before the exile, accolades had begun to pour in from Peruvians. The poet Alberto Guillén, who later broke with Haya, wrote in 1922 that Haya "brings the dawn in his arms." He went on to compare Haya to Christ.[27] Only with Haya's return, though, did the chorus of hosannas attain crescendo proportions.

With these words Antenor Orrego, one of the Trujillo bohemians, greeted the returning hero in 1931: "There marches with you the hope, the resurrection, and the victory of a great nationality in a trance of death.... You come to give direction, as the magnetic point of force, to the desires... of the producing masses of your country. Issuing from the suffering entrails of the race, these desires can only be formulated and transformed into concrete realities... by the grace of love.... We await only your expert hand to tune and harmonize these innumerable [desires]...."[28] At another time Orrego wrote: "Haya de la Torre is the transmutation in the unitary one of all the contradictions and conflicts of the continent—the prototype of the new man of America, the result of assimilation, of conjugation, of all the 'vital digestion' of two anti-thetical worlds through four centuries of bellicose friction."[29] In less high-flown and esoteric language, labor leader Arturo Sabroso observed, "the people need to personify in one man the total leadership of a social revolutionary movement." For Peru, he concluded, Haya de la Torre alone could be that man.[30] More often, though, the flowery rhetoric prevailed over Sabroso's down-to-earth style of praise. Thus, the poet Serafín Delmar wrote of Haya:

> All of us are small before him,
> His glance penetrates to scrutinize every heart;
> And when he speaks!
> His voice bathes the soul,
> Purifying us as the rain
> And the sun purify the soil.[31]

Another poet saw Haya as half Manuel González Prada, half Simón Bolívar,[32] and an Aprista song referred to Haya as the "Apostle of the new humanity."[33] Alberto Hidalgo, who had summoned Haya to his destiny with comparisons to Hitler and Mussolini, hailed him now as a man endowed with "the special mystery that envelops the heads of caudillos, a special magnetism to attract the masses and to master them . . . . He will be our Lenin."[34]

According to the poet Alcides Spelucín, like Orrego one of Haya's closest friends from Trujillo days, great heroes appear when the times are right. Before their coming, a whole people, "begins to stir and awaken." Recently, Peruvians had begun to awaken, whereupon "arising out of the bosom of the people as its most faithful interpreter and unifying force came Víctor Raúl Haya de la Torre. . . . Haya is the anxiety, the pugnacity, the will, the action, and also the conscience, the intelligence, the instinct and the feeling of the best stirrings of his medium and his time. . . . Haya is also action, deed, and palpitating reality. His life is an example, his intelligence a road, and his name a banner."[35] In his homage to Haya, Juan Seoane wrote of sentiments that palpitated in the unconscious of the rebellious masses. These "monstrous forces" awaited a man of purified intellectual power who could extract from them their essence and from this material mint the coin of a new, redemptive doctrine.[36] The imagery smacks of alchemy and Gnosticism.

Through the years, the homage continued. In 1943 the Argentine Gabriel del Mazo, Haya's close friend since the days of their collaboration in the university reform movement, wrote of Aprismo's chief as "the inspiration of Peruvian youth and the hope of his people. When he evokes the Inca patria, he becomes like one of the great sons of the Sun of the Andes. Once I thought that the Sun that Columbus brought on the sails of the caravels could have been the Andean Sun returning to its temple after having encompassed the world in a historic cycle." And now, Mazo concluded, he saw Haya de la Torre as the man who brings the sun anew.[37] In 1951, when Haya was in asylum in the Colombian embassy in Lima and denied safe conduct out of the country, a few Apristas suggested that perhaps a new *jefe máximo* (or supreme chief, the title accorded Haya since 1931) should be selected to serve until Haya regained his freedom. This suggestion was quickly squelched, the Aprista high command agreeing with Luis Alberto Sánchez that "the leadership of the party is a hierarchy sui generis, inherent in its founder, because of his being the creator of the doctrine and its principle instrument and having achieved what has been achieved. No one else could aspire to it."[38] In 1966, a young member of the party asserted that Haya's thoughts were so sublime that they could only be those of a "predestined soul."[39] And so it continued through the years, this unending tide of homage, whether he was in prison, in hiding, or pursuing his political-priestly vocation in freedom.

Helena P. Blavatsky, for many years the moving spirit behind Theosophism, has been described in terms that are uncannily applicable to Haya de la Torre: "She was an archetypal charismatic leader, an individual set apart as having exceptional or superhuman powers. If her followers at times seemed to wink at or close their eyes to her trickery, part of the reason was probably the trust that leaders enjoy from their followers: the belief that the leader has a clearer sense of goals than they and has the right to adjust the means to the ends."[40]

The sorcerer, James Frazer observed, is not necessarily a knave and imposter: "he is often sincerely convinced that he really possesses those wonderful powers which the credulity of his fellows ascribes to him."[41] To have believed in the reality of the powers ascribed to him by his Aprista followers would have required on Haya's part a certain neuroticism. And this he did not lack. A man with a marked tendency toward mystical experience, Haya had plumbed his own depths and experienced what Rolland described as the oceanic feeling: that feeling of wholeness when consciousness and the unconscious become one—or when, as some would have it today, the right and the left hemispheres of the brain "communicate."[42] Having experienced oneness with the unconscious, Haya went on to project the unconscious onto the Aprista masses. The result was a severe case of ego inflation, leading him to believe that his ego consciousness not only had been enriched by part of the psychic unconscious but also had absorbed virtually all of its treasure—and leading him also to believe that his awareness encapsulated *all* of the collective will of the adulatory masses, not just part of it. Such, at least, might be a Jungian explanation for the megalomania, bordering on feelings of "godlikeness,"[43] that Haya began to display.

Jung has observed that "every increase in consciousness harbours the danger of inflation"—the belief that because one has tapped a bit of the psychic resources within he has availed himself of their entirety.[44] For a prolonged period in his life I would assume that Haya, on every occasion when he addressed a large audience (symbolizing for him the raw forces and energy as well as the sub- and supra-rationality of his own unconscious) and began to "vibrate" with them, experienced an increase of consciousness and moved toward an ever more exaggerated degree of ego inflation. He was the victim of his own psychic inclinations and of the historical circumstances that made mass audiences available for the first time in Peruvian politics.

Heinz Kohut may be more useful than Jung in providing insights into the psychic factors that led Haya to believe he actually possessed the wonderful powers imputed to him. Charismatic leaders seem generally to display a narcissistic personality,[45] and Kohut is recognized as one of the world's preeminent authorities on narcissistic personality disorders. To put the matter in an oversimplified version, Kohut sees the narcissistic adult as a person who has reverted or regressed to infantile fantasies of grandeur. The infant believes that he can control his own small world, which he regards as the totality of the world, by manipulating parents through crying, tantrums, and exhibitionism of various sorts. Virtually by magic, without having to do anything beyond staging his performances, the infant has his world made pleasing and right. Initially, the infant's behavior is aimed at gaining the attention, support, and empathy of the "selfobject"—generally identified first as the mother, later as the father. But, when parents (selfobjects) prematurely cease to respond to the infant, he or she suffers the "traumatic withdrawal of empathy."

As he enters upon childhood and adolescence, the victim of premature withdrawal of empathy increasingly focuses love not on the self-objects in which he has been disappointed, but on himself. He may develop a "charismatic" and "messianic" personality as he reverts to an infantile, "archaic, grandiose" self, built on delusions that he can command the world, as it were, by magic. As his real self and his grandiose self merge, he begins to cast others in the role of parents; he expects to be able, by means of performances related to the tantrums and outbursts by which he tried—and largely failed—to manipulate the original selfobjects, to command them to confer on him what he covets. Those cast in the role of parents become a new selfobject: they are the right, the good, the chosen people; all others, those who cannot be controlled and manipulated, are evil. As often as not those who become selfobjects for the charismatic, narcissistic adult are weak and enfeebled, feeling the need for the support of a person who appears to be all-knowing.[46] As bonds of empathy form, not only do the people who represent new selfobjects shower love and affection upon the narcissist; he in turn showers love and empathy on them and pursues them in an excited, "eroticized" manner.[47] "At the risk of being 'overly schematic,' " Kohut writes, "I venture the opinion that those personalities who manifest charismatic strength and self-certainty (often accompanied with self-righteously expressed self-pitying and hypochondriacal complaints) have suffered a traumatic withdrawal of empathy from the side of the selfobjects who were expected to respond to the child's mirroring needs [the mother, in most cases], while those with messianic features have suffered analogous disappointments from the side of the archaic idealized object [most often the father]."[48]

From what we know of Haya's family background, it is at least plausible that he experienced traumatic withdrawal of empathy, both from the mother and father. He was closer to his "aunt-mother," his mother's sister, than to his own mother and was inconsolable when she died in 1910. He seems never to have developed an empathic relationship with his father. When the latter lay on his deathbed in 1934, Haya resorted to an unconvincing excuse in explaining his failure to come to the old man's side, although he did find it possible to play the role society almost demanded of the son by appearing for the funeral. Admittedly, there is not enough evidence for us to know if Kohut's explanation of the narcissistic, charismatic, messianic type applies to Haya. But there are indications that it does.[49]

For much of his life, Haya de la Torre acted very much like narcissistic neurotics who "are pervaded by expectations of magic,"[50] believing that the mere wish to bring about a certain objective, a wish expressed through emotional outbursts or oratory akin to the infant's exhibitionism, would cause the selfobjects to bestow that objective upon them. Moreover, Haya's "eroticized" pursuit of the Aprista faithful suggests a transfer to them of the love that had been withdrawn from the mother following her withdrawal of empathy. Responding to allegations of Haya's homosexuality, an Aprista exclaimed: "Don't you believe this. . . . Our *jefe máximo* is not a queer. . . . The situation is that he doesn't need a woman, because his woman is APRA, and to her he has dedicated everything."[51] Complying with yet another of the characteristics of the charismatic, messianic narcissist, Haya de la Torre did associate Apristas with the chosen people, with the biblical wheat and lambs, while non-Apristas dwelling in the clutches of materialism were the chaff and the goats. In a 1933 address, after excoriating the children of darkness, Haya noted that these were conspiring against and slandering Apristas. They did so "not because we own material treasurers but because we own another treasure, the spiritual treasure of our faith, of our union, of our discipline."[52]

The APRA: Spiritualism and Millenarian Beliefs

The APRA was indeed a relationship (of the type already mentioned) that established charisma in its leader, based upon "The recognition and acceptance of a leader by his followers." It was a love affair, also, in which the leader did his all to requite the love of his followers, in part to elicit from them still greater love that would inspire even more self-effacing service.[53] Beyond this, for some Apristas at least, love and service and dedication issued from the belief that Haya was a seer, endowed with supernatural powers. "Haya is a mystic," enthused one of his followers.[54] Cossío del Pomar, Haya's confidant and biographer, marveled over the chief's uncanny ability "to intuit the intimate nature of reality"; in this "Víctor Raúl shows himself to be closer to Theosophy than to the physical sciences." In Cossío's opinion, Haya was also capable of listening to the still voices of loved ones who had passed on.[55]

In late nineteenth century Europe, many a devotee of the esoteric tradition had hailed gifted poets as magi, able to feel more intensely than ordinary mortals and to transmit to those less sensitive some awareness of the divine presence that permeated the cosmos. The poet, so it was believed, could feel "the Pulses of all the infinite Deep of Heaven vibrate in his own." Sensing the spiritual, rhythmic harmony of the entire cosmos or macrocosm, the poet—who perhaps had come to his powers through a series of reincarnations that led him progressively to shed the limitations of creatureliness—could transmit to others a sense of cosmic unity.[56] What Peru witnessed in the rise of APRA attested to an important evolution in contemporary versions of the spiritualist tradition: the transfer of faith from the poet or artist as magus to the unusually endowed politician. The latter's powers enabled him not so much to feel, as poets and artists, the common rhythm of rocks and trees, streams and winds, but rather to intuit the now almost obscured pulse emanating from the masses, to make them once more conscious of its force and thereby lead them back into harmony with the macrocosm's pulse. Not only for Haya but for other Latin American leaders of the 1920s, the '30s, and more recent decades as well, the populist approach to politics arose out of the spiritualist, esoteric vision.

Surpassing all other Apristas in hailing Haya's higher powers was Antenor Orrego. According to him, anyone could acquire ideas through "the rational alchemy of books. But no one who is not an authentic creator can possess vital realities, living forces that are incarnate in him and that operate in the process of history."[57] Haya was such a creator. Beyond that, Orrego once assured a fellow Aprista, he was "hypersensitive: that is to say, a marvelous receiver of the fluids of other worlds; the states of trance for Haya were frequent and many of the political solutions that he formulated were dictated by higher spirits that became incarnate in Haya when he was in a trance."[58] In addition, then, to the sort of spiritualism without spirits discussed in the introductory chapter, Aprismo included an element of spiritualism cum spirits.

For his part, Haya did everything possible to enhance his mystique as a modern-day shaman. To an acquaintance he revealed that when in prison in 1932, his "astral body" was present in Trujillo as Apristas suffered martyrdom following their unsuccessful insurrection.[59] Some years later he informed a close companion that once when at a loss as to how to begin an address to a huge multitude awaiting his words in an outdoor plaza, he glanced at the moon, whose spirit then began to speak to him and through him to the multitude.[60]

The experience with the moon may relate to Haya's interest in astrology. An uncle in Trujillo had first introduced him to the study of the heavenly bodies, but whether he was in any way responsible for the fascination his nephew developed in horoscopes[61] cannot be known. In any event, Haya is reported (by a hostile witness, but one of integrity) once to have pointed out to some companions "his star," which ruled the destiny of his life. On this particular occasion, he noted, his star was passing into conjunction with Mars, an auspicious omen for launching a military-backed APRA golpe then in the works; for it showed that the sons of Mars were on his side.[62] Destiny for the jefe lay also under the control of Pisces (the fish, the symbol of Christ), for he had been born on February 22—just like George Washington, a coincidence he enjoyed pointing out.[63] According to astrological lore with which Haya is bound to have been familiar, a principal characteristic of the "Pisces native" is the "ability to enter into the actual feelings of those about him." Similarly, the Pisces native is likely, allegedly, to develop "a mystical temperament because of his extraordinary sense of affinity for the deeper strains he uncovers in his fellows." Purportedly, he is likely also to become a poet, "that is, the one who articulates the general race experience for those less articulate or imaginative than himself. . . . His voice as an artist . . . is always seated in his instinctive recognition of some ultimate wholeness in existence. . . ."[64]

Through the centuries, many of those drawn toward astrology have not necessarily believed in the factual control of events on earth by the movement of heavenly bodies. Rather than seeking factual understanding through astrology, they have used it as a metaphor suggesting the wholeness that can, so they hope, result from the marriage of sky and earth, consciousness and the unconscious, spirit and creatureliness.[65] Whether Haya stood in a long line of spiritualists who found in astrology a metaphorical enrichment of basically religious longings, or whether he believed in its factual applicability, we simply lack adequate evidence to know.

In addition to astrology, Haya dabbled in farther-out forms of occultism. Throughout the 1930s he maintained close contacts with the two leading occult establishments in Lima: the Centro Esotérico Nacional and the Centro Humanista.[66] The Centro Esotérico Nacional was directed by Agustín Benavides Canseco, in whose house Haya hid during much of the latter part of the 1930s when Benavides Canseco's brother-in-law, Gen. Oscar R. Benavides, was president of Peru and trying to stifle the APRA. Through this centro, Haya helped instigate the February 1939 uprising of Gen. Antonio Rodríguez against President Benavides. A key role in the plot fell to the centro's medium. In league with Haya, this young man pretended to put Rodríguez in touch with the spirit of Ramón Castilla, Peru's greatest military ruler of the nineteenth century. Speaking through the medium, Castilla of course counseled Rodríguez to rebel.[67] The golpe, apparently on the verge of success, collapsed when Rodríguez was killed by stray bullets as he delivered a speech in the patio of the Palacio de Gobierno.

The crude way in which he manipulated the spiritualist apparatus in Lima to prey upon the superstitions of Rodríguez lends substance to the appraisal of Thomas M. Davies Jr. and Víctor Villanueva. When it came to spiritualism, they contend, Haya was both a believer and a charlatan.[68] The combination of believer and charlatan is not an unusual one.[69]

Haya's recourse to the more extreme uses of occultism and his more exaggerated claims concerning shamanistic powers had only tangential bearing on the APRA as a movement that united some of Peru's leading intellectuals. What initially bound most of them to the movement was its regenerationist faith—found in many guises, both esoteric and otherwise, throughout the contemporary world—that their country and perhaps their continent and "race" stood on the threshold of a new existence. Whether the threshold would be crossed or not depended, so it was believed, more on enthusiasm and consciousness than on material determinants. While Aprista intellectuals might have little interest, on the whole, in Haya's occultism, the times were such that they would not hold it against him. What they responded to positively was the ringing message, delivered by Haya in 1933, that to be an Aprista was "to have the instinct and the capacity for the creation . . . of a new consciousness capable in turn of creating, only by its force, its energy . . . another political, social, economic, and cultural organization in the country."[70]

Like Haya de la Torre, Luis Alberto Sánchez, high in APRA's command chain and one of Peru's outstanding twentieth-century men of letters, had read Garcilaso de la Vega.[71] And, like his jefe, he had come alive to the possibility of synthesizing the dark energies of Indians with a fresh light of consciousness to forge a new Peru, and a new continent. In Aprismo, moreover, he found "a mysterious force that subdues the individualistic passions, however deeply rooted, and [reveals that] there inhere in men deeper sources of rectitude and affection than one can imagine."[72] Latin America, he declared in a 1936 Buenos Aires conference, is on the eve of a great transformation: it approaches "spiritual autonomy in the dawn of a new day."[73] A similar vision animated Carlos Manuel Cox, who formulated most of the APRA's economic program in the 1930s. Even into his advanced years, Cox clung to his belief in Peru's utopian future. His faith emerged out of German idealist philosophy[74] and the prophetic expectations of Garcilaso de la Vega.[75]

Following the death of Manuel Arévalo in 1937, Manuel Seoane, a friends of Haya's from student days at San Marcos, served for many years as number-two man in the Aprista high command. (The testimony of his brother, Juan, to Haya's charisma was quoted above.) To his practical skills as a statesman and economic planner, Manuel Seoane added an abiding inclination toward mystical musings on a millennialist world order. A work of his published in 1960 is shot through with numerological references to threes, fours, sixes, and twelves that must perforce be suggestive to anyone even vaguely familiar with esoteric thought.[76] The section on the "Twelve Wheels of Progress" smacks even of Neopythagoreanism. And yet there is also considerable hard-headed realism in Seoane, as there is in Sánchez and Cox. All three seek the fusion, so coveted by twentieth-century millenarians, of the rational and the material with the mystical and the Platonic. They mirror the concern of Haya de la Torre with, as he put it, a "cosmic interpretation" that combines science, philosophy, and religion, thereby "introducing man to the eternal."[77]

In Buenos Aires, where Peruvian Apristas often spent periods of exile, Gabriel del Mazo maintained the faith he had shown from university reform days both in the birth of a new humanity and in the unique qualifications of Haya de la Torre to serve as midwife. A profound believer in what he termed "American spiritualist politics,"[78] Mazo did all in his power to make Aprista exiles comfortable in Buenos Aires and to introduce them into the circles of leaders from other Latin American countries who also were practitioners of spiritualist politics—convinced that nations could be transformed "by the fecund, magical, and selective action of the spirit."[79] Some of those spiritualist leaders Mazo most admired were Juan José Arévalo of Guatemala, Rómulo Betancourt of Venezuela, and Natalicio González of Paraguay—in addition to their recent precursor, Argentina's Hipólito Yrigoyen. None of these men, according to Mazo, denied the material aspect of existence, but each insisted upon attaching primacy to the spiritual.[80]

Above all other Apristas, above even Haya himself, Antenor Orrego envisaged the transformation of the world through mystical powers. When it came to spiritualist politics, he was Aprismo's real extremist, as is revealed in his 1939 work *Pueblo continente*. Here Orrego maintains that man learned to use first his body and then his soul or spirit. It was initially in the Orient that the yogi, gaining absolute mastery over his body, his emotions, passions, and instincts, discovered how to convert them into the flexible servants of his most intimate and recondite spiritual reality. When the corporeal and psychic instruments reached a level of perfection and interpenetrated, there began to shine within Oriental consciousness man's third element, "the creative element, the fecundating element par excellence, the element that takes the initiative in the great transformations of the world, the consciousness of watchfulness, the consciousness that is absolutely awake, and through which man reaches a new dimension of cognition and of life."[81]

Orrego's ideas derive from the Hindu-Buddhist concept of the opening of the third eye of cognition through which humans see in such a way as to combine inward and outer sources of knowledge. They resemble also the Jungian concept of attaining the ideal balance of inward resources of cognition (intuition and feeling) with outward sources (sensation and thinking). But Hindu-Buddhist conceptualization goes further than the Jungian. As Orrego described the process, the yogi who has mastered the consciousness of watchfulness comes to apprehend that the apparently real or material world is but a reflection of the ultimate, spiritual reality: "The outward form is simply the weak reflection, a deceiving version, of the recondite reality of the spirit."[82] What the "real world contains is not more than a mere suggestion of the profound essence of truth, a suggestion susceptible to alteration by the power of the spirit." Thus, wisdom in the Orient is, above all else, power.[83] It is not just impotent "eruditism"; rather, it is the vitalizing and creative faculty.

Orrego's conclusion was this: it was first in Asia that the consciousness of watchfulness, capable of transforming the world, came into being; but now, in a new cycle of human ascent, Latin America was destined to master the wisdom that is power. Latin America was ordained to attain a more perfect fusion of the spiritual and material, the ethereal and the corporeal, and thereby create the world anew on a higher level of perfection.

To a considerable degree the APRA mystique that helped provide cohesiveness to the top level of command arose out of the faith of its leaders in the possibility of achieving a secular millennium through the powers of mind and spirit. Most of them hedged their bets and conceded important ancillary roles to technology and economic management. But, for many of them at least, there was no question that primacy lay with faith, spirit, mind-energy, vision, imagination, will, and consciousness. At the same time, most party intellectuals did not doubt that command posts should be reserved for those most abundantly endowed with the higher, nonmaterial qualities. On the whole, the party's intellectual workers, and also many of its manual workers, continued to serve the cause as long as they were able to believe that Haya de la Torre might be the best endowed of all Apristas with mystical, spiritual qualities—even if not necessarily able to transpose his astral body and talk with the dead.

Aprismo reflected, as has already been suggested, the reaction against positivism and materialism that enlisted many thinkers throughout the Western world in the period between the two world wars. However, many of the APRA's spiritualist-regenerationist facets seemed not so much to echo the general European reaction against modernity as to emerge in original fashion out of the country's Indian heritage. Like many Peruvians of the period, Apristas found in the Indian their particular symbol of millenarian reaction against the established order. At the same time, though, many Apristas linked themselves to one of the constants in millenarian, regeneration mythology by taking up the cause of feminism.

Aprismo, Indianism, and Feminism

Had Haya appeared on the scene thirty years earlier, his Indianism would have proved a hopeless handicap to his political career. But by the 1920s and 1930s, Indianism had become quite the fashion among Peruvian intellectuals and artists. Thus the Peruvian Aprista Party's assimilation of the jefe's Indianism counted in its favor, even if only among avant-garde elements. Strongly influenced by the ideology of Mexico's 1910 Revolution, Peru's avant-garde viewed their country's Indians, who constituted some 40 percent of the population by 1930, as having much to recommend them; certainly they should no longer be dismissed, as by and large they had been during the apogee of positivism except by renegades such as González Prada, as a backward and absurd species. To a considerable degree the attitudes of Peru's post-World War 1 Indianists reflected not just Mexican thought but the primitivism that had for some time been stylish among European and, more recently, North American intellectuals and artists.

One of the traits that French anthropologist Lucien Lévy-Bruhl admired in primitives was their skill as dreamers. While the rationalist met a problem by saying, "I will think about it," primitives resolved "to dream about it."[84] Thereby they gained access to a world of mystic powers that complemented "reality."[85] In the age of Freud, Jung, and Lévy-Bruhl, Peruvians could find pride in their Indians as exemplary dreamers. For confirmation of this they could turn to, among others, Garcilaso de la Vega, an incipient anthropologist of the colonial period who had noted the importance that native Peruvians attached to dreams and their interpretation.[86] Understandably, then, Indians commended themselves to Peruvians seeking life enhancement.

Peruvians in revolt against modernity could further admire Indians for their assumed mastery over astronomy and astrology,[87] for their understanding that man was linked in his life to the heavenly bodies that provided them still another source of completeness missing in the lives of moderns who had set themselves resolutely to sever such connections. Indian pantheism also appealed to Peruvians suffering the symptoms of alienation. The animism of preconquest civilizations and the natives' belief that humans are related in diverse ways to all the forces of nature and have ties involving mutual obligations and expectations,[88] no longer seemed absurd but became instead a comforting source of hope for the restoration of connectedness. Then too, Aprista mystics from Haya on down could find confirmation of their generation's visions, often connected to the myth of the eternal return, in the Indians' circular rather than linear conception of time. Moreover, Indian consciousness, it has been said, does not distinguish clearly between past, present, and future; instead, all three coexist together.[89] Here was something to appeal to the spiritualist mentality, ever in quest of the great synthesis, of explanations for clairvoyance, and of challenges to the allegedly fraudulent and incomplete perceptions of modern consciousness.

Their perceptions aglow with a new romanticism, Peru's Indianists began to see the Incas and the earlier preconquest civilizations as constructors of an ideal civilization based on a fusion of the occult and science. As shamans and sorcerers they had plumbed the mysterious world within, their inward visions sometimes enhanced by drug ingestion. As astronomers, engineers, doctors, agronomists, and the like they had forged a balanced relationship with the natural world. All the while they had recognized the interaction between their own spiritual domain and the visible, touchable world. Aware of the interconnection between the two, they had mastered the magic by which the nonsensory could shape the sensory world.

Just as Helena P. Blavatsky claimed to have found the sources of an ancient wisdom in the East and in the prehistoric mahatmas who supposedly contrived through the ages to convey their knowledge to select souls, so Peruvians of a mystical bent believed they had found in their own land the seat of an ancient wisdom. At the sacred center of the four corners in Cuzco, wise men or *amautas* had perfected a system of knowledge—according to some of the more fanciful Indianists, the amautas may even have been in touch with the eastern mahatmas, communication facilitated by the lost continents of Atlantis and Lemuria. The old wisdom now awaited rediscovery by an emerging group of contemporary amautas. Even as Blavatsky's Theosophism helped revive respect among Indians and other Easterners for their old Hindu and Buddhist wisdom, so spiritualism in its Peruvian guise helped revive admiration among the intelligentsia for some very remarkable—even when not mythologized—early civilizations.

Symbolical Masonry (described briefly in the preceding chapter), with its interest in esoteric knowledge and dreams of restoring an ancient wisdom, seems also to have played a role in vitalizing the Indianist movement. In nineteenth-century France certain Masons believed that Druids and Pythagoreans "had combined to provide an occult ideological alternative to Christianity" and that some facets of this faith, which involved sun worship, had entered into Masonry.[90] During Peru's colonial period a few mystical writers had put together accounts of a golden age in which Indians had far surpassed Christians in attainment of virtue and just social organization.[91] Various millennialist movements of the late colonial period and early nineteenth century found inspiration and justification in these myths, and it is likely that some elements of them found their way into Symbolical Masonry.

Many of the Latin American Masonic Lodges bore Indian names: thus Haya de la Torre entered the Chilam Balam Lodge in Mérida, Yucatán, named after a widely celebrated corpus of Mayan writing, which on some pages drew subtle contrasts between life under the Spaniards and a far happier preconquest existence. In Lima, both Haya de la Torre's brother Edmundo and Luis Heysen, secretary of the PAP in the early 1930s, eventually became Venerable Masters of the Túpac Amaru Lodge,[92] named for a sixteenth-century Inca chieftain and an eighteenth-centu1 namesake, both of whom led insurrections with millenarian overtones Unquestionably, there is a link between Masonry, Indianism, and Peru's spiritualist, millennialist dreams of the 1920s and '30s, but the specific details of this connection await exposition by a future researcher.

Ultimately, Indianism and Aprista use of Indian symbolism derived from a millennialist archetype: the perceived need to create the new order out of those humans who had traditionally been the most truly dispossessed and shoved to margins of society. For most Peruvians tinged with millennialist hopes, there could scarcely be a more effective symbol of the disinherited who awaited new life following the death of the old order that had dehumanized them than the country's Indians. For Magda Portal, however, and a few other Aprista feminists, the woman rather than the Indian symbolized the suppressed being in Latin America, the person with whom a genuine regeneration movement had to be primarily concerned.[94]

A companion for some years of Aprista poet Serafín Delmar and a remarkable person in every respect who awaits her biographer, Portal in 1933 gave voice to thoughts she had been formulating for some time. In that year she published two important short works: *El Aprismo y la mujer* and *Hacia la mujer nueva* (Aprismo and the woman and Toward the new woman). Together, they provide the most dramatic testimony to the awakening Peruvian feminism to be found in the first half of the twentieth century.

Aprismo appealed to Portal, who came to some of her ideas through the Russian feminist Aleksandra Kollantai, because she saw it as penetrating into the Peruvian home "to prepare a new woman," liberated from her marginal role and encouraged to develop her full spiritual and economic potential.[95] Mistress of her home, the Aprista woman would proceed to educate her husband, explaining how she joined him to form a family community and not to serve him as a domestic of inferior status.[96] Furthermore, the work of social improvement would no longer be the province of man but rather of the human pair, the man and the woman, the latter recapturing the place she had lost centuries ago. Awakening from a state of nonawareness, women would attain consciousness and thereby a new psychic balance.[97] In the basic social cell of the new society, women would be somewhat more like men, and men somewhat more like women.

In Jungian terms, Portal foresaw a new order in which women would become one with their animus (the male principle within), while men would join with their anima (the female principle within).[98] At least from the time of the Gnostics, visions of this sort (although obviously not relying on Jungian terminology before the twentieth century) have frequently underlain millenarian movements. The Gospel of Thomas in the Gnostic Gospels, for example, contains a passage in which Christ tells Mary Magdalene that she must become male in order to become a "living spirit, . . . for every woman who will make herself male will enter the Kingdom of Heaven."[99] In a Jungian context, this passage could mean that the woman who manages to become whole with the male principle within her becomes the total, integrated person who approximates the Self, a symbol of the complete fusion of consciousness and the unconscious and of the definitive ending of alienation.

Portal looked forward, then, to the advent of psychically whole and socially liberated women: women who would be equal partners with the whole and liberated men who had managed to overcome their alienation. These were the beings who would make up the new human order after the prevailing one had met its death. Initially Portal regarded Aprismo as destined to hasten the old order's passing so as to prepare the way for the new human. And, initially, Aprismo seemed receptive to feminist tenets.

While in Russia, Haya de la Torre had been impressed by "the total equality of the sexes."[100] Aprismo had introduced a revolution in Peruvian politics by insisting, in the 1931 campaign, on the mobilization of women as well as men. In 1932 party leader Luis Heysen stressed Aprismo's dedication to "equality of civil rights for men and women,"[101] while two years later Rómulo Meneses, another of the party's dignitaries, strongly endorsed the liberation of women.[102]

Throughout history, millenarian movements have often been tinged with what in recent times has come to be called feminism. Yet, for a reason that really is not elusive, these movements have generally accomplished little toward upgrading women's status. Haya de la Torre and his fellow directors of the APRA resembled, in their "feminism," the male leaders of most earlier, failed millenarian movements: they were concerned with liberating the symbolical woman that, like the Indian, lies within. Thus their quest for liberation produced little impact in the outer world, and soon many of the early women followers, Portal included, withdrew from it.[103]

In the case of women, even as in that of Indians, most anti-Aprista Peruvians were unable to distinguish between psychic and social goals, between symbolism or metaphor and reality; and they assumed that Haya meant to stand the existing social order on its head. Thus the defenders of the established order, from whom male domination and white supremacy constituted the essential and eternal order of things, saw Aprismo as the gravest menace Peru had ever confronted. Within the established order various institutions, particularly the Catholic Church, found their own and specific reasons for viewing the PAP as little short of diabolical.

Because of Haya de la Torre's role in blocking the consecration of Peru to the Sacred Heart and because of his connection to Protestantism (through John Mackay) and Masonry, the political movement he founded incurred the opposition of the Church's hierarchy and much of the clergy, even though a good portion of the baptized laity flocked to it. Aprismo's Indianism, seen as linking it with the pagan beliefs, witchcraft, magic, and occult practices of the native culture, rendered it further suspect in the eyes of the Church. Most censurable of all to the guardians of official dogma was the manner in which the APRA, with its claims to a unique reservoir of virtue, morality, and spiritual energies and its visions of a Peruvian Great Awakening, assumed the pretensions and mystique of a new religion.[104] With the "heralds of the new order" having "served formal notice of the existence of a new messianic authority superior to the traditional one."[105] defenders of the old faith struck back with all the power they could command. With the Church, the communists, and most bastions of social traditionalism aligned against it, the APRA faced a formidable coalition of enemies.

Seven

Fundamentals of Aprismo (II): Religion, Regeneration, and Synthesis

The New Religion and Its Promise of Regeneration

While in Russia, Haya de la Torre had been impressed by the Bolshevik manipulation of Christian beliefs and imagery.[1] In Russia, a political movement seemed to be confirming what Engels had understood: "To let loose a tempest in the masses one must present to them their own interests in a religious guise."[2] Then had come the exposure in England to Malinowski and Marett, impressing on Haya the social usefulness of religious energies, and after that the renewal of friendship with John Mackay, who had reassured Haya about the applicability of Biblical texts in pointing the way to social renewal. Haya returned to Peru in the years when the depression's onslaught was making a shambles of the economy, intensifying cultural stress and revitalizing the utopian hopes of the university reform movement. The sort of cultural chaos that has often spawned new religious movements was at hand, and from the outset the APRA seemed as much involved in religion as in politics.

Most accessible to the campaigners in 1931 were city and town dwellers; among them a vast mass, often composed of recent arrivals from the rural sierra, were immersed in various types of "popular Catholicism." Characterized by "a mixture of magic, syncretism, saint worship, and private devotionalism," popular Catholicism responded to a dynamic and a tradition that were "independent of the Church as an institution."[3] Into this realm of popular religion, in which occultism figured more prominently than scholasticism or the edicts of Trent and papal encyclicals, Haya de la Torre plunged eagerly. The success he soon achieved in this setting came in part from the fact that popular religion was by no means confined to the masses. It enveloped as well the middle and even upper classes, many of whose members cherished the memory of a pre-rationalist social order. And it appears to have been mainly the literate, educated persons of Peru, estranged from the official, established religious organization but longing to believe in something, who were most responsive to the combination of occultism, wisdom religion, and orthodox Catholic imagery that Haya concocted into Aprismo's new religion.[4] The truly down-and-out, the lumpenproletariat, seemed to have their doubts about the APRA's faith and voted by and large, in 1931, for Haya de la Torre's principal opponent, Lt. Col. Luis M. Sánchez Cerro.

Revolutionary mystics who initiate what Eric Voegelin describes as gnostic movements, promising paradise on earth,[5] turn frequently to the beliefs and even the language of traditional religion but twist them until at times they become little more than caricature. Precisely this occurred when Manuel Seoane at a political rally developed the theme of the mystical wonders of the Aprista Heart, drawing obviously on Sacred Heart of Jesus lore.[6] More often, it was Haya de la Torre himself who employed the religious imagery, and often he brought his act off with virtuosic skill.[7]

Speaking in Lima in November and in Trujillo in December of 1933 (following his release from penitentiary detention), Haya came across convincingly to many of his audience as he described the sacred Aprista cause of bringing salvation to Peru.[8] The APRA, he insisted at Trujillo, was no mere political party: "political parties cannot surpass what is human, and we aspire to the gigantic role of surpassing the human and surpassing it by heroic action, by magnificent daily feats, elevating ourselves, surpassing ourselves, purifying ourselves, making through our work something new, something beautiful, something eternal that transforms our sorrows into force, energy, creation, something that surges from the very soul of the people that wishes to be forgers of their future and healers of their afflictions.[9]

Referring then to the victims of the unsuccessful Aprista uprising in July 1932 in Trujillo, Haya averred that they counseled him from their tombs: "We are your teachers. Proceed ahead. Lead your party to where we wished to lead it. Make of your party a religion. Make of your party an eternal trajectory through history."[10] After reading or listening to this speech, one might well agree with Víctor Villanueva when he writes, "Haya de la Torre seems concerned with inculcating in his partisans a mystique, a faith, rather than an ideology,"[11] or with Luis F. de las Casas who contends, "Haya is not only the Chief, but the teacher of a new religion."[12]

A host of lesser Aprista dignitaries joined the jefe in fabricating the paraphernalia of a new religion. Labor leader Arturo Sabroso wrote the words to the APRA hymn.[13] Sung to the tune of "La Marseillaise," the hymn called upon Peruvians "to embrace the New Religion," assuring them that through the Alianza Popular they would attain their "longed-for redemption."[14] Another Aprista song combined hope in the good times ahead with denunciation of the movement's political enemies, the Civilistas (members of the Partido Civilista, in whose ranks Haya's father had been inscribed):

> Mothers, who doesn't know that you will teach
> our civil creed along with that of Jesus,
> to the future Apristas, who will be without fear and guilt.
> This will be brought about by those of us who today
> bear the Civilista cross.[15]

A long poem by Serafín Delmar contained these words: "Christ, the invincible revolutionary, will not return to the heavens, if he has not first made man happy on earth: this is what the New Religion says." Toward the end of his work, the poet declared: "the heart of man is such that man should become like God."[16] Little wonder that a party dignitary would attest: "To be an Aprista is not only to know the doctrine, but to have the heart inflamed by faith,"[17] or that a worker would avow, "only the person who has renewed his life is an Aprista."[18]

Just like supporters of Sánchez Cerro in 1931, Apristas had their credo. The APRA credo begins: "I believe in APRA all powerful, creator of the Popular Universities; I believe in Víctor Raúl Haya de la Torre, Founder-Director of our great Party, which was conceived by the work and grace of the Patriotic Spirit." The concluding lines are: "I believe in the Patriotic Spirit of the Aprista leaders; in the faith and union of the members; in the triumph of the Sacred Cause, . . . and that only Aprismo will bring salvation to Peru and that we will enjoy one day a better life."[19]

The conclusion of the Aprista Credo and also some of the other material quoted above shows that the APRA claimed the status of a civil religion.[20] It offered no assurances about another world, and the sort of immortality it promised the faithful was perpetual reverence by the coming generation of believers. What it promised, in addition, was rebirth into a heaven-like existence to be realized on this earth. The concept of an ideal society on earth has, of course, appeared in Christian millennialist movements extending back through the centuries. In the nineteenth century the vision of the ideal temporal order surfaced yet again in, among other guises, anarchism; and with its stress on community, anarcho-syndicalism undoubtedly contributed to Aprismo's secular religion that, toward the conclusion of its Credo, placed stress on the union of members. In this concept of union inheres a notion of a secular mystical body bound together by an animating faith. Indeed, Haya once wrote that the function of the Aprista faith was to transcend individual differences and create the community that humans aspired to because of their subliminal memory *(inframemoria)* of the original community experienced at the maternal breast.[21]

The word *religion* comes from *religare*, meaning to bind up. Thus, religion promises to tie severed parts together into a new whole.[22] But the new wholeness need not be the result of binding persons to what is transcendent. It can result from binding them to what is ineffable within the self, and also from bonding them to fellow beings in a "union of members." It was the nontranscendent salvation that the APRA offered in the most famous of all its chants: *Solo el aprismo salvará al Perú*. Generally translated as "only Aprismo will save Peru," a rendering more faithful to the nuances would be: "Only Aprismo will bring salvation to Peru"—by transforming it into the city on the hill, the site of earthly harmony that Cuzco, purportedly, once had been.

In its promise of secular salvation, the APRA was, like many of the Christian chiliastic movements that wrought havoc in times of stress throughout the middle ages and early modern period, exclusionary. Its prophet alone could dispense salvation, and he would limit salvation to those who believed in him. In constituent assembly debates at the beginning of 1932 Manuel Seoane made this altogether clear. If a person rejected Aprismo out of invincible ignorance, Seoane declared as he borrowed from Catholic theology, then the APRA would still strive to bring temporal salvation to him; but persons and groups who were consciously mistaken, who knew what they were doing and rejected Aprismo out of selfish and sordid motives, had no hope. They were condemned to "the hell of political proscription."[23]

Like all millennialist movements, whether concerned with the secular or the transcendent, Aprismo dealt in regeneration visions and myth. Haya de la Torre delighted in claiming the popular universities had allowed light to penetrate into darkness.[24] Completion of the renovating, restoring transformation in Peru, however, could not take place, Haya maintained, until revolution brought the people of enlightenment into total control within their country. Then and only then could they, and only they, bring to culmination their fecund work among the masses; then and only then could the "masculine impetus of justice" fulfill its destiny by entering "into the native soil." With the chosen people presiding from above, the new Peru would issue from "what is eternal and profound in the Peru that was."[25] Antenor Orrego added his embellishments to this imagery by suggesting that the Peruvian and Latin American masses in general were ready now to be reborn because, more than any other component of the world's populace, they had remained close to the soil.[26]

Picking up on this sort of rebirth symbolism, Aprista feminist Magda Portal wrote of a new dawn, which would see the sun arise and begin to penetrate into the dark homes of the miserable workers.[27] She went on to describe how the great pre-Columbian earth goddess, Pacha Mama, had lain for four hundred years in mourning, the sun no longer warming her mountains. But now there came at last the Aprista Inti (the Inca title for the sun). Pacha Mama would be herself again, bringing forth robust children.[28]

In developing these themes, Aprista mythologists had recourse to a paradigmatic regeneration mythology that can be traced back as readily to the first recorded instances of agricultural and human fertility rites as to the varieties of spiritualist thought in vogue during the 1920s.[29] When Haya de la Torre declared that by dying Apristas made possible the regeneration of Peru, he was attuned to the Greek myths about Persephone and others; and when he observed that Apristas had to suffer, bleed, and undergo persecution as they took the route to Calvary, "the only road adequate for renovation,"[30] he was borrowing not just from Christian mythology but from archetypal regeneration mythology of which Christianity is but one manifestation.[31] Furthermore, the old

Mithraic beliefs involved in the irrigation of soil by a bull's blood are not altogether absent from Haya's perceptions, conscious or subliminal, when he quoted González Prada to the effect that revolutions, in order to be fecund and to produce new people, must always be painful: they will spill blood, but create light; they submerge men but elevate ideas.[32] The leader of an Aprista feminist organization elaborated on this concept when she wrote that the blood of martyrs killed at Trujillo in 1932 "has had the prodigious result of fertilizing our Party, because with this irrigation our ranks have grown, and there has been revealed to us the straight and luminous path on which we, now purified, must continue." She concluded, "The great causes are always generously irrigated with blood. . . ."[33]

The imagery of society's death as a prerequisite for the more perfect resurrected society had its counterpart in the psychic death of the individual Aprista that, according to party doctrine, would make possible his or her reemergence as a more perfect person. Again and again, Aprismo's preachers harped on the need for party members literally to destroy their old identities, to obliterate their very egos, through merciless abnegation, asceticism, discipline, and self-control.[34] Thus, Haya exhorted: "I founded Aprismo in order to redeem my people. But, I desire that each son of the people prepare himself well so that he can make good use of his redeemed life. . . . Aprismo needs strong men, free from vice and ignorance, free from selfishness, who will deliver themselves totally to the work of redeeming and of bringing salvation to our brothers."[35]

Even as Dionysus, or as modern-day evangelicals, Apristas were to be twice-born. Through the ages human beings have longed, intermittently at least, for a destruction of the established order, social and psychic, for a return to the primal chaos of most origin mythologies, as the necessary prerequisite for initiating a new order. Once the old regime is destroyed, then supposedly comes that magical, liminal moment when all is possible.[36]

The millenarian frenzy in which APRA was born and which forged a mystique that endured for more than a generation was owing in large part to Haya de la Torre's ability to speak in primordial images. Carl Jung writes, "He who speaks in primordial images speaks with a thousand voices; he enthralls and overpowers, while at the same time he lifts the idea he is trying to express out of the occasional and the transitory into the realm of the ever-enduring. He transmutes our personal destiny into the destiny of mankind, thereby evoking in us all those beneficent forces that ever and anon have enabled mankind to find refuge from every peril and to outlive the longest night."[37] But, the process is not without peril, as Jung pointed out on more than one occasion in deploring the Hitler phenomenon, for he who speaks in primordial images can unleash maleficent as well as beneficent forces.

Ever since the mid-1920s Haya had thought about Romain Rolland's presentiment, one in which most spiritualists to some degree shared, of a regeneration that would originate in the East as the capitalist, Western world destroyed itself. Writing in Berlin in 1930, he speculated on Rolland's later hypothesis that the new era might actually begin in the West, as Latin America awakened to its "universal destiny as the synthesis of two worlds."[38] Yet Haya did not like to abandon the symbolism of the dawn that came inevitably in the East. He found the answer to this dilemma in 1935, and it came through his space-time theories.

Observing that only the speed of light is constant and that space and time are relative, Haya pointed out that for Europeans Russia lay in the East and that the Great War constituted the midnight of their century. Then, as the war approached its end, the Russian Revolution became visible in the East. Now, in the mid-1930s, the whole Western world approached another midnight. The subsequent new dawn had not yet begun to appear, although all kinds of John the Baptists heralded its arrival from their deserts. The new East, Haya then suggested (and here he seems to find inspiration in a visionary work by the seventeenth-century Lima creole Antonio Rodríguez de León Pinelo) was Indo-America. "Although we have been seen as the Old World's West, nonetheless owing to the relativity of space and time we are truly the Old World's East. Thus the cradle of the new dawn can be our America." While this was true, Haya cautioned his readers, it was necessary always to remember that "we must seek within ourselves the actual East and discover in it the origins of our new sunrise."[39]

My suspicions as to where Haya found part of the inspiration for the latter part of this message stem from an analysis written by Jacques Lafaye of León Pinelo's work *El paraíso en el nuevo mundo*. Lafaye writes (the inner quotations are generally from *El paraíso*):

Antonio de León Pinelo offers an example of the preoccupation with proving that the West was the new 'East.' Seeking to reconcile his faith in an 'American Paradise' with revealed truth, he recalled that Moses had written his description of the earthly paradise while he was in exile in the desert to which he had led the people of God. Although Moses had placed his paradise in the East, León Pinelo did not regard this statement as incompatible with his own claim that Paradise was in America; it sufficed to make a simple calculation of longitude: 'One can state with all geographic precision that Mexico was in the eastern hemisphere in relation to Moses when he was writing on the Sinai.' If the grass is always greener on the 'road of Saint Thomas' [assumed by León Pinelo and many visionaries of the colonial period to have preached the gospels in the Spanish "Indies" centuries before the conquest], the American prolongation of the 'road to Saint James' [according to myth, St. James had converted the early Iberians to Christianity], it was because the star which had arisen in the East of the Judaic eschatology had accomplished in sixteen centuries its revolution to the West, [becoming] the new 'North Star' of Christian hope.[40]

Whether writing in the mid-seventeenth century or in the mid-1930s, the mystic seems capable of finding logical, or extralogical, explanations for his beliefs.

The East that lies "within ourselves" is another of those concepts that has appealed to mystics through the ages. Whether within or without, the East has been stereotyped as the realm of Buddha-like resignation, of "feminine" passivity, in contrast to the acquisitive, outward-thrusting, "masculine," assertive West. In psychological terms, the West stood for ego consciousness, driven on by the urge to expand the province of what was individual and differentiated, whereas the East, symbolizing the unconscious, stood for containment of individualism and for nondifferentiation. Projected into the outer world, ego consciousness was equivalent to the capitalist spirit of possessive individualism and aggressive expansion, whereas the unconscious typified the need-to-surrender of collectivism. Some of the stereotypes of the West-East dichotomy are set forth by Jung, who saw the dichotomy as originating in the psyche. The East, Jung contended, "lies essentially within us." He saw it in terms of the collective unconscious, "constantly at work creating new spiritual forces" that may help subdue the expansive tendencies, the "boundless lust for prey" that characterized both ego consciousness within the psyche and modern, Western man in the outside world.[41]

In seeking the East, Haya revealed one of the dilemmas that plagued him through most of his life. When Haya dealt with regeneration, often he was thinking in terms of psychic rebirth, of returning to or surrendering to the inward realms of the unconscious in order to find the wholeness that had disappeared, as it does in all persons, when ego consciousness began the process of severing connections to its nest of origins. Beyond that, more as a guru than as a politician, he was thinking in terms of helping people experience, on a mass scale, the sort of "oceanic feeling" he had known at Cuzco and at other times in his life. In the next chapter, for example, we will see that Aprista rallies were more like revival meetings than political events. As he presided over mass rallies, Haya sought to put people in touch with the East that lay within.

By the end of the 1930s the vision that most beguiled Haya was no longer that of Indo-America as the East. Having toyed with this vision, Haya returned to his concept, acquired initially through Rolland and Keyserling, of Indo-America as a point between East and West, where the synthesis of the two would take place. Here was the response of the typical spiritualist to Rudyard Kipling's man-of-the-world insistence that "never the twain shall meet."

The East-West and the North-South Synthesis

The Peruvian Aprista Party espoused both a Minimum and a Maximum Program. The Minimum Program set forth the reforms that Apristas hoped to introduce into Peru, while the Maximum Program focused more on the world as it stressed, among other points, the need to achieve the solidarity of all oppressed peoples. Included as one of the Maximum Program's objectives was the internationalization—later changed to the inter-Americanization[42]—of the Panama Canal. In a 1926 essay Haya maintained that internationalization of the canal was "one of the points of greatest transcendence" in the entire Aprista program.[43] In part, practical considerations explain this stance. Control of the canal by the United States was seen as increasing Latin American vulnerability to the operation of Yankee monopolistic capitalism. And the canal in North American hands posed a special threat to Pacific coast countries that were vulnerable in their trade with Europe.[44] Beyond practical considerations, the symbolism of regeneration caused Aprista mythologists to focus on the canal. According to Gabriel del Mazo, "Indo-Hispanic America" was bound by the seas both to West and East. "Between the civilization of Europe and the cultures of the giant peoples of the other Indies, the New World must discover itself."[45] This it could do, Mazo believed, by fusing the qualities of East and West. Obviously the canal, as the great connecting passage between East and West, had far too great a metaphorical importance to allow for its unilateral ownership by one New World country—especially one that in its rampant materialism seemed to have grown unaware of the redeeming graces of Eastern mysticism.

More than any other Aprista visionaries, more even than Haya himself, who since Trujillo days had looked up to him as a savant,[46] Antenor Orrego stressed the East-West fusion and therefore attached enormous importance to an interoceanic canal as a numinous symbol. He developed these ideas at great length in his 1939 book, *Pueblo continente*, referred to earlier as the Cabala and Gnostic Gospels of Aprismo.

Known as APRA's amauta (amautas, it will be recalled, were Peru's pre-Columbian wise men who maintained the purity of sacred beliefs) and given to a prose style more esoteric and opaque than that of Haya de la Torre even in his most mystical moments, *Pueblo continente* hailed the future glories of a Latin American (Orrego chose this designation in preference to the jefe's Indo-America) "people-continent." About to lead the way to attainment of a new stage of perfection in the spiral ascent of humanity, Latin America would combine the meditation and introspection of the East with the experimental genius of the West. Thus it would resolve the problem of opposites, submerging them all into a great synthesis.[47] Orrego described Latin America as being at the crossroad, thus utilizing in his imagery the cross, that archetypal symbol of the meeting of opposites that has stirred the fancy of humans at least from the time they first learned to make pictographs and petroglyphs. Rendering the interoceanic canal all the more numinous as a crossroad symbol is the fact that it could be envisaged as a vital link joining not only East and West, but North and South—actually, the Canal flows in a north-south direction.

For a time Haya de la Torre seemed confused as he pondered the proper relationship between North and South, between the United States and Indo-America. Initially influenced by the one-sided denunciations of economic imperialism written by J. A. Hobson in England and Scott Nearing and Joseph Freeman in the United States[48] and by the Marxist ideology so much in the Latin American air following World War I, Haya delivered some pretty blistering attacks against the northern colossus and its economic outreach. To North American capitalists and to their Latin American collaborators *(entreguistas* or *vendepatrias)* who had delivered or sold out their countries he attributed much of the southern continent's ills.[49] By 1927, however, Haya (as noted in the treatment of soft Marxism in chapter 4) was beginning to attenuate his attacks.[50] In his 1931 campaign oratory occasional flashes of the anti-imperialist militant still appeared; but the tone that sounded most clearly was one of relative moderation as Haya urged the balancing of national and foreign economic interests to establish "a total and harmonious economy."[51] The anti-imperialist state he hoped to found would preside over "state capitalism." Run as a technocracy, it would be entrusted to experts in each field of economic endeavor. Within the anti-imperialist state, ample room would remain for private capital, both foreign and domestic. Foreign enterprises currently in Peru would not be subjected to confiscatory measures, although the state might modify contracts with them to obtain a fairer share of earnings.[52]

To Haya it appeared that the United States, with its Western, capitalist aggrandizing spirit ever at work, needed to expand into Latin America, just as the more passive, less acquisitive Latin America needed United States capital in order to escape from impoverishment. The anti-imperialist state would provide a just solution to the needs of North and South America, while ending the old style of contact in which southern oligarchies had placed inadequate demands on northern exporters of capital and goods.

To some considerable degree Haya's hedging on his initial anti-imperialism resulted from practical considerations. For one thing, the constituency he aimed at was made up largely of middle sectors, aspiring to capitalist status themselves and anxious to establish their own advantageous arrangements with foreign capital once they had ousted what they perceived as an oligarchy that currently monopolized those arrangements. Moreover, Haya explained that he began to revise his anti-imperialist prejudices after talking with some workers in northern Peru upon his return from exile in July of 1931. The workers explained their satisfaction with their foreign employers, noting that their wages and benefits were above average and expressing their forebodings about any move toward nationalization.[53]

In truth, Haya had a delicate balancing act to perform. Elements of the middle and lower classes whose support he wooed would be put off by cries to oust the foreign devils. On the other hand, many of the middle-sector intellectuals he courted leaned toward Marxism, and Haya would alienate them if he appeared soft on imperialism. Nor could he retain the backing of landowners in the north, whose property was being engulfed by foreign land holdings,[54] unless he promised to deal with the menace of foreign capitalism. In addition to practical considerations, however, Haya's spiritualist-tinged ideology counseled moderation and equanimity in approaching issues of economic imperialism, especially the economic penetration emanating from North America.

In *The Rediscovery of Truth*, published in Germany in 1928 and very probably read by Haya during his second European exile, and also in *South American Meditations* (published in a Spanish edition in 1931), which we know Haya read, Count Hermann Keyserling dealt at length on relations between developed and underdeveloped countries. As was to be expected, he brought the spiritualist, esoteric approach to bear on the subject. Developed countries, he asserted in the first of these books, had a high tension resulting from their faster, more "acute" rhythm, whereas the undeveloped countries existed virtually in stasis. A new era would dawn when the two areas merged so as to attain "a higher rhythmic unity." The count envisaged a "universal and all-embracing rhythm in which the existing antagonisms would enter into mutual counterpoint relations and cease their warring with one another.[55] The counterpoint world would begin only when the higher-tension rhythms of the advanced regions penetrated into the slumbering areas of the world. In consequence would come "the abolishment of imperialism" as the penetrating rhythm of the advanced country ceased to clash with the rhythm of the dormant locale, "the two rhythms now being mutually absorbed into the vibrations of a totality."[56]

In *South American Meditations*, as may be recalled from the chapter 5 treatment of Keyserling, the count became even more explicit in his two-in-one-flesh sort of sexual analogy. A spermatozoon became the symbol for the high tension areas, an ovum for those at rest.[57] Developing the sexual analogy further, Keyserling contended that every historical epoch of progress and rebirth is based on counterpoint: one "unilateralism" existing as a monad crosses with another unilateralism.[58] And the role that Latin America was destined to play in the coming epoch of rebirth arose out of its unilateral femininity. Always, the count maintained, "the salvation of mankind depends on women."

The influence of Keyserling—or some common source of esoteric enlightenment that both men frequented—seems obvious as Haya de la

Torre proceeded to give a North-South interpretation to the reawakening that Orrego had seen in terms of an East-West synthesis. It was, after
all, logical to identify Indo-America with the East and to move the East
to the South; in Haya's view, the Indian, who constituted the basic psychological stratum of all Indo-America, exemplified those traits of intuition and extrarationality imputed to the East, and to women.

As early as 1928, Haya had begun to employ the sexual analogy in
writing about North-South relations. In that year he wrote of the need
for Indo-America to unite in order to guard the productive powers of its
soil against the gigantic power—by implication a phallic power—of imperialism.[59] Without stretching the imagination too far, one can detect almost a feminist insistence that the "sisterhood" had to band together to
be able to control their bodies. Once united, they would no longer be
forced—"Against Our Will," to use Susan Brownmiller's terminology[60]—
into a situation of rape. Haya is reported to have referred to the Peruvian
oligarchy then selling out the country to foreign capitalists as "the Celestina of national prostitution."[61] Celestina, as depicted in an early sixteenth century Spanish classic attributed to Fernando de Rojas,[62] was the
prototype procurer, the bigger-than-life female pimp. In all of this,
Haya's position is certainly not one of opposition to masculine-feminine
union. But he insists that union occur under conditions of mutual dignity, under circumstances in which the feminine partner retains control
over her body and the right to enter voluntarily, on terms that she helps
establish, into relationship with her opposite.

When he wrote on the subject in 1960, Haya's views on imperialism—
and on regeneration—remained much what they had been in the late
1920s and early 30s.[63] The future might still very well belong to Latin
America (by now he sometimes used Latin and Indo-America interchangeably). In the "superdeveloped" United States as well as parts of
Europe, total domination over nature had been accomplished, a domination brought about in the interest of individual gain and material ag-
grandizement. Latin America, however, had operated at a slower rate.
Moreover, its space or geography was different from that in the developed world, often posing greater challenges. Consequently, the Latin
American historical space-time was still comparatively undefiled by the
forces of scientific technology.[64]

Underlying Haya's analysis, in which passive nature rather than the
Indian becomes a metaphor for the unconscious and the feminine prin-

ciple, was the suggestion that Latin America, still a Pacha Mama–like goddess of nature, was uniquely capable of giving birth to a new order. But she could not produce this offspring if she chose to isolate herself against penetration by the superdeveloped land. So, Latin America had to enter into marriage with the North American masculine principle. Two distinct historical space-times had to be brought together, and when this happened a gradual and pacific process could begin by which the one would be harmoniously reconciled to the other. Nature, represented by the resources of inwardness, spirituality, intuition, and the chthonic elements of the "eternal feminine," would be subjected to greater domination by the traits of outward, material development, calculation, and rationality inhering in the "eternal masculine." But this process would halt short of the extremes reached in the United States, where circumstances of historical space-time had prevented nature from achieving its fair share in the mix.

Myths that view attainment of earthly perfection through the ideal fusion of feminine and male are, of course, as old as time. The Chinese have their yin-yang vision of the universe, and in the world of Andean Indian cultures, everything is seen in terms of maleness and femaleness.[65] Furthermore, Plato had the idea (that later influenced Freud's view on the sex drive) that humans, having initially appeared on earth as four-armed, four-legged, two-headed, and bisexual beings, only to be split by a god who feared their power, were driven on by the compelling desire to reunite their separate halves in androgynous completeness.[66] In Hindu symbolism the idea of fulfillment, of wholeness, is conveyed by the joining of the female with the male principle in the androgynous Purusha, who is not unlike the Gnostic Anthropos;[67] in Tantric Buddhism of Tibet the deity Samvara is often depicted in copulation with his consort, symbolizing the perfect union of the traits of masculinity and femininity.[68] For Christians, the male God is wed to his feminine Church.[69] Thus sexual analogies recur constantly in mythical thought and are used to convey notions of spiritual wholeness that transcend considerations of the flesh.

Given Haya de la Torre's belief that the long-suffering, passive, Oriental-like Indians constituted the basic determinant of the Latin American psyche, it is not surprising that he would have assigned his continent the female role of a Sleeping Beauty who awaits the arrival of a masculine archetype. If there is any deep meaning to be read into the fact that in youthful bullfight games Haya always chose the role of the bull rather than that of the matador,[70] it could be that Haya himself identified with the symbol of the one that awaits penetration. But I do not think Haya necessarily identified with the feminine principle. In my view, he felt himself the complete representative of two worlds, the full, complete being, the hermaphrodite—a divinity symbol venerated by millenarian movements on up to the counterculture of the 1960s with its unisex ideals.[71] In the following chapter we shall see a good deal more of Haya's use of hermaphrodite symbolism in his exegesis of Peruvian regeneration.

In an essay of the early 1950s in which the metaphors are even murkier than in most of his visionary writings, Haya observes that given its mixed nature of good and evil, it is necessary "to confront and appraise imperialism with the two-faced serpentine gaze of the caduceus."[72] Because of his claimed ability to do this, Haya seems to be comparing himself to Mercury, the bearer of the caduceus. In esoteric wisdom, as taken up especially by the alchemists, Mercury was androgynous—and as employed by the medical profession as its symbol, the caduceus of course symbolizes wholeness. Often in drawings that depict Mercury, the head of one of the snakes encircling the rod points toward the sun or male principle, while the head of the second reptile points toward the moon or feminine principle.[73] Moreover, Mercury, in his earlier Greek form as Hermes, was the guide of souls to Hades and the male conduit for their return to life in the body of a new mother. He was at home in two worlds: that of living persons enjoying the sun's light as well as that of chthonic beings in the netherworld.

By comparing himself to Mercury-Hermes, Haya was also establishing an association with a trickster deity. But I prefer to see his use of this imagery as an indication of his belief that he had already become a full and complete person, "the transmutation in the unitary one of all the contradictions and conflicts of the continent, . . . the conjunction of two antithetical worlds," as Orrego (quoted in the preceding chapter) had described him.[74] Having assimilated and harmonized the respective natures and historical space-times of Indo-America and of the United States, he was the harbinger of the hemisphere's new humanity in which North and South would fuse and imperialism would be cured of its rapacious ways.[75]

The above interpretations may seem farfetched, especially in view of the possibility of explaining Haya's position on imperialism, partially at least, in terms of political expediency and practical, economic considerations. Yet for Haya de la Torre the mystical and the esoteric tended to take precedence over the practical and the empirical. This fact lies at the heart of his rejection of unilateral positivism and materialism.

As Indo-America, enveloping the central crossroads at the North-South, East-West conjunction, began to absorb and synthesize various extremes and contraries, it would become the very model of harmony, equilibrium, and balance. And some of the principal portions of the APRA's programs—specifically the corporative designs of the Minimum Program and the continental unity objectives of the Maximum Program—depicted how Indo-America would ultimately structure itself as a model of the harmonious joining of opposites. Once again, it will be necessary to examine sections of Aprista programs, usually approached through economic and political analyses, in terms of their symbolical, esoteric, and psychological meanings.

Indo-America as the Organic Center of the World

The archetypal psychic struggle may be viewed as pitting ego consciousness, which is striving for autonomy, against the collective unconscious that constantly threatens absorption and envelopment. The myth of pure capitalism by which so many in the modern world have been attracted may be seen as a projection of the psychic quest to overcome archetypal tension by awarding total victory to an expansive ego consciousness—the goal of ego consciousness being "to establish private ownership of the self, which is psychological capitalism."[76] In contrast, the myth of pure socialism (built on the premise that the emergence of consciousness constitutes a tragedy akin to original sin) projects the desire to escape tension by granting unconditional triumph to the collective unconscious or whatever one chooses to call the inward repository of what is unspecified, undifferentiated, and apparently infinite.

The inward, psychic attempt to deny total victory to either pole and instead to achieve balance between them projects into the outside world as a vision of reconciling "the aspirations of the differentiated individual with the social functions of the collective mass."[77] It projects also as a vision of reconciling the one with the many. "Perhaps," it has been writ-

146

ten, "the whole of human history is no more than the search for harmony between individual and collective."[78]

The social system that would, ostensibly, synthesize autonomous consciousness (popularly stereotyped as a male principle), which is oriented toward enterprise and self-maximizing struggle, and the collective urge (stereotypical femaleness), which seeks security through surrender of autonomy and abandonment of struggle, has received many names. Entering the political maelstrom in 1931, Haya de la Torre alternately termed his synthesizing system corporatism, organic democracy, and functional democracy.[79] Soon, however, he abandoned the word corporatism in favor of cooperativism. The former, he acknowledged, had acquired fascistic connotations; and within a few years of the inception of the PAP, Haya was at pains to deny any link to fascism. Moreover, he had acquired a liking for the term cooperativism because of its popularity among English socialist circles.[80] From the mid-1930s onward, he used cooperativism, organic democracy, and functional democracy interchangeably.[81] Whatever he called his system, Haya expected from it the dialectical synthesis of that thesis-antithesis duality of liberty and equality that has loomed so large in history.[82]

With society restructured—from the municipal on up through the national level—on the basis of functional entities, every citizen would be able to satisfy the collective yearning to retreat into the equality of a group setting without surrendering roles of individual participation. Each Peruvian could participate within his or her appropriate functional guild, corporation, or association and could strive to maximize personal productivity—but largely for the common good of the group to which he or she was associated by natural, functional ties. Within the cooperativist structure the purely selfish motivations that impelled the capitalist in the atomistic, inorganic society would, purportedly, be constrained. Unusually ambitious types with particularly strong ego-maximizing drives would enjoy opportunity for individual accumulation and thus could rise above dependence on the social-welfare mechanisms to be administered by each guild. Still, even in their case, the consciousness of being bound to a group with which they were organically united through common function would to some degree temper the urge toward autonomy. All the while the great majority of citizens, secure within their functional associations, would be shielded against the bourgeois temptations that multiplied, unchecked, in inorganic societies.

And, warmed by a sense of belonging, Peruvians would feel that they were more than ciphers in an impersonal society and thus would escape the alienation and ennui that threatened the stability of democracy in countries of unrestricted capitalism.

In line with Haya de la Torre's expressed preference for qualitative over quantitative democracy,[83] the APRA aspired to organize Peru vertically.[84] Each municipality would be structured according to functional divisions, and at this grass-roots level members would participate in determining the conduct of guild affairs. From municipal guilds would rise a vertical structure, passing through a regional level and culminating at the top in a National Economic Congress (NEC).[85] In this august body, lower-level functional groups would be represented by spokesmen who had risen through the filtering process of local and regional elections. Ostensibly, the functionally elected representatives in the NEC would be those members of the subsidiary occupational groups whose superiority was recognized by their associates. Unlike officials in inorganic societies, in which individuals were severed or alienated from natural wholes, the members of the NEC would remain organically joined to a social base. As persons who had attained to higher individual awareness or consciousness, they would remain rooted in the functional soil appropriate to them. Simultaneously, they would be one and collective. Rather than the free-wheeling atoms of elective assemblies in inorganic societies, bound to those they represented merely by "windy abstractions," they would be organically connected "through common action and common experience."[86]

The legislators of the new state envisaged by the APRA would be not merely integrated, organic persons; they would also be experts in particular fields, in contrast to the dilettante politicians of inorganic democracies.[87] In association with the national president, these experts would exercise the moderating power, the purpose of which was to coordinate the activities of the diverse functional associations that composed society. Haya compared the moderating power to the function of a watchmaker[88] who synchronized, by a system of gears, the rhythms of diverse components. What the watchmaker did with the components, the wielders of the moderating power would do with the "cells" of society.

Inclusion of functional democratic or cooperativist goals in APRA's ideology is not surprising. Cooperative ideas, in a dizzying variety of guises, some fascistic and others stoutly antifascistic, were much in the intellectual air of the times.[89] Indeed, Haya's rival for the presidency in 1931, Luis M. Sánchez Cerro, included corporatist ideas in his program. More likely than not, whenever the quest for utopia grips the human fancy, corporatist thought of one kind or another will surface. And for much of the Western world, the period between the two world wars was the age, par excellence, of utopian fancies.

Basic to the corporative lure is the millenarian dream of reconciling the opposites of the individual and the group, capitalism and collectivism, the one and the many, the hero and the great mother, consciousness and the unconscious, liberty and equality, masculinity and femininity.[90] And this dream has appeared in widely scattered locales even within fairly recent times. In Juan and Evita Perón's Argentina the system that would synthesize individualism and collectivism, capitalism and socialism, was called *justicialismo;* and, like Aprismo, justicialismo came to be viewed by its faithful as a religion. In Julius Nyerere's Tanzania the miraculous system was called first *ujamaa* and then villagization,[91] while in other parts of the "Dark Continent" the preferred denomination was "African Socialism."[92] In Muamar el-Qadaffi's Libya the system that will reconcile opposites is called *jamahirya* and it is all explained in *The Green Book.* In turn-of-the-century France the great harmonizing system bore the name Solidarism; for Hitler, the tag was National Socialism. In post–World War II Latin America, starry-eyed Christian Democrats touted the communitarian society. Actually, a paradigmatic corporatism subsumes all of these utopian systems; and it was natural and well-nigh inevitable that Aprismo would embrace corporatism from the start, although shortly rechristening it cooperativism.

What provides the common underpinning to all the systems enveloped by paradigmatic corporatism is the expectation of resolving the tensions and the opposites that inhere in the very psyche, thereby bringing into being the new human. When all goes well in the outer world, people on the whole manage to live comfortably enough with inward tensions. But when social structures threaten to collapse and outer sources of assurance disappear, the torment of the warring inner drives becomes less endurable; and it is then that people are apt to turn to the grail quest of being reborn in personal and social conditions free from polar tension. If the apocalyptic approach of annihilating one of the great polar sources of tension is not to their taste, then they will opt for corporatism's promise of synthesis. Histories of individuals and of nations teach that the quest ends always in failure. Nonetheless, it goes on, for the lessons of history are hopelessly weak in comparison with the propelling force of myths that arise out of psychically determined hopes.

The spiritualist Haya de la Torre believed that the envisaged corporative synthesis would enable Indo-America to harmonize from the vital East-West, North-South crossroad at the center of the world, the disparate rhythms and historical space-times of the human cosmos. And Peruvians had to assume the mission of teaching other Indo-Americans to fulfill their destiny. Haya recognized the need to animate persons with a great ideal if they were to utilize their energies toward transforming the world. Here was a vision for his countrymen grand enough to arouse anyone capable of eschewing mere rationality.

Apristas traded on yet another vision to galvanize Peruvians and Indo-Americans into action. Picking up on the Bolivarian dream of continental unity, revived by the university reform movement and eloquently developed in the 1920s by the Argentine Manuel Ugarte[93] and a number of lesser pensadores, Haya de la Torre joined Antenor Orrego in calling for the unity of the Latin American people-continent. (Both Peruvians appear to have been influenced in this by Count Keyserling.[94]) According to Orrego the number of potential people-continents in the world was seven. Each of the seven shared a potential for unity that transcended presently prevailing differences among component nation states. Latin America had the brightest immediate destiny of the seven because the nation-states composing it had already begun—said Orrego, in total defiance of reality—to coalesce in unity. Thus Latin America would soon realize the dialectical synthesis of nationalism and internationalism.[95] All the more, then, would the people-continent that Apristas were about to awaken to its promise qualify as the internationally harmonious center that could orchestrate the polyphonic symphony of the human cosmos.

Eight

The APRA Is Born from Death: Persecution and the Forging of a Mystique, 1931–39

Peruvians Reject Haya de la Torre and the New Religion: The 1931 Election

The time of dreaming a new Indo-America into being from across the seas came to an end in July of 1931 as Haya de la Torre returned home to head the Peruvian Aprista Party (PAP), founded the previous year by his associates, many of whom had shared the exile experience. The time for practical politics had arrived, and Haya threw himself into the campaign with abandon. From the moment he entered the capital on August 15 to the waving of palm branches by an estimated one hundred thousand limeños, enjoying an added diversion on a religious holiday,[1] Haya had to rely on his vaunted ability to function with only four or five hours sleep. On August 20 he presented his third major address since arriving in Lima as he officially accepted the PAP's presidential nomination. From that date until his death in 1979, Haya was the PAP's maximum chief—its *jefe máximo*.

During their years in exile as they hatched unrealistic plots and utilized clandestine channels for their propaganda, Apristas had acquired a reputation as dangerous fanatics filled with a sense of their own importance and disinclined to share command with those who had not suffered at the hands of the "tyrant" Leguía and had not undergone the moral purification of exile. Furthermore, some of Haya's demagogic attacks of the 1920s directed against imperialism and capitalism were recalled now, along with his attempts to radicalize the university, to indoctrinate workers with "subversive" ideas through the popular universities, and his alleged complicity with Marxists, anarchists, Masons, and Protestants—the whole array of "antinational" types excoriated by conservatives—in blocking Peru's consecration to the Sacred Heart. Finally, Haya's glorification of the Indian and his insistence upon the name Indo-America outraged many Peruvians and perhaps even rekindled abiding fears of race war. For many of the country's "decent people" *(gente decente)*, Indians were no better than savages, and civility derived exclusively from European culture. The fact that Haya de la Torre's use of Indianism was mainly symbolical mattered not; in this instance as in many others the fears that the APRA generated were no more rational than the visions around which its program was built.

Arrayed against the PAP was another new political party, the Revolutionary Union (Unión Revolucionaria, or UR), formed to back the candidacy of the lieutenant colonel who had won the gratitude of the majority of Peruvians by overthrowing the discredited Leguía dictatorship in 1930. A man of action, risen from the people and initially dismissed by most of Peru's well-born, in part because of his mixed-blood ancestry and purported lack of refinement, Luis M. Sánchez Cerro was not given to deep political theorizing. But he had a notable gift for communicating with the humble classes. Literally, he spoke their language, including sometimes its vulgarities and obscenities. "He understood them and they understood him," according to one of Peru's most astute political observers. "He loved them and because of this he won their love."[2]

The UR's platform, written principally by Sánchez Cerro, was an effective, even impressive, document. It called for hard work and sacrifice and for recognition of the capacity of all elements in the population, Indian, European, Negro, and mixed-blood, to contribute to the forging of a modern republic. In a partisan note obviously directed against the APRA, the platform stated:

Nothing could be more prejudicial to the country than to elevate to its government a closed group of narrow and sectarian spirit, especially now that we have scarcely begun the recreation of ordinary political life and institutions following the dictatorship. If the direction of public affairs were entrusted to partisan intolerance, to the hatred of a sect, to demagoguery and violence, it would be impossible to prepare the way for democracy in Peru. With a regime of sectarian hatred in power, it would be impossible to reestablish public liberties after their long, eleven-year eclipse. If a group whose goal is exclusivism in politics governs the country, it will be extremely difficult to accommodate the divergent tendencies and aspirations of organized social and economic groups to the extent that is always essential to the operation of a true democracy.[3]

Well aware of a reputation that had to be lived down, Haya de la Torre tried to attenuate the aura of extremism that attached to him. In his public appearances he took the high road, avoiding personal invective, speaking most of the time in moderate terms, and urging just as much as the UR platform a coalition of Peruvians from all social, economic, and ethnic backgrounds. And Haya was a master of ritual. The mass meetings in which he was the star attraction were skillfully planned and brilliantly executed dramatic extravaganzas. They heralded the arrival of populist politics in Peru and harked back to the pageantry of the Renaissance through which various rulers sought to enhance their legitimacy. To prescient observers, the spectacle of the Aprista mass meetings might also have revealed that Haya de la Torre was as much interested in putting on a performance as in achieving practical ends—a tendency that would ultimately cause a rift between him and some of his practical-minded followers.

In addition to the high road and the political theater of the Aprista campaign, there was also a low road that some of Haya's associates traveled. Luis Heysen, for example, in a campaign tract quoted St. Thomas Aquinas to the effect that a being whose very nature consigned it to an inferior grade could never raise itself, regardless of ambition and efforts, to a higher grade. "The ass cannot aspire to become a horse; and Sánchez Cerro must always continue to be Sánchez Cerro, imprudent, irascible, explosive." He was, concluded Heysen, illiterate and neurotic, the type of advanced paranoic, suffering from "psychic self-inflation," who "can only be studied with the books of Freud and Adler in hand."[4] Heysen further accused Sánchez Cerro and his family of trafficking in narcotics,[5] a charge that would be leveled against Haya de la Torre in later stages of his career.

Some Apristas traveled another low road, that of physical aggression. As the campaign drew toward its conclusion, UR rallies in Lima consistently outdrew those of the APRA. To this situation some Apristas responded with a violence that was probably spontaneous, perpetrated by undisciplined roughnecks, rather than planned from above. In Lima alone some twenty Sánchez Cerro supporters were killed, frequently gunned down from cars in Chicago gangland style. These acts, combined with the now widely known Aprista plots to place Haya in power by insurrection at the end of the 1920s and also shortly after Sánchez Cerro overthrew Leguía, added to the PAP's reputation for violence.

Meanwhile some Aprista campaigners abandoned the chief's restraint on issues of imperialism and went all out in their attacks both against predatory North American capitalists and their Peruvian collaborators, the latter depicted as lackeys of Wall Street—a charge, incidentally, repeated by right-wing extremists waging their own campaign against capitalist-style modernization.[6] According to a PAP propaganda tract, Peru's economy was two-thirds controlled by foreign capitalism, and virtually all the nation's problems stemmed from its neocolonial status.[7] Heysen described imperialism as "the ruin and misery" not only of Peru but of Latin America as a whole, of China, and "of all the people whose reality is similar to ours."[8] In the view of Magda Portal, symbol of the liberated Aprista woman, imperialism explained every facet of despotism in Andean America. The workers, the real people, knew enough not to permit Yankee penetration; and so the bourgeois "sellouts" who feathered their nests by collaborating with foreigners had to repress the people.[9] Latin America, she concluded, has only one problem: "imperialism, which envelops and suffocates her and makes her serve its interests, enslaving meantime her people."[10]

Just as Hitler found a scapegoat for all national problems in the Jew, so certain Apristas waging their millenarian revolt against materialism (and borrowing shamelessly from Marxist-Leninist cant) found the all-purpose scapegoat in the Yankee imperialist. E. J. Hobsbawm has observed that it is always more difficult to raise the revolt against an established national political structure than to reject the foreigner.[11] By identifying their country's collaborationist establishment with the foreigner, Aprista propagandists apparently believed they were making it easier to overthrow the domestic power structure. To some extent, however, the rhetoric of Aprista firebrands backfired, and for an obvious reason. Many Peruvians at this point—as Haya himself understood—looked forward not to the introduction of socialism but to a return to capitalism's predepression successes; and this return was assumed to require the continuing presence of foreign capital. In a personal interview, Haya managed to assure the United States ambassador to Peru that the APRA posed no menace to foreign capital.[12] But Haya could scarcely go about the entire country reassuring vested interests, and those aspiring to become vested interests, that they need not take Aprista propaganda seriously.

As the 1931 campaign progressed, Peruvians attentive to the APRA's propaganda saw the movement as engaged in "a great struggle of productive classes against a plutocratic minority, the accomplices and instruments of imperialism. . . ."[13] Some liked the image, but others registered dismay and fright.[14] Moreover, conventional Peruvians were put off not only by the content of Aprista political rhetoric but by the style in which it was conveyed. In fact, the central feature of the 1931 campaign was the Aprista style. Borrowing from Marshall McLuhan's terminology, one can say that the medium—in this case the Aprista mass meeting—was the message.

Symbol and ritual lay at the heart of Aprista mass politics, and their significance was already fully in evidence on August 23, 1931, when a crowd that partisans estimated at over 30,000[15] filled Lima's bullfight ring, the Plaza de Acho. By this date Aprista leaders had devised much of the symbol and ritual on which they would trade for over a generation. And the choice of the bullring for the political rally was important in itself. Here occurred, Sunday after Sunday during the season of the fights, the great drama that for much of the Hispanic world remained for centuries next in importance to the Catholic mass as a symbol of death and regeneration. Enacted in a circle to suggest the life cycle, the drama of the ring has the bull at first triumphant as it overcomes its tormentors, the mounted picadores, and shakes off the annoyance of the banderillas. Eventually, though, the bull, symbolizing the power of raw nature, is overcome by the superior capacities of the matador—dressed in his suit of lights (traje de luces) and embodying light. Ultimately, the bull awaits in passive resignation the penetration of the matador's sword; and even as the female and male principles join in this symbolic coitus, the blood of the dying bull irrigates the ring's soil, giving the promise of rebirth. During the drama of the bulls, moreover, the opposites of sun and shadow (sol y sombra) constantly interact and merge in their own accompanying drama of the dialectic, shaping the background for the main encounter between matador and bull. To the Plaza de Acho on August 23 Haya de la Torre brought a new kind of drama, but it embodied the same themes of life, death, regeneration, and the fusing of opposites that Lima's graceful ring customarily witnessed.

The drama of the twenty-third got underway as marchers, made up of the APRA's youthful shock troops, entered the arena bearing the Aprista flag, the gold circular Indo-America embossed on the red background—thus joining maternal blood with paternal sun. The singing of the APRA hymn, to the tune of "La Marseillaise," and other party songs followed. Perhaps it was through his contact with Romain Rolland that Haya had learned the importance of music at political rallies. Gandhi, according to the Rolland biography, understood that singing had to be a central part of mass meetings, for "music means rhythm, order." By encouraging mass singing in unison, Gandhi—as described by Rolland—made "himself the orchestra leader of his oceans of men."[16] In 1929 while in Berlin Haya wrote that, unlike Europeans, Latin Americans did not sing at political rallies. He urged that they begin to utilize singing "as in religious rites," for this would help them to curtail one of their besetting vices: excessive individualism.[17]

At subsequent Aprista rallies, singing was interspersed by the communal recitation, in highly rhythmical beats, of the Aprista Credo; but evidence is lacking as to whether this occurred at the August twenty-third assembly. On this occasion, though, Apristas did engage in the rhythmic clapping that would remain from that time on a part of their ritual. On and on the clapping continued as the Plaza de Acho resounded to a hypnotizing beat of the sort produced by drummers at African rites and at Indian ceremonies throughout the Americas: three stacatto bursts followed by a short rest, then three new bursts. The triplet rhythm was reinforced by the honking of horns from outside the plaza in unison with the clapping. The triplet rhythm also underlay the chant that now began to fill the ring: SE-A-SAP, the acronym for solo el aprismo salvará al Perú. ("Seasap" also became a salutation that Apristas exchanged upon encountering each other.)

The warm-up speakers included on this occasion Luis Alberto Sánchez, Manuel Seoane, and Luis Heysen. Subsequently, it became common to have a representative of the manual workers speak, followed by one for the intellectual workers and then by Haya himself, who symbolized the fusion of the two pillars of party strength. After the warm-up speakers on the twenty-third, Haya made his grand entrance surrounded by his special guard attired in blue shirts—symbolically the sun in the midst of the blue sky. And now the crowd raised the chant of VICTOR RAUL, VICTOR RAUL, and APRA, APRA. As Haya waited for the frenzy to subside, he presented the Aprista salute: the left arm raised, the open hand bent slightly over the head.[18] Some have seen this as a symbol of the hammer and sickle, but I think an Aprista writer caught the meaning far more accurately in referring to the "forest of raised arms"—veritable trees of life joining firmament and soil, symbolizing the wholeness of Apristas.[19] The precise origins are not certain, but I wonder if the salute might not be associated with the gesture of shamans among the pre-Inca Moches of north coast Peru, with which Haya was surely familiar. The Moche gesture took the form of a salute, but with the hand formed in a half fist, the straight thumb next to the knuckle formed (at the first joint) by the forefinger.[20] Perhaps the five peaks thus represented corresponded to those of a sacred mountain—with the central peak, formed by the third finger bent over at the first joint, being the highest and mediating between the two on either side. In the APRA salute, in any event, the number five, stressed by the extended fingers, took on a numinous significance that was present also in the five-pointed Aprista star, borrowed undoubtedly not from the Soviet Union but from Masonry.

Symbolism and ritual continued as the crowd began to wave white handkerchiefs at Haya and as he responded by waving his own handkerchief at his admirers. Perhaps this practice originated in the *marinera*, a dance associated particularly with the Peruvian north coast. In the marinera, which is almost as highly charged with sexual imagery as the tango, both partners clasp a handkerchief and synchronize its rhythmic movements with the steps of the dance. The effect can be hypnotic. With the handkerchiefs waving, Haya became "both the lover and the beloved of the masses."[21] Moreover, Haya and his audience were now, in effect, dancing with each other, and the rhythmically undulating waves of a sea of white added to the mesmerizing effects established earlier by the singing, clapping, and chanting. In most cultures throughout history, dancing has originally been associated with magic and creation. Sometimes it has been considered a part of the foreplay of a sexual union in which two will become one; at other times, it has represented the attempt of people to join with the rhythms of the cosmos, thereby ending alienation from nature. Obviously, Aprista ritual drew upon a rich panoply of symbolism as it evoked a magic spell.

Beginning his address, his sonorous voice rising and falling in wonderfully rhythmic cadence, his arms often waving as if he were flying,[22] Haya soon managed to cast an even deeper spell over the audience. Almost more important than the content of his more than two hour address[23] was the fact that before he even began to speak the audience was well on the way toward the death of individual consciousness. Just as religious revival sessions often bring about a violent psychological break with the world of established identities so that the individual may be absorbed (reborn) into the ineffable,[24] so did Aprista political rallies snuff out individual egos and immerse favorably disposed participants in the unity of the primal herd.[25]

Once the "crowd" or herd comes into being through the surrender of egos by those assembled together, it longs—according to Gustave Le Bon, whose writing on crowd psychology influenced many populist politicians in the early twentieth century—for a superior being to worship, hoping to acquire through that being a new sense of identity, purpose, and direction;[26] it hopes, in effect, for rebirth. And the person who guides the crowd out of the primal undifferentiatedness into which its components have descended in discarding the ego, who accomplishes their regeneration after death, they recognize as a god-like individual. Thus, those who compose the crowd are reborn in fusion with a charismatic, sun-like being of highest consciousness who, in joining with them in a symbol of incarnation dies for a moment himself, only to be reborn in total union with them. Haya de la Torre, a deity symbol for those who had surrendered to the psychology of the crowd, became—for many—a conduit to a new wholeness and the bestower of regeneration. Thus did Aprismo begin to establish its claims as a new religion.

As persons find themselves "in direct touch with one another, as well as with their inner selves," and also with some extraordinary personality symbolizing the transcendent, they experience a sense of power and energy.[27] From the sense of power comes the delusion that they can, literally, remake the outer world. The deluded persons have fallen into the mindset of primitives who believe in the power of sympathetic magic. The basis of this magic is the belief that if humans, as the microcosm, enact a ritual in just the right way, they can cause the outside world, the macrocosm, to replicate their ritualistic drama. If persons assembled in a giant rally could suddenly resolve social and psychic tensions, if they could for a moment die in order to be reborn, then by the power and magic of their ritualistic drama of renewal they could accomplish the death and transfiguration of the temporal order.[28]

Following the Plaza de Acho appearance, Haya took his political revivalist show on the road, traversing Peru from Tacna, in the extreme
southern desert, to Iquitos, in the northeastern Amazonian jungle area.
Occasionally in the Andes he included Quechua words in his performance.[29] Never before had a national office seeker carried out such a
campaign. The trouble was, at least from the Aprista point of view, that
Sánchez Cerro waged the same sort of campaign, proving himself thoroughly adept at populist politics. Not only did he cover much of Peru,
but in Lima he could attract a larger crowd then Haya himself. As the
military hero who had overthrown Leguía, this diminutive dark-skinned
officer with a well-earned reputation for reckless courage exuded machismo and emerged as a charismatic leader in his own right. Moreover,
he had the backing, however reluctant, of some of Peru's most well-to-
do members of the "oligarchy." However much they distrusted him as
rash and impetuous, they saw him as a lesser menace than Haya de la
Torre, whom, by and large, they simply could not fathom.[30]

The balloting took place in October. Few if any elections in Latin
American history have been subjected to more post mortems, as scholars
sought to assess the charges of fraud that Apristas began to levy immediately after the results were announced. Some thirty to forty years after
the event, a clear consensus had emerged among the scholars, and with
this consensus the Aprista historian Enrique Chirinos Soto concurred in
a 1977 publication:[31] the election was honest, and Sánchez Cerro was the
authentic victor, garnering 152,062 votes to Haya's 106,007.[32] According
to Peru's great historian Jorge Basadre, it was the popular sectors,
"above all, those of rural background, who determined that Sánchez
Cerro would be president of Peru."[33] In his authoritative account, Steve
Jay Stein concludes that although Haya had the backing of middle sectors and organized labor, Sánchez Cerro drew on a larger pool of voters,
including the artisanry and the urban lumpenproletariat.[34] Yet, Aprista
charges of fraud were so immediate and proved so persistent through the
years—and were circulated by so many friends of the APRA in foreign
countries, including United States scholars who should have known
better—that they came to be believed widely and contributed to the aura
of persecution that Aprismo assiduously cultivated.

In responding automatically with charges of fraud, Haya de la Torre
acted much like the neurotic who feels that a strong wish for something
establishes his legitimate right to it.[35] Moreover, if Haya was indeed suf-

fering from narcissism, as suggested in chapter 6, he would have found it well nigh impossible to accept the announced electoral outcome as legitimate. He had, after all, done all that was to be expected of him: he had suffered, he had performed, he had engaged in "boundless exhibitionism," and all of this was supposed to guarantee that the selfobject, namely the PAP, would gratify his wants in a way that parents had once refrained from doing.

In the period immediately following the election, Haya continued to act like a person suffering narcissistic personality disorders. When the narcissist finds that post-parental selfobjects he has pinned his hopes on also fail to respond in the desired way to his exhibitionism, and when he accepts that no additional exhibitionism or tantrums will be effective, he is overcome by shame and feels that he is somehow to blame. Now he must resign himself, he concludes, to suffering so as to render himself worthy of the future bestowal of gratification by the selfobject.[36] '

The narcissistic explanation strikes me as one that could account for Haya's actions in the months following the October electoral defeat. However, other factors, either on their own or in combination with the narcissistic aspect, could explain his conduct; central among these factors is Haya's attitude toward violence.

As early as 1925 Haya had observed that while carefully planned and controlled, limited or "surgical" violence might at times be necessary in righting the ills of the world, "anarchical violence, demented and demagogic" had at all costs to be avoided. The real task, as Haya saw it, was to prepare men so that, once they came to power, they could sustain revolutionary idealism and selfless purity. "For this we need a group of able, disciplined, studious, fully conscious workers disposed to assume any sacrifice for the common cause. Our goal is to enrich all the spontaneous capacities with a clear conscience of duty and a precise view of the route to follow."[37] Clearly, Haya shared the fears that John Mackay had voiced in 1923. What he feared, Mackay confessed, was that a social revolution, "the blind uprising of the proletariat," might take place before the spiritual revolution had been made, before "men became morally capacitated to bring a dangerous experiment to fruition."[38]

To the word revolution, Haya did not necessarily attach the connotation of violence. "One can be a revolutionary," he wrote early in 1932, "without being a proponent of violence."[39] Like Mackay, he could regard revolution in terms of inward, spiritual revival. In the outside world revolution for him had the meaning that astronomers or astrologers attached to the word: the completion of a cycle, in which a body returned to the position at which it had originated its traversal.[40] The next era of human progress, he believed, like Rolland and Keyserling, would begin as an old cycle came to an end. The cyclical view of human progress, of course, involves one in the same sort of dilemma facing many Marxists. The latter, assuming that the course of human events is shaped by economic determinants, sometimes disagree over the role of voluntarism in the making of revolution. And spiritualists, believing in cyclical determinism, are similarly puzzled. Should humans wilfully intervene to kill off what remains of a dying cycle of civilization in an apocalyptic blood bath? Or, should they simply wait for the old order to succumb to its own declining vitality, decadence, corruption, and senility, meantime exercising an ascetic discipline and cultivating the mystic's mastery over creatureliness so as to become fit to rule in the new order? Haya's actions strongly suggest that he chose the role of waiting in abnegation and suffering for the rebirth that was destined to occur. In this, he was being true to the conviction, manifested in the sexual analogy he used to depict relations with the United States, that Indo-America was essentially feminine in nature, obliged—in order to remain true to authentic cultural identity—to refrain from the actions of aggressive masculinity.

One can be a revolutionary, Haya insisted in 1932, without being a proponent of direct violence. Christ, Tolstoy, and Ghandi were all revolutionaries, he insisted. Then, in what is probably his most revealing writing on the subject, Haya added: "We deny the absurd principle of violence for the sake of violence or of revolution simply for the sake of taking power. Contrary to this, Aprismo proclaims the need of arriving at power in order to organize from it the revolution, in the sense of transformation, of evolution, of renovation...."[41] In short, the jefe máximo decreed that the APRA would not come to power by revolutionary violence; but once in power it would stage the true revolution of renovation, beginning with inward renewal. This, however, poses a question. If the APRA had been denied power through purportedly fraudulent elections, and if it rejected generalized violence as a means of achieving power, then how would it come into possession of the means necessary to carry out the resocialization of a nation? To this dilemma Haya had an answer, and, given his convictions, it was a logical answer.

Subscribing to the delusion that Aprismo was a new religion, Haya

chose to follow the example of early Christianity. Eschewing direct violence as the means to power, Aprismo would convert a general, a mighty
military leader, to its faith; he in turn, through a golpe from above rather
than a revolution from below, would entrust to the APRA control over
the nation's moral destiny. Thereby Aprismo could initiate the systema-
tized conversion of all of Peru, instilling among the burgeoning ranks of
the faithful the ego-effacing discipline that could not be reliably and enduringly implanted by the quick conversions of the political revival
meeting.[42] The election results of October had scarcely been announced
before Haya began his search for Aprismo's Constantine.[43] The search
would occupy him for the next thirty years or so of his life. At the same
time, however, that Haya took up the search for his Constantine he had
to deal with Aprismo's direct violence proponents. They would compli-
cate and disrupt not only Haya's life but the existence of the entire republic for many years to come.

The Death and Rebirth of Aprismo: 1931–33

By December, impatient Apristas were already brewing plans
for a revolution against Sánchez Cerro. Haya may have resorted now to a
ploy he would use frequently in the years ahead: feigning to go along
with plans for an insurrection, lest he alienate the more impetuous
Apristas, while hoping he could manipulate circumstances to abort the
uprising. The manipulation of circumstances was what Haya had in
mind when he delivered an address to a crowd of Apristas who had gath-
ered at party headquarters in Trujillo on December 8. As is true of all his
talks during this period, Haya's text has been reconstructed from a stenographer's shorthand version, for the jefe never used so much as notes.

The Trujillo address, delivered just a few hours after the Sánchez
Cerro inauguration in Lima, is among the most important half-dozen or
so that Haya ever delivered. By any standard, it was short: it could
scarcely have taken him more than ten or twelve minutes to pronounce
it. Anything but the customary pep talk, the Trujillo discourse was a
prophesy of immolation. Haya did not come out directly and admonish
his hearers that they must abandon hope in immediate revolution. In effect, though, this is what he told them in a talk that has been dubbed his
"Sermon on the Mount."[44]

Christianity was not the only source of symbolism Haya resorted to in suggesting to his Trujillo audience that their time had not yet come to govern Peru and that they must render themselves worthy, through purification and suffering, of their future mission to rule. He seems to have drawn also on Gandhi, by way of Rolland, in pleading the course of nonviolence. Gandhi, as portrayed by Rolland, stressed the power of "soul force," arising out of faith, sacrifice, and suffering, to transform the world: "I cultivate," said Gandhi, "the quiet course of dying without killing.... Working under this law of our being it is possible for a single individual to defy the whole might of an unjust empire and lay the foundation of that empire's fall or its regeneration."[45]

Characteristically, millenarian prophets associate their powers with asceticism, which is seen as the source of the ability to work miracles.[46] Characteristically also, they call upon their followers to emulate them in their asceticism and to join in a collective, mass sacrifice that will be rewarded by a "mass apotheosis."[47] Therefore as Haya turned to his followers at Trujillo and urged them to become, as it were, a sect of self-flagellants and as he assured them that he was and would remain preeminent in suffering, he was drawing upon regeneration archetypes that reside deep in the human unconscious. In line with an ancient tradition, of which Christ is but one exemplar, Haya sought to establish his new religion as one of heroic martyrs, not one—not yet at least—of heroic men of action in the material world. In effect, then, he counseled Apristas, as Christ had Peter, to sheathe the sword.

The initial day of a period of proof for the party was at hand, Haya informed his audience as he began his remarks. "We are going to prove, one more time, in the crucible of what will perhaps be a painful reality, the consistency of our organization, the faith in our consciousness, and the sacred immortality of our cause." True Apristas would not shy away from the prospects of suffering. Those of weak faith or limited consciousness would leave the party, and good riddance. Although their cause might appear lost for the moment, Apristas were actually stronger than ever, for their mission was not just to rule, but to set an example of moral purity and thereby to redeem. "Because we continue...giving example,...we will continue redeeming." The Aprista mission, he continued, was not to gain the National Palace, but rather "to reach the consciousness of the people before coming to the Palace"; and the consciousness of the people could not be reached by means of "wealth or guns." You enter the consciousness of the people "through the glorious example of sacrifice" and "the light of a doctrine." That light had already begun to penetrate among the masses. Therefore while others ruled by gold and violence from the palace, "we will continue governing from the people." No matter its extent, tyranny could not conquer the APRA. "More Aprista blood will run, our martyrology will augment its immortal list, terror will reinitiate its opprobrious task, but Aprismo will penetrate ever more deeply into the consciousness of the people." Then, with the epoch of blood fulfilled, "we will arise with the omnipotence of the unconquerable and will demonstrate that the great causes do not perish because of fear." Final victory, Haya assured his "comrades," would not elude them; but it would come only through resolution: "The will and only the will is the rudder of our destiny."

Next Haya developed the theme of his own suffering, in effect basing his claims to being number one among Apristas on the extent of that suffering. "I waited eight years in persecution, in prison, and in exile. Eight years of solitude which were eight years of unflagging determination. Often I was alone. Often I knew the tremendous reality of being misunderstood and forgotten. But I never faltered. The decision to conquer, in spite of all obstacles, I never abandoned for a single day." As a result of his suffering, Haya continued, the party was born and began to flourish, and so those eight years of struggle brought success. Owing to his will, and the will that his followers were now exhorted to develop in suffering, far greater successes awaited the party. "Aprismo is the child of the will which becomes incarnate in the suffering of a people, engendering in it an organic and powerful force that must serve as the vital instrument for achieving justice." Haya repeated the prediction of greater suffering to come—and in this instance he did indeed reveal prophetic powers. But he would not flinch. "Adversity does not frighten me. Easy victories are what frighten me. . . . I hope that after this hard test, in which we are going to prove our faith, our energy, our revolutionary spirit, our unassailable resolution as builders of the new Peru, we will again find ourselves pure and worthy of each other." Haya then charged Apristas to decide whether they would write the next pages of the movement's history with mud or with their blood. Until today, Apristas had nothing to be ashamed of; but, Haya implied, if they rejected the way of blood, their own blood, they would become unworthy.

Repeating a final time his prophesy of dark times ahead, Haya swore

164

to be at his post until the end: "And I trust that no Aprista will abandon his." Those who proved of insufficient mettle would not participate in APRA's resurgence when the trial ended. "Now more than ever we defend the unity of the Party, and now more than ever we will be severe with ourselves. . . . Let us be worthy of the people and let us make the people worthy of us. Solo el aprismo salvará al Perú."

Identifying with a feminine role model in the Trujillo discourse, Haya pictured himself as having given birth to the APRA child after eight years, not the conventional nine months, of suffering. But Haya took on the mantle of male qualities as well, for he claimed, in effect, to have provided the light that had penetrated the masses. In short, Haya traded on the symbolism of the hermaphrodite, the being who had become whole and complete, and thereby charismatic or godlike. Conceivably, Haya also drew on the belief, common in certain early-twentieth-century homosexual circles, that deviant males actually possessed the qualities of the hermaphrodite, being endowed with feminine souls in masculine bodies.

In the Trujillo address Haya presented himself in a way that psychiatrists, in addition to comparative symbologists, might find suggestive. In this instance, the layman seeking guidance might turn to psychiatrists who specialize in masochism; for the masochist, purportedly, is one who above all else anticipates victory through defeat.[48] And Haya predicted the apotheosis of the APRA through its virtual death by persecution and martyrdom. Further associated with masochism, it has been suggested, is the female trait, deriving from the imagery and perhaps the biology of motherhood, of welcoming pain because of an anticipated joyous outcome.[49] Another masochistic quality, according to Theodor Reik, is the endeavor to establish one's superiority over others through claims of greater, more persistent, and more prolonged suffering.[50] Reik also maintains that the display of suffering frequently arises out of a spirit of revenge, out of the hope to gain a triumph one feels he deserves but which has been denied him.[51] By arousing sympathy, by "wooing love"[52] through exhibition of suffering, the masochist hopes to inspire others to confer on him the coveted triumph. In this way the masochist is akin to the narcissist who tries to manipulate selfobjects. Also, by welcoming new suffering, the masochist-narcissist hopes to overcome the shame experienced when selfobjects originally failed to deliver the desired prize. As a masochist-narcissist, and as a probable homosexual with hermaphroditic pretensions, Haya may have drawn on the stereotype of woman's superior ability to endure suffering.

The layman, I know, should avoid conjecture of this sort on a person's psychiatric condition. Yet, conjecture in Haya's case is irresistible, because whatever inspired his actions was not primarily events of the outside world that can be quantified or detailed in some document. While by no means ignoring the events of the outside world, Haya marched primarily to an inward drum. He possessed a wide-ranging, febrile mythopoeic imagination, apparent symptoms of neuroticism, a murky spiritualist faith, and boundless confidence in his visions. This surely is the sort of personality that psychiatrists claim—not very convincingly, I fear—to be able to understand. Psychohistory, in my opinion, doesn't really work;[53] but if it did, it would be the only way to approach Haya de la Torre. As it is, psychohistory may provide an insight or two that can usefully be mixed with conventional historical methodology in seeking to understand a complex personality.

For Haya, the time of renewed travail, predicted on December 8, arrived quickly. Faced by a program of massive repression that Sánchez Cerro unleashed against the APRA, as he overreacted to rumors of revolutionary plots, Haya went underground in January 1932. The following May be was apprehended and imprisoned. The charges against him included involvement in communist activity and plotting to deliver the nation to "an international committee";[54] they focused, though, on his aborted 1929 plot to overthrow Leguía—the very man the current president had toppled, to the general plaudits of his countrymen. The flimsy nature of the charges against Haya contributed to the impression that he was being unfairly treated and aroused widespread sympathy.[55] Soon letters from abroad began to pour into Peru demanding clemency. Signatories included Upton Sinclair, Sinclair Lewis, Jane Addams, Anita Brenner, Waldo Frank, Harold Laski, Miguel de Unamuno, Gregorio Marañón, José Ortega y Gasset, and—perhaps most meaningful to Haya—Romain Rolland and Albert Einstein. Apristas contend that had it not been for his international backing, Haya's life would have been in serious jeopardy.

With the jefe in prison, his "more radical supporters, led by the legendary Manuel Barreto Cisco, 'El Búfalo,' gained the upper hand in party counsels" and staged a dawn attack on July 2 against the army garrison in Trujillo.[56] The insurrection in Haya's native city, launched against the background of a strike by northern sugar-estate workers, met with initial success, but circumstances soon turned against the insurgents. As their prospects diminished with the impending arrival of massive government reinforcements, the rebels, in one of those spontaneous acts that occur so often in military situations, massacred sixty officers and enlisted men who had been taken prisoner and held as hostages. When government troops shortly suppressed the revolution, they inflicted terrible reprisals. According to some Aprista accounts, six thousand persons were executed in cold blood. The actual number, dreadful enough, was between one and two thousand.[57]

The northern "oligarchy" had suffered a tremendous fright and one of its members, Luis Aspíllaga, expressed full approval of the "bloody, very bloody" repression and hoped it would put an end to "this damned APRA."[58] But a leader of the Aprista women's organization more accurately foresaw the outcome. The blood of thousands of martyrs, she declared, was now irrigating the Peruvian soil, producing a prodigious fertility that would cause the APRA, "now purified," to persevere and to gather strength.[59]

From his prison cell in the Lima penitentiary, Haya de la Torre, who with the help of sympathizers among the staff had managed to devise an elaborate system for smuggling messages into and out of prison (and also for exchanging letters among inmates), had learned of the Trujillo uprising when it was still in the planning stages. At first he had hoped to thwart it and to rely instead on persuading Lt. Col. Gustavo Jiménez to lead a military golpe against Sánchez Cerro. Initially Jiménez refused, expressing suspicion of the APRA because of its sectarian aspects and its ascribing of omniscience to its leader. "Believe me," Jiménez wrote in a letter of April 15, 1932, to Luis Alberto Sánchez, "this has done much harm and has created resistances that today . . . are serving the dictatorship." Apristas continued to importune Jiménez and in March 1933 he led the golpe they desired. When it failed, he was placed in prison, where apparently he killed himself.[60] Four months later came the blood bath at Trujillo.

The massive violence from below that Haya so feared, as well as the surgical violence from above that he sometimes countenanced, had failed. And from his cell Haya continued to write letters urging Apristas to seek strength in suffering and to guard against becoming embittered.

In one of these letters, written to fellow Aprista Juan Seoane, who was also in the Lima penitentiary, Haya admonished:

We must not forget that the Aprista has to suffer to be strong. We must not forget that in the Peruvian case we struggle against barbarism, against a caste sick with hatred, envy, old age, and lack of culture that sees with disdain the rise of a superior, austere, united, and young force. To have recourse to its methods or to participate in its hatreds is to yield to the contagion, to infect ourselves, to render ourselves useless for the realization of the great task that demands complete mental health and vigorous physical resistance. The civilized person who falls into the hands of a horde of savages defends himself, but does not become a savage himself. . . . We must avoid becoming barbarians ourselves, which would be to forget the civilizing mission of the party.[61]

While in prison, Haya grew more fearful than ever of releasing the tumults and passions, not only of the masses but of his own psyche. The violence that had gotten out of hand and escalated in Trujillo convinced him all the more of the need to keep the Aprista masses on a leash until they had learned the hard lesson of self-control and submission to collective discipline. And prison experiences seem to have convinced him of the need to discipline and chain the beast within, the threatening forces of his own unconscious, perceived now more as Freudian id than as Jungian anima. Up to this time, Haya had had good encounters with the "subconscious Indian who lives in us all,"[62] as at Cuzco in 1917. But the "occultists" who reach "the heights of mystical transcendence" must expect to plumb "the depths of demonic possession as well"[63] In prison, it seems that Haya suffered an experience that must have struck him as akin to "demonic possession." Going on a hunger strike (a favorite ploy to which he had resorted before going into exile when imprisoned by Leguía in 1923), he encountered frightening hallucinations and psychic disturbances that necessitated his spending some time in the infirmary.[64] This could only have confirmed Haya's persuasion that, as he expressed it in his letter to Juan Seoane written before the hallucinations, one could not abandon oneself to "bohemian ways" but must instead practice ever more rigid self-control and keep "the mind as a refrigerator," where overheated ideas and "tropical temptations" could not survive.[65] For a time, now, Haya would remain fearful of that previous source of mystical exaltation, his own unconscious; and all the more as he came to fear the wild man within did he fear the wild man without.

On the last day of April 1933, while Haya languished still in the Lima penitentiary, his nemesis Sánchez Cerro was removed from the scene, gunned down while leaving the San Beatriz racetrack by an Aprista assassin named Abelardo Mendoza Leiva. Whether this was "surgical" violence sanctioned by Haya or was committed, as the jefe maintained, by an individual acting on his own[66] remains in doubt. There is even indirect evidence to suggest that the assassination grew out of a plot between Haya—represented, from his prison cell, by emissaries—and Oscar R. Benavides, the able military officer who was chosen by congress to serve out the unexpired portion of the slain president's term.[67] While I find Basadre persuasive in his rejection of the theory of an Haya-Benavides plot,[68] the issue remains clouded and, as with the circumstances of many political assassinations, may never be clarified.

By August 1933, Haya was out of prison. There ensued a brief lull in the undeclared war between the government and an APRA that remained divided over whether to seek quick victory through a popular uprising or to follow the golpe route, meantime practicing abnegation and courting martyrdom so as to be morally ready to rule when the time came. Although no one knew it at the time, the lull in warfare was already nearing its end when Haya appeared in Lima on November 12 before a huge rally. It was the first full-scale public appearance since the Trujillo address. The Trujillo "Sermon on the Mount" had been delivered absolutely without hoopla. In its lack of trappings, it had seemed almost a spontaneous, spur-of-the-moment address. There was nothing spontaneous, though, about the November 12 performance in Lima's Plaza de Acho with an estimated thirty-two thousand in attendance. This was a grandiose Aprista "happening," with the customary warm-up speeches, the singing of party songs, the chants, the hand clapping and horn honking, the salutes and handkerchief waving, and the blue-shirted honor guard, augmented for the first time by the so-called *Búfalos:* a group of youthful activists with whom much of the party's future violence and terrorism reputedly originated.[69]

Themes that stand out in Haya's Plaza de Acho address are "togetherness," purity, the need for further sacrifice, Apristas as a chosen people, and the mission to accomplish Peru's regeneration. On this occasion more than on any previous one, the jefe offered living proof of what June Nash has noted: "Mythic symbols are part of the rhetorical devices used by ideologues in swaying opinion."[70]

Haya began by exulting in being reunited with his people under circumstances that found him, and them, still pure: "We are together again, and we are renewed in our strength, because we have always been pure. . . . But we are together again, and . . . our resolution to die many times for the triumph of justice has not been diminished."[71] Recounting how in the solitude of his cell he had often smiled as he recalled journalistic descriptions of Aprismo as "collective madness," he exclaimed: "Here we are again witnessing the resurgence of our powerful and creative collective madness." Next, he introduced the warning that added tests lay ahead and that Apristas would have to continue to back their words with drops of blood. But they should remain undaunted, for their abnegation meant that "in this country of vices, corruption and peculation, in this country of crimes and vengeance there has appeared a force propelled by the people, a force that is total purity. . . ." He conceded that some Apristas could not understand the theoretical details of the party's work. But they felt in their bones what must be done, for "our faith has the formidable force to make vibrate all of consciousness" and to reveal by intuition what is beyond the grasp of "refined consciousness." Even if Apristas cannot explain the laws of a phenomenon, they can "vibrate to it," and they can intuit the great mission "to renew and disinfect this country."[72]

A few sentences later, Haya returned to the cleansing theme: "The people follow Aprismo because they have seen in it, from the first instant, the enthusiasm to cleanse, and Aprismo began by cleansing itself with the 'blood of its blood.' " The "pure, refined, forged, and worthy" Apristas were preparing themselves for the task ahead, which he likened to Christ's raising of Lazarus: "The inheritance we have received of this bloodless and oppressed Peru may be compared to Christ's receiving the dead Lazarus in order to restore him."[73] Even though they knew that they had attained glory, Apristas must continue to seek greater perfection and to examine their consciences because, although "we do not sin mortally," Apristas might still fall into venial sin.[74]

These last words put one in mind of Saint Theresa, with whose works Haya was familiar. In *Interior Castle*, the sixteenth-century Spanish mystic writes that even after the marriage between the passionate seeker and Christ has been consummated as the two become one in the unitary stage, the person wed to the Lord will still commit transgressions, but these will be venial sins, "for from mortal sins, so far as they know, they are free....''[75] In the cited passage of his November address, Peru's charismatic prophet seems to suggest that through their cleansing by the blood they have shed, Apristas have completed their initiation rites, have consummated their wedding to him, and are henceforth incapable of major transgressions.

Words of persons far removed from Saint Theresa come to mind when reading Haya's November 12 discourse. The theme of a chosen people goes back in formally recorded history at least to Moses, who, as Freud describes him, encouraged the Jews "to progress in spirituality and sublimations. The people, happy in their conviction of possessing truth, [were] overcome by the consciousness of being chosen."[76] Moreover, no one can browse through Hitler's speeches or read *Mein Kampf* (as Haya had) without being struck by the obsession with purification and cleansing, on one hand, and germs, corruption, and degeneration, on the other. But then, these concepts are the stock-in-trade of millenarian prophets, and Haya was simply using the language of regeneration and renewal as it has echoed through history.[77] In most cases, Peruvians had never listened to such intoxicating language, although some of their forebears had heard it during earlier manifestations of Andean chiliasm. Longing for assurance and total answers in times of upheaval, many Peruvians did indeed vibrate to the words of a mesmerizing political preacher who possessed that rare talent both to penetrate into the minds of hearers, as he cogently explained the party program, and to steal into their unconscious, by way of his symbolism.

Even more dramatically in his December 18 address delivered in Trujillo's Teatro Popular did Haya resort to mythic symbols to sway opinion. His themes included agony, martyrdom and regeneration, blood and purification, suffering as the source of the spiritual energy that could transform what was material, the immanence of the divine, and finally the wholeness of androgyny. Emerging from the womb-like prison cell in a decadent Lima where his life, he said, had been constantly in danger, Haya appeared as a reborn prophet, one like St. John, who when imprisoned by the Romans had received a revelation concerning his community's trials and ultimate deliverance. Standing before a deliriously cheering audience that for many minutes he was unable to silence, Haya, his left arm raised in the Aprista salute, unashamedly wept. It was a moment, recalls Luis Alberto Sánchez, of "religious ecstasy," and Haya "seemed the ecumenical hosanna of the transfiguration." Following the address, which must be analyzed in some detail owing to its importance in creating the APRA's mystique, women dressed in mourning for "martyrs" of the July 1932 uprising came up to Haya leading children of various ages whom they offered to the jefe as new servants for his cause. Here, writes Sánchez, was the "apotheosis of the eternal. Sorrow sealed it and rendered it fecund: an indestructible pact and the cry of [continuing] war."[78]

Feeling as if a hand "was strangling his throat," Haya at last found his voice as the crowd quieted. He began with words once used by the great Cuban patriot José Martí: "I cannot do it with words [con palabras no puedo]." Overwhelmed by the immensity of the message that he wanted to communicate, Haya feared he could not do it with words. But, with words and symbols he did manage to communicate all that an overburdened psyche contained. When he had finished, his audience was limp.

Haya turned first to what he regarded as the maximum contribution of Aprismo during the two years since he had last spoken in Trujillo: Apristas had learned to work through the spirit. Heretofore, our people "lacked the breath of the cosmic, of the eternal, of the high and the pure; as they did not have this, it was necessary to seek it from the dead, it was necessary that our dead sacrifice themselves in order to give us this spirit." Until the martyrs brought about among the survivors "the incarnation of the great, of the heroic, of the sublime," Aprismo had been "only lyrical impulse." But now, Aprismo was animated by "the immortal breath of glory. Aprismo today has its glory, a glory that will not be lost, because it lives in death."[79] Thus at the outset Haya established the theme of living through death, of death and regeneration, and it was a theme from which he did not stray far in what stands as one of the most remarkable addresses in the history of Peruvian politics. Perhaps the speech could better be placed within the annals of Peruvian religion; but then, in the Indo-American world it is often difficult to distinguish religion from politics.

As he had in Lima the previous month, Haya rejoiced in being together once more with his companions—the two of them, leader and companions, finding wholeness in their union. "I return here and encounter that which in our separation we sought, you and I: I suffering there, you suffering here. Because you thought of me and I thought of you, these two forces created for the country the glory of Trujillo, and these two colossal leaps of spirit have given birth to a legend, have forged a tradition that will determine the course of history." Aprismo had now become more than a party, it had become the means of surpassing what is human, because Apristas, by purifying themselves, had become capable of creating "something new, something beautiful, something eternal in which our sorrows are transformed into force, energy, creation...." For their apotheosis, Apristas had their martyrs to thank. Because the martyrs raised their party to a transcendent level of "immortal works," Apristas now had the obligation to "make ourselves giants, to transform ourselves, to purify ourselves, to bathe ourselves in our own blood, to be pure and good, to be great and strong because we are the fathers of a new epoch of history."[80] And then Haya repeated the warnings voiced in the speech given two years previously in Trujillo and also in the one presented five weeks earlier in Lima: the period of "Calvary, of sweating blood," was still upon them. "The cross is erected. The third hour has not yet sounded. We must still wait, in the Calvary of our own hearts." By their surrender now to death and sorrow, Apristas were making possible the future birth of a luminous life of promise for the people of Peru.

Returning to the theme of being together, Haya confessed how in the long months in the penitentiary he had longed to be once more in his native city, reunited with his companions. And now he was able to present himself before his brothers, to join with them, and to hear, "head placed upon chest, the palpitation of the hearts, and to say, Brothers, I am here, we were never alone." Together in Trujillo, Apristas, the leader and the followers, would begin the work of transforming a tomb into a cradle.[81] This Apristas could begin to accomplish by seeking in their own consciousness "the sacred vessel from which spills forth the new energy, the new vibrations, the new creative trembling."[82]

A few moments more, and Haya was back to the image of Calvary and suffering. All Apristas bore the redeeming cross; "all of us have suffered, fallen, and been scourged"; all have been herded to Golgotha, where the oppressors mockingly inscribed above their heads, "This is Aprismo, King of Peru." But Apristas welcomed the weight of the cross, for it was a fecund weight that "enables us to call ourselves the saviors of Peru."[83] Then Haya returned to the theme of his imprisonment, noting that death had hovered about him many times in his lonely cell but spared him because destiny had reserved for him "the anguish of completing the work, the tremendous anguish of creating something new, blood of my blood, meat of my meat, bone of my bones." And now he referred to his wound: "My wound bleeds always, because it is the wound of the sorrow of the people, sorrow that will become victory."[84]

Much of the symbolism in the second Trujillo address Haya had employed before, and it demands no extensive commentary. The harping on martyrs recalls not only an element of the Catholic faith but of Hitler's manipulation of millenarian imagery as he dwelt upon the German victims of World War I whose blood would prepare the way for emergence of the Third Reich. It resonates, also, with St. John's prophesy in Revelation that the Lord would give the martyrs "authority over the pagans. . . to rule them with an iron sceptre and shatter them like earthenware."[85] A commentator on this passage offers an analysis that seems applicable to Haya's martyrdom imagery: "A liberal—and probably erroneous—reading of Revelation can lead to an understanding of Christian redemption as a metastatic condition in which [living] saints," through their union with martyred saints, "acquire divine strength and efficacy, elite status and authority in the world. . . ."[86] Haya's imagery may also be linked to a facet of Freemasonry: the claim of being destined to endure through eternity in part because of martyrdom and persecution suffered at the hands of the Inquisition and other institutions of intolerance and exclusivism.[87]

In the second Trujillo address Haya makes the clearest use to date of hermaphrodite symbolism, exhibiting himself as a combination Suffering Christ and Sorrowful Mother who is capable of producing redemptive birth. The imagery is by no means unique. Twelfth-century Cistercian monasticism venerated a "Jesus as Mother,"[88] and alchemists, Neopythagoreans, and other occultists also imputed to Christ—as well as to Dionysus and Hermes Trismegistus—the qualities of androgyny[89]

Especially suggestive is Haya's use of bleeding wound symbolism.[90] This could again be connected to hermaphrodite imagery if the wound is associated with the monthly bleeding of those who are capable of giving birth. Well before Christ, moreover, a spear wound inflicted on a person of charismatic potential was seen as activating his supernatural powers, with the resulting blood being deemed capable of working such miracles as reviving the sick and afflicted. In this imagery the spear was seen as a phallus, the wound as a vulva; owing to the fusion of the two in certain predestined persons, supernatural powers were set in motion.[91]

Furthermore, among primitive societies the faculties of medicine men were seen as deriving from agony of body and soul, "in confirmation of the mythological truth that the wounded wounder is the agent of healing, and the sufferer takes away suffering."[92]

Haya's wound symbolism harks back also to the imagery of the wounded Fisher King and to Amfortas in grail mythology. Amfortas, the great but wounded leader who may represent higher-than-ordinary consciousness, was released from his suffering (restored to wholeness) only when united to Parzival (or, in other versions, Sir Galahad), the guileless being who may symbolize the pure, humble masses. Outside the incarnation itself, to which symbolism it is clearly related, this was the best possible iconography for Haya as a populist leader, awaiting realization and fulfillment through union with the innocent, humble masses.

As any powerful, numinous symbol, the imagery of the perpetual wound is susceptible to many different meanings, but virtually all of them have some association with suffering that is crowned by a rebirth into wholeness and thus with apotheosis. In the wound symbolism, therefore, Haya found a way to communicate subliminally, on a level beneath and above reason, to his Trujillo companions the message that Aprismo meant the regeneration of their country and its transformation into a higher stage of existence.

Apristas in the Catacombs: 1934–39

Peace between the government and the APRA proved short-lived. For Apristas the times of affliction resumed not long after Haya predicted their return in his Lima and Trujillo addresses. The immediate cause was the refusal of President Benavides to hold special elections to fill the vacancies created in the national legislature by the arrest of its Aprista members at the beginning of 1932, when Sánchez Cerro had initiated his crackdown. By October 1933 new rumors of Aprista plots filled the air and acts of sporadic violence increased in frequency. In November Benavides appointed as his new prime minister José de la Riva Agüero, a leading spokesman of right-wing extremism. Perhaps his country's leading historian until fanaticism clouded his judgment, Riva Agüero announced, following his widely publicized return to the Catholic Church in 1932, that only Catholicism and fascism could contain the communist menace. "There can be no middle ground: either to the right or to the left." Any middle ground was either "disguised communism or else the certain road to it." The only way to avoid communism was "to return to the medieval, Catholic, Hispanic tradition as embodied now in fascism."[93] Operating on his conviction that compromise with the left was not only bound to be unfruitful but was sinful to attempt, and seeing the campaign against Aprismo's "new religion" as a holy crusade to stamp out blasphemy, Riva Agüero launched an effort to return all Apristas either to jail or to exile. Apristas began what they soon described as their time in the catacombs.

Haya de la Torre managed to escape imprisonment by going underground. It was now that he assumed the name Pachacútec. With this name he signed many of the directives and letters that issued in great profusion from his principal place of hiding, to which he gave the name of Incahuasi, or House of the Inca—strictly speaking the title Inca was reserved for the supreme ruler of the Empire of Tahuantinsuyo.[94] Even in the catacombs, Haya's delusions of grandeur did not diminish. In fact, they were nourished by events confirming his conviction that he was a predestined soul who could not be deterred from his mission. A number of assassination plots against Haya, some imagined or invented and some real, failed under circumstances that he deemed miraculous. In 1937 came the previously described encounter (see chapter 6) with the shade of Manuel Arévalo that persuaded Haya his life was under supernatural protection. Then in 1939 occurred a genuinely hair-raising episode (related at the end of this chapter) in which the jefe barely escaped death in a hail of bullets.[95]

President Benavides was no extremist and did not want Haya as a martyr. With one possible exception, involving the 1939 incident that came close to costing Haya his life, assassination attempts were neither instigated nor sanctioned by the president,[96] who seems to have known much of the time where Haya was hiding and even to have been in occasional indirect contact with him. Before the end of 1934, Benavides accepted, with apparent relief, Riva Agüero's resignation as prime minister. The scourge of leftists and centrists left office rather than sign a divorce law approved by congress. Following this, repression of the APRA eased, but Peru continued to be an embattled country where violence and revolutionary plotting abounded.

An Aprista uprising of November 1934 failed in Lima and achieved only temporary success in the Andean towns of Huancayo, Ayacucho, and Huancavelica.[97] Probably Haya was relieved, for he seems to have feared that the violence might get out of hand. He still preferred to find an officer who would stage a golpe from above. Throughout this period he searched for the right officer, but a plot with Julio C. Guerrero came to nothing in 1937, and the one worked out with Gen. Antonio Rodríguez through spiritualist intermediaries, as previously described, failed in 1939. Nor did anything come of an earlier, elaborate plan to stage an invasion from Bolivia.[98]

Throughout much of the 1930s, then, Peru carried on its unofficial civil war. The obviously partisan Luis Alberto Sánchez estimates that hostilities may have claimed five thousand Aprista lives between 1931 and the end of 1934 and an additional one thousand between that year and 1944, when peace was temporarily restored. He places non-Aprista mortalities at one hundred.[99] Body counts are notoriously unreliable, and firm figures on the struggle's victims will probably never emerge. But the casualty estimates have become a part of the APRA's lore, contributing to its mystique of martyrdom.

Anti-Apristas had their martyrs too, the most prominent being Antonio Miró Quesada and his wife. On May 15, 1935, Carlos Steer, a nineteen-year-old Aprista fanatic, fatally shot Miró Quesada as he approached the Club Nacional on Lima's Plaza San Martín. When Señora Miró Quesada tried to come to her husband's aid, Steer shot and killed her also. Miró Quesada had been for thirty years director of Lima's influential newspaper *El Comercio*, and the outspoken attacks that this paper consistently unleashed against Aprismo may have motivated the assassin. Failing in his suicide attempt after the double assassination, Steer assured authorities he had acted on his own (later in life he would change his story and implicate Juan Seoane and other Apristas in the deed); but anti-Apristas assumed from the outset that he was carrying out a party plot. Steer was imprisoned and tried by a military tribunal that sentenced him to a twenty-five-year term. Furious that the assassin had not received the death penalty, the Miró Quesada family unleashed through *El Comercio* editorials a bitter attack against Benavides, implying he had reached a secret understanding with the monstrous Apristas. For decades thereafter the anniversary of the assassination was marked "with a front page picture of Antonio and his wife and a bitter editorial condemning the

[Aprista] Party. The event and *El Comercio's* constant reminders of it did much to reinforce the anti-Aprista sentiment in Peru."[100]

Meantime, outside of Haya himself, the major figures in the PAP were either imprisoned or forced to flee into exile. Through their indefatigable propaganda efforts the "fraternity in exile"[101] managed to glorify the PAP and its cause, especially in Chile, Argentina, and Venezuela.[102] Thanks to the energy and skill of its exiles, the APRA may well have gained a higher reputation among intellectuals in those three countries, and perhaps in Colombia, parts of Central America and Mexico as well, than among the majority of their counterparts in Peru. Propaganda effort extended also to the United States, where they evoked the sympathy of a fair number of Latin America watchers, some of whom are mentioned in the following chapter.

Now that his Peruvian associates were undergoing a period of severe testing, Haya worked to retain the image of number-one sufferer. Chronically complaining in his letters of bad health and destitution, Haya acted like the narcissist who, as previously described be Heinz Kohut, self-righteously expresses self-pitying and hypochondriacal complaints. Writing to some Apristas in 1938 he noted that he knew well the agonies, mental and physical, of being confined to a cell. Nevertheless, "more difficult still is the terrain of struggle on which I must now operate."[103] To Apristas in exile Haya would occasionally direct letters chiding them for living in comfort abroad while he, remaining at his post, daily faced the threat of death. Along these lines he wrote to the Aprista Committee in Santiago de Chile exhorting its members to be on guard against being morally undermined by the security and ease of the life they enjoyed in the "rearguard." In view of his own circumstances, Haya observed, the life of the exiles seemed "a dream out of the Arabian Nights." Beware, he added, lest the good life "weaken the stimulus of your Aprista consciousness" and "effeminize your sense of responsibility."[104]

On another occasion, Haya acknowledged the sacrifice of his exiled companions, all the while urging them to seek still greater purification and moral perfection so as to be ready for their future tasks. In a 1939 letter to Apristas in Chile he referred to the terrible suffering they and their widely dispersed companions had endured in the past four years. Truly, they were suffering in "the crucible." Out of the crucible, he promised, the party would emerge stronger than ever, its "vitality and creative capacity" having been forged in adversity. Haya counseled the exiles to be of good cheer, for the right-wing parties in Peru were weakening and splintering, while "the great Aprista masses conserve their fervor and discipline with a truly stimulating loyalty."[105] Adopting a similar tone, he wrote to Apristas imprisoned in Lima: "The easy triumph is the triumph of unimportant causes. And we, the Apristas, have undertaken a truly grand endeavor: we wish to transform a country, we wish to redeem a people submitted during four hundred years to the chains of injustice, ignorance, and deceit. And to convert an oppressed people into a nation of free men is a labor that cannot be achieved except through suffering and struggle and through a long and difficult wait."[106]

During the long and difficult wait, when the party's very survival was referred to as "the APRA miracle,"[107] Haya concentrated on matters of organization. His objective was the forging of an ironclad discipline within a vertically structured PAP. Discipline was no new concern for the jefe. Indeed, from the first moment of exile in 1923 he had been obsessed with the subject. His first "Message from Exile to the Youth of Peru" had contained these words: "The modern and authentically revolutionary man must commit himself openly to his work without permitting . . . the intrusion of private actions, which are always hysterical and counterproductive actions. Individualism has died and all that is individualistic is bourgeois and therefore reactionary." In the revolutionary future there would be no room, Haya concluded, for those who did not accept the discipline imposed by "their responsibility as cells within organisms."[108] Two years later he stressed the paramount need of organization, of discipline, of unity. The task of the revolutionary movement was to "inflame consciousness" and then, by means of discipline, to guard against loss of the energy generated by inflamed consciousness.[109]

In 1929 and 1930, he turned his attention to integral education as the means of forging unity of action: "To be integral, education has to be reflected in every aspect of life: in the family, the government, the political structure. You cannot teach children to be socialists in school unless the whole governmental structure is also socialistic. . . . Education must be imparted in the school, the home, the street. The work of the popular universities in Peru is specifically to teach the workers to destroy the present social system that impedes those universities from realizing the integral education of the workers."[110] In addition to education, the organizing state would provide the means to establish unity of purpose. "All aspects of the national situation," Haya wrote in 1932, "will be directed by the state, . . . there will be grades and classes that will be determined by the state. The state will organize, discipline, and orient all classes. . . ."[111]

Within the organizing state, a single party was to play the vital role in establishing and perpetuating discipline. While in Russia, Haya had acquired strong ideas about what the right kind of party could accomplish. The Communist Party was admirable because it stressed quality rather than quantity and demanded the surrender to it of every member's personality, without reservation. Thus was assured the "conscious discipline of integral cooperation toward a common objective."[112] From Germany during the years between 1929 and 1931 Haya also acquired ideas about party structure. All that held Germany together in recent years, he argued in 1930, was the hierarchical discipline of the general staff.[113] The lessons provided by Germany were still uppermost in his mind when Haya, in 1932, compared the APRA to the German army. In a country of six to seven million inhabitants, the PAP could claim a membership of perhaps a million, he mused. The lack of a larger membership was unimportant, for the German army after the Treaty of Versailles had been limited to one hundred thousand. Nevertheless, "this cadre trained itself so well, prepared itself so well" that it produced a skilled officer corps capable of providing the organizing cell for an army that grew to between four and five million men. Apristas had a similar role to accomplish, and therefore they must acquire a discipline to match that of the German officer corps. Thereby the half million composing the Aprista core could prepare themselves for their "apostolic mission," which was to command the "four to six million new members" who shortly would seek to register in the movement. Toward the end of 1931 Haya had described his party and its aims to United States Ambassador Fred Morris Dearing. In his subsequent dispatch to Washington, Dearing commented that Haya had in mind "a pure fascist rather than a Communist organization."[114] In the light of Leninism and Stalinism, was there really any difference?

Seemingly aware of a link between "puritanism in individual behavior and . . . efficiency in organizational behavior,"[115] Haya stressed inculcating a "new puritan ethic" among Apristas.[116] When the Aprista Youth Federation (Federación Aprista Juvenil, or FAJ) was organized in 1934, members were forbidden to use alcohol, coca, or tobacco. Fajistas were also admonished to avoid cardplaying and all pursuits that wasted time and encouraged "degeneration." To guard against degeneration, they must discipline themselves through physical fitness programs. According to one source, young women Apristas were even pressured to guard against lasciviousness by denying sexual favors to non-Apristas.[117] Above all else, Fajistas should live according to the rule of "nothing for me, everything for the new Peru."[118]

The clearest expression of the disciplinarian goals that Haya pursued during his underground years may be found in the 1937 document "Vertical Organization of the Peruvian Aprista Party: Commentaries and Explanations by the Chief of the Party."[119] In it Haya explained that Aprismo "demands of each member not only the fervent conviction that "Solo el aprismo salvará al Perú"; in addition it requires of Apristas the "systematic coordination of efforts" needed "to convert this invocation into a reality."[120] To achieve coordination, Apristas were to be organized into labor brigades. Within each of the vertically structured functional brigades operated a bureau of control, its members charged with evaluating the actions, capacities, efficiency, and growth or development of brigade members. Monthly, the bureaus would transmit these ratings, together with a detailed report on the activities of each brigade member, to the National Executive Bureau of Party Headquarters.[121]

Implementation of the "Vertical Organization of the Peruvian Aprista Party" would have created a bureaucratic nightmare. Happily, the document is important not as a description of a reality ever attained but only as an exposition of Aprista objectives at one particular moment in the party's history. Supreme among these objectives, according to Antenor Orrego, was the "total replacing of the old man with the new man."[122] Apparently a principal trait of the new man would be the comprehension that lasting national transformation must come about through nonviolence, through the power of internally generated mind energy, rather than by external actions that could produce at best only ephemeral results.

During his underground years, Haya did more than concern himself with schemes to impose discipline on rank-and-file followers. In actual practice, he succeeded in imposing his will on the party's elites, whether they, like him, were in hiding in Peru or living in exile. One especially notable example of Haya's imposition of "hegemonic will" on the dispersed high command was his forbidding them to express opinions on the Spanish Civil War. The majority of party leaders, like the majority of liberal and radical intellectuals throughout the Western world, favored the Republicans in their 1936–39 struggle against the Nationalists led by Francisco Franco. However, owing to his "intransigent anti-Hispanism," Haya refused to allow his party to become involved in issues pertaining to the former mother land, or *madre patria*.[123] This fact is interesting on two counts: it demonstrates Haya's absolute control over party officials, and it attests, I believe, to the jefe's alienation from his parents that had begun many years previously in Trujillo.

The central theme of the Hispanism to which Haya showed intransigent hostility was that Spain's status as madre patria obligated Latin Americans to maintain the reverence that all children owe the parents who have given them life and shaped their natures. Hispanism thus symbolized for Haya the sort of parental ties he had disavowed. In consequence, he developed a veritably neurotic aversion to any manifestation of Hispanism. Only such hatred can fully explain his stance on the Spanish Civil War. Only an aversion of abnormal intensity, moreover, can account for the fact that Haya, who throughout his life wrote more on foreign lands than on Peru itself, virtually never referred to Spain in any of his publications. He sought to banish the madre patria, like his parents, from consciousness.

With his party in the catacombs, Haya thought increasingly about the destiny that, in his mind, linked the APRA to the United States. Nearly always, Haya's thought and actions responded to a combination of practical and mystical considerations, of realistic assessment and magical fantasies. Often the diverse elements were so intertwined as to be virtually inseparable. The intermixture of motivation was seldom more striking than when Haya turned his attention to the United States as the war clouds darkened in Europe.

On the practical side, Haya saw the possibility of enlisting the support of the United States in bringing the APRA to power. Sensitive to the indications of a coming confrontation between the fascist and the democratic nations, Haya was well aware of United States concern with checking a fascist tide, more imagined than real, in Latin America. By late 1938 Haya and the Aprista fraternity in exile, many of whose members had gained prominence as journalists in their respective countries of asylum, had launched a propaganda campaign to portray Benavides as a fascist dictator. They hoped the United States could be induced to lead Latin America in a moral intervention against Benavides, thus paving the way for the APRA's accession to power.[124]

Haya's quest for power might seem a purely practical matter, but there is more here than meets the eye, for the magical fantasies of the masochist-narcissist are also in evidence. By the proper type of exhibitionism Haya now hoped to manipulate a new selfobject, the United States, into providing the desired gratification. Increasingly, he turned his attention to persuading various North Americans that his suffering and that of his party, at the hands of fascists, had earned Apristas the right to be placed in power.[125] Often when the neurotic wants something very badly, rather than undertaking the direct personal actions that would seem best calculated to obtain it, he decides, as Karen Horney puts it, "to let George do it."[126] For a time, George had been a Peruvian general; now, he became Uncle Sam. Grasping for a deus ex machina resolution to his problems, Haya persisted in his expectations of the miraculous.

If the United States were to be lured into moral intervention on its behalf, then the APRA would have to begin to disavow the fascist, totalitarian inclinations that had concerned, among others, Ambassador Dearing. By the time World War II began, Haya de la Torre was engaged in fashioning a more democratic image for his party. Perhaps more than opportunism entered into this change of images. Haya was by no means immune to the Leninist and fascist temptations, but on the whole he responded more favorably to the methods of the British Labour Party and the ideas of Rolland and Gandhi. While the "Vertical Organization of the Peruvian Aprista Party" seems a clear enough manifestation of totalitarian preferences, one could by straining just a bit, as Aprista apologists have done, construe the document as a temporary aberration. The year 1937 was, after all, a trying one for the APRA. If the party was to survive and ultimately come to power, and if, either along the way to or once in power, it was to be restrained from initiating the sort of bloodbath that so often accompanies regeneration movements, then the most inflexible discipline had to prevail.

By 1939, in any event, Haya had begun to hope that the APRA's accession to power might be helped along by the moral intervention of the United States. Thereafter the party would be sustained in power partially through United States support, exercised through a symbiotic relationship that would develop between Lima and Washington. Was Haya actually willing, for the sake of power, to assume the role of lackey to an exploitative, imperialist foreign country? Not for a moment do I think this of him.

To Apristas and to a great many other Latin Americans the United States seemed different in 1939 from what it had been in the 1920s. In the decade that saw the founding of the APRA, the United States at one time or another had troops in the Dominican Republic, Haiti, and Nicaragua. Furthermore, in high-handed style at the 1928 Pan American Conference held in Havana, its statesmen had refused to disavow the "right" to intervene, by armed force if necessary, in hemispheric affairs. But Franklin D. Roosevelt's Good Neighbor policy appeared to have lessened the Yankee menace, and Haya was among the most starry-eyed of all Latin Americans in thinking that the new policy in Washington grew out of a true change of heart. As of 1939 there had been no Yankee occupation troops in any part of Latin America—outside of the Canal Zone in Panama and the Guantánamo base in Cuba, both of which remained under United States sovereignty—for five years. Furthermore, the United States had twice renounced hemispheric interventionism: first at Montevideo in 1933, with reservations; then in Buenos Aires in 1936, ostensibly without reservations. Haya had no intention of selling out to the nemesis against which he had raised an anti-imperialist challenge in the 1920s. However, with an apparently transformed United States he saw the possibility of a safe partnership.

Haya's perception of a changed United States would soon begin to weaken his totalitarian temptation. Initially he had seen the need for Indo-American states to organize along totalitarian lines to resist a flood of United States cultural and economic imperialism that threatened to submerge a people-continent's authentic life-style. But, if the flood no longer threatened, then Indo-America had no need for totalitarian mobilization to construct dikes.

In the coming conjunction with the United States that Haya envisioned, Peru and the entire Indo-American people-continent were cast in the feminine role. Happily, in Haya's conception there was nothing demeaning in this. He was, after all, steeped in the Hispanic tradition that hails the moral superiority of women, in part because they are assumed to be less materialistic, less capitalistically inclined than men. And, if for no other reason than his love of Wagner's operas and Beethoven's "Fidelio,"[127] Haya had to be steeped in the mythological archetype of man's dependance on a woman for redemption. Agreeing with Keyserling (as quoted in the preceding chapter) that always "the salvation of mankind depends on women," Haya perceived that the time had come for Peru and all Indo-America to fulfill their destiny of redeeming the United States—a country that had suddenly begun to show signs of being ripe for redemption.

As the 1930s ended, the fugitive Aprista jefe was downright ebullient in his optimism. Rather than practical judgment, it had to be Haya's mystical musings and his cosmic view that accounted for his optimism. In the light of any realistic assessment, the situation had to be judged bleak and unpromising for the Aprista cause.

The APRA as of 1939: Failures, Accomplishments, and Expectations

If the APRA had won the 1931 election, it might never have become more than a political party. Out of its failure, however, and out of the ensuing years of persecution it emerged with a mystique unique in the annals of Peruvian politics. In some ways this very mystique accounts for the APRA's subsequent difficulties, for the party's claims on some kind of mystical transcendence alienated probably more Peruvians than they attracted. Antenor Orrego maintained that Aprismo effected the perfect synthesis between mysticism and positivism.[128] In the 1930s, though, the PAP seemed not to have found the right balance. It outraged the positivists while appealing mainly to those with mystical predispositions who were most susceptible to millenarian fantasies—in addition, needless to say, to a host of opportunists. However, many Peruvians with a mystical bent still felt quite at home within the traditional Catholic Church and the various forms of popular religion that flourished under its umbrella. Not surprisingly, Peru's sect of "chosen people" called forth fanatical opposition from all those who did not share the new faith.

Those who identified with the old order in Peru can scarcely be blamed for the fanaticism with which they opposed the APRA, for this movement that harped on death and regeneration seemed committed to the belief that not only a few thousand Aprista martyrs but the entire old order had to die before the new humanity could appear. And a great deal of Aprista rhetoric, especially that emanating from leaders other than the jefe, indicated preference for the apocalyptic approach of speeding the old order on its way through violence, rather than allowing it to die a natural death. The actions of Aprista terrorists and assassins could only add to the apprehension of those Peruvians who were not in quest of basic transformation, either psychic or social.

When a one-time supporter grandiloquently proclaimed that Haya de la Torre "brings the dawn in his arms,"[129] he may have thrilled those who longed to have a charismatic hero bestow new life upon them. But those who did not want to see the sun set on the old order waxed ever more apprehensive. One may readily understand also how a modern-thinking Peruvian capitalist would have reacted to Romain Rolland's prediction, which Haya had proclaimed it his mission to fulfill, that Latin America was destined to speed the death of the capitalist world, thereby preparing the way for the birth of a new world that would synthesize East and West.[130] Thanks to the skillful administration of Oscar R. Benavides and to good luck in the increasing demand for its exports as the 1930s ended, Peru seemed to be surmounting its economic crisis, and the star of capitalism had begun to rise from its nadir. Thus Aprismo's mystical alternatives to positivist capitalism seemed less likely to win majority approval at the end of the 1930s than at the beginning.

Toward the end of his sixth year in office and after suppressing yet another Aprista golpe, Benavides announced in March 1939 that presidential elections would be held at the end of the year. He chose as the official candidate Manuel Prado, a banker and a member of one of Peru's most distinguished and socially prominent families. Opposition came from José Quesada, running for the Revolutionary Union (UR). It was in connection with the ensuing campaign that Benavides may have departed from his customary tolerance toward Peru's best-known fugitive, although the full story has never emerged.

When it became clear that the APRA, under Haya's direction, balked at supporting Prado and was actually negotiating with the UR, the party that Sánchez Cerro had formed and that many Peruvians regarded as fascistic,[131] Benavides may have given the go-ahead to the police agents who at dawn on a September morning in 1939 surrounded Incahuasi. With Haya in his hideout at the time were his chauffeur companion Jorge Idiáquez, his "bohemian" companion of youthful years Alcides Spelucín, Julio Aldana (like Haya, Idiáquez, and Spelucín a native of Trujillo), and Aldana's wife, who attended to domestic chores at Incahuasi. Only the courage of Idiáquez, who fled first and was mistaken—as he intended—for Haya, enabled the jefe and Spelucín to escape and shortly later even to arrange the rescue of Haya's faithful dogs and black cat from the house where all other possessions had been seized or demolished. Idiáquez was wounded and captured, and the Aldanas were likewise apprehended. "Haya should have been assassinated; he was saved by the valor of Idiáquez," writes Luis Alberto Sánchez.[132]

Shortly after this incident, Manuel Prado triumphed handily in a presidential election that was by no means a model of democratic propriety. Haya's persistent denials notwithstanding, most observers believe that just before the balloting Prado had reached a secret understanding with the Apristas: in exchange for their promise to support him or at least not to oppose him at the polls, Prado purportedly agreed to legalize their party after coming to power.[133] If such a bargain was struck, Prado did not keep his part of it until almost the end of his administration.

With Prado in office and with the failure of various Aprista golpes, Haya continued to look toward Washington, and with far greater expectations than merely becoming president of Peru. Much of what he perceived to be transpiring in the United States inspired him to believe that the cosmic union of North and South was at hand and that in consequence Indo-America was about to give birth, peacefully, to the new humanity. Strangely enough, a similar kind of belief had been germinating for some years in the United States, and in this fact Haya found confirmation of his vision.

Nine

A Convergence of Regeneration Visions:
United States and Aprista Intellectuals in the
1920s and 1930s

The Quest for New Beginnings in the United States

As World War I came to an end, many North American intellectuals stood ready to turn their backs on much of their country's prevailing order and to set out in search of new beginnings. Herbert Croly mused over a new order that would avoid "the tyranny of Bolshevism" as well as the "anarchy of unredeemed capitalism,"[1] echoing in a way Lester Frank Ward's prewar praise of sociocracy: essentially, a synthesis between collectivism and individualism.[2] Walter Lippman observed that the war "had awakened among Americans a general impatience with the nation's individualism." Along with many other·liberals, he had been "intrigued by the possibilities of wartime collectivism, but was not entirely seduced."[3] The American fascination with what Michael Kammen terms "collective individualism"[4] was asserting itself anew and spreading beyond the confines of Greenwich Village, where it had flourished during prewar years.

Out of Greenwich Village radicalism as nourished by the Lost Generation of the 1920s came, in the 1930s, full-fledged counterculture challenge to traditionally conceived American institutions and values. As the Great Depression shattered the American economy, doubts gave way, in many circles, to despair about the viability of marketplace capitalism and bourgeois individualism. Counterculture values found their way into even the highest echelons of government, for many of the intellectuals who helped assemble Franklin D. Roosevelt's New Deal hoped to forge a "constructive compromise between individual liberty" and a form of collectivism that would guarantee economic security.[5] In effect, they sought the same fusion between individualism and collectivism that Haya de la Torre hoped to find in corporatism or cooperativism. Although the fact is little appreciated, a convergence in corporatist mythology helped achieve the rapport between North and South American intellectuals that contributed to the success of F.D.R.'s Good Neighbor policy in the years between 1933 and 1945.[6]

Changing United States attitudes toward Native Americans contributed further to improved hemispheric relations. By the 1920s, glorification of the Indian became for many North American intellectuals a badge of their rejection of the capitalist ethic. Out of the glorification of the Red Man, perceived as preferring communal life and as resisting capitalism's aggrandizing spirit, emerged the Indian New Deal, presided over by F.D.R.'s Commissioner of Indian Affairs, John Collier. Basing his approach on the same assumptions that underlay Andean America's Indianism, Collier shared many of the beliefs that animated Peru's two great Indianists, José Carlos Mariátegui and Víctor Raúl Haya de la Torre.[7]

Traditionally, Latin Americans had been associated in popular United States opinion with Indians—often to the despair of upper-class Latin Americans. Usually, the assumed Indianness of the southern continent had counted against it in the minds of North Americans. In the 1930s, however, the situation changed. The people to the south of the Rio Grande no longer were viewed as refractory to civilization owing to the irremediable primitiveness of the Indian races with which they lived and bred. Rather, for some North Americans the people to the south took on the promise of a noble savagery not yet awakened to its potential. Thanks to them, the United States would have a second chance at redemption in a New World frontier. Having wasted the original opportunity to be reborn through union with the people of nature living within their own continental confines, North Americans could grasp anew after wholeness by uniting with, rather than seeking to repress and dominate, the Indianness that lay to the south.

If in the public fancy Latin America had been associated with Indians, United States cartoonists had, up to the 1920s, delighted in caricaturing the southern neighbors as unkempt blacks, as women, as children, and as idle, daydreaming people unconcerned with material advancement and therefore justly rewarded by poverty.[8] Clearly, these caricatures conveyed the notion of Latin American inferiority. But in the 1930s, the old order of values was topsy-turvy, and stereotyped characteristics once reviled become virtues. Thus, Indians, blacks, women, children, and the poor were acclaimed as natural persons, uncorrupted by the misguided constraints of capitalist culture. Furthermore, the natural preference that they exhibited for spontaneity, for bonding, for the unselfish, sharing life was now perceived to encompass Latin Americans as well. Thus stereotyped, Latin Americans held out to North America's business civilization a counterweight that could bring about a dynamic equilibrium. If the United States was no longer the redeemer nation, in which role many of its founders had cast it,[9] at least it could become an integral part of an organic redeemer hemisphere that would rescue humanity from the Old World's decline.

In 1892 an American professor of philosophy at Tokyo University speculated that Japan was on the way to becoming a unique blend of East and West, "the point of fusion for the two halves of humanity, two civilizations that had been severed in ancient times."[10] The new type of person about to be created in Japan could, he believed, "prevail through the world for the next thousand years."[11] In the isolationist mood of the 1930s (which consistently manifested an opening toward Latin America), some American dreamers saw no need to look across the Pacific for the fusion of opposite civilizations. The fusion could take place in their own hemisphere. At least a few North American seekers after a new and higher civilization had come to share the visions of Peru's Haya de la Torre.

Latin America as a New Frontier
for a Redeemer Hemisphere

The change in United States attitudes toward Latin America during the depression years was presaged by the empathy that avant-garde intellectuals and artists revealed for the Mexican Revolution that erupted in 1910. Not long after the revolution began, John Reed earned distinction among the North Americans who responded warmly to the new culture that they imagined to be emerging south of the Rio Grande.[12] By the early 1920s, Carleton Beals and Frank Tannenbaum[13] figured among dozens of visitors from the north who believed Mexico had begun the process of forging a more humane existence in which the individualistic thrust of capitalism would be constrained by the collectivist spirit that ran back to pre-Columbian times. Within the new Mexico they also anticipated the eclipse of racism as an unrestrained mingling of races and cultures gradually produced a total amalgam. They applauded also the revolution's agrarianism, seeing in it an indication that Mexico was finding its authenticity not only by returning to those natural elements of its populace most rooted in the land, but by returning to the land itself and downgrading the importance of urban, bourgeois existence. Beals and Tannenbaum obviously shared the mindset that had inspired Haya de la Torre to extol the Peruvian sierra while denigrating Lima. Moreover, they responded to the same mythological appeal of Indianism and agrarianism that had helped inspire Haya to found the APRA during the Mexican phase of his exile in 1924.[14]

Haya's Mexican inspiration came at nearly the same time that Beals and Tannenbaum were discovering the country. Beals had taken up Mexican residence in 1918 after graduating from the University of California and earning a master's degree from Columbia. Four years later Tannenbaum made his first visit to Mexico, where he met Beals and other members of a growing community of United States visitors and expatriates. Before 1922, Tannenbaum had been involved with the Industrial Workers of the World and various other radical labor movements, had earned a bachelor's degree from Columbia (1921), and had begun to dabble in journalism.

Publishing articles in a number of United States journals during the 1920s, Beals and Tannenbaum stood conspicuously among a sizeable group of North American writers and artists who defended the reform programs of the revolution and criticized the apparent designs of the State Department and Yankee business interests to turn the clock back to the days of Porfirio Díaz when the welcome mat had been out for foreign capital. On their part, State Department officials and United States diplomats sought to dismiss Beals, Tannenbaum, and other writers who defended revolutionary Mexico as Jewish Bolsheviks. Before long, Beals felt constrained to deny Soviet connections and to assert that he was not Jewish and had never spelled his name Biel.[15] While certainly not a Bolshevik, Tannenbaum did look favorably on Latin American revolutions, and he was a Jew.

By the early 1930s, American leftist intellectuals and writers who saw Mexico as America's new beginning had grown in number, and many of them joined with Beals in taking up residence in the country—among them Bertram and Ella Wolfe, who actually were Communists. As the expatriate community increased in numbers, Beals began to focus his regenerationist hopes on lands farther to the south. Like his friend Katherine Anne Porter, who also had lived in and written about Mexico,[16] he had soured on the 1910 Revolution as a source of new beginnings. Andean America now captured his fancy.

According to Beals, who had met Haya de la Torre in Mexico in 1924, the "children of the sun" were beginning to stir in Peru; they were "turning to ancient faiths" as they clamored for justice. "The tide is rising," he happily proclaimed; and when the descendants of the Quechua, Mochica, and Colla civilizations began finally to "reach for light," a new nation would be born and thereafter "a new cycle of history" would begin for South America and for the New World.[17] The coming epic of American history as Beals foresaw it would be shaped by "an organic revolution out of native culture and tradition, the fusion of elements long warring in open contradiction." Involved in the fusion would be indigenous experience, democratic theories, "Marxian economics and Fascist force," and above all "mass rhythms obeying vital life forces, new social concepts, and determinate aesthetic and ideological forms."[18] After visiting Peru in the early 1930s, Beals hailed Aprismo as the political force most likely to lead the land to its appointed task of national and hemispheric renewal.[19]

Some years before this, while briefly in the United States during the 1920s, Haya de la Torre had contact with, and lectured for, the League for Industrial Democracy, a Socialist Party group of which Norman Thomas was the major figure. At the same time, he had enthused over the anti-imperialism not only of the Socialist Party but of such men as Sen. Woodrow Borah, the novelist Upton Sinclair,[20] and the radical academicians Scott Nearing and Joseph Freeman.[21] For Haya, these and other North Americans he had met or come to know through their published works heralded a new spirit in the United States that would render the erstwhile colossus a safe and complementary mate for Indo-America in the coming marriage of opposites. Subsequently, the mounting anticapitalist spirit spawned by the depression as well as the turning of intellectuals and artists to Mexico as they sought to glimpse the future provided additional indications to Haya that the hemisphere's rebirth was at hand. The conversion of Carleton Beals to the Aprista cause provided additional confirmation for Haya's optimistic appraisal. By 1938, moreover, Haya believed he had at least a partial convert in Frank Tannenbaum, who by then had begun the teaching career in history and economics at Columbia University that would make him one of the most distinguished Latin Americanists the United States has known.

Through the mediation of the United States Embassy in Lima, Haya arranged a meeting on September 6, 1938, with Tannenbaum, who was then in the midst of a visit to Peru. Guided to Haya's hiding place, Tannenbaum had dinner with the jefe and conversed with him into the wee hours of the morning. On September 7, embassy secretary William P. Cochran, who was quick to convey the professor's impressions to Ambassador Louis G. Dreyfus, inquired if Tannenbaum thought Haya "too visionary." Tannenbaum responded that while the conversation had at times pointed in this direction, he considered Haya a skilled and adept "general."[22]

In rapport with an expanding circle of United States intellectuals, Haya also enjoyed what he deemed close relations with embassy personnel and even contrived to hold what impressed him as highly satisfactory direct conversations with some of the delegates representing the United States at the Eighth Pan American Congress, held in Lima in 1938.[23] Thus, from North Americans in various walks of life Haya derived hope that a new and mutually fulfilling relationship between the United States and Indo-America lay just ahead. Helping further to nourish this hope was Waldo Frank, who, like Haya, fancied himself a prophet of American regeneration.

Like Haya, Waldo Frank had visited Russia after the Communist takeover, had wondered if he might be witnessing the dawn of a new epoch for humanity, but on deeper reflection had concluded he was witnessing a false dawn and must turn elsewhere.[24] As it happened, he turned toward the lands to the south. From his northern vantage point he glimpsed the same kind of hemispheric destiny that Haya and his Apristas had envisioned from the south and that Rolland and Keyserling had perceived from Europe. Mistaking Frank for a genuine spokesman of North American thought, rather than as a fringe figure whose narrowly circumscribed influence would quickly ebb, Haya wondered if the moment had not arrived when vanguard United States thinkers, steeped in a new yet ancient wisdom, could begin to collaborate with Peruvian seers in realizing the destiny prophesied by the APRA.

Waldo Frank's and Aprismo's Visions of Regeneration

Born in 1889 into a Jewish family with keen literary, artistic, and musical interests (his mother was a musician who helped oversee her son's training as a cellist), Waldo Frank graduated from Yale University in 1911 and began to work as a journalist and free-lance writer. In 1916 he helped found the review *The Seven Arts* and married Margaret Naumburg, who, like Frank, was deeply interested in David Henry Thoreau and Walt Whitman, Oriental religion, and the new theories of psychoanalysis. By 1919, when he published the novel *Our America*, Frank had turned increasingly to mysticism and thrown himself into a study of medieval cabalists. Later, he fell for a time under the influence of Georges Gurdjieff and P. D. Ouspensky (dispensers of esoteric wisdom mentioned in chapter 5) and their disciple A. R. Orage. Apparently intrigued by the possibility that his generation stood on the threshold of "four-dimensional" consciousness that would free it from conventional space-time limitations, he contented that he and his contemporaries had embarked on the quest of a new America and that "in the seeking we create her."[25]

Repelled by the materialism of North Americans, their deification of the machine that had resulted from a peculiar amalgam of Protestantism and capitalism, and their propensity to approach the earth only in the lust of possession,[26] Frank saw in Latin America—which he preferred to call America Hispana—the spiritual counterbalance that the north required to be complete.[27] Frank had first intuited the importance of South America to North America while a visitor to Taos—the same New Mexican town in which John Collier had discovered that regeneration lay in the North American Indians. In northern New Mexico Frank had found people (Indians, Hispanics, and mixed-bloods) who were not psychically alienated because their conscious and subliminal selves fused into a whole; he found also a people who lived harmoniously rather than in an adversary relationship with the physical environment, a people who were one with the cosmos. New Mexico's spiritual mode of existence must be owing, he decided, not only to its Indian but also to its Iberian

194

heritage. To check on the latter possibility, Frank went to Spain, and he fell in love with the mystical tradition that he convinced himself he found there. Returning home in a state of spiritual excitement, he published *Virgin Spain* in 1926. Shortly translated into Spanish, this book helped make Frank, for the next fifteen to twenty years, one of the best-known contemporary United States authors in Spain and Spanish America.[28] Anxious to verify the presence of a mystical, intuitive, inward sensitivity resulting from the Indian and Hispanic legacies (and not averse to reaping some economic rewards from his new fame in the Spanish-speaking world), Frank undertook an Ibero-American lecture tour in 1929.

Speaking in Spanish before large and enthusiastic audiences in such centers as Mexico City, Buenos Aires, and Lima, Frank evoked an almost frenzied response among Spanish American intellectuals. His success came about because he told the Latin Americans what they wanted to hear. Instead of chiding them for their economic backwardness and challenging them to uplift themselves materially by emulating their advanced northern neighbors, Frank praised them for their mystical sensitivity and spoke of their destiny to redeem the spiritually starved United States and thereby initiate a great process of "re-creation."[29] Realization of the American hemisphere's potential for re-creation depended upon the two "half-worlds" of North and South America becoming "one mystical organic whole, existing in harmony and combining the best qualities of the materialistic North and the spiritual South."[30]

Ultimately, Frank prophesied, a new wholeness would emerge out of American chaos. America Hispana, with its "life that lacks order," and the United States, with its "order that lacks life," would join together to fulfill the hemisphere's promise.[31] Moreover, Frank insisted (totally in line with independently conceived Aprista prescriptions) that the two half-worlds must join as equals: the one rich in the spontaneity and ideals of the volk and the other brimming with rationality, order, and discipline.

In Frank's vision of hemispheric wholeness each of the two parts would become somewhat like its opposite. But this process would not proceed to the extent of total homogenization. It was precisely the promise of a harmony between individual halves that to some extent preserved their own identity that Luis Alberto Sánchez, one of Frank's most enthusiastic admirers at this time, found especially to his liking. In the coming synthesis, as Sánchez interpreted Frank's often murky message, "each part of America must conserve and allow to evolve its own individual traits."[32] In the reborn hemisphere, then, a United States that had been stripped of hegemony would continue to perform prodigies of economic production, although paying more attention to its poets and prophets and recognizing the importance of the spiritual and the mystical; and Latin America, its well-being secure within a hemisphere predicated upon the free exchange of material goods and spiritual energies, would continue its cultivation of the riches that transcend creatureliness, although acquiring greater organizational and economic skills. Here was a projected future guaranteed to dazzle a broad array of Latin American intellectuals. Understandably, they lionized Waldo Frank. Understandably, too, in their belief in miraculous deliverance from the grubby realities of material development, they helped doom their countries to continuing underdevelopment.

Among Peruvian intellectuals Frank had been in vogue even before 1929, owing to "his magnificent book *Virgin Spain*, which the poet León Felipe had translated into Spanish."[33] With the Leguía administration leery of the North American visionary and the conservative rector of San Marcos disinclined to ask him to lecture at the university in the course of the Latin American tour, a group known as the Dissident Committee of Forty Intellectuals of Peru, prominent among whom were José Carlos Mariátegui and the two future Aprista leaders Luis Alberto Sánchez and Manuel Seoane, invited Frank to lecture in Lima.[34] Obviously pleased to accept, Frank spoke both at the Teatro Municipal and the National University of San Marcos, where he received an honorary doctorate.

For the address with which he introduced Frank at San Marcos, Sánchez composed an essay that not only reveals the main ingredients of Frank's thought but also provides insights into the mood prevalent among avant-garde Peruvian intellectuals. "Cellist in his youth, and profoundly musical," Sánchez said of Frank, "he composes his literary symphonies in rhythms of music. It is only a man musically gifted who can essentialize totality from such diverse matters." Throughout his literary works, hailed in Sánchez's introduction as "symphonies," Frank based his interpretation "upon the necessity of integrating, of making one, and above all of sustaining the rhythm. This indubitably is a method that has its metaphysics, its mystic sense: a sense that is clearly Jewish."[35] Out of diversity, the Peruvian declared, Frank created synthesis, because "he has been able to detect the unitary rhythm which underlies phenomena and persons seemingly—only seemingly—discordant."

Waldo Frank had come to Latin America, Sánchez judged, to learn "the unitary rhythm of our life" that heretofore he had only dimly apprehended. Always Frank's method was to intuit, to feel the intimate harmony of a whole. Only then did the rational factor intervene, "to order, shape and discipline" what had first been grasped extrarationally. Gazing southward, Frank had intuited the possibility of an "insurrection of spirit," a "revolution of creation." And he arrived now to learn how to carry that revolution through to its destined conclusion. "His New World is not the continent which Columbus discovered; it is the New Man whose appearance he proposes and whose heralds are the rebellious minorities—the idealists—of the entire world. Minorities of Hispano-America, of Spain, of the United States, of the Jews... minorities are expressions of the nonconformity of man today, and of his need to create."[36] By 1931 when he had found, as he would describe it, "my road to Damascus"[37] and taken up the new religion of Aprismo, Sánchez could have used virtually the same language—substituting pianist for cellist and Indianist for Jewish—in hailing his jefe máximo.

Returning to the United States, Waldo Frank published the general content of his Mexican and South American lectures in the book *America Hispana*. It appeared in 1931, the same year that saw the publication of a Spanish translation of Keyserling's similarly prophetic ode, *South American Meditations*. Frank dedicated his book to the recently deceased Peruvian who had been a Marxist in his own way, José Carlos Mariátegui. In Mariátegui, Frank had discovered a kindred soul. Both of them appreciated Marxism for its "soft" side, for its mystical vision of the "organic whole"; both responded to Marxism as a "religious impulse freed of its theological form";[38] both honored the spirit, not the letter, of Marxism.[39] Mariátegui represented to Frank the American man of destiny, the new American who, having attained synthesis out of the chaos in his soul, having resolved in harmony the "dualisms of bloods and cultures," could lead the way toward the regeneration of America Hispana.[40] Above all, Frank appreciated Mariátegui for "his poet's intuition that in the ego lives the Cosmos."[41]

Shortly after Mariátegui's death in 1930, Frank concluded that his mantle had fallen to Haya de la Torre. In a note added to *America His-*

pana just before its publication, Frank wrote: "Since Mariátegui's death active political leadership of a revolutionary type has passed in Lima to Raúl Haya de la Torre, a socialist who rejects the Marxism of Russia. . . . I have, as yet, found no good cause for doubting his sincerity. Haya is a man of brilliant power—of still unproven promise. If he lacks the intellectual genius of Mariátegui, he may yet possibly be able to integrate some of the profound forces which Mariátegui aroused, and lead them into the beginnings of action."[42]

Meantime, Haya had become aware of the North American seer and commented favorably from Berlin in 1930 on Frank's Mexico City lectures, summaries of which had come to his attention.[43] Although separated by an immense geographic distance, the two men had begun to appreciate their intellectual proximity. With Haya imprisoned in Lima after the July 1932 Trujillo uprising, Frank contributed to the telegraphed pleas for clemency that foreign dignitaries from many lands directed to Sánchez Cerro.

Finally the two men met in 1942. Frank was on a second Latin American lecture tour, backed this time by the State Department in the expectation that he could help mobilize support for the war effort against the Axis powers. Amidst careful Aprista security precautions, Frank was spirited to Haya's hiding place in Lima. With Haya and Frank actually together, one might have expected their oversized egos to bump. But some element of mutual esteem survived the face-to-face meeting of the two would-be liberators of America, even though Haya appears to have retained resentment over the mild reservations that Frank had expressed about Aprismo's methods at the beginning of the 1930s.[44] Nor could the jefe have appreciated Frank's suggestion that Mariátegui's genius outshone Haya's. To Frank's type of appraisal, Haya preferred the adulation of a North American journalist who in 1935 hailed him "as the most portentous South American alive," and added: "South American intellectuals speak of him with that misty reverence reserved in this country for Abraham Lincoln."[45]

For Frank, the Lima meeting removed some of the reservations previously entertained about Haya's authoritarian leanings. In a book published the year after their meeting, Frank reported of Haya: "He is strong, solid, energetic, at forty-seven; with that natural body rhythm which one finds in all leaders whose life is strictly harmonized about a single purpose. Unlike other persecuted men, Haya has grown, spiritually, and kept his humor."⁴⁶ Here, surely, was high praise. But Haya was accustomed to still better accolades from those claiming sympathy to his cause.

In the two men conferring surreptitiously in Lima coalesced a remarkably rich sampling of the millennialist currents that through the years had surfaced sporadically in their respective continents. And their encounter can only have bolstered their mutual regenerationist hopes. Frank returned to the United States more than ever convinced that World War II was not simply a struggle pitting democracy against fascism. Beyond this, it was a "Deep War," a confrontation between the rationalistic, mechanistic, materialistic way of life that had come to characterize Western culture and the intuitive, spiritual life-style that provided hope for humanity's future. At the same time that the Axis sustained defeat, the proponents of the antimechanistic approach to life would triumph in America and embark upon the creation of a world that truly deserved to be called new.⁴⁷

On his part, Haya found confirmation of his own visions in the meeting with Frank. More importantly, in the improvement of his and the APRA's fortunes that began early in the 1940s and acquired dramatic momentum midway in the decade, Haya found harbingers of the envisaged utopian future. More than ever he now believed that his native land could be spared the cataclysmic violence that prophets so often have associated with the birth of a new humanity. Apocalyptic destruction indeed was underway, but in far-off lands. The Old World's blood bath would confer life-giving sustenance on the New World's redeemer hemisphere, facilitating the "Deep War" victory of elites who understood how to lead the way toward a millenarian order.

Ten

Emergence From and Return to the Catacombs: Haya and the APRA, 1940–48

The Years of Hope and Visionary Fervor, 1940–44

When the more or less democratically elected Manuel Prado replaced dictator Oscar R. Benavides as Peru's chief executive in 1939, the fortunes of Haya de la Torre and his APRA seemed on the upswing. The new president owed his electoral victory partly to Aprista support, even though Haya steadfastly denied that any deal had been struck, and he began early on in his six-year term to ease up on some aspects of harassment. Various party leaders, among them Carlos Manuel Cox and Ramiro Prialé, were released from prison in 1940. Even Juan Seoane and Serafín Delmar, imprisoned for their alleged roles in the 1935 assassination of Antonio Miró Quesada and his wife, were granted freedom on condition they depart at once for exile in Chile. Lesser party leaders also received their freedom not long after Prado came to power.

After initial indications of leniency on the part of the new administration, APRA's return to legality "remained suspended."[1] Haya de la Torre, who continued in hiding, and those suspected of assisting him in the clandestine direction of Aprista affairs, continued to be bedeviled by government agents, though the degree to which President Prado was directly responsible remains unclear. In any event, Haya in 1941 "miraculously" escaped another attempt on his life.[2] Two years later, police surrounded the house in which Haya had been hiding only a few hours earlier and engaged in a gun battle with the Apristas still on the premises. The latter were apprehended, but only after they had killed the colonel who directed the assault. In the melee the case containing the bones of Manuel Arévalo was somehow lost.[3]

While Haya was kept guessing as to government intentions, on the whole during the years from 1940 to 1944 he could count on security officials to turn the other way when he emerged from hiding during the night-time hours. And, provided he remained discreetly inconspicuous and avoided direct challenge to the government, he could also assume that officials would regard his hiding place as a safe haven. Relatively secure now and glowingly optimistic about the future, Haya predicted in a 1942 essay that in the aftermath of the great world struggle then underway the people of the American hemisphere would embark on the mission of forging a truly new world.[4] As the first step toward achieving their destiny, they would develop a psychological and moral approach "different from what has prevailed in the past."[5]

In 1942, it will be recalled, Haya conversed with Waldo Frank in the jefe's Lima hideout. Fully sharing Frank's conviction that in America "we are at the dawn of man's first organic era,"[6] Haya de la Torre allowed his optimism to expand, in the early 1940s, like overyeasted dough. Disgustedly rejecting the appraisal of Yale University professor William B. Fletcher that the postwar world would be much as it had been before the war,[7] Haya pronounced that a complete revolution was taking place against the background of international hostilities. A "worldwide shift to the left" was underway;[8] and if some Yankees like Fletcher could not grasp this, others, like Carleton Beals, could. Haya hailed Beals as a "brilliant North American commentator who knows the Indo-American reality"[9] and who understood that the southern continent's "revolutionary movement in changing consciousness" was being sparked by the Aprista phenomenon.[10] Encouraged by the response he detected to the north, Haya believed that the APRA approached its hour of triumph—a triumph that was guaranteed by the that had only intensified during the years of adversity.[11]

Waldo Frank and Carleton Beals were by no means the only North Americans to whom Haya looked for cooperation in forging a new hemispheric harmony and organic democracy based on the union in equality of the Americas, North and South.[12] Early in the 1940s Haya pointed to articles and books by Frank Tannenbaum, John T. Whitaker, V. J. Murphy, John Gunther, and Samuel Guy Inman that indicated, purportedly, awareness of and sympathy with Aprista visions of hemispheric transformations.[13] As late as 1939 Haya had still worried about United States reluctance to overcome its traditional imperialist approach to Latin America,[14] but by 1941 he was increasingly certain that under the inspiration of Franklin D. Roosevelt the erstwhile Colossus had embarked on such fundamental internal changes that it would emerge as a safe partner in hemispheric relations. Especially following Roosevelt's enunciation of the "Four Freedoms" in January 1941, Haya grew convinced that the United States was in the throes of a profound transformation.

Following the interpretation of Raoul de Roussy de Sales, whose 1942 book *The Making of Tomorrow* may have influenced him more than any other work he read in the early to mid-1940s,[15] Haya saw two of the four freedoms, namely those of expression and of worship, as arising out of the traditional Western democratic foundation of individual independence. However, the other two of the four freedoms, namely freedom from want and from fear, responded to the socialist instinct in humans that counseled security through surrender of the individual ego to a transcending community.[16] To gain liberation from want and fear, humans had to temper Western democracy's customary concern with self-reliance and accept dependence upon a strong central government, charged with the planned allocation of resources. In the four freedoms, Haya believed, Roosevelt combined the vertical traits of masculine individualism and nationalism with the horizontal characteristics of feminine collectivism and internationalism. Up to now, a part of the Western world, with the United States in the forefront, had exaggerated the claims of individualism, whereas Germany's National Socialism and the Soviet Union's Marxism had demanded the total surrender of liberty to state planners. But the United States, under Roosevelt, had taken up the quest to harmonize the vertical and the horizontal, the individual and the collective.[17] Thus the New Deal in the North, along with Aprismo in the south, had begun to prepare their respective spheres of influence for convergence.

De Sales had stressed the difficulty of reconciling the opposing thrusts of the four freedoms. Western men would resist a "general lowering of the spirit of enterprise," and if governments pushed too hard in the direction of planning they would impede individual freedom, "which, as we know, is the condition of all human progress." Yet he remained optimistic that the apparently insoluble dilemma would resolve itself "in the mere realities of the world of tomorrow. Contradictions

202

exist as long as no synthesis has emerged out of life itself, and it is not necessary to be able to think of a solution for that solution to exist."[18] Predictably, Haya shared the expectations of de Sales, concluding that out of the historical space-time of America had emerged a new point of view, exemplified by the very enunciation of the four freedoms, that would create a synthesis of state planning and individual liberty.[19]

Synthesis, not only between North and South America but between previously irreconcilable opposites throughout the globe, provides the key to understanding Haya's mystical ideology as influenced by the events of World War II. The fact that capitalist England and the United States had allied with the socialist Soviet Union and China in waging the struggle pointed, in Haya's mind, to the coming fusion of capitalism and socialism.[20] Moreover, Haya was influenced almost as profoundly by Lin Yutang's 1943 book *Between Tears and Laughter* as he had been by de Sales' *Making of Tomorrow*. From Lin Haya acquired the conviction that within the worldwide revolution then underway, Asia was affecting the West more than it was being affected by the West. From this it followed, in Haya's mind, that Indo-America, which he saw as having a great deal in common with the India of Gandhi and the China of the Kuomintang, was destined in the postwar era to change its northern neighbor more than the United States would alter Indo-America.[21] Just as in the Asian people-continent the Kuomintang was destined to defeat communism while absorbing some of communism's philosophical and social tenets, so in the American people-continent Aprismo would overwhelm its Marxist adversaries while incorporating some of their perceptions into a new American synthesis.[22] The simultaneous awakenings of the East and of Indo-America heralded, Haya believed, the end of imperialism; these awakenings meant that areas previously dominated and exploited would soon be able to live in peace and equality with the powers that once had exploited them.[23]

Lin Yutang struck another theme of East-West convergence that reinforced Haya's view of the future of South-North relations in the American hemisphere. According to Lin, the new physics as explained by Sir James Jeans had begun to affirm the correctness of Taoist and Confucian theories of matter, according to which constant transitions occurred between particles and waves.[24] In the worldwide process of decay and regeneration, the East, with its perceptions of ultimate reality confirmed by the latest breakthroughs in science, would begin to undermine the materialism of the West while negating the latter's imperialist thrust. In all its ramifications, the old world order would give way to a new one, for already the distinctions of high and low were, in line with the teachings of relativity, being altered: the nadir (which represented the underdeveloped world) was beginning its upward ascent, while the zenith (symbolizing the developed world) was on a descending curve. Taoists had always understood that the zenith was not high, nor the nadir low, but that the two were merged together by the relativity of time and space that collapsed the past and the future into the now.[25] Furthermore, Lin Yutang expressed his visions of regeneration in much the same terms that Haya, drawing on Antonio Rodríguez de León Pinelo, had himself utilized in 1934.[26] Lin wrote: "With the roundness of the earth, the Far East has already become the Far West of America. . . . The same thing must be true of the lines and directions of a round universe, of which the earth is considerably less than a suggestion of a microscopic speck."[27]

Thus were the concepts of the seer from Trujillo, who envisioned time in circles and layers rather than straight-line progression and who saw reality (the object) as determined by both the viewer (subject) and the point from which the subject viewed the object, confirmed by the man who for a time became the East's best-known guru. Nor could Haya have failed to respond to Lin Yutang's conviction (expressed in a chapter titled "Government by Music") that the approaching world synthesis would rest upon the proper combination of ritual (expressing the order of the universe) and music (expressing the harmony of the universe), together with the punishments and inducements that governments found necessary.[28]

Lin Yutang and de Sales served, of course, only to reinforce Haya's previous convictions about the coming convergence of the materially developed West or North with the spiritually developed East or South, of individualism with collectivism, of the one with the many. At the same time, the signs of fundamental transition that he found in the United States heightened his conviction of the New World's appointed role in initiating the new order.

Even more than to Roosevelt, with his four freedoms, Haya looked to Henry Wallace as the political leader who would lead North America toward the convergence of capitalism and socialism,[29] thereby preparing his country to enter into a new relationship of harmony with its hemispheric neighbors. By 1942 Haya was hailing Wallace, elected in 1940 as Roosevelt's vice-president, as the philosopher of revolution who intuited the true dimensions of the trial by fire currently afflicting the world and out of which would emerge integral democracy.[30] Very probably, Haya knew and approved of Wallace's well-established reputation for associating with astrologers.

In the 1930s, Wallace had written that the challenge for the world was to retain the sacredness of the individual, a holdover from "pioneer Protestantism," while teaching people "not to compete with each other for enough of this world's goods, but to learn how to live with each other in abundance." Specifically, Wallace had added, "it becomes a modern duty to make individual and group interest coincide."[31] In the new democracy, Wallace believed, properly thinking individuals should feel as committed as ministers of the Gospel. These highly motivated men would "not be Socialists, Communists, or Fascists, but plain men trying to gain by democratic methods the professed objectives of the Socialists, Communists and Fascists: security, peace and the good life for all."[32] Whether or not Haya knew the details of the new world Wallace envisioned, the Peruvian had no doubt that the North American was his country's leading politician-activist prophet of "neo-democracy."[33] In the field of action, he complemented Waldo Frank in the realm of ideas.

When Wallace visited Peru in 1943 during a Latin American goodwill tour, Haya's enthusiasm rose to new heights; and an article that he wrote on the United States vice-president was one sustained paean of praise. In particular, Haya delighted that the distinguished visitor, in a speech delivered at a banquet in Lima's presidential palace, had praised the ancient Incas for their communal labor practices and their agricultural expertise. Warming to his subject, Wallace had extolled the Incas for inventing the concept of social justice in America. In another speech about which Haya wrote admiringly, Wallace pointed to the Indian foundations of Andean America and maintained that the "persistent vitality" of the Indian races promised an imminent rebirth in Latin America. Having seen the remains of Inca civilization in Peru, Wallace averred, he had come to understand that the past would provide the future.[34]

In Henry Wallace, Haya de la Torre saw the culmination of the anti-imperialism that he had first encountered in Senator Borah and in certain other political leaders and intellectuals during his rapid sojourns of the 1920s in the United States. In Wallace he also found the spiritualist, visionary strain that he had encountered among certain sensitive North Americans in the 1920s, beginning with Anna Melina Graves, who had been a colleague at Lima's Colegio Anglo Peruano. This visionary strain, Waldo Frank had assured Haya and countless other Latin Americans, was a constant in United States culture, winding its way back to Whitman and Thoreau and even to figures of the colonial background and resonating with the mystical beliefs of the North American Indians. For Haya, Wallace offered confirmation that the United States was unshackling its spiritual, mystical potential. Liberation of that potential would set in motion a train of consequences, including the end of capitalist exploitation of the weak. This change in domestic conduct would then spill over into hemispheric relations and result in abandonment of imperialist exploitation.

As it turned out, Wallace no more set the tone of the postwar United States than the Kuomintang established the patterns of a new China. This, however, Haya could not foresee; and as World War II approached its end, the erring prophet found enormous comfort in his hopelessly inaccurate perceptions of a future marked by convergence between the Soviets and the free world. As he awaited fulfillment of his grandiose visions, Haya's ever-present shrewd, pragmatic, and opportunistic strain led him to seek out practical ties with the United States. Thereby he strengthened a relationship that through the years would provide partial compensation for the failure of his mystical dreams of regenerative symbiosis between the United States and Indo-America.

During the war years Haya saw to it that his Aprista lieutenants who had not been forced underground or into exile collaborated with FBI personnel in ferreting out Japanese and German agents operating in Peru. For these efforts, Haya purportedly received compensation from the United States Embassy in Lima.[35] Moreover, Haya frequently took his nightly outings in a luxury automobile bearing United States diplomatic license plates.[36] While rewarded with minor attentions, Haya never received from the United States the major service he may have been angling for: internal intervention in the affairs of Peru, conducted through diplomatic and economic pressures, aimed at toppling an incumbent administration and replacing it with an Aprista government. While Haya did not abandon hope that an internal military golpe might place him in power, he expanded the efforts begun in the 1930s to involve the United States. Operating still on the basis of a narcissistic personality, Haya expected some outside agency to bestow on him the power that he coveted.

In 1942 and 1943 Haya sought to secure the "moral intervention" of Washington in Peruvian affairs by convincing United States Embassy officials in Lima that President Prado had fascist leanings and was thwarting the democratic aspirations of the people.[37] Although failing at the time to ensnare the United States in his scheme, Haya persisted on this tack. Apparently hopeful of preparing the way for future assistance against dictators who might deny power to Apristas, Haya in 1944 polished his arguments that the United States was morally obligated to intervene in Latin America to help assure democratic procedures.[38] And, once he sensed the beginning of a Cold War mentality in Washington, he would begin to brand his internal foes not as fascistic but as Communist totalitarians.

Although Haya's wooing of Washington never produced an optimum payoff, his posture did contribute to a generally favorable attitude toward the APRA, not only in the State Department but among United States intellectuals. As the Cold War began, State Department officials appreciated the role of APRA as the principal rival of Communists, both in labor and student movements. And intellectuals, especially those who refused to see free-enterprise capitalism as a panacea for problems both within the United States and abroad, hailed Apristas as men of the democratic left who would forge a better society through a mixture of capitalism and socialism. If an exalted international reputation in the free world was very nearly as important to Haya as the direct exercise of political power in Peru, which it may well have been, then he did not go without substantial rewards for his efforts of the early 1940s to ingratiate himself with North Americans.

The APRA Returns to Legality:
Haya and His Party, 1944–45

In 1944 Aprista political activities were still banned. Accordingly, discretion prevailed when the party held its second national convention in late July. To the assembly, which convened in a private residence, came a group of Haya's hand-picked acolytes. To avoid noise that might attract the attention of neighbors and police, it was agreed that orators would not be applauded; instead, listeners were to register approval by raising their left arms in the APRA salute.[39] Among other points, the assembled Aprista leaders agreed to change the name of their national movement to Party of the People (Partido del Pueblo), for many Peruvians objected to the internationalist implications of the APRA denomination. (From this point forward, I shall use the designations Party of the People and Peruvian Aprista Party, or PAP, interchangeably, in line with the custom that prevailed in Peru.) Also, the participants toned down the radical language of the 1931 party platform (the Plan of Immediate Action), dropping for example the demand for separation of church and state that many Catholics had found offensive. This reflected the decision of its directors that the Party of the People, as a purportedly democratic organization, must respect the wishes of the majority of Peruvians.[40] Moreover, the new platform was singularly free of inflammatory language directed against the oligarchy.[41] Following the convention, publicly circulated remarks by Haya were noteworthy for their temporizing tone. Obviously Haya and his subordinates fully understood that chances for the speedy relegalization of their movement depended upon their creating an image of moderation.

The long-awaited day arrived in May 1945, when President Prado bestowed almost full legal rights upon the Party of the People, the one remaining restriction—and a major one, at that—being that the party could not present its own presidential candidate for the coming election. With their days in the catacombs at an end after thirteen years, Apristas laid plans to celebrate their political resuscitation with a suitably impressive ritual. The date for Haya de la Torre's "re-encounter" (reencuentro) with his followers was set for May 20. As that day dawned, multitudes began to assemble at the Campo del Marte on the outskirts of Lima. By the afternoon they set out on their march to the central Plaza San Martín, where by late evening Haya finally appeared on a balcony to address them. It was one of the most emotion-charged moments in Peru's political history.

Few details had been left to chance in arranging the symbolism and ritual that preceded Haya's appearance on the balcony. Many of the people assembling at the beginning of the day at the Campo del Marte had gone without food, thereby preparing themselves by fasting for the evening's re-encounter. The march to the Plaza San Martín was conceived as a pilgrimage. Here, according to an Aprista zealot, were "fast and pilgrimage, as in the sacred hours of collective mysticism."[42] Estimates as to the number of people who finally assembled in the plaza range from 150,000[43] to 300,000,[44] with most Aprista authors settling on the figure of 200,000, thereby qualifying the event as "the largest political manifestation in Lima's history."[45] As the shadows of evening appeared, the plaza exploded in the noise of Aprista three-beat handclapping and horn honking and the singing of party songs. The Aprista salute and shouts of approval greeted the preliminary speakers, and then, after the masses had sung the Aprista "Marseillaise" and begun to wave white handkerchiefs, Haya de la Torre appeared at last before them.

Obviously overcome with emotion, and understandably so, Haya waited long moments for the tumultuous ovation to subside. Finally, he launched into his address by stressing the martyrdom that Apristas had endured for long years.[46] "We have known how to suffer for our ideals," he began, and he proceeded to develop the theme that only those who know how to suffer for their country truly love the patria. Abruptly, Haya then swung to the subject of forgiveness, averring that all true martyrs must know how to pardon those who have wronged them. To be citizens worthy of the historic mission that corresponds to them "as the paramount democratic force of the nation," Apristas must learn to cast aside rancor and thoughts of vengeance.

Addressing next the themes of economic development and justice, Haya came remarkably close to endorsing the turn-of-the-century positivist position (discussed in chapter 2), which the APRA had initially rejected in scorn. Haya noted that wealthy nations could afford to experiment with redistribution schemes. In Peru, however, the solution for those who lacked wealth was to learn to create it. Above all, in order to develop its potential Peru required citizens under the discipline of political parties. In this respect, Apristas were qualified above all others, for they had acquired a civic education through fifteen years of suffering. With the "magnificent moral capital" accumulated through suffering, Apristas would proceed to the "forging of a great patria. With our power, our discipline, our unity, we are going to demonstrate that we are not an element of destruction, that we are not phantasms that must be feared, that we do not bear words of revenge on our lips."

After returning to the martyrdom theme and utilizing the populist ploy of declaring that he was "speaking through the mouth of all Peru's Apristas," Haya concluded with a reference to Winston Churchill. If Peruvians had lacked a Churchill to call them to blood, sweat, and tears, he observed, this nevertheless had been the tenor of his admonitions to the movement since 1931. Owing to the spirit of sacrifice, which had tempered their party, Apristas could establish a unique claim among Peruvians: to them belonged the responsibility for building the nation, always in the spirit of unity, discipline, and sacrifice.

Haya's re-encounter address was short, lasting not much over half an hour. In comparison with past performances it was decidedly restrained. Haya did not attack the oligarchy; nor did he call upon youth to wrest power from their selfish and myopic elders. At age fifty a portly figure with a balding head, Haya had the taste to realize that he could no longer present himself as a fire-eating bohemian radical. Instead, he had begun to assume the posture of an elder statesman who found rancor beneath his dignity. In his conciliatory tone it may also be that, as Víctor Villanueva suggests, Haya was not addressing merely the two hundred thousand people standing in the plaza.[47] Much of his rhetoric he may have aimed at the relative handful of aristocratic Peruvians comfortably seated in the Club Nacional. No one present in this bastion of Peruvian high society, located at the Plaza San Martín, could have failed to hear Haya's words as they thundered from the numerous loudspeakers scattered about the jam-packed plaza. To the occupants of the Club Nacional, close to which Carlos Steer had assassinated the Miró Quesadas in 1935, Haya directed his words of concilation and pledge of nonviolence. To them he offered assurances that Aprismo would now hitch the zeal of populist politics to the conservative practicality of the old positivist school.

For all of its conciliatory tone, Haya's address could only have emitted alarm signals to gradualist Peruvians. In spite of the lip service to democracy, Haya still judged members of his party as a chosen people, uniquely purified by the suffering that had conferred on them the right to lead Peru toward its destiny. Moreover, Haya's words may well have fallen within the context of neurotic behavior. An eminent psychiatrist affirms that the neurotic intent upon the manipulation of people predictably assumes the pose of "utmost. . .generosity, consideration, justice, dignity,. . .unselfishness. . . . He should be able to endure anything, should like everybody. . .should never feel hurt, and he should always be serene and unruffled."[48] According to another psychiatrist, the masochist hopes ultimately to gain power over people by inducing them to injure him; once injured, he feels what amounts almost to gratitude, mindful of the hold he has gained over his victims as a result of having been victimized by them.[49] By inference at least, Haya throughout his re-encounter speech had clung to the image of Peru's number-one sufferer. Thereby he subtly claimed the deference not only of Peru's chosen people but of those who in their blindness had persecuted those people. In his mature years, Haya was acquiring subtlety, but his manipulative devices remained essentially unchanged.

By placing Haya's forgiveness message in the context of an earlier address, one delivered in November 1933, it is possible more readily to detect the fervor of religious messianism that Haya still conveyed, if in a less blatant manner. In the 1933 discourse, Haya had also stressed the need to forgive prodigal Peruvians who had initially remained outside the Aprista fold because of invincible ignorance. "It is necessary, comrades," he had stated, "that we open the arms to the adversary of yesterday when he comes loyally to us. The enlightened adversary who repents and returns is always recognizable by the light in his eyes."[50] In effect, Haya in 1945 simply indicated anew his willingness to embrace sinners who had seen the light, repented, and gravitated toward the true cult of redemption. Assuming a Christ- or Gandhi-like demeanor in 1945, Haya played to the hilt the role in which an admirer had cast him six years earlier: "With his piety and with his faith, he [Haya] has been able to penetrate into the hearts of all Peruvians. His work has been fecund because he has brought to it faith and charity: the charity that flowed from the side of Christ, the Divine Master."[51] In the Party of the People, religion and politics remained as thoroughly intermixed as they had been in the PAP. And it would soon become apparent that for obdurate sinners Haya remained as unforgiving as he had been a decade earlier. For the unrepentant, there would be no honorable role to play in Peru's coming secular salvation.

Even more than by reading between the lines, with the help of psychiatrists, or by placing these lines in the context of earlier rhetoric, moderate Peruvians would have been alarmed by hearing the conversation of May 21 that passed between Haya and three of his devoted supporters: the journalist Eduardo Jibaja; Haya's chauffeur-secretary-handyman and rescuer from assassination in 1939, the Trujillo-born (1907) bachelor Jorge Idiáquez; and the poet Alcides Spelucín, Haya's companion of Trujillo bohemian days. According to Jibaja's account, the four men were seated in a car on the evening following the re-encounter address, discussing Haya's triumphant return to public life. Haya revealed that when he had stepped onto the balcony and beheld the sea of waving white handkerchiefs and felt the "palpitating rhythm" of two hundred thousand persons, he had been altogether overwhelmed. Tears welled in his eyes, and even when the fifteen-minute ovation began to subside, his throat remained knotted. He had lost his composure and did not even know how to begin his discourse. Then he had glanced up at the sky and caught sight of the moon; as he gazed on it, composure had returned, his rhythm had calmed, and the words for his speech had come to him— not, after all, through "the mouth of all the Aprista people of Peru," but through the moon. Haya's account, as reported by Jibaja, puts one in mind of the transvestite shamans (berdaches) common among North American Indian tribes, who claim to receive visions and supernormal powers from the moon goddess, enabling them to take on the hermaphrodite's qualities of wholeness and to serve both as the father and nourishing mother of their people.[52]

Continuing his account of the conversation in the automobile, Jibaja relates that he commented on the effect of Haya's words that fell on the "silence of 200,000 souls in tension." Haya's words, Jibaja declared, had "rolled [across the people] in the miracle of Pentecost with its tongues of fire." And the jefe's soul had become whole in the Plaza San Martín as Haya "purified his wounds through the pardon extended to his enemies." Thereby the people of Peru had found salvation "in the immaculate conscience of Aprismo and of Haya de la Torre." Thus, although Haya had never held political office, he could now lay claim to commanding the moral destiny of Peru.[53] Apparently none of the other three passengers in the car dissented from this opinion.

Social anthropologist Victor W. Turner notes that many of the world's preeminent revolutionaries have "walked a *via crucis.*" They have preached their message, achieved initial success, but then endured frustration and physical suffering, betrayal, and even execution. And then, they "have experienced a curious resurrection, . . . a political canonization. . . ."[54] Thus had it been with Haya, or so at least he might well have imagined it had been. After preaching regeneration and arousing hopes, he had disappeared into the Aprista catacombs, ultimately to be reborn thirteen years later amidst the greatest ritualistic spectacle that Aprismo ever staged. The following evening his canonization, indeed his virtual deification, had been confirmed within the confines of an automobile by three of his most loyal disciples. The canonization scene, with its indications that Aprismo still revolved about the neurotically inflated ego of its jefe máximo, scarcely boded well for the political tranquility of Peru in the months ahead.

Another incident, occurring soon after the re-encounter address, also boded ill for political tranquility. Directly following delivery of his speech, Haya proceeded to the suite in the Hotel Bolívar occupied by José Luis Bustamante y Rivero. In a state of euphoria occasioned by his rapturous reception in the plaza, Haya expected an enthusiastic, emotional encomium from Bustamante. Instead, the always restrained Bustamante simply placed a hand on Haya's back and observed, "How tired you must be, Víctor Raúl." Haya de la Torre "was genuinely infuriated,"[55] and from this fury may have stemmed part of the APRA's refusal to collaborate honorably with Bustamante when, a few months later, he became president of Peru.

Following the re-encounter experience, Haya and the Aprista high command, some of its members quickly returning from exile, threw themselves into the campaign as Peruvians prepared to choose a successor to Manuel Prado. With ex-dictator Oscar Benavides pulling many of the strings, a National Democratic Front had been formed to back the candidacy of Bustamante, a highly respected professor, attorney, and diplomat from Arequipa. Following an ill-fated attempt to seize power through a military golpe touched off in Ancón, Apristas gave their support to the National Democratic Front. In the June 1945 election Aprista backing helped Bustamante triumph over Gen. Eloy Ureta, the hero of a 1941 war with Ecuador, by a vote of approximately 300,000 to 150,000. For a moment it appeared that democracy had arrived and that Prado, "having received a dictatorially governed Peru, had turned it over to his successor as a democratic country."[56]

This appearance would prove deceptive, primarily because Benavides and Prado, in masterminding the strategy of the 1945 election, had made two serious errors. They had chosen as their favored candidate a man who would have made a superb justice of the supreme court, head of a bank or legal firm, rector of a university, or minister of foreign relations. But, the calm, reflective, and lackluster, the punctiliously honest, conscientious, and responsible Bustamante had no stomach for the political infighting in which the president of Peru would, as it turned out, have to engage. That Peru's president in 1945 would have to be a master of no-holds-barred political combat was owing in large part to the second error in judgment committed by Benavides and Prado. This arose out of the belief that the APRA, having undergone changes including the discarding of much of its radical rhetoric of the 1930s, had become a safe and cooperative political organization ready to work with other groups within a democratic framework. As it turned out, either Haya himself was unreformed and incapable of taking the democratic high road in his approach to politics or he was unable to discipline his followers into hewing to a moderate approach. No one, I believe, can really know which of these two possible explanations is the more accurate.

With Bustamante in the Palace of Pizarro, Apristas approached politics in a spirit of arrogance suggesting the conviction that only they were morally qualified to rule Peru—a conviction Haya had done nothing to counter in his May 20 address. To judge from their actions, Apristas from Haya on down deemed Bustamante a mere caretaker president who would preside nominally over the country until its proper masters took over. Meantime, the president was to be treated as a puppet. Aprismo's numerous enemies, of course, were not about to accept this scenario; nor was Bustamante, who, however ineffective as a politician, did have a mind of his own. As the political climate warmed, Haya threw himself with undiminished energy into scheming and plotting. Never in his career had he had such an opportunity as he would enjoy between 1945 and 1948 to apply in real life the political skills that he had first begun to sharpen while manipulating spools with his brothers and sisters as they grew up in Trujillo.

Far from devoting all his mental energies to the labyrinthine ways of Peruvian politics in late 1945, Haya continued to refine his historical space-time concepts (his major, book-length exposition of this subject, *Espacio-tiempo-histórico*, appeared in 1948) and persisted in his vision quests. Indeed, even in late 1945 Haya continued to give the impression that politics was for him an exciting hobby, pursued at times with fanatical concentration but just as likely to be superseded by the still more absorbing activity of seeking, and sharing, mystical visions. On October 9, 1945, Haya presented in Lima's Teatro Municipal a mystical discourse that for richness of occult allusions and esoteric symbolism is unmatched in all his oeuvre. Sections of the speech, perhaps imperfectly recorded by a stenographer, are extremely obscure; but the greatest difficulty arises from Haya's apparently helter-skelter, capricious organizational scheme. Therefore, in the description that follows, I deal topically with the themes to which Haya referred, rather than attempt to follow him step by step in the order in which he presented them.[57]

According to Haya, all Peru should be envisioned, and ultimately organized, as three circles of production: one in the north, one in the south, and one in the center. The central circle, which overlapped into each of the other two, would integrate and synthesize the activities of the northern and southern circles, for it would, among other things, process the primary goods produced in the north and the south. Here, then, is a time-honored mystical conception of a process in which out of two comes one. But this is only the first of several processes in which out of two, one would emerge. In each of the three circles of production, government would mediate between labor and capital to harmonize these opposites into a unified whole; furthermore, in each circle the opposites of production and consumption would be resolved through planned and orderly processes of distribution.[58]

Haya then asked his audience to add to their three-circle view of Peru two vertical or longitudinal axes, one running just inside the eastern perimeters of the circles, the other just within the western perimeters. The eastern column stood for the Andes, while the one to the west depicted the coast. Haya's vertical columns put one in mind of the two columns at the entrance of a Masonic temple, depicting the masculine and the feminine principles.[59] Inside the temple the two principles symbolized by the columns fuse in the squared and polished stone altar that, in turn, may be seen as symbolizing—according to one's esoteric preferences—the squared circle, the philosopher's stone, or the great lapis of the alchemists. The altar, the squared circle, the philosopher's stone, and the lapis are all mandalas: symbols of wholeness or even of the godhead.[60] Just as the two opposite principles fused into wholeness in the altar stone, so Haya envisioned the coming together of the two principles symbolized by the two vertical axes. Thereby Peru would achieve redeeming wholeness as the two became one through a dialectical process of the sort that has fascinated thinkers as far removed in time and space as Heraclitus and Hegel. As he proceeded in his Teatro Municipal discourse, Haya explained, sometimes metaphorically and sometimes directly, the nature of the two axes and the process whereby their opposite principles would merge.

Given his long-held belief that the Andes represented repose, inward-ness, tranquility, and the spirit of sharing, Haya scarcely had to belabor the feminine nature of Peru's eastern axis. At some length, though, he described the western axis, extending from Tumbes southward to Tacna, in such a way as to specify its masculine characteristics. He noted, for ex-ample, the energetic, aggressive competitiveness of coastal life. Then, in order to characterize the two axis areas more fully, Haya returned to symbolism he had first employed in his August 23, 1931, address pre-sented in Lima's Plaza de Acho: the symbolism of a car in chaos.

Peru, Haya suggested, should be compared to a car with wheels that turn faster on one side than on the other. He noted that he had affec-tionately preserved this image through the years, for it had become a fa-vorite "toy car."[61] He proceeded, then, to compare the side of the car on which the wheels turned slowly to the Andes. There, the pace, the in-tensity, the rhythms of life seemed sluggish; but they were perfectly at-tuned to the reality of their setting, in consequence of which harmony prevailed between psychic and telluric factors. Traveling across Peru, which Haya compared to using the "Time Machine" described by H. G. Wells in his 1895 novel of that title, brought one to the coast, where, largely because of foreign influences, life proceeded at a faster pace. In many ways, he conceded, this pace was suitable to the coast. What was needed was a gearing mechanism to harmonize the two velocities, for otherwise Peru, like the toy car, would continue to go in circles. Here, Haya seems to draw on alchemical imagery and also to revert to his pre-viously described notion of Mercury's power to reconcile the opposite principles embodied in his caduceus. Chaos, for alchemists, consists of things going aimlessly in circles. Frequently alchemists' drawings de-picted Mercury, as the sun-moon hermaphrodite, standing on a round chaos, the implication being that through the union of opposites chaos had been overcome.[62]

In Haya's vision, the western and eastern axes, corresponding to the tracks of the fast and the slowly moving wheels of the car, proceeded in straight lines. Somehow, then, a gearing mechanism had been intro-duced that overcame chaos. The miracle, evidently, had been accom-plished by a governmental quaternity located at the precise center of the central circle—a situs that through the ages has been regarded as a sym-bol of the divine. The four components of the government were the tra-ditional legislative, executive, and judicial, plus a fourth one to which

Haya attached the greatest importance: a chamber that integrated and harmonized all of Peru's functional energies. This chamber, the fourth component of the governmental quaternity (advocated many years earlier as an essential ingredient of Haya's corporatism or cooperativism), he called the National Economic Congress (NEC). The great wonder of the NEC was that it would "endow the numerical [or quantitative] in Peru with voice," that is, with a qualitative, identifying characteristic. Old style democracy allegedly had considered only quantity; the new democracy would take into account also the qualitative distinctions of humans. Each man (it is not clear if Haya envisaged feminine representation in his NEC) would sing in a different voice, one that was tuned to the particular function he fulfilled in society. Representatives of all functions would converge ultimately in the NEC, within whose chambers all the different voices of Peru would be harmonized. "In Pythagorean terms," Haya declared, "it [the NEC] will give to what is numerical a symbolical, almost a mystical, function in our new democracy."[63] Moreover, within each functional group whose members selected a delegate to the NEC, the problems of the one and the many would be resolved; for the member of each functional group would maintain an individual identity within his group, but his voice would merge to become one with the voices of his fellow members. Once again, then, out of opposites, in this instance the individual and the several, the unified one would issue.

Stressing such concepts as harmony and convergence, Haya described how the NEC would relate to and interact with the traditional parliament. The NEC, he explained,

considers a man according to the function that he represents and fulfills in the bosom of the collectivity. On the other hand, political democracy [whose functions in the new democracy would pertain to the parliamentary assembly] only considered man as a conscious and responsible citizen, capable of emitting a vote that helped constitute national sovereignty. Now [in the envisioned new order], these two factors of democracy coincide, converge, and are harmonized so as to coordinate and resolve the great problem of our day of economic, political, and social democracy.[64]

The political parliament, in Haya's scheme, would synthesize the voices already rendered harmonious by the NEC, thereby creating in Peru a unity corresponding to that of the cosmos. It would be possible to say,

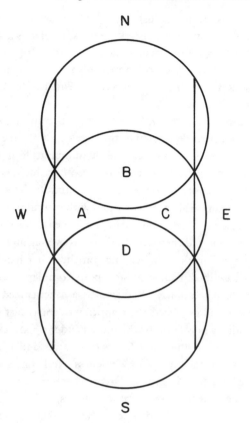

Figure A

"with Galileo," as Haya put it, that "political science will speak in the language of mathematics, a language that, as Pythagoras insisted, was the language of music."

In Peru's sacred center, then, all of the country's diverse voices and rhythms would be integrated and divergent velocities would be geared. As a result the tracks of the sierra and the coast on which Haya's toy car traveled would proceed in straight lines. Chaos would be resolved, and feminine and masculine principles would converge in unity.

Reduced to diagram form, the vision that Haya sought to share with his Teatro Municipal audience may be depicted by the accompanying sketch (figure A). The circles represent, of course, Haya's three circles of production. The two longitudinal axes stand for coast and sierra, masculinity and femininity, and serve also as the tracks of Haya's imaginary car that has been delivered from chaos. The diagram recalls Jung's observation that an underlying obsession in much esoteric thought "seems to be the interaction of two heterogeneous systems by the sharing of a common centre."[65]

Note that the central area of the drawing has become a quaternity or a mandala, its four parts designated by the letters ABCD. In effect, then, the numinous three has become the equally numinous four. One of the overriding concerns of alchemists and other esoteric thinkers had always been to effect the transition from trinity to quaternity. This may be because three has traditionally been associated with masculinity: it suggests striving and constant mutation in terms of a Hegelian formula in which the two become one and then start the process over again in an endless chain of becoming. To the number four, on the other hand, feminine traits have been ascribed. Four suggests repose, completeness, stasis, and being—rather than becoming.[66] Reduced to a schematized depiction, Haya's October 9 address effects the transition of the trinity to the quaternity, suggesting a new Peru in which the gender opposites have been fused.[67] With their pyramids, made up of squares and triangles, the Egyptians manifested their quest for wholeness. And Haya sought to apply in Peru the "ancient wisdom" of Egypt, as preserved (or invented or distorted) through the years by esoteric thinkers.

Finally, if one wished to doodle, he or she could construct a diminutive circle with four dots, representing Haya's four branches of government, at the center of the central circle. This would provide a mandala within a mandala, with the four dots even hinting at the squaring of the circle. One could also (see figure B) complete a square in the central portion by drawing two lines to connect the longitudinal axes, and this likewise would hint at the squaring of the circle.

Through the years many a person has regarded this sort of doodling, and above all what is symbolized by it, as the most meaningful thing in life. These persons have a psychological compulsion to find an all-embracing universal order—along the lines of Kepler, who hoped to find God in the geometrical relationships of the universe. Often, these persons have as their ultimate objective the enclosing of "the boundless in a finite image."[68] Haya de la Torre must have been such a person. Other-

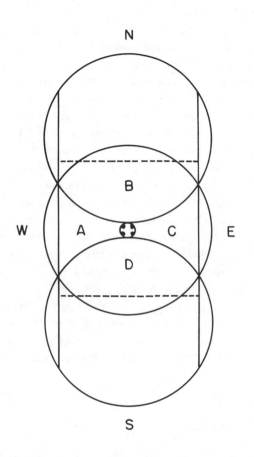

Figure B

wise, as Peru's leading political figure in 1945, engaged in some of the most important political activities of his entire life, he could not have taken time out to deliver a Pythagorean address[69] to an undoubtedly perplexed audience in the Teatro Municipal.

The October 9 discourse indicates that Haya had not outgrown the fascination with matters esoteric that had led him, during his years of European exile while plotting his country's political future, to take up the study of Pythagoras,[70] as mentioned in chapter 5. Shrewd, suspicious, and even cynical in his personal and political dealings, Haya ap-

220

proached the visionary and the hermetic with all the passionate belief of the inveterate flat-earther.

Above all else, an almost desperate hope gave rise to Haya's propensity for belief: the hope that Peru and all Indo-America were about to find lasting political stability. Ultimately, this stability would result from a governmental system that derived legitimacy not from the vote of the half plus one, but rather from that system's charismatic, miraculous power to reconcile opposites in harmony. From spiritualism, from an ancient wisdom as confirmed by particle physics, a new sect of rulers would derive the numinous powers needed to establish legitimacy.

Undoubtedly, the desperate hope for effective political order and stability nourished the occultist penchant not only in Haya de la Torre but also among dozens of Indo-American political actors and theorists through the years. Out of sustained chaos has come the conviction that there *must* exist some secret method that will confer order. And discovery of the method would have nothing to do with mere rationality or the pragmatic spirit. Just as faith healers hope to cure the afflicted by brining them back into harmony with cosmic rhythms, thereby restoring wholeness and "centeredness," so have political healers longed to conjure up the mystical powers needed to provide a holistic solution to secular ills, thereby restoring Indo-America's body politic to wholeness. Seeking total solutions, they are wont to disparage merely economic palliatives.

The Political Arena in Peru, 1946–48

Speaking in celebration of Haya de la Torre's birthday in 1943, Manuel Seoane, living in exile at the time in Santiago de Chile, maintained the jefe would always be recognized as number one, because of his unstinting sacrifice and unflinching resolve in the face of danger. Always strong enough to resist temptation and to scale the mountain by the most difficult path, he preached from the mountain top both with words and deeds.[71] After APRA's 1945 relegalization, except for the right to proclaim its own presidential candidate, Haya's words afforded hope of peaceful times ahead. Before long, though, his deeds gave rise to apprehension among those desiring an era of gradualism.

Living in luxury and maintaining two residences in the fashionable environs of Lima,[72] Haya traveled about accompanied by youthful bodyguards armed to the teeth. Frequently he was accompanied also by handsome young devotees, chosen for their ideological fervor and loyalty to the chief, who had been recruited into an organization with the mysterious, astronomical name of the Bureau of Conjunctions. The favorites with whom Haya surrounded himself customarily greeted him with the Aprista salute and with the "Seasap" salutation, the shortened version of "Solo el aprismo, salvará al Perú."[73] At this time there appeared also, to complement the ranks of the notorious Búfalos, an additional goon squad known as the Aprista Vanguard of Assault Troops (Vanguardia Aprista de Choque, or VACH). They whipped up enthusiasm at public meetings, painted slogans on walls, and, having taken oaths of absolute obedience to the jefe, carried out sundry less savory enterprises.[74] Perhaps Haya had still not managed to place altogether behind him the examples of Leninist Russia, Mussolini's Italy, or Germany in the immediate pre-Hitler days.

The above material comes from a writer notoriously hostile to the APRA, but the picture it presents of a man who cast himself more in the role of a vainglorious totalitarian than a democratic politician is confirmed even by partisans of the Party of the People. Manuel Seoane himself, writing in collaboration with Aprista official Luis Barrios Llona in 1954, severely criticized the jefe for his actions during the 1945–48 years. According to the joint letter, Haya had distanced himself from the people and remained sequestered with a small clique of sycophantic intimates while doing nothing to chastise his lieutenants who sought only personal gain from the party's return to political legitimacy.[75] Others in the party maintained that between 1946 and 1948 the National Executive Committee of the Party of the People met only six times, and then simply to be informed of decisions taken by an isolated hierarchy, which often included only the triumvirate of Haya, Jorge Idiáquez, and the staunchly conservative Fernando León de Vivero, political secretary of the Party of the People.

All the while, Haya missed no opportunity to enhance his charisma through ritual or to bask in the adulation of his followers. It was now, in fact, that some of the worst extremes of hero or saint worship described in earlier chapters came most prominently into public view. When Haya

In March 1947, Haya de la Torre arrived in the United States on a speaking tour and was photographed in his suite at the Waldorf Astoria. His Aprista lapel pin depicts a condor, Peru's symbolical counterpart to the American eagle, and a figure tied strongly to the Indian past. New York Times Pictures.

received the special oath of absolute obedience from Apristas elected to the national congress in 1945, he was standing before a statue of Christ as the Good Shepherd.[76] In 1946 Haya's birthday was converted into a day of nationwide Aprista celebration. On this first official celebration of the annual Day of Fraternity (Día de Fraternidad), Manuel Seoane compared Haya's Aprista heart to the Sacred Heart of Jesus[77]—an incident already alluded to in chapter 7. Here, apparently, was a sacred heart to which all Peru should indeed be consecrated—unlike that of Jesus, to which Haya had prevented consecration in 1923. In a book published shortly after the APRA's return to legality, Gustavo Valcárcel maintained that Haya's oratory surpassed that of Demosthenes; he hailed the chief as "our most illustrious citizen of all time. . . . He is the saint most loved by the people. He is the teacher, father, brother of the people. He is the civil prophet descended from the Old Testament. I have seen him bear on his shoulders the tragedy of Peru."[78]

In 1947 and again in 1948 Haya undertook lecture tours in the United States, appearing mainly on college campuses.[79] When he returned from the second of these tours, during which he had met with Walt Disney in Hollywood, addressed a luncheon meeting of the Americans for Democratic Action in Washington, and conversed with Einstein at Princeton, the Aprista newspaper *La Tribuna* assured its readers that Haya had been received as one of the world's great men, as a Gandhi or a Roosevelt. The writer welcomed Haya back to his post as the political and intellectual captain of all Indo-America and continued, "We salute you because your voice has resounded in the consciousness of a great people [the people of the United States] as the rumblings of a new world which is born in Indo-America. . . . We salute you as the Cid Campeador, a glorious soldier who has discharged into eternity the creative force of his genius. . . . Víctor Raúl Haya de la Torre returns today. . . . He returns covered with glory to deliver himself to his people, and his people will hail his heart and luxuriate, as happy as people on the first day of the world, in his embrace, as wide as eternity."[80]

A few days later *La Tribuna* reported Haya's address to an Aprista convention. The discourse ended as a new day was breaking, and as the listeners departed they had the feeling that "they had returned from God."[81]

In 1947 appeared more of the dreadful verse that had hailed Haya de la Torre at the beginning of the 1930s. J. H. Chávez penned the following lines:

> A salute to you, Víctor Raúl, giant of a man,
> To the immense orbit of your glory,
> Which has brought a continent together in fraternity,
> By the eternal routes of history.
> Like the volatile condor that cuts the heavens,
> Goes the message of your word and your action,
> Redeeming from suffering all those people
> Who listen with patriotic emotion to you.[82]

In a Plaza de Acho address of September 7, 1946, Haya made it clear that redemption was reserved for those who heeded him "with patriotic emotion." Apristas, the jefe told his audience, must attempt to convert those who had lived in error by being generous and forgiving. But, if the vanquished had not yet learned their lesson, if they still endangered "democracy," if they still entertained "dark intentions," then "I authorize the Party to defend itself with all the means available to it"; we "are the only majority force in Peru, and therefore the only responsible force." Peruvians outside the fold were dismissed as opportunists who did not know how to suffer and to struggle.[83]

In the same speech, as well as in one delivered the preceding July at the Plaza San Martín, Haya dwelt on regeneration and other themes of religious content. The APRA, he maintained, was the party of eternal youth, because it knew how to renew itself. Twice, in 1934 and in 1946, it had released all members from their promises, and on both occasions it returned to life more powerful than before. No intelligent observer could deny, Haya claimed, that "when a political or ideological movement endures and maintains its vigor and sprouts forth anew in youth every ten years, it is always a young party."[84] After explaining to his hearers the essential features of Aprista ideology, Haya had concluded the July address with a variation on the theme "as it was in the beginning, is it now, and ever shall be" that figures prominently in Christian ritual. Although Aprismo had undergone and would continue to undergo rebirth, the doctrine he expostulated, Haya stated, constituted "Aprismo as it was, as it is, and as it will be. The popular cry that 'Aprismo never dies' is without any doubt the authentic expression of an undeniable truth." As Haya's voice faded, the faithful took up the chant "Aprismo never dies" (el aprismo nunca muere).[85]

In the years between 1945 and 1948 Apristas showed a mastery not only in staging rituals and orchestrating hosannas to their chief. They proved adept also at constructing efficient mass organizations. Ousting Communists from the positions of control they had gained in the Confederation of Laborers of Peru (Confederación de Trabajadores del Perú, or CTP), founded in 1944,[86] Apristas converted the country's major labor organization into an arm of political action. Apristas also moved effectively to gain control over student organizations at the University of San Marcos. At the same time they infiltrated elementary and secondary school teacher groups and organized the Peruvian Aprista Youth movement (Juventud Aprista Peruana, or JAP) to instill loyalty to the sacred cause among those aged ten to eighteen. As a result, not just the university but the high schools and primary schools were politicized. Both in the classroom and outside of it, Aprista teachers led their pupils in singing the Aprista hymn. Moreover, especially in the provinces, they established the custom of marching their students to political rallies.[87]

Whether owing to party policy established from on high or—more likely—to the spontaneous hooliganism of youthful zealots, Aprista-related violence soared. Apristas bombed the houses of political enemies and burned the headquarters of the rival Revolutionary Union party, assassinated the departmental prefect of Cerro de Pasco, and in general contributed to an explosive atmosphere. When Lima's two leading newspapers, El Comercio and La Prensa, undertook a concerted campaign to denounce these activities and began to publish exposés, factual and fabricated, of Aprista terrorism, the party's congressional bloc induced a law calling for press censorship. Thereupon students assembled at the University of San Marcos on the night of December 7, 1945, to protest the proposed legislation. Aprista Búfalos attacked the demonstrators, injuring many of them.

Determined not to play the role of puppet that Apristas expected of him, President Bustamante faced a mounting tide of difficulties.[88] Apristas and their allies formed nearly a two-thirds majority in the senate. In the chamber of deputies, with fifty-three of the one hundred fifty-three members, they formed alliances that provided them an effective majority. This enabled them to enact legislation permitting congress to override presidential vetoes by a simple majority. Aprista strategy was clear: the party would claim that Peru should be governed by congress, where the people with the moral right to rule prevailed.

In addition to his political troubles, Bustamante faced sharp economic problems. From the previous Prado regime he had inherited a troublesome inflationary spiral. Immediately after World War II came to an end the United States had cut back its purchase of Peruvian commodities, and thus the yield of export taxes declined alarmingly. Peru's major food producers, furthermore, taking advantage of the high world prices prevailing directly after the war's end, exported most of their crops, and the country in consequence confronted serious food shortages. This forced the government to expend dwindling foreign currency on food imports. Even so food supplies fell short of demand. Produce prices soared and each day long lines formed early in the morning outside grocery stores. Under these conditions Apristas derived important political dividends from the low-cost public dining halls operated by the Party of the People.

In his days of trouble, Bustamante found one issue on which he could agree with Apristas. The president was desperately anxious to increase petroleum production so as to ease some of the country's financial difficulties. Accordingly his administration signed a contract with the International Petroleum Company (IPC) providing that this Standard Oil subsidiary, which had controlled exploitation of Peru's major petroleum and natural gas deposits along the northern coast since the Leguía administration, should explore for new deposits around Sechura, on land set aside as a national reserve by the Benavides administration. Apristas warmly backed the agreement, known as the Sechura Contract, when it came up for congressional approval, even claiming credit for having conceived the arrangement.[89] Undoubtedly, Aprismo's friendly attitude toward the IPC strengthened its good standing in Washington.

The proposed Sechura Contract brought to life a group of economic nationalists, among them Communists as well as some of Peru's wealthiest capitalists anxious to form their own petroleum company, who denounced the agreement as a sellout to Yankee imperialists. The two major newspapers, *El Comercio* and *La Prensa*, united to condemn the contract, both of them tending to hold Apristas responsible for the alleged betrayal of national interests and dealing rather leniently with Bustamante. One of *La Prensa*'s editors, Francisco Graña Garland, launched especially sharp attacks against the APRA because of its support for the Sechura Contract. On January 7, 1947, Graña was shot down in Lima. An apparently carefully conducted investigation produced strong evidence that Apristas had planned and executed the assassination, though it shed no light on how high up the chain of command the plot might have originated. Not very convincingly, Apristas sought to portray the assassination as a Communist plot hatched in Moscow and intended to discredit the APRA through a frameup.[90] Here, if nothing else, was an indication of Aprista sensitivity to Cold War issues. They had come to understand that the best way to enlist United States support was to depict themselves as implacable foes, and therefore as the preferred victims, of Soviet machinations.

The United States and the Frustrations of Visionary Aprismo

While he still hoped to accrue benefits from the United States, Haya de la Torre by 1948 was awakening to the unreality of the exalted hopes that he had placed, as recently as 1945, in the northern republic. While World War II had been in progress, Haya had responded to the prophetic views of the Waldo Franks and the Carleton Beals and had dismissed William G. Fletcher's prediction that the postwar United States would revert to its traditional life-style, values, and prejudices. As it turned out, Fletcher was right. With the United States returning to its old ways and suffocating the counterculture of the 1930s, the mystical hopes of Frank and Haya for a symbiotic North-South union that would herald the appearance of a new humanity seemed little more than the dream of madmen. Rather than create a new world in the American hemisphere based on a North-South connection, the United States dedicated itself after 1945 to shoring up the Old World. From their attention to Europe most North Americans anticipated not a new spirituality but a new wealth, created through the old methods of pragmatic capitalism. Still, the quest for new material well-being had an accompanying idealism.

Turning their attention to the battle-ravaged Old World, United States statesmen hoped to create out of Europe's chaos a universal organization for the maintenance of peace and security. "With all the élan of the Wilsonian age," Arthur P. Whitaker has written, "newspaper editors, columnists, and radio commentators rallied to the cause of universal internationalism." In the process, inter-Americanism fell by the wayside. In fact, inter-Americanism, which had been regarded during the early days of the New Deal as opening up "a large vista of international cooperation for the United States, came to be regarded by some as an obstruction to the more spacious view of a world order...."[91] Most decidedly, then, idealism suffused the new internationalism. But this idealism took on an Old World focus that was neither anticipated nor appreciated by Haya de la Torre or by Latin Americans in general. Between 1945 and 1948 they endured a cruel awakening as they discovered the extent to which the hopes aroused by the Good Neighbor policy and prophetic utterances of a handful of gringo intellectuals had been based on delusion.

With United States capitalism resuscitated and soaring to new heights in the postwar era, and with the country's intellectuals turning away en masse from socialism as they awakened to the new potentials of capitalism and to the horrors of Stalinism,[92] Americans ended their brief flirtation with Marxism and their fascination with convergence. As the United States left collapsed in tatters, the visionary and extrarational gave way to practicality and empiricism. In consequence, North Americans withdrew from the latest of their periodical infatuations with spiritualism and the occult. Beginning in 1945, they passed into a more characteristic cycle of extolling bourgeois values. A manifestation of the new cycle was the total eclipse of Henry Wallace, whom Haya had expected to lead the United States into an era of hemispheric regeneration. Running for president in 1948 at the head of the Progressive Party, Wallace was repudiated by all save a handful of American voters.[93]

Attesting further to North America's departure from the route Haya de la Torre had expected it to follow was the emergence of the "national character" obsession. Beginning with Margaret Mead's And Keep Your Powder Dry (1942), "studies of American character became a leading growth sector of the knowledge industry."[94] United States intellectuals, and before long their popularizers, harped on national identity; and, facing the perils of mass society, many of them began to extol such old-fashioned attributes as individualism and competitiveness. Often they sought to bolster the home-grown virtues that had ostensibly made the country great through invidious contrasts with negative identity traits, such as communalism and a preference for Eros over Logos, that they associated with insidious "others," including blacks (who definitely passed out of vogue after 1945), Native Americans (who faced the termination of John Collier's New Deal for Indians), and Latin Americans (whose economic underdevelopment once more became the badge of character deficiences).

In the 1920s and 1930s Latin America had been perceived by some North Americans as a frontier where they might become whole by surrendering to the mores of the "other," regarded as a more natural person. By the later 1940s, however, Latin America had become a frontier to be dominated and improved in the quest of sustained economic growth. If in the process Latin Americans could assimilate North American ways, well and good. But they had little value so long as they remained the "other." The swing in national mood brought North Americans back to their more customary way of regarding themselves and the rest of the world. This return to normalcy helped obliterate the vision of hemispheric convergence, inspired by an underlying faith in the operation of a cosmic dialectical process destined to synthesize opposites, that had excited United States counterculture prophets in the 1920s and '30s while raising the hopes of Haya de la Torre.

An additional "other" who passed out of vogue as the establishment's patriarchy regained its grip on American life was the woman. In no time at all after the war, feminism gave way to a resurrected cult of domesticity. And this, too, had at least a subtle bearing on United States–Latin American relations, for, as will be recalled, Latin Americans had often been stereotyped in the United States not only as black-like and Indian-like, but also as woman-like. If North American women were expected to return to domesticity, then Latin Americans were counted upon to take up once more the role customarily ascribed to them. The natural function of women and Latin Americans was to accept dependence and to provide an atmosphere that the hard-working capitalist would find tranquil and refreshing.

So long as he had been in the throes of his wild delusions about the hemisphere's future, Haya de la Torre could not have seen his incautious pursuit of intimate relations with the United States as threatening to Peru's or Indo-America's interests. In the postwar world, however, it was plain for all to see that the United States had settled into the old routine of assuming that whatever good came to Latin America could only come in consequence of a greater good garnered by United States capitalists as they developed the southern frontier over which they had reassumed their natural right to hegemony. In these circumstances, Latin Americans had ample reason to approach the United States with caution. But Haya refused to exercise caution, and this refusal led to a watershed in APRA's history.

As long as there had been hope that the United States was on the way toward transforming itself into a land in which socialism and capitalism converged under the direction of a triumphant counterculture headed by men who had attained higher consciousness, Haya de la Torre could champion the northern superpower and still retain his radical credentials. By 1948, though, he could no longer have it both ways. By then, his continuing deference to the United States branded him, among most Latin American intellectuals, as a staunch conservative—and this at the very time when radical Apristas began to insist on guiding the movement in an anti-imperialist direction. Perhaps already in the 1930s there had been two APRAS, but the cleavage in the movement had never before been so evident as it was in 1948.

The Return to the Catacombs: Haya and Aprismo in 1948

Following the assassination of Graña Garland at the beginning of 1947, a mounting tide of anti-Aprista sentiment led to the formation of the National Alliance. Membership in the Alliance included Communists, anxious to wrest control over organized labor from Apristas, and a broad variety of centrists who blamed the Party of the People for perpetuating a superheated political ambience that interfered with the pursuit of business as usual. However, the Alliance's driving force came from the "extreme right,"[95] and understandably so. It might be true that Haya and the higher echelons of Aprista power wielders no longer raised verbal objections against the wealth of the oligarchy or even the capitalist practices and political favoritism that had contributed to the accumulation of wealth. But it was also true that many Apristas showed impatience to displace the old oligarchy so as to monopolize for themselves the rewards of business acumen and political influence.

The National Alliance applied pressure on President Bustamante to take a firmer hand in disciplining Aprista troublemakers, even if this meant repudiating the democratic procedures that he cherished. Ultimately despairing over Bustamante's disinclination to adopt forceful measures, elements of the Alliance started plotting to replace the president with a more forceful leader. Well aware of what was transpiring, Apristas decided to strike first. In fact, ever since mid-1947 they had been working, with some success, to enlist support of lower-echelon officers of the army, navy, and air force in a revolution against Bustamante. Learning of these activities, Gen. José del Carmen Marín, with the backing of Gen. Juan de Dios Cuadros, approached Haya de la Torre with the warning that if the APRA persisted in its plots the country would once again suffer a violent confrontation in which the higher-level, more conservative military officers, backed by the oligarchy, would inevitably triumph. General Marín then held out an attractive alternative to the jefe máximo. If Haya would cooperate with what was expected to be a bloodless golpe that certain highly placed officers and civilian collaborators were planning against Bustamante, then Apristas would be allowed to participate and present their own presidential candidate, in the subsequent free elections. There are strong indications that Haya decided to go along with Marín's plan. At the time, an all-or-nothing challenge to Peru's power establishment simply seemed too great a risk to take. Although possessed in many ways of the gambler's instincts, Haya always refrained from risking his full stake on matters of chance, and this helps explain why he remained a survivor in Peru's tumultuous political struggles.

Undoubtedly Haya approved the nonviolent aspects of Marín's proposal. Haya could still be tempted toward the use of violence, but he operated by and large now under the spell of Rolland, Gandhi, and Tolstoy—a fact not grasped by detractors who attributed the jefe's conduct to spinelessness and bourgeois decadence. Furthermore, Haya was surely shaken by Gandhi's assassination at the beginning of 1948. By the time of his death, Gandhi's political success had been marred by a bloodbath of awesome proportions spawned by sectional and religious animosities in northern India. Even the great Indian mystic had not been able to control his followers or to transform his country in line with his peaceful intentions; this fact could only have given pause to Haya de la Torre.

In 1948 Haya remained reluctant, as he always had been, to have the APRA assume power before its ranks had been subjected to the iron discipline of its directors. And as the year progressed, the jefe faced mounting evidence that many of his troops lacked indoctrination and that they failed to appreciate that true revolutions were wrought through the power of the will rather than through violence—in short, through spiritual, rather than merely physical, means. Probably in his own mind Haya had not yet fully resolved whether the road to Peruvian regeneration lay through obliteration of the forces and sectors that he found uncongenial or through the resolution of all opposites in harmony. But, despite the intimate coterie of sycophants who clouded his judgment by assuring him of his god-like supremacy and therefore of his right to total power, he seemed on the whole to incline toward the visionary, second approach; and he did not want to be pushed toward the first alternative by violence-prone underlings who had not progressed adequately toward attainment of higher consciousness. Enjoying, moreover, the sort of adulation he had received since 1945 from large sectors of the public, Haya did not wish to risk a return to the underground life or even imprisonment by a putsch that, if unsuccessful, could entail these possibilities and one that was even worse: the obliteration of the party on which his ego had come to depend. In the final analysis, though, how Haya felt about matters had become irrelevant, for he had ceased to be the master of events even within his party.

Revolutionary scheming had been initiated with Haya's consent even before General Marín's warning. Involving lower-level military officers and remnants of the anarchist elements in the APRA who had precipitated the 1932 Trujillo uprising, it assumed a dynamic of its own. Ignoring the wishes of the party's elders, and apparently taking them by surprise, militant Apristas, both military and civilian, arose in Callao against the Bustamante government on October 3, 1948.[96] The higher officers, including General Marín, backed the government and, with the larger part of the armed forces following their orders, crushed the uprising.

President Bustamante declared the APRA illegal and ordered the apprehension of its leaders. But, so far as the PAP's more implacable enemies were concerned, Bustamante had by his past complacency demonstrated an inability to deal adequately with the national menace. Justifying their actions on the grounds of Bustamante's proven ineffectiveness, military officers in Arequipa launched a revolution on October 27. They christened their movement the "Restorative Revolution," and to the post of "supreme general" they named Manuel A. Odría, a brigadier general who had served in one of Bustamante's cabinets. When Gen. Zenón Noriega, commander of the troops in Lima and the man who had directed suppression of the October 3 insurrection, disobeyed the president's orders to advance upon Arequipa, claiming he did not wish to instigate a bloodbath, Bustamate realized he was powerless and withdrew from the Palace of Pizarro on October 29. Arriving quickly in Lima, Manuel Odría assumed the powers of provisional president and launched an all-out assault on Apristas.[97] Party leaders unable to find hideouts or to flee into exile were jailed. At the same time the new administration vented its anger on rank-and-file party members, firing them en masse from their jobs. The worst days of the 1930s were relived as Apristas returned to the catacombs. Only now they had less visionary faith to sustain them, for almost as much as in the United States, the cult of the extrarational had—for the moment—passed out of vogue in Peru.

As soon as the Callao uprising began on October 3, Haya de la Torre went into hiding, knowing full well that the government would blame him for masterminding the insurrection. With General Odría in power, a massive manhunt commenced and Haya moved at night from one hiding place to another, his life genuinely in danger. Finally on January 3, 1949, he found sanctuary in the Colombian Embassy on the outskirts of Lima. He would not leave its premises until April 1954.

Time spent in the embassy proved a milestone in Haya de la Torre's personal development, marking the first step toward his recovery from narcissism. Cut off from the handful of adulatory acolytes who had surrounded and largely isolated him since his return to Peru in 1931, Haya began to develop his own psychic resources and strengths. He emerged from his confinement a far less psychologically disturbed person than he had been at any point in his public career up to that moment.

Eleven

From Middle Age to Old Age: The Mystical and Political Worlds of Haya de la Torre, 1949–63

Haya in Confinement and Abroad, 1949–57

From January 1949 until April 1954, Haya de la Torre remained confined within the Colombian Embassy. Throughout this period, in spite of pleas from abroad and attempts to invoke international law on Haya's behalf, General Odría's administration refused to grant APRA's leader safe conduct out of the country, claiming he was guilty of common crimes that ranged from masterminding the 1947 Graña Garland assassination to inciting the 1948 Callao insurgency.[1] At first, Haya could not even correspond with his followers. Not until the end of 1951 or the beginning of 1952 did associates manage to establish a reliable clandestine network that made possible the exchange of letters.

In spite of grave inconveniences and occasional concern that his life was in danger, Haya's spirits did not flag. In a revealing letter of late 1952 to Luis Alberto Sánchez, in exile in Santiago de Chile, Haya noted happily that his time in the embassy had been like "years at the university," because of his extensive reading schedule and his various writing projects. Unlike his Incahuasi years when he had chronically complained about his ailments, Haya now informed Sánchez that he had never felt better, physically or mentally. His various intellectual undertakings he found so absorbing that he never slept more than four or five hours a night. Rather than lamenting his penury, as in the Incahuasi letters, Haya informed Sánchez that he had received a small inheritance from

Adriana de González Prada, the recently deceased widow of Manuel González Prada, Peru's socialist and anarchist precursor who had exercised strong intellectual influence over Haya in his youth and after whom the popular univerisities had been named. Also, Haya's mother had left him some jewels, and he speculated in his letter over the best way to sell them and divide the proceeds with his surviving brothers and sister. On a small radio, Haya reported, he listened to broadcasts from abroad; and a doberman dog as well as pigeons on the embassy roof kept him company—at first Odría's troops surrounding the embassy suspected the birds were carrier pigeons.[2]

Toward the end of 1950 rumors circulated that Odría's troops were about to storm the embassy. Thereupon, its personnel burned many documents and Haya consigned to the flames the manuscripts he had produced up to that time in his enforced seclusion. When the danger evaporated, Haya resumed his writing and enjoyed the most prolific period he had known since his underground years. From an embassy typewriter that he complained was terrible[3] issued the pages of a book that Haya would publish as *Treinta anōs del aprismo*, as well as two other books that Haya ultimately decided not to publish. Toward the end of his confinement, Haya reported that he had two secretaries working on his manuscripts.[4] By this time he had completed a book on Arnold Toynbee's theories of history that is discussed below.[5]

Throughout his involuntary residence in the embassy, Haya's letters remained comparatively free from the nagging, petulant, and self-pitying qualities that had characterized many of his missives written some fifteen years earlier from Incahuasi. It was as if the narcissist had begun, tentatively and haltingly at least, to discard his efforts to manipulate selfobjects into bestowing what he conceived of as his due. One quality, however, remained as much in evidence in the communications of the early 1950s as in those of the 1930s, and this was exuberant optimism about the future. Aprismo, Haya assured Sánchez in one of his letters from the embassy, was like a tree dropping seeds: throughout Indo-America parties cast in the Aprista image were emerging. Haya apparently expected them to help fulfill the destiny he had long ago foreseen for his continent. Haya and his associates had always looked on Rómulo Betancourt's Democratic Action in Venezuela as an Aprista-like party; now he observed the degree to which Argentina's Peronism had been influenced by APRA ideology[6]—although he would subsequently distance himself from Perón, dismissing his ideology as a demagogic copy of Aprismo that lacked substance.[7]

Haya's optimism during the confinement period fed also on what he regarded as conclusive evidence that influential North Americans had come increasingly to appreciate Aprismo's importance and destiny. In 1953 he applauded Carleton Beals for a recent assertion that all progressive movements in Latin America derived from Aprismo.[8] He praised also the 1953 book *The Envoys*, by Hoffman R. Hays, as the best foreign work he had read on Latin America, Peru, and Aprismo.[9] In addition, he lauded Harry Kantor's *The Ideology and Program of the Peruvian Aprista Movement*, also published in 1953. A political scientist at the University of Florida, the impressionable Kantor had spent long sessions in 1948 with Haya, in which the jefe explained Aprista ideology. Although Kantor failed to capture the mystical essence of APRA, this weakness in his book probably was to the movement's advantage, given the comparative lack of interest in occultist millennialism in the United States during the 1950s. Under these circumstances, Kantor proved a better apostle for Aprismo than Waldo Frank would have been. In any event, Haya exulted over the great service rendered by Kantor's book, which, he noted, "seems an homage to Aprismo."[10]

In the same letter to Sánchez in which he enthused over Kantor's study, the jefe noted the degree to which his image had been enhanced when another North American writer, Ray Josephs, had reported in the October 16, 1948, edition of *Colliers* that Albert Einstein regarded Haya as one of the few persons in the world who understood the theory of relativity.[11] Turning then to practical politics, Haya noted that Odría's collaboration with Communists in organized labor left the dictator vulnerable to United States censure. In a subsequent letter, Haya mentioned to Sánchez that Mario Laserna, "a good friend of Aprismo," was in touch with Sen. Joseph McCarthy on the matter.[12] Anticipating a propaganda campaign that would bombard the United States with information on Odría's Communist ties, Haya saw considerations of realpolitic as well as intellectual sympathy as contributing to North American support for Aprismo.

In the real world existing immediately beyond the confines of the Colombian Embassy, the status of Aprismo hardly seemed to coincide with its jefe's cheerful assessments. In fact, with the chief for all practical purposes in solitary confinement, the Party of the People faced the most serious challenge to date to its very existence.

By the end of the 1940s, Aprismo lacked the esprit and mystique that had inspired the faithful in the first era of the catacombs. "The cycle of emotional enchantment had come to an end," a well-informed observer has written, and Apristas had grown tired of "promises of miracles" and the "preaching of jeremiads."[13] Many who until now had followed the APRA through thick and thin grew disillusioned with a leadership that had brought the party to the brink of power but had somehow lacked the final reserves of talent and resolve needed to grasp the elusive prize. Coveting power, whether to effect revolutionary change or merely to serve their own interests, Apristas from the higher to the lower ranks were coming to suspect that the jefe might personally fear the prospects of becoming president.[14] Some of the party's one-time partisans even detected "a political death wish" at the top level of command.[15] Understandably, then, when Manuel Seoane from exile conducted a "postal congress" of the party in 1951, he discovered that many Apristas felt it was time to choose a new jefe.[16] Under these circumstances, it was scarcely surprising that many an Aprista dignitary gave up the struggle and renounced party membership. In doing so, they could often advance persuasive ideological justifications.

Luis Eduardo Enríquez and the well-known novelist Ciro Alegría left the party even before the 1948 fiasco at Callao, accusing Haya of having abandoned his opposition to both foreign imperialism and the Peruvian oligarchy. With ample grounds, they charged that whereas Haya had once preached the nationalization of land and industry, he now exhorted people to avoid socialistic ways and to think only in terms of individually producing more wealth.[17] In 1952 Eduardo Jibaja, one of the four persons present at the "canonization" scene in the automobile on the night after Haya's re-encounter address, had tendered his resignation, although he later rejoined the Party of the People.[18] Around the end of Haya's embassy confinement came a bombastic renunciation from Alberto Hidalgo. A poet who in 1931 had summoned Haya to his destiny and hailed him as the "instrument history has chosen to move the air of all Latin America,"[19] Hidalgo in 1954 charged Haya with having made peace with the oligarchy, the military, and the foreign imperialists, with being a homosexual, with running his party as an absolute monarchy, and, finally, with responsibility for the murder of Graña Garland.[20]

Accused by Hidalgo of responsibility for the perpetration of violence, Haya was charged by Magda Portal, and by many other defectors from Aprismo, with lacking a stomach for violence. Explaining her abandonment of the party in 1950, Portal voiced the complaints of many when she attributed the failure of the Callao uprising to Haya's loss of nerve. She was tired, she averred, of a party that continued to weep over martyrs, "always martyrs from the working classes, never from among the leaders." The suitable words to direct to Haya, she concluded, were those spoken by the mother of the last Moorish king of Granada when he surrendered in 1492 to the forces of Ferdinand and Isabella: "You who did not know how to defend it as a man, weep now as a woman."[21] Ironically, the woman who had joined the APRA in the hopes that it would spearhead a feminist movement left the party with the charge that its jefe had become too much like a woman. Perhaps Haya did not feel unduly maligned if he had in mind the words of his idol, Gandhi: "Ever since I have taken to nonviolence," Gandhi had once observed, "I have become more like a woman."[22]

Those who withdrew from the APRA on the grounds of Haya's accommodation with the oligarchy, the military, and the foreign imperialists or on the basis of his lack of appetite for revolutionary violence had never adequately understood the jefe in the first place. This was not altogether their fault, for Haya's pronouncements on such matters as capitalism and its practitioners, both native and foreign, as well as on violence, had frequently been ambiguous and expressed in opaque, esoteric language. While Haya had attacked capitalism and imperialism he had, even from the late 1920s, reserved a place in his ideal future for capitalism—once it was properly geared to be brought into harmonious coexistence with the collectivist spirit. Unlike Marxists who pronounced for a universe free of capitalism, Haya had consistently advocated a "multiverse,"[23] where capitalism and socialism would function side by side as parts in an all-prevailing solidarity of opposites. Thus, Haya had not so much betrayed his one-time followers as they had deceived themselves by failing to follow his arguments to their conclusion. Furthermore, Haya from 1930 onward had never publicly castigated the military as a class. Clearly, he found a place for them in his multiverse. Indeed, he had looked consistently upon the military as the instrument for the APRA's nonviolent ascent to power.

On the matter of the comparative merits of violence and nonviolence, Haya may have led some of his earlier followers astray, owing to his own long-enduring ambivalence regarding the means for obtaining a millennialist order. In the 1920s and in his Pachacútec (the "cataclysm") days of the 1930s, Haya certainly appeared to toy with a cataclysmic approach to the envisioned new order, one that called for annihilation of the prevailing order; but he had never failed, even then, to speculate on the possibility of the peaceful synthesis of old and new within the multiverse of the future. By the late 1940s and the '50s Haya's Pachacútec days were behind him; he had attained resolute consistency in the esoteric faith in diversity as the key to transcendent harmony. His burgeoning tolerance of diversity helped propel from the party those who refused to include the "other" in their utopian visions, and this fact may very well stand to Haya's credit. However credit or blame is assessed, the fact is that after 1948 the APRA had been divested of its shock-troop component. From that time on Aprismo was a different kind of factor in Peruvian politics than when it had appeared in the country following the fall of Leguía.[24]

Convinced more than ever by the time of his embassy confinement that his ordained life was one of revelation rather than violent revolution, Haya de la Torre now found what satisfied him as proof that his revelations had been right all along. In the course of his captivity, he came upon Arnold Toynbee's *Study of History*. The discovery of the English historian who, like Oswald Spengler—the German historian who had fascinated Haya in the 1920s—found "spiritual comfort in the discovery of vast imaginary symmetries in the irregular stream of human history"[25] proved enormously exhilarating to Haya. Soon he was busily writing what turned out to be a nearly two-hundred page book that analyzed the historian's thought.[26]

Toynbee, in whose historical analyses the influence of Bergson is unmistakable,[27] saw the rise of civilization not so much in piecemeal efforts as in "miraculous spiritual improvement" and in periods of "creative evolution" that owed everything to the élan vital.[28] In this approach Haya thought he found confirmation of his own visionary musings. Predictably, he expressed delight in the mystical elements of Toynbee's approach, "which other critics had disparaged." In particular, he praised the Englishman's tendency to see history in the fourth dimension, in a space-time continuum, and in "concentric circles, in terms of the enormous segments of an immense sphere which cuts through planes located at varying distances from each other." These segments could unite or separate, could become "as fathers and sons or could open among themselves profound fissures, but without ever ceasing to be correlative to the maximum arc of the circle of their total universality."[29] Clearly, the years had not diminished Haya's penchant for obfuscated prose in describing obscure thought. One can only imagine the results had Haya come upon the thoughts of another man very much after his own heart, Pierre Teilhard de Chardin, and composed his own variations on them.

In addition to praising Toynbee's "extraordinary geometry of history and his cosmic vision of space-time,"[30] Haya applauded the historian's vision of the passing away of nationalism and the birth of a new era that would be characterized by awareness among national communities that they were mere parts of a larger order.[31] To Haya, Toynbee's thought coincided with Aprista notions about the emergence of people-continents that would subsume the old nation-state configurations.

Toward the conclusion of his analysis of Toynbee's thought,[32] Haya returned to some of his earlier speculations on United States–Indo-American relations. Within its historical space-time, Indo-America operated, he maintained, with a slower and less dynamic rhythm than the one that prevailed in the United States, where both space and time were less expansive. Predictably, Haya then cast Indo-America in the role of the feminine Yin element and the United States in that of the masculine Yang. According to Toynbee, as Haya interpreted his writings, new civilizations dawned when the Yin was awakened by the intrusion of the Yang.[33] As the two worlds of America came together, Haya believed, they would produce a new civilization that vibrated to the "general rhythmic impulse that runs through the whole universe."[34] In Toynbee, then, Haya found a new and, at the time, respectable guru who confirmed the teachings imparted many years earlier by Romain Rolland and Count Keyserling, and more recently by Waldo Frank.

Concluding his exposition of the applicability of Toynbee's insights to the Aprista vision of the New World's destiny, Haya wrote: "The American or New World civilization . . . must join in its creative powers the deep conceptual values of 'pronto' and 'mañana,' action and lassitude, celerity and repose, together with the profound roots of 'yesterday.' It must confront the summits of the future, without ceasing to attend to the multiple slopes of the past that nourish with eternal vital fluids the brusque changes of the dynamic civilizations."[35]

When imprisoned in 1933 during the Sánchez Cerro crackdown on the APRA (see chapter 8), Haya had suffered illness and a frightening hallucinatory experience that left him, for the moment, wary of plumbing his own psychic depths where the "subconscious Indian lives in us all."[36] Perhaps his fear of idle, solitary moments explains the frenetic activity that marked his life in subsequent years, even those spent underground when his reading and writing regimen was constantly interrupted by political plotting, letter writing, and nocturnal sallies. In contrast, his five-year "retreat" in the Colombian Embassy, as Odría sought to match the rigors of Sánchez Cerro in repressing the APRA, proved actually a time of relaxed and happy contemplation, free from psychic terror. In fact, during these years Haya learned to turn inward consistently and to abandon his flight from the self. Comforted by Toynbee and other authors and by his own writing, Haya actually came to practice and to relish the life of meditation to which he had previously done little more than render lip service. Ultimately, he left the embassy a changed person. More at peace with himself after having exorcised some of his interior demons, he emerged to find a Party of the People that had also changed, having experienced the flight of its demons of radicalism and violence. By the time he was reunited with his followers, Haya was able to live more comfortably not only with himself but also with them.

More tranquil in his private life, and satisfied that his visionary musings on America's future had been confirmed by Toynbee, Haya received the news early in 1954 that international pressure had at last caused Odría to relent and to grant him safe conduct out of the country. Haya departed Peru in April, traveling first to Mexico City and Caracas. June found him in Montevideo, where he received the lengthy joint letter signed by Manuel Seoane and Luis Barrios Llona, respectively the secretary-general and secretary of foreign affairs of the Aprista Central Committee. In their letter (mentioned briefly in the preceding chapter), the two Aprista officials, who had been living in exile, questioned their leader's negative attitude toward Peronism and strongly criticized his unabashed espousal of capitalism. Above all, they urged Haya to reverse his uncritically pro–United States stance. The United States, they stated, had abandoned its Good Neighbor approach to hemispheric affairs. Behind a barrage of Cold War rhetoric, they charged, the United States had embarked upon a new policy of self-serving intervention, focusing at the moment on Guatemala, which it justified by the need to stamp out

Communism in the Americas. To the fresh threats of North Amercian intervention, the APRA must respond by dedicating itself anew to its pristine anti-imperialism.[37]

The Seoane-Barrios letter was dated June 11, and on June 27 Guatemala's leftist president Jacobo Arbenz was forced to resign as a result of an invasion launched from Honduras that was, as even the United States press at the time made clear, masterminded in CIA headquarters. Even so, Haya refused to be swayed by the arguments that Seoane and Barrios had presented. For many years, he had been convinced that Marxism posed the greatest ideological challenge to his historical space-time theories. Furthermore, on the practical level Communists threatened Aprista designs to control Peru's organized labor movement. On ideological as well as practical grounds, Haya was as dedicated a Cold Warrior as Pres. Dwight D. Eisenhower's Secretary of State John Foster Dulles. Moreover, Haya continued to look on Washington as a well-nigh indispensible agency for shielding the APRA from persecution and thereby providing its members with the access to power that was essential to prevent the party from withering away. From Haya's viewpoint, then, the shrewdest tactic to follow was to play up APRA's staunch anticommunism and all the while to encourage the United States to pursue a hemispheric policy of intervention aimed at fostering democratic processes and ending military harassment of purportedly democratic movements. If Washington could be convinced that democracy was the great antidote to communism and that the APRA was democracy's paladin, then all would be well for the party's future.

From the standpoint of shrewd political tactics, Haya's position probably made more sense than the one advocated by Seoane and Barrios; and ultimately, his position prevailed. Still, when the jefe departed Montevideo to make his way to Puerto Rico before embarking on a tour of the Scandinavian countries, Greenland, Germany, Geneva, London, and Paris, he left behind him a troubled and divided party. At least Odría, in part because he wanted to present a political demeanor more pleasing to the United States (he would in due course be decorated by the Eisenhower administration for his contributions to the free enterprise system, a fact that intensified Haya's preference for Democrats over Republicans), eased his repression of the APRA. Although the party technically remained outlawed, "government agents simply looked the other way. They pretended not to know what was going on."[38] Returning from exile, Ramiro Prialé became the party's secretary-general (replacing Manuel Seoane) and worked indefatigably and with some success to heal the party's wounds and reinstill its esprit. On Prialé, the traveling Haya conferred what amounted to "viceregal powers."[39]

In his travels, especially in the Scandinavian countries, Haya confirmed his belief of the early 1940s that United States capitalism did not pose a threat to Indo-America because, throughout the world, capitalism was set unmistakably upon a course of convergence with socialism and in consequence was about to discard its aggressive and expansionist ways. Throughout the world, Haya wrote in a 1955 essay, an incomplete and frustrated capitalism, incapable of "advancing farther as an economic system," faced "a congealed communism whose philosophical principles are in crisis." Already elements of the two systems had begun to coalesce in the Scandinavian countries, which offered the model for the future to the rest of the world. Meantime, science had introduced into the world a new force of such prodigious power as to make international violence a thing of the past. With the power of atomic energy channeled into peaceful uses, the world would be on the brink of solving its problems. Employing the classical symbolism of destruction and rebirth through fire, Haya suggested that the atomic explosion over Japan marked the birth of a new era that would incorporate and subsume the heretofore warring forces of capitalism and communism. This was a thesis, Haya wrote, that had first occurred to him in 1948; now, seven years later, he found that in the last volume of *A Study of History*, just now made available to him, Toynbee had reached a similar conclusion.[40] Reassured in his millennialist vision of the world's future, Haya could scarcely waste time on the concerns that less prescient persons voiced about such ephemeral matters as United States imperialism in Latin America.

At this point it seems that Haya's vision of coming world harmony no longer focused on the American hemisphere. With Europe moving toward a capitalist-socialist convergence, Haya foresaw the rise of a new world order based on the type of harmony that he once had expected to originate in his hemisphere. Europe might still be distinct from Indo-America, he wrote Luis Alberto Sánchez in a letter of January 14, 1955, but there were obvious lessons to be learned from it[41] as humanity approached its next stage of existence.

Choosing to remain above the political skirmishing in Peru that must have struck the cosmic visionary as inconsequential, Haya passed through Switzerland, where he might have mused on what a long way he had advanced since his 1925 meeting with Romain Rolland, and continued on to England. In that country he renewed his acquaintance with Bertrand Russell and various Labourite politicians and university professors. He attended a reception in his honor at the London School of Economics and presented a lecture series at Oxford. Then, moving on to Paris, he lectured at the Sorbonne on "el Inca," Garcilaso de la Vega, as a philosopher of history.[42] Finally, by July 1957 Haya was ready to return to his native country and to enjoy a new re-encounter with his followers.

Visions and Politics: Haya de la Torre from 1957 to 1963

Politically, Peru in 1957 had changed dramatically from the country that Haya departed some three years earlier. Odría's eight-year rule had ended with democratic elections in 1956, resulting in Manuel Prado's reelection. Backed by Apristas, Prado had garnered some 568,000 votes. Ominously, so far as Party of the People fortunes were concerned, a new political figure, Fernando Belaúnde Terry, a University of Texas–trained architect backed by the National Front of Democratic Youth, ran a strong race and gained the support of some 458,000 voters. Youth had found a new candidate in Peru. The Popular Action party that Belaúnde established after the election would shortly begin to whittle into other Aprista constituencies as well. For the moment, what most alarmed the Party of the People was the loss of general electoral support in the 1956 elections. In the departments where it had presented slates, the party won some 27 percent of the ballots. In contrast, voters had rewarded its candidates with about 50 percent of the ballots in 1945.[43]

Haya's official re-encounter with his long-suffering partisans occurred on July 25, 1957, and in the same location as the more dramatic 1954 re-encounter: Lima's Plaza San Martín. Conspicuously missing from Aprista sources covering the event are the usual boasts about crowd size, a sure indication of disappointment in the turnout. To those on hand for the occasion, Haya delivered a rather low-key address. He devoted much of his time to setting forth the Aprista program and to asserting the party's ideological consistency. And, he repeated the call for forgiveness of enemies as he urged reconciliation among Peruvians. Only one highly mystical utterance found its way into the jefe's remarks, one that recalled a section of his memorable 1933 address delivered in Trujillo. On that occasion, which came shortly after his release from the penitentiary, Haya had informed his hearers: "My wound bleeds always, because it is the wound of the sorrow of the people."[44] Now, as he commenced his 1957 speech, Haya addressed these words to his audience: "Each one of you understands how deep is this wound of love and how profound is the vibration of my spirit before this truly fraternal gathering."[45]

The "wound of love" terminology appears to derive from Saint Theresa's *Interior Castle*. In it, the Spanish mystic referred to the "wound of love" that is suffered when the spiritual seeker, who has once encountered God in the unitary state, agonizes over the inevitable withdrawal from ecstatic union and the return to an existence that is lacking in transcendence.[46] Haya may have meant to convey the meaning that his moments of ecstatic wholeness came only when he was united to the Aprista faithful, conceived as a symbol of the ineffable. If this interpretation is valid, it suggests a lessening of Haya's megalomania. In the 1930s he cast himself as the charismatic leader who could fulfill his followers. Now, in 1957, these followers had become the symbol of the ineffable, of the godhead, that Haya required for his own fulfillment.

In closing his 1957 discourse, Haya returned to another theme from Saint Theresa that he had first sounded in his 1933 speech at Trujillo. In both addresses Haya maintained that while Apristas might sin venially, they were incapable of sinning mortally.[47] In 1933, Haya had been shouting in the wind in an attempt to allay his own apprehensions, for he fully understood that Apristas might indeed sin mortally by taking to violence and immersing Peru in a bloodbath. In 1957, he was confident that Aprismo was no longer capable of this kind of sin. Between 1933 and 1957 Haya had overcome his own lingering temptation to violence. And between 1948 and 1957, believers in the efficacy of violence had withdrawn in disillusionment from the Party of the People. By 1957, neither Haya nor his Aprista followers could be tempted by the mortal sin of seeking regeneration through violence, however much they might still stoop to commit the venial sins of political dirty tricks.

The life-style that Haya settled into after the 1957 re-encounter differed enormously from that of the three years that followed the 1945 re-encounter. The more mature Haya neither encouraged nor received the type of saint worship that had set the style of Aprista politics between

1945 and 1948. Apparently his ego no longer required this sort of abnormal nourishment. And, with party ranks now reflecting Haya's moderation, there was less need to trade on charisma as a disciplining mechanism. One welcome consequence was that the party propaganda ceased to include hagiographic paeans penned by hack poets.

After July 1957, party headquarters, designated the House of the People (Casa del Pueblo), became the center of Haya's life. Here he lectured and engaged in dialogue with party members as often as twice a week, being especially anxious to attract Aprista youths to these sessions. On another evening of the week he attended to the party's labor contacts by presiding over popular university classes, which met also in the Casa del Pueblo. At last Haya had found the large household or extended family that he nostalgically imagined latifundistas to have presided over in the golden days of his native Trujillo. In the Casa del Pueblo, Haya played a paternalistic role, guiding his wards toward political virtue and spiritual development and sharing his visions with them. In his household, Aprismo's patriarch dedicated himself to far more than political mobilization in any ordinary sense of the word. Unlike ordinary politicians who are content to describe, comment upon, and offer suggestions for the reform of "reality," Haya attempted to expand, beyond the senses, the realm that his followers experienced. In all, he functioned as a professor, a patriarch, and a priest or shaman. And the Casa del Pueblo served as a classroom, as the "big house" of the patrician's extended family, as a political forum, and as a church. Moreover, on days of special ritual, particularly on Haya's birthday, overflow crowds spilled out of the Casa del Pueblo, filling the street in front and enabling Haya to renew his mystical experiences of wholeness as he merged, vibrated, and pulsated with the people who fulfilled him.

For a part of 1959 and 1960 Haya set aside his political vocation and patriarchal-priestly duties. Taking what amounted to the professor's sabbatical, he sought to expand his knowledge and deepen his spiritual development by living in Europe. Such, at least, was the rationalization that Haya's disciples provided for his extended residence in Europe. They bristled at charges that the jefe was living in luxury and idleness off a government subvention and party contributions. Instead, as they more accurately told the story, Haya lived frugally, dedicating himself to constant study and to meetings with the great intellectual, spiritual, and political leaders of the world. Thereby he was preparing himself more fully "to bring to the people of America . . . the message of culture, of preparation and spiritual superiority which he understands how to achieve and how to transmit."[48]

Apristas insisted that their chief gained his meager sustenance not from subventions but from the sale of articles to various American and European journals. The Party of the People even circulated a pamphlet that listed an impressive number of essays that Haya published during the June 1959–March 1960 period when he resided in Rome. According to figures provided in the pamphlet, Haya received as little as ten dollars for some of his newspaper pieces but averaged around two hundred dollars for his journal essays. In addition he received a thousand-dollar honorarium plus transportation and expenses for several days of participation in a University of Chile summer program.[49]

In the same pamphlet that detailed Haya's writing income, the anonymous compiler included an encomium authored by the well-known Colombian man of letters, Germán Arciniegas. Arciniegas's words are worth quoting at some length, for even if they do not provide an altogether accurate portrayal of the traveling jefe, they do indicate the new image that Haya was cultivating. The new image, while altogether flattering, did not impute to Haya the superhuman, even divine, traits that admirers had extolled in the past. Here is how Arciniegas described Haya's life-style:

There are those who would expect the great *Jefe* of the APRA while in Rome to live in luxury as a splendid caudillo. In reality, he lives as a student. He lives, as he has ever been, as a dreamer; he lives, with his great ideas for the future of America, in his small studio where he is his own servant, his own teacher. . . . Haya reads and writes every morning, and in the evening attends courses in Italian at the Dante Alighieri Center, as a punctual student: ferociously punctual. No one can invite Haya out before eight o'clock at night, because this is the hour when the class ends. . . . Haya as a politician knows that the first obligation for a statesman is to study. And he studies humanely, in books, in men, in whatever place of the world.[50]

While in Europe Haya worked to exalt his image as a statesman and also as a world-class visionary and savant. In an article that he published at the beginning of 1960, Haya referred to Aristotle, Heraclitus, Kant, Hegel, Bertrand Russell, Werner Heisenberg, Alfred North Whitehead, and others as he speculated on the ultimate consequences of new scientific discoveries. Subatomic matter was, he observed, neither material nor predictable, and this provided the definitive refutation to Marxist theories of scientific materialism and economic determinism. Harping on concepts of relativity, space-time, and the fourth dimension, Haya referred to a meeting with Einstein in 1948 at Princeton. At one point Einstein, according to the story, had become so excited by one of Haya's suggestions that he switched from his slow and methodical English to German so as to express more rapidly his total agreement.

At last recognizing that they were no longer constrained by material determinants, Haya continued in his early 1960 article, human beings would attain to true spiritual liberation and usher in a new era. Presiding over a utopian world would be a "new class." Rather than the political manipulators to whom Milovan Djilas had scornfully given this title, Haya's new class would be formed by persons who had mastered the new science and its spiritual implications. Soon outer space would be explored by incredible vehicles, and robots would begin to perform the dreary work that heretofore had kept humans trapped in creatureliness. Together with drudgery, class conflict would disappear from human existence. Moreover, the confrontation that many predicted between the Soviet Union and the United States would not occur, for their supposedly incompatible systems were every day approximating each other more closely. Already, both countries were capitalist, although in Russia property had one owner, the state, while in the United States it had many owners. The Soviet Union, however, was in transition, for its citizens were no longer paid according to needs but rather in accordance with a capitalist scale that stressed productivity and facilitated the acquisition of individual property. Meanwhile, the United States and with it the entire capitalist world were moving toward a "synthesis of the contradictory duality of capitalism which still includes exploitation of man by man." In all, according to Haya, it seemed likely that atomic warfare would be avoided and that humanity would attain a new cosmic wholeness as the earth was linked to outer space through the conquest of the planets.[51]

In another of his visionary articles, this one written in Rome in March 1960 (and already described in some detail in chapter 7 in the section titled "The East-West and the North-South Synthesis"), Haya reverted to historical space-time analysis as he noted that Europe and North America operated according to an accelerated time. But ever since Einstein discovered space-time relativity, "we have known that solar

Although Haya spent most of his time abroad in the late 1950s and early '60s, he delivered a political address in Lima in March 1961. Wide World Photos.

time is not the real measure of time," for time has to be recognized as subjective, produced and distinguished by different kinds of consciousness. In Latin America time has had a slower rate, and space, which includes geography and environment, has not yielded to those intent upon its domination as it has in the super-developed countries. In consequence, Haya prophesied that the world would be reborn in Latin America, which had remained comparatively dormant with its space relatively unmastered and undefiled by human exploitation. Here, once more, was the familiar symbolism of rebirth out of a virgin matrix, resulting from the conjunction of Yang and Yin space-times.[52] Here also was an indication that although Haya after the embassy interlude concerned himself primarily with international harmony, he could also revert to an outlook that attached primary importance to Indo-America in pointing toward greater worldly perfection.

Living abroad during an interlude of exile that for once was self-imposed, Haya de la Torre retained his status as a visionary and also demonstrated that he had lost none of his mastery over ritual. He did not need the Plaza de Acho or the Plaza San Martín, or even the Casa del Pueblo, as a setting for his ritual. Just a hotel room would suffice. When Haya in 1961 received a visitor in a hotel room in Paris, the stage was carefully set. To begin with, Haya was in a modest hotel, in keeping with the legend of his abnegation. The props were few, but effective. On a table lay a copy of a flattering biography by Felipe Cossío del Pomar. The visitor would have had to peruse only a few pages to discover that Haya was indeed an extraordinary person. Next to the book was a lithograph, also the work of Cossío del Pomar, depicting the execution by firing squad of six Aprista's at Chan-Chan in 1932, in consequence of the ill-fated Trujillo uprising. Here was a reminder of Aprista martyrdom and of the party's destiny to preside over a process of rebirth that would follow on the heels of death.[53] Not even a shaman was more attentive to his ritualistic paraphernalia than the jefe ensconced in his Paris hotel.

With Haya operating on the higher level of the international statesman and visionary, his more worldly minded followers back in Peru enjoyed at last a taste of political power, thanks to their large congressional bloc, to their resurgent control over organized labor, and to their understanding with President Manuel Prado. Apristas benefited now from the *Convivencia*, meaning "a living together in harmony." The term applied specifically to the collaboration between Apristas and President Prado, but in broader context it signified accord between the Party of the People and the country's upper-class establishment. Chastened by their repression at the hands of Odría and willing to bide their time until the next elections, Apristas did not harass Prado as they had Bustamante—perhaps in part because Haya had begun to find Prado *simpático*, whereas he could never really abide Bustamante.[54]

The tone of Aprismo during the Convivencia was set by Secretary General Ramiro Prialé when, in a 1956 interview published in the Latin American edition of *Time* magazine, he contrasted his party's initial program with its current goals. Regarding the objective of a unified Latin America, Prialé confessed that Apristas now considered it utopian. Concerning the nationalization of lands and industries, Apristas now had in mind only the nationalization of public services. Furthermore, the objective of an internationalized Panama Canal had been abandoned. Also, Apristas now welcomed the investment of private North American capital, having learned to distinguish between exploitative capitalism and capitalism as currently practiced in the United States.[55]

Manuel Seoane, former secretary-general of the PAP, who had come close to abandoning the party at the time of the letter coauthored with Barrios Llona on June 11, 1954, voiced the feelings of many Apristas when he continued to complain behind the scenes over the party's accommodation with the status quo. During a notable three-hour address of July 30, 1957, on the occasion of the party's Third National Congress, Seoane looked back nostalgically on Aprista accomplishments. The party, he insisted, had inspired a sense of dignity and a new sense of justice in Peruvians. Resisting the temptation to betray their principles, however great their fear and suffering, Apristas "through the long cruel times" had presented the serene example of a people "marching on the route of their Calvary, . . . keeping always high the banner of their faith."[56] Seoane seemed to be lamenting the Aprista present by holding up the image of its past. Disgruntled by Aprismo's apparent abandonment of reform in the present, Seoane increasingly curtailed his participation in party affairs.

By the end of the 1950s, the current and the past secretaries-general personified the Party of the People's division into stand-pat and reformist branches. From his Olympian heights, Haya de la Torre did little to resolve the split. Actually, from a political standpoint, it made sense to retain the liberty to tell one type of audience one thing, and a different type the opposite. Thereby, as Gilbert and Sullivan put it in *Utopia Limited*, "yes" became "but another and a neater form of 'no.' " Opportunism, however, outraged some Aprista sectors. A residue of leftists withdrew from the party following its convention in October 1958. Two years later they formed their own Rebel Aprista party. Spokesman for the new group charged that the original party had betrayed, for a mere "plate of lentils," its mystique, its doctrine, its glorious trajectory, and its history of martyrdom.[57]

Not only Aprista leftists showed signs of discontent. Conservative middle sectors, who had once embraced Aprismo as their means of practical salvation from the forces of an impersonal marketplace economy, chafed as the party's high command locked in an embrace with the oligarchy, which during the Convivencia experimented with laissez-faire policies that seemed to benefit only the well-to-do. As the 1962 elections approached, Peruvian middle sectors, growing more rapidly than the country's employment opportunities, found little to enthuse over in

Aprismo's new demeanor.[58] In contrast, many did find a ray of hope in the Popular Action party headed by Fernando Belaúnde. Long-established middle sectors, fearful of a decline in status because of their difficulty in coping with a lackluster economy, and new middle sectors, only recently arrived at bourgeois respectability and fretful over their ability to remain there, responded approvingly to Belaúnde's promise to achieve rapid economic development and also to provide an expanding array of social services.

As the 1962 elections approached, Gen. Manuel Odría, the dictator from 1948 to 1956, announced his candidacy and quickly demonstrated that he would be a formidable contender. He had considerable support among law and order–obsessed elements of the oligarchy who still feared Apristas as violence prone and also among the urban poor of Lima who had benefited from the social programs conspicuously presided over in the early 1950s by the dictator's wife. To no one's surprise, the Party of the People nominated Haya de la Torre as its standard-bearer. While Haya may well have been reluctant to return to the political trenches, he realized there was no other way in which he could retain command over the party and thereby enjoy all the privileges, material, psychological, and spiritual, that accrued to him as jefe máximo. Backed by the outgoing Prado administration, candidate Haya de la Torre was described as "the sort of conservative we need in Peru."[59]

In 1962, the year of the missile crisis in Cuba, the Alliance for Progress was one year old. Through the Alliance, the John F. Kennedy administration hoped to accomplish wonders of economic revitalization and social reform in Latin America and in the process turn back the communist threat personified by Fidel Castro, who had come to power in Cuba at the beginning of 1959. On all counts, the APRA seemed to be what Washington was looking for as a partner in transforming Peru into an Alliance for Progress showcase. In its present form, Aprismo was sufficiently supportive of the notion that private foreign investment represented the best road to development to satisfy North America's staunchest free-market capitalists. At the same time, though, North American reformers found Aprismo to their liking.

Intellectuals in the Kennedy administration, among them Arthur M. Schlesinger Jr. and Richard Goodwin, had their input into the Alliance for Progress and, in a very restrained way, harked back to some of the hopes of Waldo Frank and his coterie in the 1930s. Indeed, a new generation of leftist-reformist intellectuals of the Democratic party in its New Frontier stage dreamed not only of effecting sweeping internal reforms in the United States but of forging hemispheric solidarity among parties of the democratic left that sought to combine private initiative with state planning and capitalism with non-Marxian socialism. Many intellectuals of this persuasion looked approvingly on the Party of the People as a champion of the democratic practices and leftist socioeconomic reforms that would halt communism in its tracks.

As to Aprismo's democratic leanings, the optimistic New Frontier intellectuals did not altogether misconstrue the nature of the movement in the early 1960s. As Haya's millennialist visions had switched from self-righteous exclusivism to a mystical inclusion of opposites, from the totalitarian temptation to a pluralist persuasion, his party had indeed settled into a pattern of democracy—albeit of patronalist democracy that required an enlightened leader to channel, uplift, and ennoble the spontaneous wishes of the masses. But, were the North American intellectuals correct in judging Peruvian Aprismo to have remained a movement of the left? The straightforward, unnuanced answer would have had to be no. However, Haya de la Torre could scarcely have found the question relevant, for in the coming age as he envisaged it, left and right, like socialism and capitalism, would coexist in harmony.

In the June 1962 election none of the presidential candidates received the third of the 1,689,618 votes cast that would automatically have resulted in accession to the presidency. As a result congress, in line with constitutional provisions, had to choose between the three highest candidates: Haya de la Torre with approximately 557,000 votes, Belaúnde with slightly more than 544,000, and Odría with some 520,000. At this time, had his heart been in the effort, Haya might have exerted all his energies and guile to persuade Washington, which might well have been favorably predisposed, to threaten dire consequences if congress sought to thwart the will of the people. In fact, however, Haya made no effort to play his Washington card, thus abandoning the tactics he had begun to develop in the 1930s. Instead, the man who on the night when the returns were being counted whiled away the hours discussing with a handful of friends such topics as the music of Erik Satie and the difficulties of translating Keats and Shelley into Italian[60] appeared in the auditorium of the Casa del Pueblo on July 4 to announce that he was renouncing his claim on the presidency. As his dumbfounded listeners exploded in shouts of "No!" and raised the chant of "with you until death," Haya explained that the outgoing president had asked for his renunciation in the interest of maintaining the nation's tranquility. To his incredulous audience, Haya then announced: "My response [to Manuel Prado] could not have been other than that of any other responsible Peruvian from whom there is demanded the sacrifice of his aspirations or of his legitimate right or of his very life. . .so as to guarantee the stability of the country." He would leave it to the future to decide whether Prado had been justified in his request. On his part, he could only have replied, without a moment's hesitation, affirmatively: "For Peru, everything; for liberty, everything; for the defense of my people and their justice, everything."[61]

Then, in what a sympathetic historian describes as the most formidable discourse of his life,[62] Haya proceeded to praise the man who had imprisoned him and placed his very life in jeopardy, Luis M. Sánchez Cerro. There is, I believe, a simple explanation for this amazing conduct. In the late years of his life, having come to find in his roles as professor, patriarch, priest, and visionary statesman of international repute a higher calling then the mere presidency of Peru, Haya could feel sincere gratitude toward the man who had originally come between him and the country's highest political office. It might also be that in honoring the man who humiliated him, Haya was revealing that a masochistic streak still inhered in his psyche. Be that as it may, Haya concluded the address, which is said to have convinced even non-Apristas of the jefe's "moral and intellectual stature," by admonishing his listeners to recognize that the APRA was no longer—actually, it probably never had been—the party of the national majority. It was necessary, he declared, to take this claim that Apristas had advanced for thirty years and "put it in the refrigerator, and to hope that we will recover in other elections."[63]

Having found a graceful if disingenuous explanation for backing away from his presidential bid, so that he might remain free to pursue his higher calling, Haya now attempted the master political stroke of his career. He reached an accord with Manuel Odría, who in the course of his dictatorship had proclaimed Aprismo's chief morally unworthy of Peruvian citizenship and who had spilled more Aprista blood than any ruler since Sánchez Cerro. In essence, the accord provided that when congress met to select a president, Apristas would support Odría. By renouncing his own claim on the presidency, which otherwise the military might well have blocked through a golpe, Haya felt he had guaranteed the actual seating of the large bloc of Aprista senators and deputies elected to congress at the same time that Peruvians had cast their ballots for a president. The military, he believed, would not prevent one of their own from occupying the presidency, even though he had pacted with the APRA. Once Odría was in office, Apristas could effectively govern the country from the congress that they expected to dominate through already-planned alliances with other political groups. By assuring Apristas political office, power, and patronage, Haya would guarantee the continuing strength of his party, his extended family, his students, and his cultists. He could then continue to minister to the higher needs of his followers while lesser Apristas discharged their functions in the national congress.[64]

In his master political stroke, Haya miscalculated. To begin with, the pact with Odría so outraged many Apristas as to drive them from the party.[65] Far more damaging to Haya's expectations than the defections was the unanticipated military reaction that the understanding with Odría provoked. Beginning to regard their professional mission as including the maintenance of internal stability through timely social and economic reforms intended to ease revolutionary pressures that, if unattended to, could result in uncontrollable upheavals from below, many military officers balked at the prospect of rule by Apristas and Odriistas. Regarding these two groups as defenders of a status quo sorely in need of reform, and also still inclined to exercise the military veto over APRA that had become an ingrained reaction since 1932, officers under the leadership of Gen. Ricardo Pérez Godoy ousted President Prado from the Palace of Pizarro on July 18, ten days before the legal end of his constitutional term. Proclaiming a program of extensive reforms, the military announced that they would govern the country for one year, at the end of which they would hold new elections. Outraged that Peru would not be transformed into an Alliance for Progress democratic showcase of economic development, fashioned by Apristas in close collaboration with United States experts, the Kennedy administration at first refused to extend diplomatic recognition to the military government. Few persons in Washington seemed to understand how disinclined Aprismo's jefe was to serve as president or how indifferent many members of the movement he headed had grown toward matters of political and social reform.

After beginning with a flourish of agrarian-reform plans and housing projects for the poor, the military government ran out of momentum and devoted its remaining energies to a crackdown on alleged Communists.[66] Precisely at this moment, the Kennedy administration saw fit to extend diplomatic recognition to the military, heartened perhaps by its dropping of threats to nationalize the International Petroleum Company. Fundamentally, though, what prompted recognition was the officers' renewed pledge to hold elections in June 1963 and the feeling among Kennedy advisors that continued nonrecognition would accomplish nothing. Furthermore, Apristas themselves argued in behalf of recognition.

Between July 1962 and June 1963, Fernando Belaúnde campaigned indefatigably. As he carried his message to the sierra, Belaúnde struck an Indianist tone reminiscent of that of the early APRA and of José Carlos Mariátegui. Unstintingly praising Inca traditions, including those of communal landownership and labor, Belaúnde called upon the native communities to advance themselves through the energetic use of the same cooperative methods employed by their distant ancestors. The Indian, he proclaimed, must be allowed to develop in his own way, as a collectivist being. Thus the five thousand or so Indian comunidades should be protected, even if this meant expropriating land from private sierra estates to permit restitution of property illegally seized from the natives. Beyond this, surplus Indian population in the Andes was to be drained off: not toward coastal cities, already plagued by unemployment, but rather toward the selva, the eastern range of Andean foothills and the river valleys formed by Amazonian tributaries. To facilitate this, Belaúnde urged colonization projects and above all construction of a giant north-south selva highway that would provide the transportation infrastructure necessary to support new colonies. Belaúnde addressed his reform program to coastal Peru as well. Recognizing the many accomplishments of coastal capitalism, he promised to allow room for the free exercise of private business initiative. But he also pledged governmental planning efforts to stimulate economic expansion.

The only candidate with fresh ideas to offer voters in the 1963 election, Belaúnde steadily gained support as he traveled throughout Peru to explain his program of reform within a framework of moderation and compromise. Not since the 1931 campaign, when Haya and Sánchez

Cerro had both crisscrossed the country, had a presidential aspirant worked so hard to carry his message to so many.[67]

At age sixty-eight, Haya de la Torre showed understandable reluctance to take on the burdens of another presidential campaign. Yet, with the party badly divided between those counseling support of Odría and those favoring Belaúnde, it appeared that Apristas, to retain some semblance of unity, would have to field their own candidate. Although "it was clear even to many of the Aprista leaders that it was not in the interest of Haya, the party, or Peru" to have the jefe run again, "Haya himself apparently would not concede this."[68] Unwilling to share his party, his family, and his coreligionists with another chief, Haya took once more to the campaign trail. This time his message, essentially one of patience and assurances that Peru's social and economic problems were not really terribly pressing,[69] failed to generate excitement. Both Haya and Odría fell considerably behind their 1962 ballot tallies; Haya, in fact, ran consistently behind Aprista congressional slates.[70] Receiving more than the required third of the ballots cast, Belaúnde was inaugurated for a six-year term on July 28, 1963.

According to Luis Alberto Sánchez, who had been elected to the senate, Haya observed once the electoral results were known: "We have won the majority of congress; now we will be able to control the executive and co-govern. I have lost, but not the party." Here were precisely the results that Haya very probably most desired, even though Sánchez thought he detected a trace of sadness in Haya's smile when he mused, "Perhaps this has been my last opportunity."[71]

It turned out that Haya was right, in a way: the 1963 campaign had indeed been his last opportunity to win the Peruvian presidency. Yet, Haya would live for another sixteen years, and toward the end of that period he would render what was arguably his most valuable political contribution to his country and hold his first public office. Out of apparant political death, new life would issue.

Twelve

Success Born of Failure: Haya's Final Years, 1963–79

Apristas Regroup for an Election That Never Came: 1963–68

Contributing to Haya de la Torre's political resuscitation after 1963 was the inability of Pres. Fernando Belaúnde to satisfy the hopes of those who had placed him in office. For this inability, the aprista congressional majority bore some responsibility, as it forced the president to modify certain features of the sierra agrarian reform program he had initially proposed[1] and to scrap the selva highway plans—which may not have been economically feasible anyway. Belaúnde suffered also from the denial of large-scale Alliance for Progress funds as Washington retaliated for the president's purchase of jet fighters from France and for a projected new contract with the International Petroleum Company (IPC) and his threat to nationalize the firm if it rejected the contract.[2] Ultimately, though, Belaúnde had principally himself to blame for his failure to satisfy his followers. That failure had begun during his campaign when his populist exuberance had raised false hopes.

Basically responsible for Belaúnde's downfall was his insistence upon being both a developmentalist and a populist president. Thus he spent money on economic development projects at the same time that he increased the social spending intended to safeguard the masses and struggling middle sectors in a secure clientel status vis-à-vis a patronalist government. He did not want to impose steep taxes on the wealthy— nor could he have done so in view of the congressional control exercised

Haya is pictured here at Oxford on May 7, 1964, the fortieth anniversary of the founding of the APRA. He had taken up a fellowship at St. Catherine's College the previous month. Wide World Photos.

by the Aprista-Odriista watchdogs of oligarchy interests—for he placed a basic faith in the ability of private capitalism, with only a modicum of government stimulus and direction, to solve urban-sector problems. His access to foreign funds severely curtailed and unable to stimulate adequate domestic capital formation because some of his reformist rhetoric frightened the oligarchy into increasing their deposits abroad, he watched helplessly as mounting inflation estranged the insecure middle sectors who had so recently placed their trust in him. As Belaúnde's stock declined, Haya de la Torre began to reap the success of his past failures as a candidate. Having never held a public office, his record in some respects remained unblemished.

As Belaúnde began his administration, Haya had returned to his functions at the Casa del Pueblo. Engaging in his Socratic-method colloquia with Aprista youth and other interested citizens and presiding twice a week over popular university classes, Haya appeared intent upon verifying the judgment of his old mentor in England, the anthropologist R. R. Marett. According to Marett, "Moral progress will be not only possible but inevitable as soon as our statesmen become educators and our educators statesmen."[3] By patiently fulfilling his mission as an educator, both within the halls of the Casa del Pueblo and in the world at large, Haya was proving himself to be, according to an admirer, "one of the greatest statesmen of Western Christian culture."[4] At the same time, by listening patiently to accounts of personal problems and sometimes arranging for loans and jobs, Haya continued to play his role as family patriarch.

Mass meetings, held on the street in front of the Casa del Pueblo, afforded Haya the opportunity to add the religious dimension to his functions as a statesman-educator. One of Aprismo's most impressive ritualistic celebrations, rich in religious overtones, occurred on February 22, 1966, in conjunction with the Day of Fraternity that marked Haya's seventy-first birthday. According to Serafino Romualdi, a North American labor leader who sympathized deeply with the APRA, nearly one hundred thousand people "paraded through the streets of Lima, past the Casa del Pueblo, . . . chanting 'Víctor Raúl! Víctor Raúl!' " The paraders "are Indians from the uplands, slum dwellers from the barriadas, workers, peasants, students, intellectuals, professionals." For hours, the jefe stood on the reviewing stand, "waving the white handkerchief, held aloft in a crooked arm, in the traditional party salute of the APRA." According to Romualdi, the event constituted "the supreme tribute to a leader who has entered the autumn of his life and was now resigned to fade away."[5]

As the crowds filed by Haya, they shouted at intervals, "With you until death." Here was religious symbolism not commented upon by Romualdi. Haya, who exulted in this chant and may very well have devised it, was familiar, at least since his association of the 1920s with John Mackay, with St. John's Revelation; he knew that the people who were saved, who spurned false faiths in spite of Roman persecution, bore witness for Jesus "even unto death."

The importance of religious symbolism was not lost on Andrés Townsend Ezcurra, one of Aprismo's ablest leaders. According to him, the style with which the 1966 Day of Fraternity had been celebrated attested anew to the fact that the PAP was not just a political movement. It was, in addition, a deeply emotional and spiritual movement that addressed the religious hopes of its adherents. While Aprismo as a political body was subject to the same contingencies and errors of any such organization, "as an emotional movement, deep, charismatic, and mystical," it overcame its crises and the errors of those in its fold. "It matters not that the APRA might err or that some of its men might turn out to be inconsequential or not up to their responsibilities. Bad priests do not deprive the Church of its divine origin or its supernatural character." While the religious aspect explained Aprismo's endurance, Townsend concluded, it also tended to undermine the party's concern for changing temporal society and to impair its ability to attract the mass entry of new recruits, for many Peruvians simply failed to respond to Aprismo's religious faith.[6]

By September 1968 the campaign for the following year's election was already underway. Although Haya had relaxed his control over Aprista affairs and had continued to spend considerable time in Europe, his party did not hesitate for a moment in nominating him once more as its standard-bearer. And the party's prospects seemed bright. True, the APRA had continued to suffer defections and had lost its control over university youth to radical adherents of a Fidel Castro type of revolution,[7] but Peru's other political groupings, including Belaúnde's Popular Action party, had suffered more serious losses and splits. To many observers, "the victory of the Apristas in the 1969 election seemed virtually assured."[8]

The likelihood of an Aprista victory goaded the military into action. Fearful, as they had been in 1962, that the exercise of power by a party grown indifferent to temporal reform posed a threat to internal security, the military decided once more to thwart constitutional processes. On October 3, 1968, the officers ousted Belaúnde and assumed power on their own. The pretext for their action—and it was only a pretext—was that Belaúnde had betrayed national interests by signing a new contract with the IPC in August. Capitalizing on this issue, the officers promptly nationalized IPC holdings, thus initiating a nationalistic revolution from above. In the process, they hoped to forestall revolution from below. Once again Apristas were frustrated, but Haya himself very likely regarded the military golpe as deliverance from the burdens of the presidency. Now he would not risk impairing his guru status by revealing shortcomings as a chief executive, a fate that had befallen Argentina's mystical president Hipólito Yrigoyen—Haya's role model in the early 1920s—when he had proved unable to cope with the problems of the Great Depression.

Gen. Juan Velasco Alvarado, who emerged as Peru's chief executive following the military takeover, proclaimed: "To cancel the traditional dependency of our country is the fundamental objective of our nationalist revolution and the central goal of the full development of Peru."[9] Proceeding to translate words into deeds, Velasco launched the most sweeping revolutionary program that Peru had ever witnessed. Not only did he strike out against dependence on foreign capital, a policy symbolized by the IPC nationalization, but he and his advisors moved also to initiate sweeping agrarian reform in the sierra while at the same time confiscating the main components of Peru's export economy, the sugar and cotton estates of the northern coast, and transforming many of them into worker cooperatives. For many years, the APRA had received its most solid support from the organized laborers of the northern coast, and Velasco's determination to impose reform in that area undoubtedly arose in part from the desire to deal Aprismo a mortal blow.

Promulgating a corporatist mythology strikingly similar to that which underlay Aprista reform programs dating back to the early 1930s, "the Revolutionary Government of the Armed Forces" denounced both capitalism and Marxist socialism and set out to forge a new economic structure that would synthesize the positive elements of each. Capitalism's evil effects, according to Velasco Alvarado, led to alienation by destroying the ability of humans to control their own development. Communism, on the other hand, suffered from an all-absorbing centralized bureaucratic structure that left no room for particularisms. Like capitalism, then, it "dehumanizes and alienates." Peruvians must be wary and selective as they confronted the two systems forged in other lands. By insisting on authenticity, they could become "the discoverers of their own solutions."[10] Carlos Delgado, a former Aprista who emerged as one of the leading civilian theoreticians collaborating with the military in shaping Peru's nationalist revolution from above, saw the country's challenge in a similar light. Peru, he affirmed, must develop its social system on the basis of its own historical reality, being guided by the past as it approached the future: "To know who we will be or ought to be, it is necessary, beforehand, to know what we have been and what, in reality, we are today."[11]

In the sierra, owing largely to prevailing assumptions about the inherently collectivist nature of Indians,[12] the military government stressed a socialist approach. Indians were to be organized into producer cooperatives, often on land confiscated from latifundistas. Within the cooperatives, "social property" would prevail, virtually eliminating the possibility of fee-simple ownership. On the other hand, the officers recognized the existence of a strong capitalist dynamic in coastal Peru, and they announced their intention to leave room, especially in the manufacturing industry, for private ownership and management. At the same time, they sought to establish, side by side with private industry, various "industrial communities" in which workers would participate in ownership, management, and profits.[13] In explaining the industrial community, President Velasco stated its primary purpose was to forge "a new personality" by allowing workers to become "the true creators of a human community which they feel is truly theirs."[14]

Endeavoring to establish points of contact with all Peruvians, the revolutionary government moved to eliminate intermediaries, such as political parties, between the people and the state,[15] and to claim control over all citizens in the national interest. Thus, through nationalism the officers hoped to achieve the integration of Peruvians into a common political form, even though people would be exhorted to contribute to the nation in different ways according to their particular status and function within the body politic. It would be the task of cultural elites "to legitimize the social revolutionary ideal by formulating a convincing national ideology that would bind all . . . [citizens] together"[16] and persuade them to join, in the appropriate manner, in building a nation.

The cultural elites, whose role was to harmonize the functional and regional components in Peru's new corporatism, were to include technicians, engineers, members of the military and civilian intelligentsia,[17] and a sprinkling of bishops and priests. Government's legitimacy was to rest upon recognition by the masses of the elite's cultural superiority and its mastery over the mysterious knowledge, unattainable by the rank and file, of how to forge a nation and achieve the security of its citizens. Including select beings who knew the proper approaches to spiritual development as well as those who knew how to bend the material world to their wishes, the wielders of this moderating power were expected to devise a proper blend of nonmaterial and material rewards as they proceeded toward their goal of joining multitudes of variegated Peruvians and dozens of disparate aggregations into one nation.

Rather than from force, the new leaders would derive the perquisites of sovereignty from their ability to act as teachers—as intellectual workers capable of raising the consciousness of manual workers. Especially during the early years of military rule, a fairly high percentage of Peruvians seemed willing to accept, even if somewhat glumly, Velasco Alvarado's typically populist contention that "our legitimacy has its origins in the incontrovertible fact that we are bringing about the transformation of this country in order to defend and interpret the interests of the people against those who would deceive them."[18] The general apparently had taken to heart the Marxist-Leninist belief in the duty of the vanguard to liberate the masses from so-called false consciousness.

Millennialism New and Old: Peru from 1969 to 1976

However deep-seated their aversion to Aprismo, the revolutionary generals from the outset rendered the movement a supreme compliment: they borrowed from the ideology and imitated the populist tactics that Apristas had unveiled in the 1930s—even though Velasco Alvarado, try as he might, never developed into a charismatic leader. Haya was not slow to draw attention to the origins of much of the military program. In his 1971 Day of Fraternity speech he claimed that the APRA program, denounced by the military for forty years, had now become the guide for the reforms and transformations proclaimed by the military revolution. "The program now in effect that aims at making a new country was first developed in 1931, first promulgated in the country in 1931."[19] Returning to this theme in his 1972 birthday discourse, Haya declared:

We are the initiators of these [military] reforms. We are the vanguard of Peru's transformation. Read the Aprista Program of Government of 1931. Recall our struggle, our suffering, our martyrdom in the service of these very ideals that the movement of October 3, 1968, now proclaims. We have urged "progressive nationalization of wealth" since 1924.... We urged cooperativism and proposed a law of cooperatives of agroindustrial enterprises in the valleys of the north in 1945 and 1956.... The Apristas, I repeat, have struggled more than twenty years for these aspirations, which now are the programs of renovation and change.[20]

With enthusiasm for reform very much the mood of the moment, a new generation responded approvingly, at least for the first four or five years, to the military promises of renovation. Under these circumstances, Haya found it advisable to refurbish the APRA's revolutionary image and to recall the innovative programs that had been downplayed since the Convivencia (1956–62).[21] Moreover, by the early 1970s Haya had to protect APRA turf not only against the incursions of a now revolutionary armed forces but also against those of a radicalized Catholic clergy.[22] Resolved to claim for themselves the uses of religious symbolism in prophetically proclaiming the advent of a millennialist era, some Peruvian churchmen had begun to make effective use of "liberation theology." In the 1930s, Haya had been allowed virtually to monopolize religion (or what passed for religion) in the service of revolution. As the 1970s began, however, that monopoly was broken; and Haya realized that only by moving to the left could he persuade a new generation that the Aprista faith might be a better instrument of transformation than the Catholic faith in the hands of a radicalized and often politically opportunistic clergy. A challenge to him as a politician Haya could face with relative equanimity, at least by this point in his career. But a challenge to his prerogatives as a mystical prophet and visionary required an energetic response and a refurbishing of Aprismo's credentials as a millennialist movement in order to meet liberation theology on its own ground.

With its stress on *concientización*—or raising into consciousness an awarenesss of the dazzling human potential that purportedly had been snuffed out by an exploitative capitalist order—liberation theology sometimes minimized divine transcendence and traded on concepts of the immanence of God that have appealed to millennialists through the centuries. Proclaiming a preferential option for the downtrodden, onto whom was projected or transferred the repressed divine spark that awaited spiritual independence within each individual, some liberation theologians intended to stand the existing order, social and psychic, on its head. In consequence of an inward, psychic, or spiritual inversion, and of a complementary outward or social inversion, a liberated person would emerge in a liberated society.

As Peru's most eminent peddler of the new millennialism, Father Gustavo Gutiérrez, explained in 1971, the goal of liberation theology was "a new man in a qualitatively different society."[23] As the new and liberated person evolved, human brotherhood and economic well-being would emerge within a just society. With economic problems overcome miraculously through the creation of new persons with fully developed *conciencia* (similar in many ways to the "cosmic consciousness" that had titillated spiritualists at the turn of the century), the world would settle into an altogether higher stage of existence. However, an initial period of suffering and struggle (praxis) against the established order would be required to establish group consciousness and to usher in the golden age. Here was the message not only of Gutiérrez but of numerous liberation theologians as they began to write what appears to some observers as a new chapter in the history of soft Marxism. And, just as the old millennialism of Aprismo had appealed to victims of early twentieth century modernization, the new millennialism attracted the victims of Peru's dramatic but also sporadic and woefully uneven post–World War II modernization.

According to one of its defenders, liberation theology was new to the Latin American scene.[24] Any Peruvian who had attended to the new religion of Aprismo in the 1930s, however, could only have regarded the recently surfacing variety of the politics of the miraculous with a sense of déjà vu. Unfortunately for the purposes of Aprismo at the beginning of the 1970s, the fresh generation of Peruvians was unfamiliar with Haya's use some forty years earlier of archetypal religious symbolism of regeneration. To attract this new generation that was able to select its favorite package of utopianism in a veritable supermarket of millennialisms— where, among others, the military, the clergy, and the communists displayed well-stocked shelves—Haya de la Torre had to revert to his initial role of charismatic prophet.

Far more than opportunism inspired the jefe's restored enthusiasm for dreams of heaven on earth. After all, the military and the church, two institutions that had generally joined in denouncing the early APRA, had now actually taken up the starry-eyed prophesies of Haya's youthful days. Perhaps, then, fulfillment of his prophetic visions was at hand. If so, the time had come for Haya to abandon the caution coun-seled by the unpropitious circumstances obtaining in Peru between the mid-1940s and the mid-1960s, when rationalism in a neopositivist guise had triumphed, and to return joyously and openly to the exuberant op-timism with which he had contemplated the country's future in the 1930s.

Even in 1960, Haya had not doubted that the world was about to ad-vance into a higher stage of existence, and two essays of that year dis-cussed in the preceding chapter attest to this conviction. At that time, however, Haya had doubted that Peru was in a position to lead the ad-vance. Now, that doubt was giving way to rekindled confidence. In a fi-ery address of September 21, 1969, commemorating the thirty-ninth anniversary of the PAP, Haya reminded party members of the moral splendor they had already achieved. He congratulated them for never having been businessmen and sordid materialists, praised them for hav-ing scaled the peaks of virtue, and predicted that they were now about to ascend to such heights as to bring altitude sickness to ordinary mortals. From their lofty heights they would understand how to resolve all na-tional problems as they began to prove that "only Aprismo will redeem Peru."[25]

During the course of the military dictatorship Haya continued occa-sionally to tour the Peruvian provinces and to travel to Europe. When in Lima, however, he could generally be found five or six evenings a week at the Casa del Pueblo. There he met with party officials, received visi-tors from the provinces and abroad, offered popular university classes, and every Thursday conducted a colloquium on current economic and political problems, often with several hundred people in attendance.[26] He continued also to be the star attraction at mass rallies, generally held on his birthday, as well as in May and September to commemorate, re-spectively, the founding of the APRA in Mexico and the establishment of the PAP in Peru. Whether in the setting of an auditorium or the open-air mass meetings, Haya returned incessantly to the themes he had first begun to stress in the 1920s and '30s, apparently obsessed with dem-onstrating his movement's ideological consistency. Again and again, for example, he advocated the functional or corporative organization of the state and the creation of a National Economic Congress as the fourth branch of government.[27] The envisioned results of a government formed on this basis were as utopian as ever: a state of "harmonious equilibrium and coordination" that invested capital according to the needs of the people.[28]

While in Israel in 1957, Haya had described David Ben Gurion, the young nation's prime minister, as presiding, like a prophet of old, over the building of a state of four powers—the fourth being the Histadrut, which Haya described as a syndical and cooperative organization of manual, intellectual, industrial, and agricultural laborers. Crowning a life of fecund struggle, Ben Gurion, Haya maintained, had arrived at the point where he was creating a state resting on a foundation of cooperativism that combined individual and collective labor.[29] Nineteen years later, in February 1976, Haya addressed a sizeable turnout on the occasion of his eighty-first birthday. As he lingered over the wonders that could ensue from the government of the four powers,[30] Haya might well have thought that, assisted by the military's newly proclaimed belief in corporatist harmony, he was about to see the creation of a Peruvian state modeled after the sort of vision that he had always proclaimed and that had ostensibly helped give life to the new state of Israel. Perhaps his own life "of fecund struggle" was about to achieve its culminating glory.

Although Ramiro Prialé in his 1956 *Time* magazine interview had dismissed the old Aprista goal of continental unity as utopian, Haya de la Torre in his late years returned repeatedly and insistently to this objective, professing to believe that its attainment was close at hand. In February 1973 he told the Fraternity Day celebrants that the vision originating with Simón Bolívar was about to be fulfilled as a result of the impetus supplied by Aprismo, for Aprismo had taught South Americans to think in terms of continental patriotism and "to prescind from the nationalism of the little fatherland [*patria chica*]."[31] Two years later Haya told the throng assembled to commemorate another birthday that Peru had revitalized the old Bolivarian dream. Since 1924, he maintained, the APRA had provided the "missionary leadership" for the movement of continental solidarity. And because Apristas had urged the surrender of certain perquisites of nationalism in the interest of a transcending patria, "we have suffered persecution, martyrdom, and incomprehension. We are truly the preachers in the desert of ignorance and malice, who were not heard." However, times had changed, Haya concluded. In the present moment, "not only in the continental area but throughout the world, APRA enjoys vindication," because the Bolivarian dream is on the way to realization.[32]

Like corporatism, Indo-American integration conveyed a mystical meaning to Haya, and this is why he labored in behalf of its attainment. Integration, he told the crowd assembled before the Casa del Peublo on May 7, 1976, meant the coming together of "liberty and union."[33] No one familiar with the jefe's thought can fail to grasp the significance of this statement. Just as corporatism would harmoniously fuse within Peru the opposites of liberty and union, masculine independence and feminine bonding or collectivism, the Yang and the Yin, so the integration of Indo-American republics into a true people-continent would accomplish the same miracle of reconciling the one and the many on a supranational level. Thereby Peru, the nation, and Indo-America, the people-continent, together would emerge into a new and higher stage of existence. Appropriately, Haya stressed both the functional, four-power organization of Peru[34] and the integration of Indo-America in his May 7 address—the last one, it turned out, that he would deliver before a mass audience, owing to deteriorating health.

During the period of military government, Haya returned to still other themes out of the Aprista past as he addressed the party on its festival days. In 1969, for example, he employed symbolism suggestive of the cabalist's and the alchemist's discovery of something precious amidst dross, or of the individual's discovery of a spark of divinity within the uncharted morass of his own unconscious. Aprismo, he declared, had reached down into the depths of the Peruvian reality and liberated unsuspected and sublime treasures: the love for justice and liberty and the ability to die for the truth that points the way to a future destiny.[35] Several times in the 1970s Haya also returned to the populist metaphors, favorites of his since the 1930s, alluding to the integral wholeness of the leader and his followers who had achieved fusion. In a 1971 address he claimed he was not delivering his own remarks but was serving only as the passive agency of expression for the aspirations of his people. "I wish to say to you at the conclusion of this night that I did not think about what I have said to you." No preparation had been required, because his message "had been dictated" by "this grand, magnificent, mass presence of a great people, who have never bowed before authoritarian decrees."[36] On another occasion, he declared: "Those who direct the party are you, those who direct the party are the mass of militants who always inspire me, who always give me nourishment, and who always help me advance along this difficult path."[37] Still another time, after some remarks were greeted by an ovation, Haya confided that he welcomed such applause and chants, for they indicated that he and his hearers had entered into unity.[38] In these moments comparable to the mystic's unitary state, Haya continued to experience the "oceanic feeling."

Toward the end of his life Haya harped also on the predominance of consciousness over material determinants. "Our people," he declared, "do not make the revolution with money." Instead, they understand that the revolution must be made in the consciousness of the people.[39] Great deeds proceeded out of an "integrated intuition and an animating faith."[40] Therefore, it was necessary always "to strengthen our faith, to confirm our consciousness."[41] To strengthen faith and confirm consciousness, Haya in all of the public addresses of his last years continued the tradition he had established at the beginning of the 1930s: he devoted considerable time to a review of party doctrine. Thus Aprismo's ceremonial days continued to be rather more like church meetings, which include lessons drawn from the Gospels, than ordinary political rallies.

Decidedly more religious than conventionally political in tone was the theme of death, martyrdom, and the mystical union of the living with the dead that Haya returned to again and again. In September of 1969, for example, he saluted the party's martyrs: "They are with us now, glorified by their martyrdom. . . . Our dead are with us, our permanent companions."[42] Three years later Haya maintained that Apristas who had died in willing sacrifice, or even of natural causes, were the *penates*—pre-Columbian household gods—of the party. "The dead of the APRA, among whom are young and old, men and women, form the sacred communion of the great guardians on the other side of life."[43] In this instance Haya was more the Indo than the Latin American, for he drew more on Tahuantinsuyo's reverence for the dead than on Catholic doctrines of purgatory and the mystical body.

In addition to death, Haya dealt, as in the past, with themes of immortality and regeneration. The APRA, he insisted, was "a militant brotherhood of the dead, the living, and those to come."[44] Truly historic causes are immortal, and APRA's perpetual youthfulness assured its immortality.[45] These statements came in a September 1969 address. In February 1973 Haya sounded the theme anew: "The Peruvian Aprista Party proceeds with a torrential entry of youth. We are a young party, a new party. Those of us who fall, we fall. And you will continue over our graves gaining new victories." To this the crowd responded with the familiar chant, "Aprismo never dies."[46]

When Apristas staged their annual birthday salute to Haya in February 1976, tens of thousands of citizens spread out before the Casa del Pueblo on Avenida Alfonso Ugarte. The homage to Haya on his eighty-first birthday turned into one of the largest "human concentrations" that limeños had witnessed in recent years:[47] and this in spite of the facts that the national press, controlled by the military government, withheld publicity for the event and that Aprista machinery for mobilizing mass demonstrations was seriously impaired by government harrassment. On this occasion, the next-to-last time that he was to preside over a mass audience religiopolitical ceremony, Haya fittingly returned to the death-and-regeneration theme. "A man of eighty-one years says, long live life, and after death, then long live the Aprista Revolution."[48] Predictably, the multitudes responded with "Aprismo never dies." In the past, beginning with the Trujillo address of 1933, Haya had professed that the death of Aprista martyrs would bring rebirth to the country. Now, he implied that his own death might be the essential prerequisite for Peru's rebirth. Understandably, Haya's thought had turned to his death, for his health had been failing of late and for a year now friends had expressed concern over his sickly appearance and demeanor.[49]

As it turned out, Haya's death would virtually coincide with the passing of a repudiated and increasingly detested military government from power. The circumstances under which the military peacefully relinquished power owed a great deal to Haya de la Torre, and at the time many Peruvians hailed these circumstances as preparing the way for their country's rebirth. Seldom has a would-be prophet been more fortunate than Haya in the timing of his death, for he died just as a national regeneration he had long prophesied seemed—to the credulous at least—at hand.

Haya de la Torre's Last Encounter with the Peruvian Military, 1969–78

Under the heavy-handed rule of the Revolutionary Government of the Armed Forces, Peruvian affairs by 1975 proceeded from bad to worse. A broad variety of causes contributed to the deteriorating situation, ranging from the government's incompetence to factors beyond human control. Whatever their causes, the national misfortunes that accompanied military rule helped revive Aprismo's fortunes.[50]

Problems beyond human control that confronted the generals included a disastrous earthquake in 1970 that resulted in over fifty thousand deaths and left some three hundred thousand homeless. In 1972 serious floods occurred, and all the while the fishmeal industry continued its decline because of the persisting absence of the anchovy schools caused by a change in the patterns of offshore ocean currents. Velasco Alvarado responded in 1973 by nationalizing the fishing industry and placing it under a huge state monopoly. And now human failure compounded natural disaster, for the monopoly proved grossly inefficient in its management. The government fared no better in organizing the nationalized sugar estates of the northern coast,[51] which had operated efficiently before their seizure.

Converting a part of the copper industry into "industrial communities" worked out no better than the fishing and sugar enterprise experiments. In addition to bureaucratic bungling, the nationalization of portions of the copper industry led to the drying up of loans from the Export-Import Bank and other international lending agencies. This changed in 1974, when Peru reached an agreement on compensation with the expropriated firms. With the foreign money lenders propitiated, the military government plunged into reckless international borrowing. While the generals obviously cannot be blamed for the steep decline in world copper prices that contributed to heavy trade deficits in 1974 and 1975 and apparently necessitated heavy borrowing, their conversion of portions of the economy into industrial communities discouraged local capitalists. Productive investment of national private capital lagged alarmingly as government propaganda vilified native capitalists, and in these circumstances borrowing from abroad seemed the only salvation. Meantime, despite the generals' rhetoric of economic nationalism, Peru in 1975 received more United States private capital than any other South American country with the exception of Venezuela. While outraging Peruvian leftists, the foreign capital inputs barely compensated for the 1969–74 decline in private foreign investment that had preceded the compensation agreement.

The vast program of land redistribution in the sierra, which the generals pointed to with special pride as proof that they were forging a new Peru, often did little more than replace private landowners with government bureaucrats, charged with organizing dubious Indians into state-controlled cooperatives. Moreover, the military government proved unwilling to transfer capital from the modern, urban, industrialized, export sectors into the traditional agricultural sector. This being the case, the rural sector remained starved of capital resources, and land reform on the whole stopped short of producing broadly based social and economic transformations among the peasantry.[52]

As agrarian reform bogged down, middle sectors and working classes of the coast grumbled over the inflation of upwards of 20 percent a year, led by increases in food prices, as well as unemployment and underemployment that together afflicted just over 50 percent of the labor force. These circumstances sparked sporadic protest riots and strikes. A serious challenge to the administration came with a strike by Lima's 7,000-man police force. Suppression of this strike by the armed forces in February of 1975 resulted in over one hundred deaths. Many of the victims were working-class supporters of the striking policemen. Enraged mobs retaliated against what they considered government brutality by burning the Officers' Club on Plaza San Martín.[53]

The events of February unleashed a pent-up discontent with military rule that had been growing since 1972. Discontent resulted not only from the declining economy but also from the curtailment of freedom of expression and of the press, from crude attempts to turn the schools into centers of indoctrination intended to inculcate revolutionary consciousness, from the inflamatory preaching of hatred against all who questioned the policies of the military rulers, and from such inept public relations ploys as changing the name of the national palace from Palacio Pizarro to Palacio Túpac Amaru—the latter having led a 1780 uprising mainly of Indians and mestizos against the Spanish government in an act that most Peruvians, rightly or wrongly, saw as a race war. All the while the public reacted with mounting derision to the officers' claims that their revolutionary goal was democratic participation. In fact, it had become altogether clear that the revolution was made from above, by a relatively small number of officers and civilians.

Velasco Alvarado may well have been a man of good intentions, anxious to serve his country's overall interests. Prone to believe, however, in simplistic and indeed miraculous solutions, he had been duped by the Marxist propaganda[54] then rife among Peruvian officers and emanating from the High Center of Military Studies (Centro Alto de Estudios Militares, or CAEM). Dispensing the so-called dependency theory that ascribed all national ills to foreign imperialists and their sellout collaborators among the oligarchy, various instructors at the CAEM, buttressed by ancillary agencies of opinion molding, had spread the message that nation building was a relatively simple matter. It could be accomplished by leaders of exalted consciousness once they banished from society the false consciousness imposed on Peruvians by generations of cultural malformation caused by the predominance of an alien life-style of capitalism and materialism. The ideology that inspired Peru's military reformers descended out of the university reform movement and soft Marxism that flourished in the 1920s; it may even have been tinged by the spiritualism that fascinated so many officers in the 1930s. The extreme good fortune of Haya de la Torre and the Apristas lay in the fact that not they but rather Velasco Alvarado, the most gullible product of the new currents of military thought, sought to put into practice the theories of creating the new human through massive resocialization and of building a new nation through conciencia.

However decent his intentions, Velasco Alvarado proved himself the most inept and at the same time the most ideologically inflexible president that Peru has suffered since the end of old-fashioned military caudillo days in the nineteenth century. The revolution he headed, despite many positive features, ended in more ways than not in failure. Thus the public responded favorably when a bloodless military golpe ousted Velasco in August 1975 and replaced him with the more moderate and pragmatic Gen. Francisco Morales Bermúdez. Toning down the excesses of his predecessor, Morales Bermúdez sought to rebuild the shambles of the economy by arresting the drift toward control by state functionaries with high consciousness but low levels of practical skills. The new president afforded encouragement to the private sector. Unquestionably, though, so far as most citizens were concerned the greatest boon Morales Bermúdez conferred was his decision to return the country to civilian rule.

In many ways, Haya de la Torre received, and deserved, equal credit for the ending of military rule, owing to the effective role he had played since 1969 in mobilizing public opinion against the generals. Haya's criticism had been unfailingly civil and temperate—otherwise it would not have been tolerated. At the same time, it had been effective and had earned him the sort of massive, society-wide respect and even affection that had previously eluded him.

Haya was the made-to-order gentlemanly critic of the military government because, even in his advanced years, he remained as much a believer in utopian visions of the new person and the new society as Velasco Alvarado. In consequence, Haya did not criticize the general's objectives, which he continued to associate with the goals of Aprismo. But, with a light-handed approach often laced with humor, Haya complained about the amateurism of a government that lacked command over details, that "surprises us each night with a decree and two nights later with the rectification of that decree."[55] Above all, Haya complained about the authoritarian features of the military revolution from above, demanded the right of citizens to dialogue with the government concerning the most effective approach to reform, and insisted that no reform efforts could be effective unless they involved participation of the people in their formulation and implementation. No true revolution is possible, he proclaimed, "without the participation of the people."[56] Haya derided the notion that effective government derived from *dirigismo*, or centralized economic control from above, and urged that the various political and economic forces of the nation be allowed to seek equilibrium in freedom.[57]

Tracing Aprismo's concern with individual freedom not only to its advocacy of democracy but also to the anarchist strain of its ideological origins,[58] Haya criticized the overweening collectivization of the social property concept that underlay the industrial communities.[59] While the APRA had always advocated cooperativism, which preserved individual ownership of property, it opposed, Haya declared, out-and-out collectivization. Accordingly he criticized the collectivization that he detected in the military approach not only to industrial but to agrarian reform: "We do not want a collectivization learned from Asiatic countries and transferred here...under a new form of imperialism."[60] Apristas stood for justice *and* liberty, according to Haya, and Peru was in a better position than foreign countries to synthesize these two elements that many persons considered incompatible.[61] Indeed, Peru's Incas in their cooperative state had known how to fuse justice with liberty.[62]

In September 1975 a reporter from the magazine *Oiga* came to Haya's home, the Quinta Mercedes in Vitarte on the outskirts of Lima, to conduct an interview. He was overwhelmed by the presence of books in Haya's eight-by-twelve-foot study: books in many languages on shelves reaching to the ceiling; books and journals and magazines on the floor, on small tables, and piled on the desk. He noted also three typewriters, a stereo set, a pile of records with a Beethoven selection at the top, a handsome German shepherd, and a cat. Outside an old gardner puttered, accompanied by more dogs and an alpaca. An "amiable" Jorge Idiáquez, Haya's loyal servant-companion of many years who probably had saved his life in 1939, served refreshments as the conversation began. Obviously, the conversation—or better, Haya's monologue—overwhelmed the reporter as much as the books. Displaying a "prodigious memory" and frequently reaching for books so as to read passages that confirmed his statements, the octogenarian ranged over topics including the internationalization of the Panama Canal, the new constitution of China and Mao Zedong's activities, and the Cuban Revolution. He dealt at length with recent Peruvian history and the role of the APRA in shaping it, reserving his lengthiest observations for the military revolution then underway.

"We have never denied the revolutionary character of the [military] government," Haya began, "because we have seen that it follows the programmatic points that were the banner of the Aprista party, as can be proved by reading our 1931 Program." The military revolution embodied "magnificent goals, excellent intentions"; but these were imperfectly carried out by inexperienced administrators, and above all they suffered from the lack of popular participation and dialogue with experienced men of divergent persuasions. Haya then expressed optimism that under the recently installed Morales Bermúdez important rectifications would be forthcoming. In fact, Haya considered it likely that a constituent assembly would be convened before long to prepare for a return to democratic procedures.[63] For once, Haya's optimism proved justified. A constituent assembly did convene in 1978. This event might have been long delayed had not the ancient Aprista jefe managed to dominate opposition politics between 1969 and 1978 and to set the tone of criticism of the military government.

Throughout the years of military rule, Haya de la Torre refused to impugn the honor or question the integrity and motives of the generals. And this contributed to the ultimate ability of the officers to withdraw from politics with at least a modicum of dignity.[64] Had the climate been charged with vituperative denunciations of the officers, they might well have responded with the vindictiveness of wounded pride and delayed restoration of power to civilians. Playing the role of elder statesman to the hilt and chastising the officers in sorrow rather than anger, Haya earned the gratitude of Peruvians for the manner in which he was able, with the collaboration of Morales Bermúdez (who happily did not believe the rumors linking Apristas to the assassination many years previously of his officer father), to finesse the generals back into the barracks. Never in his long life had Haya given a more striking demonstration of his political sagacity. Despite constant prodding from impetuous party elements to abandon restraint and to assail military intentions as well as practices, Haya stuck to his course. He knew that intemperate denunciation of the officers' goals would only have encouraged leftists to rally to their cause, while weakening the case he sought to make in behalf of the consistency of Aprismo's revolutionary ideology.

In the 1930s, Haya and his Apristas had contributed spiritually to the nation by inspiring hope—albeit exaggerated hope—in the midst of suffering, anxiety, and alienation. In the 1970s, against the advice of many associates, Haya contributed tangibly to his country by voicing noninflamatory criticism of an unpopular regime and thereby defusing an explosive situation. The impetuous and megalomanic Haya de la Torre of the 1930s would not have made this kind of a contribution. By the 1970s, though, the jefe had changed, and altogether for the better. Gone were his cataclysmic visions of an ideal future to be achieved by elimination of all those mortal sinners who did not agree with Aprista prescriptions or who contrived to keep Apristas out of power. The cataclysmic vision of regeneration had given way, clearly, consistently, and unambiguously, to the pluralist quest of the harmonious accommodation of opposites. At last the tension between two distinct approaches to an envisioned utopian future had been resolved. The Gandhis, the Romain Rollands, and the Keyserlings, had triumphed, definitively, over the Lenins, the Mussolinis, and the Hitlers in the struggle for Haya's mind. Neither approach to utopia is ever effectual, but at least the first one is relatively innocuous and occasionally even uplifting for those who pursue it.

Perhaps the most profound change of all that Haya had undergone in his old age was this: he had been cured of narcissism. Free at last from obsessive preoccupation with personal grandeur, he no longer expected adoring followers to lift him in some miraculous way to the pinnacles of power to which he felt entitled by a unique spiritual endowment.

The Recovery from Narcissism

In a 1960 article dealing with the Congo and its Marxist strongman Patrice Lumumba, Haya de la Torre criticized the cult of personality and the "megalomanic spirit" that feeds on "the poisonous potion of adulation and deification." Men believing themselves to be providential figures, Haya observed, had all come to "the saddest ruin." And the providential delusion brought with it more than personal ruin, for invariably it dealt ruin to those who had been deceived into rendering obeisance to the "predestined" man. Indeed, the contagion of providentialism undermined entire societies.[65] The remarkable essay on Lumumba by a man who above all others had assumed the providentialist mantle in twentieth-century Latin America stands, I believe, as Haya's veiled confession and as an act of contrition for his own sins in trading on the "megalomanic spirit." By 1960, however, Haya was changing: he was well on the way to overcoming his narcissism.

From chapter 6 it will be recalled that, according to Heinz Kohut, narcissistic personality disorders can ensue from early psychological injury to a child caused by "the unreliability and unpredictability of the empathic response" of the child's mother and/or father. Psychologically maimed by denial of the nutrients of steady and sustained empathy at a crucial stage of development, narcissists as they grow up and mature reveal their injury by, among others, the following symptoms: "They are sensitive to injustices done them, quick to accuse others—and very persuasive in the expression of their accusations—and thus are able to evoke guilt feelings in others, who tend to respond by becoming submissive to them and allowing themselves to be treated tyranically by them."[66] These symptoms manifest themselves in the relationship that narcissists establish with persons and groups onto whom they transfer the expectations that originally centered on parents. To manipulate them, narcissists assert their own perfection and resort to exaggerated behavior patterns that are comparable to the tantrums by which as children they vainly sought parental fulfillment of wishes. Above all, narcissists seek admiration and approval through "the boundless exhibitionism of the grandiose self."[67]

Often, Kohut observes, persons suffering from narcissistic disorders can begin to effect a cure through reading. In the words of various authors they find the supportive and nutrient responses denied by parents who had prematurely withdrawn empathy.[68] The narcissist can also be cured if he begins to find consistent empathic response from the persons or groups onto which he has transferred the expectations that once centered on parents. Once he has built up confidence in the parental substitutes, he begins to curtail his exorbitant demands, to discard his tantrums, and to abandon the "exhibitionism of the grandiose self."

Beginning only in 1957, after he had grown more comfortable with his nature during the embassy confinement, did Haya have the opportunity for sustained and consistent periods of "togetherness" with the projection of that nature: his extended family, the rank-and-file Apristas who, purged of the shock troop elements, no longer made the jefe uneasy. Only from 1957 on did Haya and the family members have the opportunity to begin to know each other intimately and, in the process, to take mutual reliability for granted. By 1972, when his followers raised their familiar chant, "With you until death," Haya could reply with serene confidence: "Yes, I know it. And this is why I wish always to be with you."[69] The following year, Haya exulted in union with his family with these words: "We are together and we will be together tomorrow, when all of you return to work, to the classrooms, to the workshops, to the fields and when you then remember the cry of the Party. We are here! This is our Casa del Pueblo."[70]

Confident of the love of his followers, and of his for them, Haya by the early 1970s had settled into a sharing relationship with them in which he expected to give as much as to receive. He had recovered from his narcissism. It had taken a long time, and but for a long life Haya would have failed of this accomplishment. In the end, though, integrated into a community of unquestionable mutual affection, he had become a relatively unalienated man and had accomplished—to use the words that serve as the title for one of Kohut's books—the restoration of the self.

Toward the end Haya also put behind him the masochist's glorification of suffering that had characterized his youthful and middle years. In his 1975 Oiga interview he stressed that persecution of the APRA had long since ceased. The *via crucis* was in the past, and Haya spoke as if he had no interest in dwelling on those bygone days.[71] Well on his way to overcoming his vindictiveness so as to emerge as his country's great conciliator, Haya informed his interviewer that he had decided not to write his memoirs, for inevitably these would have given offense to some, opened old wounds, invited retaliation, and thus have perpetuated a political climate of acrimony and recrimination. "With eighty years of life and sixty of political struggle," Haya stated, "one learns many things—among others, to pardon."[72]

Having discovered how difficult it is to change oneself into a better person and how in the final analysis it depends largely on the luck of one's circumstances, Haya had developed tolerance for the foibles of others. Thus he had abandoned his old dream about fashioning a new human through authoritarian resocialization. Ultimately it was this change in Haya—one not likely to be forgiven by Peruvian revolutionaries who pin their hopes on schemes of the enforced remaking of human nature—that permitted Haya late in life to develop a genuine commitment to democracy and to disavow the role of the social engineer who in his hubris believes he can in short order reshape all of humanity into a uniform mold. While Haya never accomplished Peru's regeneration, in late years he did effect the only sort of miracle that really is possible, that of personal rebirth originating from within, rather than from outside coercion. As a result of his transformation, Haya was ready to assume perhaps the most important political role of his life as he presided over the sessions of Peru's 1978 constituent assembly.

The 1978 Constituent Assembly and the Death of Haya de la Torre

In June 1978, with the way smoothed for them by Haya's skills at conciliation, the military set the stage for their return to the barracks by holding elections for a constituent assembly. Apristas won the largest bloc of votes, about 36 percent of those cast, and Haya de la Torre, with some two hundred and thirty thousand ballots, drew the most popular support of any of the candidates.[73] Shortly later, garnering 66 of the 92 votes cast, Haya was elected president of the assembly. Showing an astounding "political staying power,"[74] Haya at age eighty-three accepted his first public office. In a remarkable culmination to an extraordinary life, he had come to be recognized as his nation's moral director.

The July 28, 1978, speech with which Haya convened the assembly may have been his finest hour. Renewing the commitments to many of the tenets of the early APRA program, including the uplifting of marginal social sectors and "equality of women in all fields," he called for the integration of Indo-America into a people-continent. Exhorting the delegates to produce a constitution that reconciled personal with communal interests, Haya reminded them of the four freedoms proclaimed by Franklin D. Roosevelt—which, the reader will recall, had combined individualistic with collectivist objectives; and he spoke in behalf of a National Economic Congress that would serve as the fourth branch of government and provide the balance of functional representation to the representation of individuals furnished by the traditional parliament.[75]

Toward the end of his approximately thirty-minute address, Haya struck again at the theme of continental unity. In line with this objective, Peruvians, on the one hundred fifty-seventh anniversary of their country's declaration of independence, must begin to admit limitations on national sovereignty. Without these limitations, Indo-America would remain "Balkanized" and thus vulnerable to "imperialism from whatever source."

Concluding his address, Haya stated he represented all members of the assembly. And he saluted all citizens who had sacrificed their lives to the goal of creating a Peruvian nation in which justice prevailed. In the past, the reader need scarcely be reminded, Haya had tended to reserve praise for Aprista martyrs. Now, he hailed well-intentioned Peruvians of all stripes: "I remember and render homage to all the fallen and to all the heroes, to all the parties whose men have become one with the people. It is up to us to justify the sacrifice and the hope of those who have struggled politically and socially and who, with sincerity and commitment, wished that Peru would be rebuilt upon the bases of justice and liberty."[76] In effect, Haya declared that all the martyrs and heroes of Peru's history could, by their sacrifice, bring redemption to the country. Here was a dramatic departure from the early claims that "Solo el aprismo salvará al Perú."

Even before the assembly began its plenary sessions, Haya de la Torre had begun to confer with the spokesmen of the various political persuasions represented in the body, hoping to find a basis of mutual respect and accord. Once sessions began, Haya showed, according to an observer, "the patience of a grandfather."[77] Especially with the long-winded oratory of his old-time adversaries on the Marxian left did Haya demonstrate patience without end. "They are good boys," he would say; "let them talk." Why shouldn't the delegates be long-winded, he wondered. Not having had the chance to debate political issues publicly for ten years, Peruvians of all political persuasions "had a lot to say."[78] Obese and aged, Haya had difficulty ascending the stairs into the assembly hall. Yet he endured the lengthy sessions that sometimes ended only with the first rays of dawn.

In the constituent assembly, Haya clearly manifested the change that he had undergone in the past twenty years or so. In 1955 a friend of Luis Alberto Sánchez had inquired why Haya de la Torre showed such suspiciousness of intellectuals. Sánchez, Haya's long-time and long-suffering associate, provided a fair and penetrating answer. Intellectuals, he observed, had independent opinions, and Haya tended to object to and belittle all opinions that differed from his own.[79] By 1978, however, Haya had become the complete pluralist and was able to live by, not just believe in, the starry-eyed esoteric faith that order and harmony could emerge from the wildest and widest assortment of opposites.

Finally, after eleven months of deliberation, the assembly produced its constitution. But Haya was no longer on hand. During the final months of debates, Aprista elder statesman Luis Alberto Sánchez presided over assembly sessions, for Haya was suffering from advanced lung cancer, diagnosed at Houston's M. D. Anderson Hospital in March 1979. When the constitution was finally approved at the end of June, Haya from his deathbed on July 12 could only affix a shaky signature.[80] Since his return from Houston on April 12, he had lived in seclusion in his beloved Quinta Mercedes home. Located close to Lima in Vitarte, Quinta Mercedes, which had belonged to a sister of Haya's, afforded a mixed rural-urban setting. In his last days, Haya was accompanied still by his ever-loyal secretary and comrade from Trujillo, Jorge Idiáquez, whose relationship with the jefe through the years constitutes one of Latin America's greatest sagas of friendship and love.

The constitution, which Haya had managed to sign only by dint of a supreme effort, elicited this description from Luis Alberto Sánchez: It was not, he insisted, altogether capitalist or socialist or democratic-socialist or Christian democratic or populist or communist. Instead, "as all great symphonies, it has something of everything: violin, trumpet, snare drum, and bass drum."[81] What more fitting homage could the constitutional fathers have rendered their dying president, who had liked to say, "If Bolívar was the Liberator, I am the Unifier."[82]

On July 20, Haya received the last sacraments at Quinta Mercedes.[83] With elements of the clergy having taken up the politics of the miraculous as they professed the possibility of attaining justice on earth, Haya may have found reason toward the end to bury his early animosity toward the Church, assuming that the need for a new religion no longer existed. Also at Quinta Mercedes, on the 27th, in a bedside ceremony attended by only a handful of intimates, the about-to-depart military government conferred on a gaunt and nearly comatose Haya de la Torre the decoration of the Order of the Sun in its highest grade. An unidentified reporter writing on the event for the Lima magazine *Caretas* observed: "The government seemed to interpret a vast national sentiment tending toward a reevaluation . . . of the personality of Haya de la Torre. Forty-seven years after the revolution of Trujillo and the executions at Chan-Chan, in the same month of July . . . a military government admitted the merits of the old and mortally sick enemy. In this there is something of grandeur."[84] Peruvians could indeed take pride in the bedside rite of passage from death to apotheosis.

At 10:45 on the night of August 2, Haya succumbed to cardiac arrest. On August 3, declared a day of national mourning, the coffin containing Haya's ravaged remains was conveyed to the Casa del Pueblo. Behind it filed thousands of admirers carrying red geraniums and white handkerchiefs.

On the day of mourning, Lima's newspapers presented column after column of praise for the departed leader. One of the most eloquent of the tributes appeared in *El Comercio*, the paper that for so many years following the 1935 assassination of Antonio Miró Quesada and his wife by an Aprista had specialized in fanning hatred of Haya and all his followers. *El Comercio's* anonymous editorialist lamented that Haya, "a Moses of politics," would not be on hand to enter, with his fellow citizens, "into the promised land of constitutionality and democracy to which he had so much aspired." Instead, Haya de la Torre, "who clearly figured among the greatest men his country had produced," and whose political postulates "transcend our frontiers and resonate throughout the continent that he called Indo-America," had now begun "to dialogue in the eternal regions with the greatest figures of our nation." Both a revolutionary and a democrat, the writer contended, Haya in the name of the first had spent his life pursuing the objectives of the second. Finally, the editorialist excused Haya's cult of personality. Such a cult is inescapable, he maintained, for a charismatic leader "who more than once knew how to interpret the desires and hopes of a majority of citizens."[85]

From Caracas, Bogotá, Buenos Aires, Montevideo, and other Latin American capitals leading statesmen and intellectuals rendered homage to Haya.[86] Nostalgia contributed to the eloquence of their eulogies. Well might the continent's leaders in 1979 have looked back longingly on those days of the 1920s when all had seemed possible and on a man who, up to the moment of death, had confidently anticipated deliverance through the miraculous. With the death of Haya de la Torre, a bit of the magic and the mythic disappeared from Latin America's ideological landscape. Statesmen at the end of the 1970s mourned not only the passing of Haya but also the relentless march of modernity, with its denial of miraculous solutions, of which it reminded them.

Following the solemn rituals at the Casa del Pueblo on August 3, the mourners accompanied Haya's coffin to the Miraflores Cemetery. There the intense party rivalry that only the old jefe had managed to contain during the last years of his life surfaced publicly. Luis Alberto Sánchez, doyen of Aprismo's right wing, left the cemetery before Armando Villanueva, the leader of the left wing, delivered the final farewell oration.[87] Already, the consequences of the Unifier's departure had appeared, and these consequences would contribute to the resounding defeat that Villanueva sustained at the hands of Fernando Belaúnde in the 1980 presidential election.

In the early 1980s, Haya's admirers could not point to the sort of political monument the jefe would have prized the most, for intra- and inter-party strife had intensified throughout the land, and a new group of Marxist-Maoist terrorists had begun to extend their activities from the sierra into Lima itself. However, admirers could point by the end of 1983 to a fitting artistic monument: a larger-than-life-size sculpture of the jefe, picturesquely set in a small Lima park close to where the Avenida 28 de Julio intersects with Avenida El Inca Garcilaso de la Vega (once named Avenida Wilson, but now happily rechristened to honor a Peruvian mestizo hero rather than a North American president). The sculpture's likeness to Haya is striking, and the choice of pose is alto-

Monument to Haya dedicated in December 1983. The sculptor, Miguel Baca Rossi, appears at the right. Juan Mejía Baca Archives.

gether inspired. Haya appears as the orator, his right hand raised to emphasize a point, his left hand reaching down to grasp the top of the desk or table before which he stands. More than a mere orator, Haya emerges in this pose as a Buddha-like figure, for the positioning of his arms recalls the legend of the infant Buddha pointing up with the right and down with the left arm to assert mastery over sky and earth, over worlds above and worlds below. However, rather than asserting mastery, Haya, as portrayed by sculptor Miguel Baca Rossi, symbolizes the joining in harmony of those opposites worshipped by his Indian ancestors: the world above, with its sun god Inti, and the world below, with its earth goddess Pacha Mama. Haya helped rekindle in twentieth-century Peru the reverence for duality that had inspired Indo-America's original inhabitants. It remains to be seen if this spirit will ever match the passion for exclusiveness, and for stamping out all that is "other" instead of absorbing otherness through synthesis, brought by the conquistador with his militant and intolerant brand of Christianity.

The Accomplishments of Haya and Aprismo:
A Final Assessment

The rise of Aprismo reflected, in part, the resurgent cult of spiritualism apparent in much of the Western world at the turn of the twentieth century. In the developed world, rampant spiritualism never became strong enough to threaten the dominance of empiricism in the quest for ongoing material progress. Spiritualism's resurgence did produce, however, a salutary leavening of materialistic society. It sparked, in addition, a revitalization of the arts and in general helped many people find more balanced and richer lives. In contrast, less beneficial consequences flowed from spiritualism's new wave in Peru and the rest of Indo-America. Here, a rational, empirical approach had appeared only recently and had not established intellectual hegemony; here the new faith in the supremacy of mind and spirit over matter threatened to overwhelm the currents of thought that elsewhere had contributed to material development. By spearheading the reaction against positivism and leading the revival of esoteric thought and Neoplatonism in Peru, Aprismo in its early manifestations impeded the march toward economic progress. Even Aprismo's Neoplatonism, however, was not without salutary consequences. It contributed to Indo-America's ability to resist North American cultural imperialism, with its siren call to obsessive materialism and its compulsive, even demonic, pursuit of growth—regardless of the costs exacted from nature, within and without. Suspicious of but not altogether hostile to the North's capitalist ethic, Haya's movement urged moderation in the competition for material goods and rendered homage to the limitless creative power of the spirit. Depending on the criteria used, APRA's nourishing of an esoteric tradition produced results both good and bad. In many other respects, however, the movement played a more clearly positive role. It is the positive element I choose now to emphasize, while ignoring the features—frequently conceded in the course of this book—that are blameworthy.

To many of society's most alienated sectors, Haya and Aprismo provided a sense of spiritual community; and, in a development unique in Peru's history up to that time, they bestowed this sense of spiritual community through politics. Providing a meaningful spiritual brotherhood-sisterhood for the marginal and afflicted is a task to which the Catholic Church in Peru should have, and occasionally through the years has, addressed itself. In the 1920s and '30s, however, the official Church either did not try or did not know how to fulfill this function. Ultimately the APRA, by taking upon itself a religious function, helped goad the Church into seeking new approaches for bringing spiritual wholeness to distressed persons. In recalling the Church to a part of its mission and thereby providing a reminder that throughout history functions of a religious nature are often best fulfilled by persons outside the organization of official churchs, the APRA played an important role, even if some of its utopian excesses eventually found their way into certain elements of the clergy.

However important its function in the religious realm, Aprismo's major contribution to the generation of Peruvians who reached maturity in the 1920s and '30s lay elsewhere. The significance of that contribution can, I think, best be described by an analogy drawn from psychiatry.

When an individual attempts, often unconsciously, to repress a part of the psyche, symptoms of mental distress are apt to appear, prompted (if Freud and Jung are right) by flashes of an involuntary return of the repressed. Similarly, when the dominant members of society make a collective effort, which may become so ingrained in their character as to fade from conscious awareness, to repress the social counterpart of the unconscious, i.e., the ostensibly instinctual creatures of raw nature, then society begins to show symptoms of pathology, for the repressed elements make spasmodic attempts to return from the marginality to which they have been consigned. This is how it was in Peru when the APRA appeared on the scene. Suppression of the Indians, as well as non-Indians who were stereotyped by the seekers of progress as deficient human beings comparable to aborigines, had become such an established way of life that elements within the dominant sectors had virtually ceased to be aware of the degree of repression they practiced. Furthermore, old members of privileged society, joined by an even less socially attentive array of parvenus, ignored the increasing marginalization that uneven modernization had imposed on once-accommodated sectors. The result was damaging both to the oppressors and the oppressed. Multiple symptoms of malaise appeared in Peruvian society, spawned by attempted returns of the repressed. More than any other Peruvian, Haya de la Torre through his APRA was responsible for raising consciousness by spreading awareness of the degree to which Peruvian ruling sectors had established social repression. The resulting awareness of repression lead to what may be described as "social individuation."

Jung, it will be recalled from chapter 4, equated psychic individuation with the individual's rebirth accomplished by incorporating into conscious awareness some aspect or perspective of the unconscious that had previously remained beyond the grasp of cognition.[88] Persons reborn through individuation experience a euphoric glow of wholeness. Shortly, though, they perceive that they have lifted up only a small portion of the treasure that lies at the roots of consciousness, and so they are gripped anew by feelings of incompleteness. They become aware that the dynamics of the psyche demand a never-ending repetition of individuation cycles. The process of social individuation is analogous.

Becoming aware of their social substratum in a new manner, the Peruvian establishment began to comprehend the need for social reintegration as they underwent unwelcome therapy or analysis at the hands of Haya and his Apristas. With conscience and consciousness partially awakened, ruling elites eased up ever so slightly on the repressive pressures directed against the social substratum, and they assimilated enough of the raw material lying at the roots of society to relieve at least a few of the most glaring symptoms of social pathology. Up to a point, Peru was reborn, and in the process it escaped the massive eruption from below that can sometimes virtually destroy both the individual psyche and also societies when no provision is made for the return of the repressed. But, just as the individual through individuation never attains more than an infinitesimal fraction of the overall potential of psychic wholeness or integration, so societies in their collective individuation achieve results so miniscule as to leave many unaware that the process has taken place at all. And, lest serious pathology reappear, new avenues for the return of the repressed must be provided every generation or so—as Thomas Jefferson understood in his prescient advocacy of what was, in effect, periodic social individuation.[89]

Among his generation, Haya de la Torre fostered awareness, however begrudging, of the need for some measure of social reintegration. He thereby gave a social application to his own experience of individual rebirth. At Cuzco he experienced for the first time the oceanic feeling: he became one with the suppressed elements within, and these elements he then discharged onto the Peruvian Indian as the most likely symbol of the repressed in the outside world. From then on he began to goad society into a collective act of individuation. While the way had been paved for him by Manuel González Prada and various anarchists and socialists, and while his approach was reinforced by José Carlos Mariátegui and a host of other Indianists, Haya through his uncanny skills as a propagandist and political activist was the primary agent in fostering, for a brief moment at least, a new mindset in Peru. But for that new mindset, Manuel Prado in his first term (1939–45) neither would have nor could have taken the important steps toward Indian integration that Thomas M. Davies, Jr., has described in a book of major importance.[90]

By the mid-1940s Haya and the Apristas, it is true, seemed to curtail their interest in Indians and other components of marginalized Peruvians, however much they still posed as champions of the downtrodden. Was this a betrayal, as critics have charged? Or, was it a result of a realistic understanding that no single generation will permit an unimpeded and continuous return of the repressed?

By late middle age, Haya showed himself content with the limited fruits of a regeneration process that had produced in Peruvian society an offspring that differed only in detail from the parents. He desisted from pressing on toward the millennialist goal of a change in essence. This restraint is rarely exhibited by persons with proclivities toward transcendent experiences and prophetic visions who are at the same time endowed with charismatic powers to inflame the masses. Ultimately this restraint made Haya supremely valuable to his country—although apocalyptic millennialists will continue to berate him for his restraint.

Notwithstanding his restraint after 1945, Haya bestowed guarded blessings on the 1968 revolution. Unlike many Apristas, content with the worldly privileges they had finally grasped, the jefe understood that a younger generation had to provide new conduits for the return of the repressed. It was as if he recognized the military revolution as a new generation's act of social individuation that had, by and large, to be condoned.

When Haya first appeared on the political scene, he seems to have believed that Aprismo's ideals could be largely realized through one massive miracle. At the end, he was willing to settle for a recurring series of minor miracles. Manifesting his conviction about the need for the recurring renewal of Aprismo's quest, Haya at the end bequeathed his meager worldly goods to the support of the needy children of the Party of the People.

Consistent in his fascination with regeneration mythology, even if at the close of his life he expected less dramatic consequences in any one cycle, Haya also remained steadfastly committed to the cornerstone of Aprista ideology: the historical space-time theory. Even in his last address to a major outdoor rally on May 7, 1976, he explained historical space-time once more.[91] The theory lay at the very heart of his hope to forge a new awareness in Indo-America by fusing the modern and the aboriginal mindsets. In the final analysis, Haya understood that Indo-America could achieve no true social integration until two distinct ways of reckoning time and interpreting the cosmos had been reconciled.

Above all, historical space-time rested on a relativist approach to time. The theory accepted a subjective-objective relationship in the cosmos in consequence of which the perceiver helped shape the perceived. The theory further assumed the possibility of perceiving the different layers of time existing simultaneously in an all-embracing now, which collapsed past and future and within which cycles recurred and time had no universal, linear progression. Here was the way in which American aborigines, whether south or north of the Rio Grande, traditionally thought. Haya's hopes for the rise of Indo-America rested ultimately on the possibility of encouraging the Europeanized elements of his people-continent to incorporate into their space-time perceptions the outlook of the Indian. His hopes rested also on the possibility of persuading Europeanized Americans to fuse with their modern realism the Indian's concept of reality. For the Indian, reality "includes equally and indistinguishably all that we call mental—everything that appears or exists in the mind...and behind and within all the forms and appearances of nature." Reality includes, finally, the entire realm of thought, "thinking itself out of an inner realm...into manifestations."[92]

In turn-of-the-century Peru, most members of participating society looked at the Indian and saw in him an inherited, genetic nature that rendered him inferior, a nature that probably could not be elevated even by prolonged contact with enlightened culture. Haya, on the other hand, by the time of his Cuzco experiences looked at the Indian and saw consciousness as the inherited, genetic ingredient; he saw, in short, a spiritual element, one that existed not in Cartesian isolation from but rather in holistic, interpenetrating union with the external environment, cultural and physical. Owing to the union, humans interacted in an ongoing dialectical process through which they were not only influenced by but actually exerted influence over an outer world that constituted the interpenetrating opposite of consciousness. While such inter-action with the physical environment might not result in its tangible im-provement and material enrichment, the interaction did at least result in a total life-style that, because it was whole, proved more reassuring and satisfying than the one favored by atomized moderns. Such, at least, ap-pear to have been the early musings of Haya de la Torre as he contem-plated the Indian.

Having perhaps no more than dimly intuited Indian holism as the ba-sis for the awe he felt when in the presence of Peru's native culture, even its architectural ruins at Chan-Chan, Haya during his European travels became better acquainted with the cosmology of an esoteric tradition that posited the unity of humans with the universe, of microcosm with macrocosm. Whereas modern positivist thinkers had sought to deny the connection, Indians still—or at least so Haya believed—recognized it and constructed their lives about it. During the years in Europe, Haya re-solved, as a part of his mission, to lead Peruvians back to the unalienated cosmology of the Indians and the esoteric tradition. In Europe he dis-covered that he had no need for Marxism in his quest to transcend alien-ation. From a non-Marxist perspective first suggested by Peru's Indian culture he was able to formulate a dialectical vision that foresaw transfor-mation of human life as the result of interaction among the components of a complete, unitary system made up of the interpenetrating opposites of consciousness and environment.

Haya's initial fascination with Indians set him on the road toward al-most all the major ingredients that constituted the program he devised for the spiritual-intellectual and socio-economic improvement of Indo-America. This original fascination, however, did have to be fortified and rationalized—or extrarationalized—by a more systematic immersion in a spiritualist, esoteric tradition—an ancient tradition ostensibly buttressed by quantum mechanics. It was not just esotericism and fragments of the new science that led Haya back to concepts of pre-Columbian civiliza-tion. Rather, it was the entire zeitgeist of the advanced, Western world in the early years of the twentieth century. Donald M. Lowe has noted that a perceptual revolution occurred between 1905 and 1915, with mani-festations in virtually all fields of knowledge, including science, art, liter-ature, and music. The effect of the revolution was to undermine faith in "rational linearity." Emerging in its stead was "multi-perspectivity, i.e., the perception of different perspectival relations." Lowe continues:

"With the displacement of linearity by multi-perspectivity, time, space, and the individual are no longer absolute coordinates in perception." As a result, "common sense and reason lost their unity and finally disintegrated."[93] Within the newly conceptualized cosmos, "instead of developmental order within objective space-time,...perception posits synchronic system without temporal continuity." On up to the late decades of the twentieth century, however, many persons continued to "work under the old suppositions," unable to adapt to the multi-perspectival approach that "expresses an entirely different sensibility."[94]

In Indo-America, Haya de la Torre stands in the first rank of artists and intellectuals who managed to attune themselves to the new sensibility. Among those who spent their lives actively engaged in politics, Haya's ability to intuit that the new sensibility led back to the pre-Columbian mentality and that the two, together, had somehow to complement the modern mindset while in the process avoiding heavy borrowing from Marxist insights, renders him unique. His attempt to forge a new Indo-America that incorporated along with the modern bourgeois perception the primal and the postmodern approach to apprehending the cosmos may have been chimerical. Nevertheless, this attempt helped spark a regeneration of Peruvian politics that yielded abundant fruits. At the same time, Haya's life and politics suggest that Indo-America's enduring spiritualist, esoteric tradition is a more effective stumbling block to Marxism-Leninism than the official religion of Catholicism with its tendency to denigrate nature, its preference for hierarchical stratification, and its spurning of eclecticism in favor of a lavish theology that carefully defines orthodoxy.

Challenging the precepts of positivism and of modernity in general, Haya played the leading role in introducing into Peru a political style that provided "some release from the confines of the ordinary bourgeois life," one that rendered once more respectable a concept of life in which "reality and dreams are perceived to merge and miracles are thought to be daily occurrences."[95] Through the art of politics he succeeded far more than the artists, writers, and composers of his period, whether in Peru or the rest of Indo-America or even in the capitals of the developed world, who challenged modernity by seeking to reinforce personal and societal inclinations toward fantasy. Under Haya's leadership, Aprismo helped bolster Peru's cultural authenticity, thus fulfilling the principal goal of the university reform movement. What is more, Aprismo through its populist politics exercised an influence far beyond the realm of the classrooms

During a long life, Haya de la Torre helped delay the proliferation of conventional bourgeois perceptions of reality throughout Peru. In the process he dispensed enough nonmaterial rewards to make many Peruvians welcome the delay. Thereby he worked a minor miracle. The great unanswered question this book raises is whether the miracle ultimately contributed to Peru's long-range interests.

Trading on Haya's mystical legacy at the end of Fernando Belaúnde's disastrous five-year term when Peruvians suffered the worst socio-economic problems in their modern history, Alan García Pérez carried the Aprista banner to overwhelming triumph in the 1985 presidential election. Groomed by Haya as his successor, the young, charismatic, populist, and ego-inflated García will be hard-pressed to continue the tradition of spiritualist politics.

Pushed along by runaway population increases, the Peruvian rhythm has quickened. In the past a generation and more could safely be allowed to intervene between cycles of social individuation. Now, the country demands the process every ten to fifteen years. Furthermore, six years after Haya's death Peruvians seemed less inclined to settle for psychic substitutes for the return of the socially and economically repressed. Yet the heritage of spiritualist politics facilitates only the psychic surrogates of socio-economic amelioration.

United States observers of the Haya phenomenon tend to question whether it is the politician's proper role to deal primarily in enhancing inward states, in nourishing popular culture through myth, fantasy, and ritual, while persuading followers that the world of outer reality is but a part of reality. In the Indo-American context, however, such a role has been accepted as natural and proper to the politician. Here is a major manifestation of the gulf between the two half-worlds that Haya de la Torre sought, and inevitably failed, to bridge.

Notes

Abbreviations

HAHR *Hispanic American Historical Review*

LARR *Latin American Research Review*

OC Víctor Raúl Haya de la Torre, *Obras completas*, 7 vols. (Lima, 1976–77).

Preface

1. This tale is a bit much even for Josephs, who concedes that it could be apocryphal but notes that it has contributed to making Haya a legend.

Chapter 1

1. Gloria Durán, "Dolls and Puppets as Wish-Fulfillment Symbols in Carlos Fuentes," in *Carlos Fuentes: A Critical View*, ed. Robert Brody and Charles Rossman (Austin, 1982), p. 180.

2. Ethnohistorians and chroniclers of popular religions, with Roger Bastide, Ralph Della Cava, June Nash, and Michael T. Taussig prominent in their ranks, have in recent years contributed significantly to an understanding of the mythological and the mystical, the ritualistic and the symbolical, as determinants and reflections of rural and even urban culture among marginal sectors in Latin America. John Phelan stands preeminent among several writers who have dealt with the millennialist visions of regeneration that inspired many of the first Franciscans to reach New Spain. Luis Villoro and Jacques Lafaye figure among several writers who have drawn attention to the visionary Christian occultism that contributed to the independence movement in New Spain. In his novel *The War at the End of the World*, trans. Helen R. Lane (New York, 1984), Mario Vargas Llosa deals sensitively with some of the occult and millennialist beliefs that helped spark a famous rebellion in the backlands of Brazil in the 1890s. Instances of regenerationist frenzy appearing specifically among Peruvian marginals have been recorded by Jeffrey Klaiber, Vittorio Lanternari, Juan Ossío, and Steve J. Stern. Juan Larrea, a Spanish emigré who helped found *Cuadernos Americanos* in Mexico City

296

shortly after the fall of the Second Republic, provides a suggestive instance of a link between leftist utopianism in Spain and Spanish America. He also figures among the many writers who have pointed to the surrealist visions of wholeness that inspired some of Latin America's best writers and poets, among them Peru's César Vallejo. In *Rubén Darío and the Romantic Search for Unity* (Austin, 1983), Cathy Login Jrade points to the importance of esoteric influences on Nicaragua's great writer. By and large, though, the occultism and secular chiliasm flourishing up to the present time among the rich, the powerful, and the sophisticated persons who wield political power, or aspire to do so, remain largely unexplored.

3. Porter, "Hacienda" (1934), in *The Collected Stories of Katherine Anne Porter* (New York, 1965), pp. 158–59.

4. Lately the enduring importance of the extrarational in the Native American mindset in South and Central America has received attention from a number of anthropologists and ethnohistorians, including Joseph W. Bastien, Victoria Reifler Bricker, Benjamin N. and Lore M. Colby, Alvaro Estrada, Peter Furst, James B. Greenberg, Francisco Guerra, Billie Jean Isbell, Juan Víctor Núñez del Prado Béjar, Karen B. Reed, Gerardo Reichel-Dolmatoff, James D. Sexton, Douglas Sharon, James M. Taggert, and Barbara and Dennis Tedlock. A review of some of this literature is found in Frank Salomon, "Andean Ethnology in the 1970s: A Retrospective," LARR 17 (1982), 75–128. The new field of archaeoastrology has begun to show the extent to which ancient native views of the cosmos, of time and of space, persist into the present. See, for example, Anthony F. Aveni, ed., *Native American Astronomy* (Austin, 1977); David L. Browman and Ronald A. Schwarz, eds., *Spirits, Shamans, and Stars* (The Hague, 1979); and Gary Urton, *At the Crossroads of the Earth and the Sky: An Andean Cosmology* (Austin, 1981).

5. Germán Arciniegas has described Haya as a dreamer, taken up with "his great ideas for the future of America." See Partido del Pueblo, *¿De qué vive Haya de la Torre? Documentos reveladores* (Lima, 1960), p. 23. Ricardo Luna Vegas, *Mariátegui, Haya de la Torre y la verdad histórica: La verdad en sus documentos originales; refutación de las versiones Apristas; una polémica cuya vigencia se mantiene viva* (Lima, 1978), p. 127, makes a telling point in his analysis of Haya de la Torre's *Obras completas:* in a total of 3,388 pages, Haya devoted 906 to Peru. The majority of the pages deal with Haya's thought not on national problems but on the world at large and on projected solutions for the ills of humanity in general.

6. See Aileen Kelly, *Mikhail Bakunin: A Study in the Psychology and Politics of Utopianism* (New York, 1982), pp. 291–92. On the totalitarianism inherent in Bakunin's approach and in that of utopianists like him, see also the classic biography by E. H. Carr, *Michael Bakunin* (London, 1937), as well as Arthur P. Mendel, *Michael Bakunin: Roots of Apocalypse* (New York, 1981).

7. Yates, quoted by E. H. Gombrich in his "On Frances Yates," *New York Review of Books*, March 3, 1983, p. 11.

8. According to Hyatt H. Waggoner, *American Visionary Poetry* (Baton Rouge, 1982), passim, this view of interaction is the distinguishing characteristic of visionaries.

9. Above all, Haya must be seen against a Peruvian background that is only now beginning to receive serious attention from historians. See, for example, Fernando Silva Santisteban's monograph "El pensamiento mágico-religioso en el Perú contemporáneo" in vol. 12 of *Historia del Perú*, directed and coordinated by Silva Santisteban, 12 vols. (Lima, 1980). In the same volume of this superb collection—brought to fruition after years of labor not only by Silva Santisteban and the distinguished contributors but also by the vision and patient efforts of Juan Mejía Baca, director of the firm that published the set—see Wilfredo Kapsoli Escudero, "Los movimientos populares en el Perú."

10. Haya de la Torre, who claimed to know him personally, maintained approvingly that Werner Heisenberg (winner of the Nobel Prize for physics in 1932) had gone "much further than Einstein in the matter of indeterminacy." See Eduardo Jibaja C. [pseud. Ignacio Campos], *Coloquios de Haya de La Torre* (Lima, 1977), pp. 55–56. A better mentor than Heisenberg for Haya to have followed on indeterminacy would have been Max Born. See Heinz R. Pagels, *The Cosmic Code: Quantum Physics as the Language of Nature* (New York, 1982), pp. 64–65.

11. *Caretas* (Lima), Aug. 6, 1979.

12. Robert J. Alexander, comp. and trans., *Aprismo: The Ideas and Doctrines of Víctor Raúl Haya de la Torre* (Kent, Ohio, 1973), p. 3.

13. Vasconcelos, "Política peruana," *Novedades* (Mexico City), Nov. 1948, quoted by Luis Eduardo Enríquez, *Haya de la Torre: La estafa política más grande de América* (Lima, 1951), p. 80.

14. Alberto Hidalgo, *Por qué renuncié al Apra* (Buenos Aires, 1954), pp. 24–30.

Chapter 2

1. For an excellent treatment of Peruvian economic development, 1890–1918, see Jesús Chavarría, *José Carlos Mariátegui and the Rise of Modern Peru, 1890–1930* (Albuquerque, 1979), pp. 7–21. Chavarría also discusses (pp. 21–26) some of the disruptions occasioned by rapid modernization. See also Gianfranco Bardella, *Setenta y cinco años de vida económica del Perú, 1889–1964* (Lima, 1964).

2. Eugene W. Burgess and Frederick H. Harbison, *Casa Grace in Peru* (Washington, D.C., 1954), p. 3.

3. Mira Wilkins, *The Emergence of Multinational Enterprise: American Busi-*

ness Abroad from the Colonial Era to 1914 (Cambridge, Mass., 1970), p. 176. See also Fredrick B. Pike, *The United States and the Andean Republics: Peru, Bolivia, and Ecuador* (Cambridge, Mass., 1977), pp. 143–73.

4. Luis Alberto Sánchez, *Un sudamericano en Norteamérica: Ellos y nosotros*, 2d ed. (Lima, 1968), p. 14.

5. Frederic M. Halsey, *Investments in Latin America and the British West Indies* (Washington, D.C., 1918), p. 322.

6. J. Fred Rippy, "British Investments in Paraguay, Bolivia and Peru," *Inter-American Economic Affairs* 5 (1953), pp. 43f.

7. Rosemary Thorp and Geoffrey Bertram, *Peru, 1890–1977: Growth and Policy in an Open Economy* (New York, 1978), p. 338.

8. William S. Bollinger, "The Rise of the United States in the Peruvian Economy, 1869–1921" (M.A. thesis, University of California, Los Angeles, 1971), p. 14. See also Dale William Peterson, "The Diplomatic and Commercial Relations between the United States and Peru from 1883 to 1918" (Ph.D. diss., University of Minnesota, 1969).

9. See Jesús Chavarría, "La desaparición del Perú colonial (1870–1919)," *Aportes* (Paris) 23 (1972); 138–40). On some important aspects of economic development see Benjamin S. Orlove, *Alpacas, Sheep, and Men: The Wool Export Economy and Regional Society in Southern Peru* (New York, 1977).

10. Carl F. Herbold Jr., "Peru," in *The Urban Development of Latin America, 1750–1920*, ed. Richard M. Morse (Stanford, 1971), p. 108.

11. For reliable coverage of this period see Ernesto Yepes del Castillo, "Los inicios de la expansión mercantil capitalista en el Perú (1890–1930)," in vol. 7, and Baltazar Caravedo Molinari, "Economía, producción y trabajo (Perú, Siglo XX)," in vol. 8 of *Historia del Perú*, directed and coordinated by Fernando Silva Santisteban, 12 vols. (Lima, 1980). See also Yepes del Castillo, *Peru 1820–1920: Un siglo de desarrollo capitalista* (Lima, 1972).

12. On the Peruvian positivists, see Fredrick B. Pike, *The Modern History of Peru* (London, 1967), pp. 159–68.

13. On structural binds, see F. LaMond Tullis, *Lord and Peasant in Peru: A Paradigm of Political and Social Change* (Cambridge, Mass., 1970). On the simultaneous consolidation and dislocations of the Peruvian oligarchy and its hangers-on during the early twentieth century, see Dennis L. Gilbert, "The Oligarchy and the Old Regime in Peru" (Ph.D. diss., Cornell University, 1977), esp. pp. 37–82.

14. For background on the psychological effects occasioned by modernization and its dislocations, see J. F. C. Harrison, *The Second Coming: Popular Millenarianism, 1780–1850* (New Brunswick, N.J., 1979), p. 219. See also Robert Waelder, *Progress and Revolution* (New York, 1967).

15. Eric J. Hobsbawm, *Primitive Rebels* (New York, 1965, originally published in 1959), p. 3.

16. See César Lévano, *La verdadera historia de la jornada de las ocho horas en el Perú* (Lima, 1963); and Víctor Villanueva, *El Apra en busca del poder, 1930–1940* (Lima, 1975), p. 75.

17. On the rise of labor unrest in Peru see Luis Felipe Barrientos, *Los tres sindicalismos* (Lima, 1958); Peter Blanchard, *The Origins of the Peruvian Labor Movement, 1883–1919* (Pittsburgh, 1982); Heraclio Bonilla, *Gran Bretaña y el Perú,* vol. 5: *Los mecanismos de un control económico* (Lima, 1977), the concluding volume in a valuable work describing an economy dependent on the uncertainties of world markets; Alberto Flores Galindo, *Los mineros de la Cerro de Pasco 1900–1930* (Lima, 1974; Wilfredo Kapsoli, *Las luchas obreras en el Perú, 1900–1919* (Lima, 1976); Wilfredo Kapsoli and Wilson Reátegui, *El campesinado peruano 1919–1930* (Lima, 1972); Piedad Pareja, *Anarquismo y sindicalismo en el Perú, 1904–1929* (Lima, 1978); Denis Sulmont, *El movimiento obrero en el Perú* (Lima, 1975); and Denis Sulmont, *Historia del movimiento obrero en el Perú de 1890 a 1977* (Lima, 1977).

18. On fears of "impending annihilation" among marginal Germans as a contributing factor to the rise of Hitler, see James M. Rhodes, *The Hitler Movement: A Modern Millenarian Revolution* (Stanford, 1980), pp. 193–95.

19. William G. McLoughlin, *Revivals, Awakenings, and Reform: An Essay on Religion and Social Change in America, 1607–1977* (Chicago, 1978), p. 207.

20. Victor Turner, *Dramas, Fields, and Metaphors: Symbolic Action in Human Society* (Ithaca, 1974), p. 13, passim.

21. James H. Billington, *Fire in the Minds of Men: Origins of the Revolutionary Faith* (New York, 1980), p. 429.

22. Gaius Glenn Atkins, *Modern Religious Cults and Movements* (New York, 1923), p. 223.

23. Robert Wohl, *The Generation of 1914* (Cambridge, Mass., 1979), p. 47.

24. Peter Gay's analysis of the background to the Hitler movement contains portions strikingly applicable to the post–World War I period in Peru—except that in Peru spiritualism rather than anti-Semitism emerged as a principal force directed against the established capitalist order. See Gay, *Freud, Jews, and Other Germans: Masters and Victims in Modernist Culture* (New York, 1978), esp. pp. 20–21.

25. Carleton Beals, *Fire on the Andes* (Philadelphia, 1934), p. 179. Beals writes also (pp. 176–77) of the Peruvian tendency to approach health problems through the quest for miraculous cures.

26. Alma Karlin, *The Death-Thorn: Magic, Superstitions, and Beliefs of Urban Indians and Negroes in Panama and Peru,* trans. Bernard Miall (London, 1934).

27. Wohl, *Generation of 1914,* p. 176.

28. See Franklin L. Baumer, *Modern European Thought: Continuity and*

Change in Ideas, 1600–1950 (New York, 1977), p. 370; James Webb, *The Harmonious Circle: The Lives and Work of G. I. Gurdjieff, P. D. Ouspensky, and Their Followers* (New York, 1980), p. 103; and Hayden White, *Metahistory: The Historical Imagination in Nineteenth-Century Europe* (Baltimore, 1973), pp. 331–34. Henry Pachter brilliantly discusses the hopes of German youth in the Weimar Republic for total reform and for a community that would be freed from the burdens of history and tradition and also cleansed of materialism and cynicism. This generation's fascination with Nietzsche, he contends, made them susceptible to such utopian flights of fancy and contributed to the rise of Hitler. See especially the essays "Irrationalism and the Paralysis of Reason" and "Aggression as Cultural Rebellion" in Pachter, *Weimar Études* (New York, 1983).

29. On the enormous influence of Bergson, see H. Stuart Hughes' landmark study, *Consciousness and Society: The Reorientation of European Social Thought, 1890–1930* (New York, 1958).

30. Hans L. C. Jaffé, *Pablo Picasso*, trans. Norbert Guterman (New York, [1964]), pp. 23–24.

31. Augusto Salazar Bondy, *Historia de las ideas en el Perú contemporáneo*, 2 vols. (Lima, 1965), 2:288–89.

32. Jorge Basadre, *La vida y la historia: Ensayos sobre personas, lugares y problemas* (Lima, 1975), p. 199; and Luis Alberto Sánchez, *Testimonio personal: Memorias de un peruano del siglo XX*, 4 vols. (Lima, 1969–76), 1:136–38. The two leading Bergsonians in Peru were Mariano Iberico (see his *El nuevo absoluto* [Lima, 1926]) and Alejandro O. Deustua, one of the most influential figures at the University of San Marcos.

33. See Michael Adas, *Prophets of Rebellion: Millenarian Protest Movements against the European Colonial Order* (Chapel Hill, 1979), pp. 43, 184.

34. Luis Alberto Sánchez, *Haya de la Torre o el político: Crónica de una vida sin tregua*, 2d ed. (Santiago de Chile, 1936), p. 33. On changing social and economic conditions in turn-of-the-century northern coastal Peru see the excellent study by Michael J. González, *Plantation Agriculture and Social Control in Northern Peru, 1875–1933* (Austin, 1984). See also Manuel Burga and Alberto Flores Galindo, *Apogeo y crisis de la república aristocrática: Oligarquía, aprismo y comunismo en el Perú, 1895–1932* (Lima, 1979), presenting an anti-Aprista interpretation; Lauro A. Curletti, *El problema industrial en el valle de Chicama*, 2d ed. (Lima, 1972); Peter F. Klarén, "The Social and Economic Consequences of Modernization in the Peruvian Sugar Industry, 1870–1930," in *Land and Labour in Latin America*, ed. Kenneth Duncan and Ian Rutledge (Cambridge, 1977); Pablo Macera, *Cayatlí 1875–1920: Organización del trabajo en una plantación azucarera del Perú* (Lima, 1975); Pablo Macera, *Palto: Hacendados y yanaconas del algodonal peruano (documentos 1877–1943)* (Lima, 1976); Solomon Miller, "Hacienda to Plantation in Northern Peru: The Process of Proletarianization of a

Tenant Farmer Society," in *Contemporary Change in Traditional Societies*, vol. 3: *Mexican and Peruvian Communities*, ed. Julian H. Steward (Urbana, 1976).

35. See Felipe Cossío del Pomar, *Víctor Raúl: Biografía de Haya de la Torre* (Mexico City, 1961), pp. 36–37. Like Luis Alberto Sánchez, Cossío was a close associate of Haya, although he did not play nearly as important a political role as Sánchez. Each man has written more than one biography of Haya. Taken together, their works provide some of the best insight into his life and times, even though many of the pages must be seen in the light of political propaganda. Sánchez has noted that Haya always preferred the biographical treatment rendered by Cossío, who, "as a good artist and without the restraints of objectivity from which I have always suffered," was more "systematic" in his praise. See the note with which Sánchez introduces his March 14, 1955, letter to Haya, in Víctor Raúl Haya de la Torre and Luis Alberto Sánchez, *Correspondencia, 1924–1976*, 2 vols. (Lima, 1983), 2:220.

36. Beals, *Fire on the Andes*, pp. 200–201.

37. Reminiscences of Macedonio de la Torre, quoted in Jean Franco, *César Vallejo: The Dialectics of Poetry and Silence* (New York, 1976), p. 7. On Macedonio de la Torre and his recollections of Trujillo see also Ernesto More, *Vallejo en la encrucijada del drama peruana* (Lima, 1968), p. 73. Víctor Raúl's well-to-do cousin, Macedonio became a fairly well known painter in Peru. See Alcides Spelucín, *La pintura de Macedonio de la Torre: Ensayo de estética* (Lima, 1948). Although a bit older than his cousin, Macedonio developed a fast friendship with Víctor Raúl when the two were growing up in Trujillo. Later, Macedonio became one of Haya's staunchest political partisans.

38. See Cossío, *Víctor Raúl*, pp. 19–22, and Sánchez, *Haya de la Torre*, p. 15.

39. Cossío, *Víctor Raúl*, p. 38.

40. Haya de la Torre interview with José A. Barba Caballero, Nov. 25, 1976, in Barba, *Haya de la Torre y Mariátegui frente a la historia* (Lima, 1978), p. 40.

41. Haya de la Torre interview with Steve Jay Stein, May 20, 1971, in Stein, *Populism in Peru: The Emergence of the Masses and the Politics of Social Control* (Madison, 1980), p. 134.

42. Cossío, *Víctor Raúl*, p. 49.

43. Partido Aprista Peruano, *Llamiento a la nación* (Lima, 1931), p. 4.

44. Peter E. Klarén, *Modernization, Dislocation, and Aprismo: Origins of the Peruvian Aprista Party, 1870–1932* (Austin, 1973), stresses the fear of status loss among old-line elites as a factor contributing to Haya de la Torre's founding of a populist movement of social protest. His thesis was anticipated by Liisa North, "The Origins and Growth of the APRA Party and Socio-Economic Change in Peru" (Ph.D. diss., University of California, Berkeley, 1970). Haya indignantly denied the Klarén-North thesis when the former's book, *La formación de las haciendas azucareras y los orígenes del APRA* was published in Lima in 1971. If not

convincingly, Haya took especial pains to deny the downward mobility of his family. See César Hildebrandt, "Los varios papeles de Haya," *Caretas* (Lima), Aug. 6, 1979, p. 13. Indeed, as early as 1953 Haya had expressed outrage over books by Eudocio Ravines and Luis Eduardo Enríquez that depicted his family as representative of aristocrats who had fallen on evil days. See Haya's letters of May 21, 1953, and Jan. 4, 1954, to Luis Alberto Sánchez, cited and extracted in *Literature and Politics in Latin America: An Annotated Calendar of the Luis Alberto Sánchez Correspondence, 1919–1980*, trans. and comp. Donald C. Henderson and Grace R. Pérez (University Park, Pa., 1982), pp. 249, 256. For all of Haya's protestations, the fact is that he received no inheritance from his financially struggling father, and his mother left him only some modest jewels, the proceeds from which had to be shared with his brothers and a sister. See Haya's Nov. 8, 1952, letter to Sánchez, extracted in Henderson and Pérez. *Literature and Politics*, p. 246.

45. OC, 1:205.

46. Cossío, *Víctor Raúl*, p. 51.

47. Haya revealed his antifather feelings in the exhortation he made in 1922: "Let us be different from our fathers." See Sánchez, *Haya de la Torre*, p. 77.

48. Haya de la Torre interview with Stein, Dec. 12, 1970, in Stein, *Populism in Peru*, p. 156.

49. See Robert J. Alexander, comp. and trans., *Aprismo: The Ideas and Doctrines of Víctor Raúl Haya de la Torre* (Kent, Ohio, 1973), p. 3.

50. On the significance of anarcho-syndicalism in Haya's early intellectual formation, see his "Nota prologal," OC, 1:xxiii.

51. Antenor Orrego, "Prólogo" to Alcides Spelucín, *Antología poético*, ed. Pedro Morán Obiol (Bahía Blanca, Argentina, 1971), p. 27.

52. See Alcides Spelucín, "Haya de la Torre en mi recuerdo," *APRA* (Lima) 14, no. 3 (Feb. 22, 1946): 14.

53. See Alberto Baeza Flores, *Haya de la Torre y la revolución constructiva de las Américas* (Buenos Aires, 1962), p. 169. Uncritical in its approach to Haya and Aprismo, the work nonetheless has considerable value.

54. Franco, *César Vallejo*, pp. 2–3.

55. Ibid., pp. 13–14.

56. Vallejo, quoted by Franco, ibid., p. 20.

57. Percy Murillo Garaycochea, *Historia del APRA, 1919–1945* (Lima, 1976), pp. 60–61. Written by an Aprista militant, the work contains much useful information. Murillo had access to APRA archives and cites newspaper sources profusely.

58. Orrego, "Prólogo," pp. 23–24.

59. See, for example, Alcides Spelucín's *El libro de la casa dorada* (Trujillo, Peru, 1926).

60. This theme is most clearly brought out in Spelucín's 1938 poem "Las paralelas sedientes." See Julio Galarreta González, "Alcides Spelucín, hombre y

poeta," in *Publicaciones* (Universidad Nacional Federico Villarreal, Lima) 2, no. 3 (Jan. 1977).

61. Luis Alberto Sánchez, *Apuntes para una biografía del Apra*, 3 vols. (Lima, 1978–81), 1:230.

62. Orrego, quoted by Franco, *César Vallejo*, pp. 12–13.

63. Erik H. Erikson contends that in forming identity the youth must establish some congruence between what he sees in himself "and what his sharpened awareness tells him others judge and expect him to be." See Erikson, *Young Man Luther: A Study in Psychoanalysis and History* (New York, 1958), p. 14. See also Erikson, "The Problem of Ego Identity," *Journal of the American Psychoanalytical Association* 4 (1957); 68–69.

64. Karlin, *The Death-Thorn*, pp. 60, 67.

65. Beals, *Fire on the Andes*, p. 199.

66. See OC, 4:288–310.

Chapter 3

1. Quoted in Manuel A. Capuñay, *Leguía: Vida y obra del constructador del gran Perú* (Lima, 1952), p. 151.

2. See Fredrick B. Pike, *The Modern History of Peru* (London, 1967), p. 220.

3. See Fredrick B. Pike, *The United States and the Andean Republics: Peru, Bolivia, and Ecuador* (Cambridge, Mass., 1977), p. 181.

4. Steve Jay Stein, *Populism in Peru: The Emergence of the Masses and the Politics of Social Control* (Madison, 1980), pp. 65, 70.

5. Max Winkler, *Investments of United States Capital in Latin America* (Boston, 1929), pp. 148–53.

6. Quoted in Stein, *Populism in Peru*, pp. 53–54.

7. Waldo Frank, *America Hispana: A Portrait and a Prospect* (New York, 1931), p. 163.

8. See Carl E. Schorske, *Fin-de-Siècle Vienna: Politics and Culture* (New York, 1980), pp. 24–115.

9. See the first two chapters in Baltazar Caravedo Molinari, *Burguesía e industria en el Perú, 1933–1945* (Lima, 1976).

10. Quoted by Víctor Andrés Belaúnde, *Palabras de fe* (Lima, 1952), p. 166. See also pp. 279f.

11. See editorial in *Estudios* (Lima) 1, no. 1 (July–Aug. 1928): 1–2, commenting on the founding of the Catholic University.

12. Belaúnde editorial in *Mercurio Peruano* (Lima) 1, no. 1 (July 1918): 50f.

13. See Mark Van Aken, *Pan-Hispanism: Its Origin and Development to 1866* (Berkeley, 1959).

14. Among the most prominent Peruvian Hispanists was Manuel G. Abastos.

304

See his "El Perú y España," *Mercurio Peruano* no. 28 (1920), esp. p. 269, in which he predicts Peru's return to the spiritual values of the mother country as now embodied in Hispanism. Also prominent in the Hispanism movement was Rodrigo Zárate, a Peruvian army captain stationed in Spain during World War I. See his *España y América: Proyecciones y problemas derivados de la guerra* (Madrid, 1917). See, in addition, Fredrick B. Pike, *Hispanismo, 1891–1936: Spanish Conservatives and Liberals and Their Relations with Spanish America* (Notre Dame, Ind., 1971), esp. chs. 8 and 9.

15. See Pike, *Hispanismo*, pp. 176–78.

16. See Lin Yü-sheng, *The Crisis of Chinese Consciousness: Radical Antitraditionalism in the May Fourth Era* (Madison, 1979), esp. p. 27.

17. For background material see Joseph Maier and Richard W. Weatherhead, *The Latin American University* (Albuquerque, 1979).

18. Gabriel del Mazo, *Vida de un político argentino: Convocatoria de recuerdos* (Buenos Aires, 1976), p. 79.

19. Gabriel del Mazo, *El radicalismo: Ensayo sobre su historia y doctrina*, 2d ed. (Buenos Aires, 1951), p. 221.

20. On anti-imperialism and university reform, see José Ingenieros, *Antimperialismo y nación*, ed. Oscar Terán (Mexico City, 1979). Although an elder statesman of the Argentine intellectual community, Ingenieros (d. 1925) took to the university reform movement with great enthusiasm and was hailed as one of its outstanding proponents. See also Gabriel del Mazo, comp., *La reforma universitaria*, 3d ed., 3 vols. in 1 (Lima, 1968), 1:135–50.

21. Mazo, "Una conciencia de la emancipación en desarrollo," in his *Reforma universitaria*, 3:292.

22. Gabriel del Mazo, *Reforma universitaria y cultura nacional*, 4th ed. (Buenos Aires, 1955), p. 22.

23. Mazo, *Radicalismo*, p. 215.

24. Mazo, *Vida de un político*, p. 79.

25. Héctor Ripa Alberti, "Renacimiento del espíritu argentino," in *Reforma universitaria*, comp. Mazo, 1: 196–97.

26. Quoted by Mazo, *Vida de un político*, p. 85.

27. Alberto S. Kornzaft, introduction to Mazo, *Vida de un político*, p. 10.

28. Ibid., p. 11.

29. Héctor Ripa Alberti, president of the Argentine delegation to the Congreso de Estudiantes that convened in Mexico City in 1921, quoted in *Reforma universitaria*, comp. Mazo, 3:8.

30. Mazo, *Reforma universitaria y cultura nacional*, p. 32.

31. See, for example, OC, 6:320.

32. See Mazo, *Vida de un político*, p. 215, and a 1926 article by Haya in OC, 2:236–38.

33. On Haya's role in the eight-hour strike, the importance of which is exaggerated by his partisans, see OC, 1:228–38, and Arturo Sabroso, *Réplicas proletarias* (Lima, 1934), pp. 9–13.

34. See Jorge Basadre, *La vida y la historia: Ensayos sobre personas, lugares y problemas* (Lima, 1975), pp. 135–36.

35. OC, 1:389.

36. The best account of the eight-hour strike is found in Peter Blanchard, *The Origins of the Peruvian Labor Movement, 1883–1919* (Pittsburgh, 1982).

37. See Enrique Cornejo Köster, "Crónica del movimiento estudiantil peruano," in *Reforma universitaria*, comp. Mazo, 2:11–23. An ardent Aprista, Cornejo Köster spent much of his life as an expatriate in Buenos Aires. See Luis E. Heysen, *El apóstol del APRA en Buenos Aires* (Lima, 1973).

38. Basadre, *La vida*, p. 180.

39. Ibid., p. 152.

40. The idea for popular universities had come to Haya in Trujillo in 1916. But his initial endeavors to implement the idea in his native city had ended in stark failure. See Stein, *Populism in Peru*, p. 253 n. 18.

41. See OC, 1:219–20.

42. Message of Haya de la Torre to the president of the Unión Ibero-Americana, dated Lima, May 10, 1920, published in *Unión Ibero-Americana* (Madrid), June 1920, p. 15. The guiding spirit behind Spain's Institución Libre de Enseñanza derived from a mystical and utopian movement known as krausismo. Inspired by Krausist objectives, as well as by some of the ideals of Freemasonry, the Institución sponsored university extension work through which cultural-spiritual elites sought to enhance the consciousness of the working classes. The ultimate objective seemed at least in part to be the establishment of a hierarchical social structure based on cultural and moral refinement rather than wealth. See Fredrick B. Pike, "Making the Hispanic World Safe from Democracy: Spanish Liberals and *Hispanismo*," *Review of Politics* 33 (1971): 307–322. Similar goals and purposes helped motivate the establishment in England in 1899 of "labour colleges," in which some thirty-two thousand were enrolled by 1926. See Stuart MacIntyre, *A Proletarian Science: Marxism in Britain, 1917–1933* (New York, 1980).

43. On labor ties formed by Haya and fellow intellectuals through the popular universities see Luis Alberto Sánchez, *Apuntes para una biografía del Apra*, 3 vols. (Lima, 1978–81), 1:24; and Stein, *Populism in Peru*, p. 141. On Haya and the popular universities in general see José A. Barba Caballero, *Haya de la Torre y Mariátegui frente a la historia* (Lima, 1978), p. 48; and Jeffrey Klaiber, "The Role of the González Prada Popular Universities in the Development and Formation of the Peruvian Aprista Movement" (M.A. thesis, Loyola University, Chicago, 1968). See also Klaiber's "The Popular Universities and the Origins of Aprismo, 1921–1924," *HAHR* 55 (1975): 693–715. By the time of Haya's exile in 1923, popular uni-

44. OC, 1:127. The selection was written in 1926. Haya saw in the popular universities "the living hope of the work of renovation" through which youth would accomplish the "ideal of the integral redemption of the disinherited" (ibid., 2:72).

45. Antenor Orrego, "La cruzada por la libertad del estudiante," an essay written in 1932, in *Reforma universitaria*, comp. Mazo, 3:110–11.

46. James H. Billington (writing on the phenomenon specifically in Russia and Italy), *Fire in the Minds of Men: Origins of the Revolutionary Faith* (New York, 1980), p. 453. See also pp. 404, 430.

47. Mazo, *Vida de un político*, p. 25.

48. Basadre, *La vida*, pp. 158–64, 196–97.

49. Ibid., p. 150.

50. Haya de la Torre interview, Feb. 13, 1971, in Stein, *Populism in Peru*, p. 120.

51. Grant Hilliker, *The Politics of Reform in Peru: The Aprista and Other Mass Parties of Latin America* (Baltimore, 1971), p. 85, notes that most of those leaders who gained and retained prominence in APRA "were drawn together as leaders of the university reform and protest while students in Trujillo or Lima. Their family backgrounds were not typically bourgeois, however; more than likely they resembled that of Haya de la Torre, aristocratic in tradition but reduced to modest circumstances by the political and financial upheavals of the late nineteenth century."

52. OC, 2:96–98.

53. Born in Scotland in 1889, Mackay studied at the University of Aberdeen, following which he served for eight years as an educational missionary in Latin America. He studied also in Madrid and earned a doctorate in the Faculty of Philosophy, History, and Letters at Lima's San Marcos University. Subsequently settling in Princeton, he served as president of the Princeton Theological Seminary from 1936 until his retirement in 1959. The author of thirteen books, Mackay died in 1983 at the age of ninety-four.

54. John A. Mackay, *Los intelectuales y los nuevos tiempos* (Lima, 1923), p. 25. According to Haya (OC, 2:237), Mackay was one of the few British intellectuals who genuinely understood Latin America.

55. Mackay, *Intelectuales*, p. 27.

56. Luis Alberto Sánchez, *Haya de la Torre o el político: Crónica de una vida sin tregua*, 2d ed. (Santiago de Chile, 1936), pp. 92–93.

57. Ibid., p. 82, and Cornejo Köster, "Crónica," pp. 24–25.

58. Felipe Cossío del Pomar, *Víctor Raúl: Biografía*, 2 vols. (Lima, 1969–70), 1:183–86.

59. See Barba Caballero, *Haya de la Torre y Mariátegui*, pp. 52–53, and Basadre, *La vida*, p. 189.

60. See OC, 5:214 and 7:479; Mazo, *Reforma universitaria*, 2:11; and "The Story of Haya de la Torre," *The Nation*, April 9, 1924, pp. 406–10.

61. Quoted in Stein, *Populism in Peru*, p. 145.

62. Quoted in Sánchez, *Haya de la Torre*, p. 105.

63. OC, 2:481.

64. See the discourse Haya delivered on May 7 in *Reforma Universitaria*, comp. Mazo, 3:94–95.

65. See Arrell Morgan Gibson, *The Santa Fe and Taos Colonies: Age of the Muses, 1900–1942* (Norman, 1983), pp. 207–8. Austin's thought about the American Indian arises from common assumptions shared by Haya de la Torre and by many modern Western admirers of premodern, non-Western culture. For example, Janet and Colin Bord in their book *Earth Rites* (London, 1982) contend that early man in Britain recognized, respected, and entered into beneficial union with the earth's energy forces and thereby maintained fertility in humans and in nature.

Chapter 4

1. On the local sources of Indianism in the Peruvian sierra, centering especially around Cuzco, see José Tamayo Herrera, *Historia del indigenismo cuzqueño, siglos XVI–XX* (Lima, 1980), with a valuable prologue by one of the fathers of twentieth-century Peruvian Indianism, Luis E. Valcárcel. Noting that cycles of Indianism have appeared in Cuzco since the sixteenth century, Tamayo shows how the movement gained prominence with the Escuela Cuzqueña between 1909 and 1920 and then expanded dramatically after the 1920 student congress. The twentieth-century movement had its origins in a small intelligentsia of decidedly anticlerical persuasions. Nourished by Valcárcel's vision of an Indian Renaissance, Cuzco's Indianism interacted with European currents of primitivism. On Valcárcel's role in early twentieth-century Indianism, see his *Memorias*, edited by José Matos Mar, José Deustua C., and José Luis Renique (Lima 1981). Also indispensable are Manuel Burga and Alberto Flores Galindo, "Feudalismo andino y movimientos sociales," in vol. II of *Historia del Perú*, directed and coordinated by Fernando Silva Santisteban (Lima, 1980); and Thomas M. Davies Jr., *Indian Integration in Peru: A Half Century of Experience, 1900–1948* (Lincoln, 1974).

2. See Edward Said, *Orientalism* (New York, 1978), p. 188.

3. Quoted in ibid., p. 167.

4. James H. Billington, *Fire in the Minds of Men: Origins of the Revolutionary Faith* (New York, 1980), p. 220.

5. Joseph Featherstone, "Rousseau and Modernity," *Daedalus*, Summer 1978, pp. 182–83, explains the myth of the "lost community" and "long revolution," which I prefer to call long march to avoid the connotation of circularity.

308

6. On aspects of the myth of the return to the lost community to undergo re-creation, see Meyer Howard Abrams, *Natural Supernaturalism: Tradition and Revolution in Romantic Literature* (New York, 1971), p. 225; and James George Frazer, *The Golden Bough: A Study in Magic and Religion,* abridged ed. (New York, 1922), pp. 675–76.

7. Erich Neumann, *The Origins and History of Consciousness,* trans. R. F. C. Hull (Princeton, 1970), p. 322.

8. See Ronald T. Takaki, *Iron Cages: Race and Culture in Nineteenth-Century America* (New York, 1979).

9. See Stanley Diamond, *In Search of the Primitive: A Critique of Civilization* (New Brunswick, 1974). Peru's Indianism not only reflected the turn-of-the-century Western world's cult of primitivism but also the widespread and closely related *völkisch* movement. In one manifestation of völkisch thought, eastern Jews *(Ostjuden)* became symbols of rooted, whole, authentic, communal, myth-inspired, fully alive human beings. Neoromantic Jewish thinkers contrasted the Ostjuden to Europe's acculturated Jew who purportedly had sacrificed what was noblest in humanity to the Enlightenment's positivistic and individualistic rationalism. Like Peru's Indianists, glorifiers of the Ostjuden tended to be socialists intent upon eradicating allegedly dehumanizing capitalism. See Steven E. Aschheim, *Brothers and Strangers: The East European Jew in German and German Jewish Consciousness 1880–1923* (Madison, 1982).

10. See Richard Slotkin, *Regeneration through Violence: The Mythology of the American Frontier, 1600–1860* (Middletown, Conn., 1973), p. 179.

11. Indian artist Oscar Howe quoted in *Southwest Art,* June 1982, p. 123.

12. Carl E. Schorske, *Fin-de-Siècle Vienna: Politics and Culture* (New York, 1980), p. 214.

13. Waldo Frank, *America Hispana: A Portrait and a Prospect* (New York, 1931), p. 174.

14. Typical of the "eternal" Indian school, in which the native is viewed as inherently communalist rather than individualistic, is Hildebrando Castro Pozo, "Social and Economico-Political Evolution of the Communities of Central Peru," in *Handbook of South American Indians,* vol. 2: *The Andean Civilizations,* ed. Julian H. Steward (New York, 1963), pp. 483–99. The literature that propounded this viewpoint was extensive in Peru during the 1920s and '30s. See Fredrick B. Pike, *The United States and the Andean Republics: Peru, Bolivia and Ecuador* (Cambridge, Mass., 1977), pp. 275–80. See also David Guillet, "The Individual and the Collectivity in Andean Studies," LARR 18 (1983): 240–51 (a review essay); and William Foote Whyte, "Conflict and Cooperation in Andean Communities," *American Ethnologist* 2 (1975): 373–92. See also note 52, ch. 12.

15. See Lucien Lévy-Bruhl, *How Natives Think* (London, 1926), and *Primitive Mentality* (London, 1923), both translated by Lilian A. Clare.

16. Gaius Glenn Atkins, *Modern Religious Cults and Movements* (New York, 1923), pp. 280–81.

17. In a 1917 letter to his father, Haya noted he had just finished reading Garcilaso's *Royal Commentaries* for the second time. See the anonymously edited collection, *Haya de la Torre, fundador del aprismo: Rasgos biográficos, opiniones, anecdotas: Homenaje en el Día de la Fraternidad* (Lima, 1959), p. 47. On the centrality of the Garcilaso work to the ongoing Peruvian polemic over the true nature of the Indian, see Jim Marshall Baker, "The Role of Garcilaso de la Vega el Inca in the Eighteenth-Century Debate on America" (Ph.D. diss., University of Texas, Austin, 1973).

18. Peru's early archaeologists and anthropologists were in a way forerunners of Claude Lévi-Strauss, whose fascination with anthropology derived in part from his distaste "for the century in which we are living, for the total ascendancy of man over nature, and of certain forms of humanity over others." His temperament and tastes, Lévi-Strauss confessed, carried him "towards more modest periods when there was a certain balance between man and nature, the diverse and the multiple forms of life" (E. Nelson and Tanya Hayes, eds., *Claude Lévi-Strauss: The Anthropologist as Hero* [Cambridge, Mass., 1970], p. 10).

19. OC, 2:57–59. The essay appeared originally in *Construyendo el asprismo* (Buenos Aires, 1933).

20. OC, 2:106. The quoted passage occurs in what is Haya's most notable Indianist essay. It was published originally in *¿A dónde va Indoamérica?* (Santiago de Chile, 1935). In a letter of November 1938 to Luis Alberto Sánchez, Haya referred to his constancy and pronounced it "worthy of the Indian that I carry within." See Haya de la Torre and Luis Alberto Sánchez, *Correspondencia, 1924–1976*, 2 vols. (Lima, 1983), 1:336.

21. OC, 2:109.

22. Ibid., 1:42–45.

23. See note 45, ch. 3.

24. Jung's most succinct and approachable writing on individuation is found in his *Memories, Dreams, Reflections*, trans. Richard and Clara Winston, recorded and edited by Aniela Jaffé, rev. ed. (New York, 1965), pp. 196, 209, 296, 346, 383f.

25. Romain Rolland thought highly of Jung. Hermann Keyserling not only dealt a great deal in Jungian imagery, especially in *The World in the Making*, trans. Maurice Samuel (New York, 1927), but also sought advice from the psychiatrist through correspondence when wounded in his self-esteem by Victoria Ocampo's rejection of his amatory advances. See Doris Meyer, *Victoria Ocampo: Against the Wind and the Tide* (New York, 1979), pp. 81–82.

26. Haya felt much like Arnold Toynbee vis-à-vis Jung. Toynbee, Haya notes, acknowledged that had he known Jung's works earlier, he could have spared him-

310

self a great deal of exploration on his own of the mythological and symbolical as keys to understanding history. See Haya, *Toynbee frente a los panoramas de la historia* (Buenos Aires, 1955), also in OC, 7:122.

27. The quoted passages are from Michael A. Dorris, "The Grass Still Grows, the Rivers Still Flow: Contemporary Native Americans," *Daedalus*, Spring 1981, p. 46.

28. OC, 1:188.

29. Ibid., 4:283.

30. George Leonard, *The Silent Pulse* (New York, 1978), p. 18.

31. OC, 2:56–57.

32. Quoted in Luis Alberto Sánchez, *Haya de la Torre o el político: Crónica de una vida sin tregua*, 2d ed. (Santiago de Chile, 1936), p. 165.

33. OC, 2:451.

34. Ibid, pp. 55–56. John Fisher, "Regionalism and Rebellion in Late Colonial Peru: The Aguilar-Ubalde Conspiracy of 1805," *Bibliotheca Americana* (1982): 45–59, notes a long line of millennialist rebellions in the sierra, aimed at establishing the predominance of Cuzco over Lima, of the mountains over the plains. Often the millennialist movements shared Garcilaso de la Vega's vision of Spaniards joining in perfect harmony with Indians to re-create the romanticized splendors and grandeur of the Inca past. Only the sierra, the seat of the golden community of preconquest times, could launch the country into its new golden age. Fisher provides, then, one more indication that just as Peruvians clung to one myth that posits the bloodthirstiness of the Indian and his readiness to launch a genocidal movement against the non-Indians, they also have tended through the centuries to mythologize the Indians as the source of regeneration.

35. See James M. Rhodes, *The Hitler Movement: A Modern Millenarian Revolution* (Stanford, 1980), p. 77.

36. Melvin J. Lasky, *Utopia and Revolution* (Chicago, 1976), pp. 145–56. See also W. Y. Evans-Wentz, *Cuchama and Sacred Mountains*, ed. Frank Waters and Charles L. Adams (Athens, Ohio, 1981).

37. See Barbara Haskell, *Marsden Hartley* (New York, 1980), p. 17.

38. OC, 1:61.

39. Ibid., 5:384.

40. See Sontag, *Illness as Metaphor* (New York, 1978).

41. OC, 2:55, 3:55. See also Thomas M. Davies, Jr., and Víctor Villaneuva, comps., *300 documentos para la historia del APRA* (Lima, 1978), p. 75.

42. Frank, *America Hispana*, p. 156.

43. Burr Cartwright Brundage, *Lords of Cuzco: A History and Description of the Inca People in their Final Days* (Norman, 1967), p. 11. For a stunning indication of how an idealized Cuzco fits into the archetypal model of the perfect city,

see James Dougherty, *The Fivesquare City: The City in the Religious Imagination* (Notre Dame, Ind., 1980), esp. p. 1.

44. Brundage, *Empire of the Inca* (Norman, 1963), p. 209. In the 1917 letter to his father in which he comments upon reading the *Royal Commentaries* (see no. 17, this chapter), Haya reported that he had been especially impressed by the sections on Pachacútec.

45. Eduardo Sierralta Lorca, *El Apra y la sombra* (Mexico City, 1957), p. 162. Written by a Chilean who at one time was an Aprista and an associate of Haya but who subsequently broke with the movement and its *jefe* and became a bitter critic of both, this novelistic approach to the history of Aprismo must be used with caution. By Apristas, it is dismissed as worthless, but I believe that in many of its passages it is both accurate and insightful. Jorge Basadre, moreover, finds the work reliable in many of its sections. See Basadre, *La vida y la historia: Ensayos sobre personas, lugares y problemas* (Lima, 1975), pp. 554, 575 n. 7. Apristas dismiss many of Basadre's historical assessments, regarding him as biased against their movement.

46. See Alfred Kazin, *Starting Out in the Thirties* (New York, 1980, originally published in 1965), pp. 69–70.

47. See Alvin W. Gouldner, *The Two Marxisms: Contradictions and Anomalies in the Development of Theory* (London, 1980). See also Norman Levine, *The Tragic Deception: Marx contra Engels* (Santa Barbara, 1975). Levine argues that Engels misunderstood Marx's message and accordingly reduced a humanist doctrine to a mechanistic and unilinear theory of technological determinism, opening the way for the positivistic dogmatics of the Stalinists. Somewhat related interpretations were advanced many years ago by Georg Lukács, by Erich Fromm, and by the latter's fellow members of the "Frankfurt School." For a strong argument on behalf of "hard" Marxism, which insists that history is shaped by the development of productive forces at the level of the base, see G. A. Cohen, *Karl Marx's Theory of History: A Defence* (Princeton, 1978); and William H. Shaw, *Marx's Theory of History* (London, 1978).

Works that I have found especially helpful in revealing the "soft" aspect that places Marxism within the stream of reaction *against* materialistic realism include, above all others, Robert C. Tucker, *Philosophy and Myth in Karl Marx* (Cambridge, 1961), and the following: Marshall Berman, *All That Is Solid Melts into Air: The Experience of Modernity* (New York, 1982); Katerina Clark, *The Soviet Novel: History as Ritual* (Chicago, 1981), an incredibly rich analysis that stresses, among other points, the "Neoplatonism" of high Stalinist culture and Marxism's "neo-religious doctrine" of salvation and rebirth; Russell Jacoby, *Dialectic of Defeat: Contours of Western Marxism* (New York, 1981), arguing that while thinkers such as Georg Lukács, Antonio Gramsci, and Rosa Luxemburg may have lost their political battles, they won the battle of the faith; Leszek Kolakowski, *Main Currents of Marxism: Its Rise, Growth, and Dissolution*, trans. P. S. Falla, 3 vols. (New York, 1978), a masterful account by a Polish former Marxist that often stresses the salvationist and mythological side of Marxism; Michael Levin, "Marxism and Romanticism: Marx's Debt to German Conservatism," *Political Studies* 22 (1974): 400–413; Jules Monnerot, *Sociology and Psychology of Communism*, trans. Jane Degras and Richard Rees (Boston, 1953), depicting one element of Marxism as the search for immortality by joining with the Volk, the proletariat, and thereby with what is durable and ineffable to compensate for loss of faith in individual immortality; J. L. Talmon, *The Myth of the Nation and the Vision of the Revolution: The Origins of Ideological Polarisation in the Twentieth Century* (London, 1981), showing how the Western world, following the catastrophes of World War I, was susceptible to messianic compensation and ready to grasp at two opposed "religions" promising secular redemption—communism and fascism; Arend T. van Leeuwen, *Critique of Heaven* (New York, 1972), depicting Marx largely as a romantic humanist, on the basis of the poetry he wrote as a young man; and Leonard P. Wessell Jr., *Karl Marx, Romantic Irony, and the Proletariat: The Mythopoetic Origins of Marxism* (Baton Rouge, 1979). Finally, Walter Benjamin stands as one of the most intriguing figures to find his way into Marxism through messianic mysticism. See *Philosophical Forum*, 15 (1983–84), an issue devoted to Benjamin, and especially the article by R. Triedemann, "Materialism or Messianism?" See also Gershom Scholem, *Walter Benjamin: The Story of a Friendship*, trans. Harry Zohn (New York, 1981); and Richard Wolin, *Walter Benjamin: An Aesthetic of Redemption* (New York, 1982). Martin Jay's study, *Marxism and Totality: The Adventures of a Concept from Lukács to Habermas* (Berkeley, 1984), came to hand too late for its bountiful insights to be incorporated into my text.

48. Robert C. Williams, *Artists in Revolution: Portraits of the Russian Avant-Garde, 1905–1925* (Bloomington, Ind., 1978), p. 24.

49. The "as if" philosophy, articulated by Hans Vaihinger in the latter part of the nineteenth century, sheds much light on the subjective truth value of suprarational beliefs. His major work is available in English: *The Philosophy of "As If": A System of the Theoretical, Practical, and Religious Fictions of Mankind*, trans. C. K. Ogden, 2d ed. (London, 1968).

50. Williams, *Artists in Revolution*, p. 40.

51. Ibid., p. 46.

52. Richard Whelan, "Fragments of a Shattered Dream: The Russian Avant-Garde, 1919–1930," *Portfolio*, Sept.–Oct. 1980, p. 59.

53. Kazin, *Starting Out in the Thirties*, p. 20.

54. Billington, *Fire in the Minds of Men*, p. 7.

55. Ibid., p. 254.

56. Ibid., pp. 256–57.

57. Edmund Wilson, *To the Finland Station: A Study in the Writing and Acting of History* (New York, 1940), p. 180.

58. Bruce F. Campbell, *Ancient Wisdom Revived: A History of the Theosophical Movement* (Berkeley, 1980), p. 13.

59. See Jesús Chavarría, *José Carlos Mariátegui and the Rise of Modern Peru, 1890–1930* (Albuquerque, 1979), probably the most satisfactory of the "life-and-times" books dealing with Mariátegui. Abounding in imaginative insights into Mariátegui's intellectual eclecticism that combined elements both of Marxism and Catholicism is the most recent of many valuable books by the Peruvian man of letters, Eugenio Chang-Rodríguez: *Poética e ideología en José Carlos Mariátegui* (Madrid, 1983). Mariátegui's major work has been expertly translated into English by Marjory Urquidi, with a valuable introduction by Jorge Basadre: *Seven Interpretive Essays on Peruvian Reality* (Austin, 1971).

60. See José Carlos Mariátegui, "La crisis mundial y el proletariado peruano," *Amauta* (Lima) 5, no. 30 (April–May 1930): 7–9.

61. Barbara Goodwin and Keith Taylor, *The Politics of Utopia: A Study in Theory and Practice* (London, 1982), basing part of their analysis on Karl Mannheim, argue that utopianism envisions the total transcendence of the prevailing order, which implies standing that order on its head. Consequently, utopian hopes inevitably focus on a class or a group excluded from existing society. As the most excluded of all Peruvians, Indians became the center of utopian hopes. Psychic rebirth also contains a world-turned-upside-down element, with the unconscious gaining for a moment the upper hand over consciousness.

62. See *Amauta* 2, no. 7 (March 1927): 38.

63. Wilson, *Finland Station*, p. 302.

64. José Carlos Mariátegui, review of Miguel de Unamuno, *L'agonie du christianisme*, in *Libros y Revistas* (Lima) 1, no. 3 (Sept. 1926): 3.

65. José Carlos Mariátegui, *Ediciones populares de obras completas, primera etapa* (Lima, 1959), 3:22.

66. José Carlos Mariátegui, "Defensa del marxismo," *Amauta* 3, no. 19 (Nov. 1928): 10f. See also Fredrick B. Pike, *The Modern History of Peru* (London, 1967), p. 362 n. 53.

67. See Antonio San Cristóbal-Sebastián, *Economía, educación y marxismo en Mariátegui* (Lima, 1960).

68. See Rhodes, *Hitler Movement*, pp. 74–75.

69. Luis Alberto Sánchez, *Apuntes para una biografía del Apra*, 3 vols. (Lima, 1978–81), 1:40–41. Anna Melina Graves, an American, taught at the Colegio Anglo Peruano from 1917 until 1923. She remained for many years a friend, admirer, and benefactor of Haya de la Torre. It is puzzling, therefore, that Haya in a Feb. 28, 1935, letter to Sánchez referred to her as a neurotic not to be taken seriously.

314

Three years later, nontheless, Graves took considerable pains to correspond with Haya, and as late as Sept. 29, 1953, in a letter to John Mackay at Princeton, Sánchez inquired how Miss Graves could be contacted. See Donald C. Henderson and Grace R. Pérez, trans. and comps., *Literature and Politics in Latin America: An Annotated Calendar of the Luis Alberto Sánchez Correspondence, 1919–1980* (University Park, Pa., 1982), pp. 181, 226, 309.

70. OC, 3:32–35.

71. Ibid., 2:437.

72. Ibid., 2:430–31.

73. Ibid., 3:66, 71.

74. Waldo Frank, *Aurora rusa*, trans. Julio Huici (Madrid, 1933), pp. 216–17. The work appeared originally in English as *Dawn in Russia* (New York, 1932).

75. OC, 2:436.

76. Mariátegui, review of Unamuno, p. 4.

77. Percy Murillo Garaycochea, *Historia del APRA, 1919–1945* (Lima, 1976), pp. 60–61.

78. Jack J. Roth, *The Cult of Violence: Sorel and the Sorelians* (Berkeley, 1980), pp. 17, 47. Additional clues to Marxism's appeal are provided by Régis Debray, a heretical Marxist himself, in his book *Critique of Political Reason*, trans. David Macey (New York, 1983). Debray finds that Marxism has appealed to those with penchants for millennialism, for concepts of the sacred that can vitalize secular myths, for faith rather than critical reason, and for ritual, charisma, and personality cults.

79. Haya mounted extremely strident and simplistic arguments against imperialism in a 1925 address to an anti-imperialist assembly in Paris. See OC, 1:74–75. For similar rhetoric, see OC, 1:88, 102, 110. See also "The Story of Haya de la Torre," *The Nation*, April 9, 1924, p. 410. In 1926 Haya called for the nationalization of land and industry and the organization of the economy on a socialist basis to block Yankee imperialism. See OC, 1:34. By 1928, however, he had begun to attenuate this line. See Víctor Villanueva, *La ideología pequeñoburguesa inglesa publicada en "Latin American Perspectives"* (Lima, 1977), pp. 19–23; and Ricardo Luna Vegas, *Mariátegui, Haya de la Torre y la verdad histórica: La verdad en sus documentos originales; refutación de las versiones apristas; una polémica cuya vigencia se mantiene viva* (Lima, 1978), pp. 13, passim. A one-time member of the Partido Aprista Peruano, Luna Vegas withdrew in 1954 and has subsequently been an outspoken critic. On the other hand, he is uncritical in his admiration for Mariátegui. Unfortunately many Peruvians to this day feel that they can either admire Mariátegui or Haya de la Torre and that if they approve one they must disparage the other.

80. For a succinct résumé of the last-stage, first-stage thesis on imperialism, see Haya, "Nota prologal," OC, 1:xvii; Haya de la Torre, *Ideario y acción aprista*

(Buenos Aires, 1931), esp. pp. 77–109, 129, 148, in which he quotes from his 1928 writings; and Haya de la Torre, *El antimperialismo y el Apra* (Santiago de Chile, 1935). See also Sánchez, *Apuntes*, 1:62. Haya's stance on anti-imperialism, as it actually existed and as it was perceived by apprehensive United State officials, is studied by Richard V. Salisbury, "The Middle American Exile of Víctor Raúl Haya de la Torre," *The Americas* 40 (1983): 1–16.

81. Among anti-Aprista sources mentioning the incident are César A. Guardia Mayorga, *Reconstruyendo el aprismo (Exposición i refutación de la doctrina política i filosófica hayista)* (Arequipa, 1945), pp. 94–109; and Víctor Villanueva, *El Apra en busca del poder, 1930–1940* (Lima, 1975), p. 20. Aprista Luis Alberto Sánchez touches on the matter in *Testimonio personal: Memorias de un peruano del siglo XX*, 4 vols. (Lima, 1969–76), 1:240. For a sampling of the bitterness with which communists and Marxists have attacked APRA, going back to the 1927 Brussels Congress when Haya first began to soften his anti-imperialism, see, in addition to Guardia Mayorga, Ricardo Martínez de la Torre, *Apuntes para una interpretación marxista de historia social del Perú*, 4 vols. (Lima, 1947–49); Julio Antonio Mella, *¿Qué es el APRA?* (Mexico City, 1928), an attack by a Cuban communist (subsequently assassinated in Mexico) in response to which Haya wrote *El antimperialismo y el Apra;* and Eudocio Ravines, *The Yenan Way* (New York, 1951). A friend of Haya's and an Aprista while in Europe in the mid-1920s, Ravines subsequently became a Communist and founded the Peruvian Communist Party. His book is a highly readable but grossly unfair portrayal of Haya as an out-and-out fascist. Ravines later abandoned communism and became a staunch conservative.

82. See OC, 4:esp. 84–87. In an adulatory article on Haya, Jonathan Mitchell avers that the Peruvian had become disenchanted with the Soviet Union as soon as he perceived that its political system afforded "no place for middle-class intellectuals like himself." What most impressed Haya while in Russia, according to Mitchell, was the communist hymn, the "Internationale." Haya learned it phonetically, syllable by syllable, and from that time on insisted "on breaking up whatever gathering he was in by having everyone stand up and sing the 'Internationale,' in Russian, at his direction." See Mitchell, "End of the Conquistadors," *New Republic*, Jan. 2, 1935, p. 210.

83. Haya, "Nota prologal," xxix.

84. OC, 2:58.

85. Haya "Nota prologal," xxii.

86. Sánchez, *Apuntes*, 1:56, contends that the Arielism-Marxism fusion was "perhaps the most fecund and genuine amalgam of Latin American reality at that time [i.e., the 1920s]."

87. See, for example, Eduardo Jibaja C. (pseud. Ignacio Campos), *Coloquios de Haya de la Torre* (Lima, 1977), pp. 34–35; OC, 1:366–86, 5:158–59.

88. G. D. H. Cole, *What Marx Really Meant* (London, 1934), p. 22. Cole later revised this book, publishing it in 1948 as *The Meaning of Marxism*.

89. See, for example, Haya's 1935 article "Sinopsis filosófica del aprismo," published originally in the Buenos Aires review *Claridad* and found in OC, 4:399–404. The theme is repeated in an article published in *Cuadernos Americanos* (Mexico City) 108 (1960), found in OC, 1:366–86.

90. Franklin L. Baumer, *Modern European Thought: Continuity and Change in Ideas, 1600–1950* (New York, 1977), pp. 467–70, notes that Lenin thought to strengthen Marxist claims on materialism and empirical, positivist criteria. Lenin seemed to think that Marxism maintained itself or fell on the materialistic interpretation of human conduct. But during the years 1908–25 there occurred a formidable challenge to the whole principle of the determinacy—and even the materialism—of matter. Though Lenin boasted that the majority of scientists, especially physicists, espoused materialism, Alfred North Whitehead reported just the opposite, Baumer notes.

91. Haya first adumbrated this argument in 1935 (OC, 4:399–404) and developed it in 1942 (OC, 6:168–75). See also notes 93 and 98, ch. 5.

92. Haya suggests (OC, 4:433) that in the age of new understanding, it is becoming apparent that idealism, thought, and psychological processes are on the way to overcoming materialism.

93. See Ernest G. McClain, *The Myth of Invariance* (New York, 1976), and *The Pythagorean Plato* (Stony Brook, N.Y., 1978).

94. See Mircea Eliade, *Myths, Dreams, and Mysteries*, trans. Philip Mairet (New York, 1960), p. 26.

95. Haya complained often that Peru's middle classes were being drained by foreign capitalists and their oligarchical associates. Under this assault, the middle classes were becoming ever weaker, more oppressed, and more threatened by "proletarianization." See OC, 1:153–59, 174; 4:100–101, 109. He also praised Sun Yat-sen for understanding the need for a multiclass alliance to protect the middle classes against the threat of imperialism (OC, 4:107). The remedy Haya envisaged was state capitalism, which would strengthen the endangered middle sectors (OC, 1:153–59, 174). He showed further solicitude for Indo-America's middle classes in maintaining they were in their heroic age, ready to struggle against domination by latifundistas and the grand bourgeoisie. But the struggle of the middle classes had to be controlled by the "iron discipline" of the anti-imperialist state, lest it simply release self-seeking greed (OC, 4:178–79). Late in life Haya returned to these themes, stressing it was the middle classes of Indo-America—urban and rural—who as principal victims of imperialism raised the first cry of protest ("Nota Prologal," xl).

96. Haya de la Torre, *Construyendo el aprismo* (Buenos Aires, 1933), p. 121. A central thesis of his book *El antimperialismo y el Apra* was the need for a multi-

class party to accomplish the social revolution. Haya returned to the need for a multiclass approach to social problems in a Sept. 21, 1969, speech (OC, 6:31–32).

97. See Stein Ugelvik Larsen, Gernt Hagtvet, and Jan Petter Myklebust, eds., *Who Were the Fascists: Social Roots of European Fascism* (Bergen, 1980). Many of the essays in this praiseworthy volume stress the protean nature of fascism and the impossibility of producing an inclusive, generic definition. They reveal, too, the extent to which Soviet observers have shifted away from the 1928 caricatures that Stalinists applied to fascism and are now ready to concede fascism's "progressive" features. See also Ernst Nolte, *Marxism, Fascism, Cold War* (Atlantic Highlands, N.J., 1982).

98. Alan Cassels, "Communication," *American Historical Review* 84 (1979): 1232.

99. There were, of course, adequate attractions in Marxism-Leninism for the intellectual seeking an authoritarian or even totalitarian society. On Leninist authoritarianism, see Leonard Schapiro, *The Origin of the Communist Autocracy* (Cambridge, Mass., 1955). Whether the authoritarian-totalitarian tendency inhered initially in the thinking of Marx and Engels remains a highly charged issue.

100. See A. James Gregor, "African Socialism, Socialism and Fascism: An Appraisal," *Review of Politics* 29 (1967): 324–53. Many of the insights this article provides on so-called socialism in Africa are uncannily applicable to Aprismo in Peru. See also A. James Gregor, *The Fascist Persuasion in Radical Politics* (Princeton, 1974), *Italian Fascism and Developmental Dictatorship* (Princeton, 1979), and *Young Mussolini and the Intellectual Origins of Fascism* (Berkeley, 1979). In a way, Peruvian Indianism correlated with the agrarian streak present in many European fascist movements that assailed financiers and industrialists. With paradigmatic fascism, Aprismo also shared a glorification of poetic, artistic vision as part of the repudiation of positivism.

101. Robert Wohl, *The Generation of 1914* (Cambridge, Mass., 1979), p. 176, notes that fascism "affirmed the superiority of spirit over matter, of action and instinct over thought, and of the impetuousness of youth over the vacilation and corruption of age." For Haya's comparable glorification of youth, see his *Dos cartas* (Lima, 1923), p. 26. See also OC, 1:8, 17–19, 29, 125, 126; and Rómulo Meneses, *Por el Apra (En la cárcel, al servicio del P.A.P.)* (Lima, 1933), esp. pp. 106, 109.

Chapter 5

1. Max Weber quoted by Franklin L. Baumer, *Modern European Thought: Continuity and Change in Ideas, 1600–1950* (New York, 1977), p. 477. The cult of the irrational, which Weber mistakenly believed to be on the way out, is examined in Gerald Chapple and Hans H. Schulte, eds., *The Turn of the Century: German Literature and Art, 1890–1915* (Bonn, 1981). See also Brian Inglis, *Science*

318

and *Parascience: A History of the Paranormal, 1914–1939* (London, 1984).

2. See Terence H. Qualter, *Graham Wallas and the Great Society* (New York, 1979).

3. Gershom G. Scholem, *Major Trends in Jewish Mysticism*, 3d rev. ed. (New York, 1954), p. 326.

4. See Jean Pierrot, *The Decadent Imagination: 1880–1900*, trans. Derek Coltman (Chicago, 1981). Many avant-garde thinkers associated socialism with the advent of a new age that would strike the death knell for materialism. In socialism, they found proof of evolution "toward a generalized spiritualization." See Valerie J. Fletcher, *Dreams and Nightmares: Utopian Visions in Modern Art* (Washington, D. C., 1983), p. 23.

5. Bronislaw Malinowski, *Magic, Science and Religion, and Other Essays* (New York, 1948), pp. 69–70. The essay from which the book takes its title appeared originally in 1925. See also S. F. Nadel, "Malinowski on Magic and Religion," in *Man and Culture: An Evaluation of the Work of Bronislaw Malinowski*, ed. Raymond Firth (London, 1957), esp. p. 197.

6. See Georg F. Vicedom, *The Challenge of the World Religions*, trans. Barbara and Karl Hertz (Philadelphia, 1963), pp. 99–100.

7. Bruce F. Campbell, *Ancient Wisdom Revived: A History of the Theosophical Movement* (Berkeley, 1980), pp. 36, 42.

8. On this phenomenon see Victor Turner, *Dramas, Fields, and Metaphors: Symbolic Action in Human Society* (Ithaca, 1974), p. 172.

9. See Michael Adas, *Prophets of Rebellion: Millenarian Protest Movements against the European Colonial Order* (Chapel Hill, 1979), xx.

10. The literature on Gurdjieff is vast. For a succinct account of his life and works, see James Webb, *The Harmonious Circle: The Lives and Work of G. I. Gurdjieff, P. D. Ouspensky, and Their Followers* (New York, 1980). Ouspensky met Gurdjieff in St. Petersburg, Russia, in 1915 and writes about his discipleship in *In Search of the Miraculous: Fragments of an Unknown Teaching* (New York, 1949).

11. P. D. Ouspensky quoted by Webb, *Harmonious Circle*, p. 130.

12. P. D. Ouspensky, *Tertium Organum: The Third Canon of Thought, A Key to the Enigmas of the World*, trans. Nicholas Bessaraboff and Claude Bragdon, 2d. American ed. (New York, 1922), p. 197. The work appeared initially in Russian in 1912. By 1938, the English edition of 1922 was in its thirteenth printing.

13. James H. Billington, *The Icon and the Axe: An Interpretive History of Russian Culture* (New York, 1966), p. 478.

14. Webb, *Harmonious Circle*, pp. 400–401. See also Webb, *The Occult Underground* (La Salle, Ill., 1974).

15. Ouspensky, *Tertium Organum*, p. 206.

16. Ibid., pp. 258, 314–15. For insights into turn-of-the-century English spiritualism, see Charles Howard Hinton, *A New Era of Thought* (London, 1900), and *The Fourth Dimension* (New York, 1904). Strongly spiritualist in approach is the journal edited by A. R. Orage (himself a disciple of Ouspensky and Gurdjieff), *New Age*. The journal also manifests comtemporary Nietzschean thought in England. The animating spirit behind *New Age* found expression in a 1911 article that poet Allen Upward published in the journal: "In no other age since the birth of Christianity has there been manifested the same devouring curiosity about the future, and the same disposition to expect a new earth if not a new heaven" (quoted by Fletcher, *Dreams and Nightmares*, p. 17).

17. See Jacob Leib Talmon, *Political Messianism: The Romantic Phase* (New York, 1960).

18. See L. J. Rather, *The Dream of Self Destruction: Wagner's Ring and the Modern World* (Baton Rouge, 1979); and Fritz Stern, *The Politics of Cultural Despair: A Study in the Rise of Germanic Ideology* (Berkeley, 1961), esp. pp. 97–188.

19. Campbell, *Ancient Wisdom*, p. 29. In the early 1950s, Haya quoted approvingly from James Frazer's *The Golden Bough* (OC, 4:126): "In the final analysis, magic, religion, and science are only theories of thought; and just as science has supplanted its predecessors, so, at a later time, it can be surpassed and replaced by some more perfect hypothesis."

20. Ouspensky, *Tertium Organum*, pp. 231, 233–34.

21. Alfred North Whitehead, *Science and the Modern World* (New York, 1925), p. 257. John B. Cobb Jr., *God and the World* (Philadelphia, 1969), p. 45, presents interesting material on Whitehead's belief concerning God as "the call forward," a push toward creativity, beyond our present selves and the existing world. See also Craig R. Eisendrath, *The Unifying Moment: The Psychological Philosophy of William James and Alfred North Whitehead* (Cambridge, Mass., 1971).

22. Kirk Varnadoe, "In Detail: Rodin and Balzac," *Portfolio*, May–June 1982, p. 96.

23. Bertrand Russell, *The Analysis of Matter* (London, 1927), p. 7.

24. Ibid., p. 385.

25. Ibid., p. 393.

26. See, for example, OC 6:175.

27. James Jeans, *Physics and Philosophy* (New York, 1942), pp. 215–16.

28. See Carl Friedrich von Weizsäcker, *The Unity of Nature*, trans. Francine J. Zucker (New York, 1981). The author studied with Heisenberg, and he saw the uncertainty principle not as a threat to common sense but as a welcome insight that abolished the old illusion that humans could totally separate themselves from the rest of nature. For Weizsäcker, the uncertainty principle rendered meaningless the conceptual contrast between realism and idealism.

29. Ronald W. Clark, *Einstein: The Life and Times* (New York, 1971), p. 412. Heinz R. Pagels, *The Cosmic Code: Quantum Physics as the Language of Nature* (New York, 1982), pp. 65–66, explains that it is always the same entity that is being observed or represented, whether its wavelike properties or particlelike properties are emphasized; what occurs is that two symbolic means of representing the same entity are employed.

30. Gary Zukav, *The Dancing Wu Li Masters: An Overview of the New Physics* (New York, 1979), p. 219. On the alleged connection between the new physics and spiritualism or Oriental extrarational wisdom, see Fritjof Capra, *The Tao of Physics* (New York, 1975). Zukav and Capra are two of the better-known popularizers of quantum mechanics who stress a purported connection between the new physics and the esoteric wisdom of the Orient.

31. Baumer, *Modern European Thought*, p. 462.

32. Ibid., p. 470.

33. Ibid., p. 471.

34. Pagels, *Cosmic Code*, is effective in denying an actual link between esoteric wisdom and the new physics.

35. Romain Rolland, *The Life of Ramakrishna*, vol. 1: *Ramakrishna, the Man-Gods, and the Universal Gospel of Vivekananda: A Study of Mysticism and Action in Living India* and vol. 2: *The Life of Vivekananda and the Universal Gospel*, trans. E. F. Malcolm-Smith, 7th ed. (Calcutta, 1965, originally published in 1929).

36. Rolland, *Life of Vivekananda*, p. 262.

37. The ability of man the microcosm to influence the macrocosm figures prominently in the thought of Count Hermann Keyserling, as revealed especially in his book *The Recovery of Truth*, trans. Paul Fohr in collaboration with the author (New York, 1929). The book, I believe, had a strong influence on Haya de la Torre. See note 58, this chapter.

38. Rolland, *Life of Vivekananda*, p. 341.

39. Jeremy Bernstein, "Scientific Amusements," *New York Times Book Review*, Sept. 6, 1981, p. 5.

40. Luis Eduardo Enríquez, *Haya de la Torre: La estafa política más grande de América* (Lima, 1951), p. 67. While the work, published not long after the author's abandonment of the Peruvian Aprista Party in which he had held high posts, must be used with caution, Enríquez appears to have the facts straight in relating Haya's entry into the Chilam Balam Lodge.

41. See the anonymous essay in *Boletín de Masonería Boliviana* (La Paz) 26 (1946): 80–81. In this and various other numbers the *Boletín* provides some of the best insights into Symbolical Masonry that I have encountered. See also Manly Palmer Hall, *The Secret Teaching of all Ages: An Encyclopedia Outline of Masonic, Hermetic, Qabbalistic, and Rosicrucian Symbological Philosophy* (Los

Angeles, 1945). A more recent book of enormous importance for one wishing to track down the symbolical and esoteric origins of Freemasonry is Peter Partner, *The Murdered Magicians: The Templars and Their Myth* (New York, 1982). Partner investigates the possible connection between Freemasonry and the Templars (suppressed by the papacy in 1307), who were assumed by many to have gained access to the "wisdom of the East" while serving in the Holy Land. As depicted through Partner's massive research, Freemasons emerge as ostensible bearers of eternal verities and not merely as members of a benevolent society or social club.

42. Luis Alberto Sánchez, *Apuntes para una biografía del Apra*, 3 vols. (Lima, 1978–81): 1:45, states that Rolland lured Haya away from the positivist and materialistic ideological strains of the Mexican and Russian revolutions, providing him with a healthy antidote of philosophical idealism. Actually, though, Rolland served primarily to strengthen a spiritualist strain in Haya's nature apparent already in Trujillo days and nourished by Bergson's works and by soft Marxism and Freemasonry. Moreover, it was the idealist, spiritualist strain in Mexican revolutionary ideology that seemed most to influence Haya—as well as Mexico's university youth—in the mid-1920s.

43. Martin Green, *The Challenge of the Mahatmas* (New York, 1978), pp. 210–11. While he deals primarily with Leo Tolstoy and Gandhi, Green is enormously perceptive in his treatment of Rolland. Green has expanded his treatment of Tolstoy and Gandhi in a highly original study, *Tolstoy and Gandhi, Men of Peace (A Biography)* (New York, 1982). Haya de la Torre responded to many of the same currents of anti-imperialist thought that Tolstoy and Gandhi shaped and by which they were shaped. India's anti-imperialist ideology produced considerable impact on Mexican intellectual circles in the 1920s and may, in consequence, have come to influence Haya de la Torre during his years of exile.

44. See Romain Rolland, *Mahatma Gandhi: The Man Who Became One with the Universal Being*, trans. Catherine D. Groth (New Delhi, 1968, originally published in London, 1924), pp. 17–18.

45. Rolland, *Ramakrishna*, pp. 11–12.

46. OC, 2:320–23.

47. Antenor Orrego, *El pueblo continente: Ensayos para una interpretación de la América Latina* (Santiago de Chile, 1939).

48. Quoted in Luis Alberto Sánchez, *Haya de la Torre o el político: Crónica de una vida sin tregua*, 2d ed. (Santiago de Chile, 1936), p. 113. The letter was published originally as part of a Letter-Prologue to Haya's first book, *Por la emancipación de América Latina: Artículos, mensajes, discursos, 1923–1927* (Buenos Aires, 1927). To a remarkable extent, Rolland's letter echoes the closing passage of his lengthy, mystical, and symbolical novel of regeneration, *Jean-Christophe*. See the Gilbert Cannan translation of this work in the Modern Library edition (New York, [1913?]). Children of the sun cults flourished in England and parts of Europe

in the early twentieth century. They may have reflected some of the same esoteric thought that inspired Rolland and may conceivably have influenced Haya de la Torre. See Martin Green, *Children of the Sun* (New York, 1976), esp. p. 437; Frederic V. Grunfeld, *Prophets without Honour: A Background to Freud, Kafka, Einstein, and Their World* (New York, 1979), pp. 71–73; and Thomas J. Perry, *Children of the Sun* (London, 1923).

49. Sánchez, *Apuntes*, 2:100. A picture of Haya taken in Germany in 1926 shows him with the cane (it appears to be bamboo) in hand. See the unpaginated pamphlet by Felipe Cossío del Pomar, *Datos biográficos de Haya de la Torre* (Lima, 1946). Haya lost the cane two years later in a border-crossing incident when entering El Salvador.

50. Abraham Valdelomar, *Our Children of the Sun: A Suite of Inca Legends from Peru*, trans. Merritt Moore Thompson (Carbondale, Ill., 1968), p. 22.

51. Hermann Keyserling, *The World in the Making*, trans. Maurice Samuel (New York, 1927), p. 11. A sympathetic sketch of the count is found in Roger Hinks, *The Gymnasium of the Mind: Journals 1933–1963*, ed. John Goldsmith (Salisbury, Eng., 1983), and is quoted by Stephen Spender in his review of the Hinks volume in *Times Literary Supplement*, June 29, 1984, p. 715. Keyserling's faith in the emergence of a new consciousness, reflecting the all-pervasive thought of his era in esoteric circles, is akin to the faith enthusiastically set forth by Marilyn Ferguson for a subsequent generation of believers. See Ferguson, *The Aquarian Conspiracy: Personal and Social Transformation in the 1980s* (Los Angeles, 1980).

52. Max Weber once commented on his "religious unmusicality" (quoted by Victor Turner, *The Ritual Process: Structure and Anti-structure* [Chicago, 1969], p. 6). Devotees of spiritualism and the occult, on the other hand, seem to think musically. In the works of Rolland, himself a musicologist, musical imagery is often employed to communicate mystical visions. See David Sices, *Music and the Musician in "Jean-Christophe": The Harmony of Contrasts* (New Haven, 1968). A massive literature is devoted to the ties between music and mysticism, and at least a cursory sampling of it is necessary, I believe, in order to understand the thought of Rolland, Keyserling, and Haya de la Torre. A good point of departure is provided by *The American Theosophist* 70 (1982), and *Parabola* 5 (1980), each containing valuable articles that explore the connecting links between music and mystical or extrarational thought. See also Hans Kayser, *Akróasia: The Theory of World Harmonics*, trans. Robert Lilienfeld (Boston, 1970); Ernest G. McClain, *The Pythagorean Plato: Prelude to the Song Itself* (Boulder, 1978); Wilfred Mellers, *Bach and the Dance of God* (New York, 1980); and Guy Murchie, *Music of the Spheres* (Boston, 1961).

53. Keyserling, *Recovery of Truth*, p. 6.

54. See OC, 4:513, and Robert J. Alexander, comp. and trans., *Aprismo: The Ideas and Doctrines of Víctor Raúl Haya de la Torre* (Kent, Ohio, 1973), p. 23.

Most mystics regard seven as an especially sacred or numinous number.

55. Keyserling, *Recovery of Truth*, p. 12.

56. In his 1920 *Outline of History*, Wells presented a pessimistic, cyclical viewpoint in assessing the prospects of the West, much in line with the Spenglerian view. On Spengler and his *Zeitgeist*, see Eric R. Bentley, *A Century of Hero-Worship: A Study of the Idea of Heroism in Carlyle and Nietzsche, with Notes on Wagner, Spengler, Stefan George, and D. H. Lawrence*, 2d ed., rev. (Boston, 1957); and H. Stuart Hughes, *Oswald Spengler* (New York, 1952). On the prevalence of Spenglerian concepts in Europe both immediately before and after World War I, see Franz Borkenau, *End and Beginning: On the Generations of Cultures and the Origins of the West*, ed. Richard Lowenthal (New York, 1981). Borkenau draws attention to the apocalyptic element in Spengler's thought that was typical of the era. The central concept pertained to doomed civilizations that might receive new sparks from barbarian turmoil or chaos and thereby enter upon regeneration.

57. Keryserling, *Recovery of Truth*, p. 6.

58. Those who read some of Haya's formulations of historical space-time and note how he uses his theory as the foundation for his visions of international harmony and synchronous rhythm (see OC, 1:239–41, 322–23; 4:214, 329, 376–81, 392–93, 418–19, 513; 5:368–72) and then compare this treatment to Keyserling's *Recovery of Truth*, pp. 6–30, 60–67, may share my suspicion that one of Haya's sources of inspiration was the colorful count. *The Recovery of Truth* appeared in a German edition in 1928, and Haya probably read it during the 1929–31 period of his exile, spent largely in Germany. Conceivably, the similarity in Haya's and Keyserling's approaches could derive from recourse to a common store of esoteric thought. For a masterful exposition of the main features of esotericism, see Geoffrey Ahern, "Esoteric 'New Religious Movements' and the Western Esoteric Tradition," in *Of Gods and Men: New Religious Movements in the West*, ed. Eileen Barker (Macon, Ga., 1983), pp. 165–76.

59. Robert Lawlor, "The Resounding Cosmos and the Myth of Desire," *Parabola* 5, no. 2 (1980): 78.

60. Felipe Cossío del Pomar, *Víctor Raúl: Biografía de Haya de la Torre* (Mexico City, 1961), p. 313. According to James H. Billington, *Fire in the Minds of Men: Origins of the Revolutionary Faith* (New York, 1980), pp. 100–103, Pythagoras became a favorite source of symbolism among revolutionary Masons and romantic revolutionaries in general in eighteenth-century France.

61. Isaiah Berlin, *Russian Thinkers*, ed. Henry Hardy and Aileen Kelly (New York, 1978), p. 142.

62. In many passages of *South American Meditations*, trans. Theresa Duerr (New York, 1932), Keyserling appears intent upon insulting Latin American womanhood in general. Probably this attitude arises from his pique with Victoria

324

Ocampo, an Argentine deeply involved in the mystical thought of the era, for having spurned his sexual overtures. See Ocampo, *El viajero y una de sus sombras: Keyserling en mis memorias* (Buenos Aires, 1951). See also n. 25, ch. 4.

63. Hermann Keyserling, *Meditaciones suramericanas,* trans. Luis López-Ballesteros y de Torres (Santiago de Chile, 1931), p. 59.

64. OC, 4:281.

65. Linda Dalrymple Henderson, "The Merging of Time and Space: The 'Fourth Dimension' in Russia from Ouspensky to Malevich," *Soviet Union* 5 (1978): 173. Henderson suggests that the originator of hyperspace philosophy may have been Charles Howard Hinton, an Englishman who eventually moved to the United States, where he died in 1907 after serving as an untenured professor of mathematics at Yale University. See note 16, this chapter. See also Richard Whelan, "Fragments of a Shattered Dream: The Russian Avant-Garde, 1910–1930," *Portfolio,* Sept.–Oct. 1980, pp. 54–61; and Robert C. Williams, *Artists in Revolution: Portraits of the Russian Avant-Garde, 1905–1925* (Bloomington, Ind., 1977), p. 109.

66. John Adkins Richardson, *Modern Art and Scientific Thought* (Urbana, 1971), p. 106. See also Linda Dalrymple Henderson, *The Fourth Dimension and Non-Euclidian Geometry in Modern Art* (Princeton, 1983). On the extent to which changing concepts of time and space influenced Marcel Proust, Pablo Picasso, and Sigmund Freud, among other leading figures of literature, art, and science, see Stephen Kern, *The Culture of Time and Space, 1880–1918* (Cambridge, Mass., 1983). For a summary of spiritualists' perceptions of space-time and fourth-dimension concepts, some passages of which seem almost interchangeable with portions of Haya de la Torre's works, see Rodney Collin, *The Theory of Celestial Influence: Man, the Universe, and Cosmic Mystery* (New York, 1975, originally published in 1954), esp. pp. 156–71.

67. See Ouspensky, *Tertium Organum,* p. 119.

68. Webb, *Harmonious Circle,* p. 111.

69. *Tertium Organum,* p. 252. Much of Ouspensky's analysis derived from Gurdjieff, who, "having destroyed the Newtonian world of inherited conditioning, erected an astonishing Einsteinian universe where nothing was what it seemed, and where relationships of cause and effect were blurred or rearranged in new patterns" (Webb, *Harmonious Circle,* p. 548).

70. Henderson, "Merging of Time and Space," p. 182.

71. On this, see Claude Bragdon's introduction to Ouspensky, *Tertium Organum,* pp. 3, 5. Bragdon, a leading American Theosophist, authored books such as *A Primer of Higher Space, the Fourth Dimension, to Which Is Added, Man the Square, a Higher Space Parable,* 2d ed. (New York, 1923).

72. OC, 4:411. Haya first began to write about space-time in a 1928 essay, published in 1935 in his *El antimperialismo y el Apra* (included in OC, 4:9–22). The

major work in which he set forth the ideas he had been formulating on the subject since the late 1920s is *Espacio-tiempo-histórico* (Lima, 1948), consisting of five essays and three dialogues. For an English translation of some of Haya's spacetime writings, see Alexander, *Aprismo*, pp. 34–85.

73. OC, 4:329.

74. Ibid., p. 376.

75. Ibid., p. 378.

76. Ibid., 1:322–23.

77. Ibid., 5:368–72.

78. C. G. Jung, *Psychology and the Occult*, trans. R. F. C. Hull (Princeton 1977), p. 139.

79. Cossío, *Víctor Raúl*, p. 69; OC, 5:367.

80. On Hinton, see note 65, this chapter. On the Hinton-Wells connection, see Webb, *Harmonious Circle*, p. 119.

81. Cossío, *Víctor Raúl*, p. 313.

82. See Bruce Mazlish, *The Riddle of History: The Great Speculators from Vico to Freud* (New York, 1966), p. 329. Probably Haya was drawn to Spengler because the German was what Mazlish (pp. 320–21) calls an "astrological historian." Spengler saw himself, according to Mazlish, "as the modern Kepler, drawing up the Faustian horoscope. . . . Spengler's astrological view of history is, I believe, of the greatest importance in his work. It allows him to see a cyclical movement in history—an eternal recurrence—that results from the astronomical theory of the revolutions of the heavenly bodies." On Spengler, see also note 56, this chapter. Given Haya de la Torre's interest in horoscopes, his predisposition toward eternal recurrence beliefs is understandable; this predisposition may have accounted for part of his attraction toward Spengler.

83. Clark, *Einstein*, p. 119.

84. Haya met Einstein and shook hands with him in the home of the economist Alfons Goldschmidt during the winter of 1929.

85. OC, 3:172–75.

86. Ibid., pp. 168–70. Haya seems also to have been acquainted with Einstein's article in *Encyclopaedia Britannica*, 14th ed., 11:105 (See OC, 4:402). During his underground years in the mid-1930s, Haya had his own set of the *Encyclopaedia Britannica*, sent to him by John Mackay from the United States. On this, see n. 133, ch. 8.

87. OC, 3:394.

88. Ibid., p. 171.

89. See ibid., 4:389–92.

90. See Joaquín Edwards Bello, "Asaltos y mitomanias," *La Nación* (Santiago de Chile), Dec. 27, 1943; and Enríquez, *Haya de la Torre*, p. 44.

91. OC, 1:304.

92. Ahern, "Esoteric 'New Religious Movements,' " p. 167.

93. For communist attacks against historical space-time, see: Rodney Arismendi, a prominent Uruguayan communist theoretician, *La filosofía del marxismo y señor Haya de la Torre* (Montevideo, 1946); Héctor Cordero, *Aprismo, espacio-tiempo-histórico y marxismo* (Lima, 1958), subsequently published in a revised edition as *Crítica marxista del APRA: Aprismo, espacio-tiempo-histórico y marxismo* (Lima, 1979); César D. Guardia Mayorga, *Reconstruyendo el aprismo: Exposición i refutación de la doctrina política i filosófica hayista* (Arequipa, 1945); César Jiménez, *Perú: Revolución popular o reformismo burgués* (Lima, 1980). A more restrained, though highly opaque, Marxist critique of historical space-time is found in José Leopoldo Decamilli, *El pensamiento filosófico de Haya de la Torre: Parte expositiva* (Asunción, 1969). Decamilli maintains that the fundamental point of divergence between Aprismo's ideology and Marxism arises from the fact that Haya does not actually believe in matter; instead, going back to Heraclitus for confirmation (pp. 16–17), he professes that all is movement. Decamilli further accused Haya of rejecting all absolutes of truth in consequence of his total relativism. Actually, rather than denying matter, Haya, in the esoteric tradition, refused to accept a matter-spirit dualism. And, rather than strict relativism, his position accorded with the esoteric concern for bringing all approaches to truth into some sort of harmonious unity.

94. Haya, OC 4:432, foresees the fusion of philosophy and science as heralding the dawn of a new day.

95. Ibid., p. 380.

96. Ibid., 5:337, from Haya's December 1933, Trujillo address, which is discussed in ch. 8.

97. Ibid., 4:381.

98. For Gabriel del Mazo, *Vida de un político argentino: Convocatoria de recuerdos* (Buenos Aires, 1976), pp. 220–24, historical space-time explained virtually all the fundamental puzzles of human existence and was perhaps the most monumental intellectual discovery of the modern era. Jesús Véliz Lizarraga, *Principios fundamentales del aprismo: Filosofía, doctrina y programa* (Lima, 1956), pp. 17–45, 55–64, hailed historical space-time as one of the great intellectual-scientific breakthroughs in the history of human thought.

99. Robert K. Merton, *The Sociology of Science: Theoretical and Empirical Investigations*, ed. Norman W. Storer (Chicago, 1973), pp. 263–64.

100. See n. 20, ch. 2, for reference to Victor Turner's discussion of the liminal moment.

101. Sánchez, *Haya de la Torre*, p. 123. See also the unpaginated campaign booklet *Biografía y gráficos de Haya de la Torre* (Lima, 1931), for whom no author or compiler is listed.

102. Enríquez, *Haya de la Torre*, pp. 69, 72.

103. On Haya's views that liberalism was dead, see OC 2:388–89.

104. See Sánchez, *Apuntes*, 1:231, and the anonymously edited *Haya de la Torre, fundador del aprismo: Rasgos biográficos, opiniones, anécdotas: Homenaje en el Día de la Fraternidad* (Lima, 1959), pp. 10, 42–43.

105. See G. D. H. Cole, *A Short History of the British Working Class Movement, 1789–1937*, 3 vols. in one (London 1937, originally published 1925–27), 3:23.

106. Haya, "What is the APRA?" *The Labour Monthly: A Magazine for International Labour* (London) 8 (Dec. 1926): 75–76. See also Sánchez, *Apuntes*, 1:48.

107. Cole, *Short History*, 3:24–25.

108. OC, 7:91–92.

109. See Andrew Lang, *The Making of Religion* (London, 1898).

110. Richard M. Dorson, "The Founders of British Folklore," *Times Literary Supplement* (London), July 14, 1978, p. 787.

111. Mazlish, *Riddle of History*, p. 315, describing the views of Spengler.

112. Ernest Gellner, "What Is Structuralism?" *Times Literary Supplement*, July 31, 1981, p. 881.

113. Weston La Barre, "The Clinician and the Field," in *The Making of Psychological Anthropology*, ed. George D. Spindler (Berkeley, 1978), p. 267.

114. Gellner, "What Is Structuralism?" p. 881.

115. See Weston La Barre, *The Ghost Dance: Origins of Religion*, rev. ed. (New York, 1972), pp. 31–68.

116. Malinowski, *Magic, Science and Religion*, p. 24.

117. Ibid., p. 22, and Robert Redfield's introduction to the book, p. 10.

118. OC, 3:81. Haya's observations may have arisen primarily out of his experience in Russia, where he was impressed by how the cult of the "incorruptible Lenin" was used in the manner of a resurrection myth. For perspective on this subject, see Nina Tumarkin, *Lenin Lives! The Lenin Cult in Soviet Russia* (Cambridge, Mass., 1983).

119. OC, 2:268.

120. Alfred North Whitehead, *Religion in the Making* (New York, 1960, originally published in 1926), p. 43.

121. See, for example, R. R. Marett, *The Diffusion of Culture* (Cambridge, 1927), *Faith, Hope and Charity in Primitive Religion* (New York, 1932), and *Psychology and Folk-lore* (London, 1920).

122. R. R. Marett, *Heads, Heart and Hands in Human Evolution* (New York, 1935), p. 15.

123. Ibid., pp. 13–14. Marett also argued (p. 19) that "the mind is not merely exploring experience but is literally creating it."

328

124. Ibid., p. 19.

125. See Richard V. Salisbury, "The Middle American Exile of Víctor Raúl Haya de la Torre," *The Americas* 40 (1983): 1–16.

126. See "Advertencia," the biographical sketch provided by the compilers of Haya's *Obras completas* (OC 1:x–xv). Haya's account of being refused permission to land in Panama is found in OC, 2:141–46, 157. See also Felipe Cossío del Pomar, *Haya de la Torre, el indoamericano* (Mexico City, 1939), pp. 176–77; and Sánchez, *Apuntes*, 1:104.

127. OC, 2:76.

128. John A. Mackay, *The Other Spanish Christ: A Study in the Spiritual History of Spain and South America* (New York, 1932), pp. 194, 196–97. Cossío, *Víctor Raúl*, p. 311, also relates the Haya-Mackay meeting in the outskirts of Berlin.

129. For background, see Roderick Stackelberg, *Idealism Debased: From Völkisch Ideology to National Socialism* (Kent, Ohio, 1981).

130. OC, 2:229–30.

131. Ibid., 3:224.

132. James J. Rhodes, *The Hitler Movement: A Modern Millenarian Revolution* (Stanford, 1980), p. 69.

133. La Barre, *Ghost Dance*, p. 268.

134. This is a key point in the interpretation that Rhodes presents in his masterful study, *The Hitler Movement*.

135. The most blatant charge of homosexuality came from the bombastic and unstable Alberto Hidalgo, after he broke with Haya and Aprismo. See his *Por qué renuncié al Apra* (Buenos Aires, 1954), pp. 24–30. Eduardo Sierralta Lorca, *El Apra y la sombra* (Mexico City, 1957), p. 238, notes it was widely bandied about that Haya was a homosexual *(maricón)*, but he does not necessarily seem to lend credence to the allegations. Víctor Villanueva (like Hidalgo and Sierralta, an ex-Aprista), *El Apra en busca del poder, 1930–1940* (Lima, 1975), p. 29, comments that Haya is "sexually indifferent." Perhaps with a mind to countering the homosexual allegations, Cossío, *Víctor Raúl*, p. 307, states that Haya had a sweetheart of the opposite sex while in Berlin, but he is not convincing. Cossío adds that Haya was not the typical Latin American male who in order to avoid being called maricón indulged in macho exhibitionism. In his 1948 interview with Ray Josephs, discussed in this book's preface, Haya, it will be recalled, referred cryptically to a failed romance at eighteen that ended his interest in women.

136. Ricardo Martínez de la Torre, *Fascistas y pro-nazis* (Lima, 1941), and Eudocio Ravines, *The Yenan Way* (New York, 1951), are not reliable witnesses in depicting Haya as a fascist. See n. 81, ch. 4. On Martínez de la Torre, see also Sheldon B. Liss, *Marxist Thought in Latin America* (Berkeley, 1984), pp. 138–39.

137. Luis Alberto Sánchez, *Testimonio personal: Memorias de un peruano del*

siglo XX, 4 vols. (Lima, 1969–76), 1:353. Sánchez, *Apuntes*, 1:231, mistakenly identifies August 15 as Corpus Christi.

138. Felipe Cossío del Pomar, *Víctor Raúl: Biografía*, 2 vols. (Lima, 1969–70), 1:341. (Heretofore in this chapter I have cited Cossío's one-volume *Víctor Raúl: Biografía de Haya de la Torre*, published in Mexico City in 1961.)

139. Steve Jay Stein, *Populism in Peru: The Emergence of the Masses and the Politics of Social Control* (Madison, 1980), p. 175.

140. See, for example, Samuel Ramírez de Castilla, *La anti-república, o el Congreso Económico Nacional* (Lima, 1947), p. 22. Haya himself, I believe, was conscious of the resemblance and liked to be photographed in Mussolini-like poses—though never the bare-chested pose Mussolini was known to choose.

141. See, for example, OC, 3:7–12.

142. See Enríquez, *Haya de la Torre*, p. 100; Ravines, *The Yenan Way*, p. 19; and Sánchez, *Apuntes*, 1:46–47.

143. Sánchez, *Testimonio*, 2:828.

144. Alberto Baeza Flores, *Haya de la Torre y la revolución constructiva de las Américas* (Buenos Aires, 1962), p. 150.

Chapter 6

1. This is the description of Weber's concept of legitimacy and of charisma provided by Talcott Parsons, *The Structure of Social Action*, 2 vols., 2d ed. (New York, 1968, originally 1949), 2:669. On the subject see also Arthur Schweitzer, "Theory and Political Charisma," *Comparative Studies in Society and History* 16 (1974): 150–81. For a probing and imaginative analysis of the topic, in which the case studies often seem at least partially applicable to Haya de la Torre, see Ann R. Willner, *The Spellbinders: Charismatic Political Leadership* (New Haven, 1984).

2. Lucian W. Pye on Erikson, "Personal Identity and Political Ideology," in *Psychoanalysis and History*, ed. Bruce Mazlish, rev. ed. (New York, 1971), p. 171.

3. See Franz Neumann, "Anxiety and Politics," in Neumann, *The Democratic and the Authoritarian State: Essays in Politics and Legal Theory*, ed. Herbert Marcuse (Glencoe, Ill., 1957), pp. 290–91. See also Aristide R. Zolberg, "Moments of Madness," *Politics and Society* 2 (1972): 183–207.

4. William G. McLoughlin, *Revivals, Awakenings, and Reform* (Chicago, 1978), p. 207.

5. Hugo von Hofmannsthal, quoted by Carl E. Schorske, *Fin-de-Siècle Vienna: Politics and Culture* (New York, 1979), p. 172.

6. Raoul de Roussy de Sales, *The Making of Tomorrow* (New York, 1942), p. 268.

330

7. Jung, interview with H. R. Knickerbocker, in Knickerbocker, *Is Tomorrow Hitler's?* (New York, 1941), p. 46.

8. OC, 5:342. Haya is referring to his Dec. 8, 1931, Trujullo speech.

9. Ibid, p. 154.

10. Through "consciousness raising" of the type described, a group can become subject "to the truly magical power of words." See Paul Roazen, *Freud and His Followers* (New York, 1974), p. 186.

11. Haya interview with Steve Jay Stein, Nov. 4, 1970, in Stein, *Populism in Peru: The Emergence of the Masses and the Politics of Social Control* (Madison, 1980), p. 176.

12. OC, 1:168.

13. Ibid., p. 139.

14. Ibid., p. 7.

15. Ibid., 2:98–99.

16. Alberto Hidalgo, *Diario de mi sentimiento (1922–1936)* (Buenos Aires, 1937), pp. 46–47. In this work, Hidalgo includes his 1931 article calling Haya to his destiny, as well as Haya's letter of response, much of which I have quoted in the text.

17. OC, 2:481.

18. Ibid. 7:209: letter of Dec. 4, 1932, to Juan Seoane, when both Haya and Seoane were in the Lima penitentiary.

19. Quoted by Felipe Cossío del Pomar, *Haya de la Torre, el indoamericano* (Mexico City, 1939), pp. 254–55.

20. The Arévalo incident is recounted in Percy Murillo Garaycochea, *Historia del APRA, 1919–1945* (Lima, 1976), pp. 368f. As Haya's friend and young political associate, Murillo would not have published this account without the jefe's imprimatur. On Haya's carrying the bones of Arévalo in the trunk of his automobile, see Thomas M. Davies Jr. and Víctor Villanueva, eds., *300 documentos para la historia del APRA* (Lima, 1978), pp. 19–20. See also Gustavo Valcárcel, *Apología de un hombre, Haya de la Torre* (Lima, 1945). To place the Arévalo matter in context, one must recall that throughout much of provincial Peru there still obtained the conditions described by William A. Christian Jr. in *Local Religions in Sixteenth-Century Spain* (Princeton, 1981), p. 130. In rural Castile and much of Western Europe, Christian notes, and "All through the early modern period and up to the present . . . there have been people revered while alive and venerated after death, whose bodies are seen as working miracles."

21. OC, 7:260–61.

22. Ibid., 4:281, a selection written in 1938. See also Felipe Cossío del Pomar, *Víctor Raúl: Biografía de Haya de la Torre* (Mexico City, 1961), p. 12.

23. OC, 6:13.

24. See J. F. C. Harrison, *The Second Coming: Popular Millenarianism, 1780–*

1850 (New Brunswick, 1979), p. 17. See also Abner Cohen, *Two-Dimensional Man: An Essay on the Anthropology of Power and Symbolism in Complex Society* (Berkeley, 1974), p. 17; and Bryan R. Wilson, *Magic and the Millennium: A Sociological Study of Religious Movements of Protest among Tribal and Third-World Peoples* (London, 1973), p. 499.

25. Carleton Beals, *Fire on the Andes* (Philadelphia, 1934), p. 427.

26. "The Story of Haya de la Torre," *The Nation*, April 9, 1924, p. 406.

27. OC, 1:21.

28. Orrego, quoted by Alcides Spelucín in his introduction to *El proceso Haya de la Torre*, originally published in Guayaquil in 1933, included in OC, 5:233–34.

29. Orrego, "Haya de la Torre: El hombre acción," in *Radiografía de Haya de la Torre* (Lima, 1946), p. 29. The anonymously edited pamphlet is filled with selections glorifying Haya.

30. Arturo Sabroso, with Rómulo Meneses, *Réplicas proletarias* (Lima, 1934), p. 13. The piece from which the quotation in the text is taken appeared in 1923.

31. Serafín Delmar, "Haya de la Torre," in Alberto Hidalgo et al., *Cantos de la revolución* (Lima, 1934), p. 39.

32. See the poem by Juan José Lora in ibid., p. 8.

33. See "Vals ideal," in *Cancionero aprista* (Lima, 1941). It may also be significant that companions of Haya referred to him as Wotan and as Jove. See Donald C. Henderson and Grace R. Pérez, trans., and comps., *Literature and Politics in Latin America: An Annotated Calendar of the Luis Alberto Sánchez Correspondence, 1919–1980* (University Park, Pa., 1982), pp. 323, 324.

34. Alberto Hidalgo, "Haya de la Torre en su víspera," in *Radiografía de Haya de la Torre* (Lima, 1946), p. 9.

35. Spelucín, introduction to *El proceso*, OC, 5:226.

36. Juan Seoane, *Hombres y rejas* (Santiago de Chile, 1937), p. 118.

37. Gabriel del Mazo, *Reforma universitaria y cultura nacional*, 4th ed. (Buenos Aires, 1955), p. 31.

38. Luis Alberto Sánchez, *Testimonio personal: Memorias de un peruano del siglo XX*, 4 vols. (Lima, 1969–76), 3:969–70.

39. Pablo Silva Villacorta, *¿A dónde van las ideas de Haya de la Torre? Una nueva visión sobre las ideas que conforman la doctrina del APRA* (Lima, 1966), p. 28.

40. Bruce F. Campbell, *Ancient Wisdom Revived: A History of the Theosophical Movement* (Berkeley, 1980), p. 100.

41. James George Frazer, *The Golden Bough: A Study in Magic and Religion*, abridged ed. (New York, 1922), p. 42.

42. On right and left brain hemispheres see especially Julian Jaynes, *The Origins of Consciousness in the Breakdown of the Bicameral Mind* (Boston, 1977). See also n. 93, ch. 7. Currently, hemisphere theories are being questioned.

332

43. See Volodymir Walter Odajnyk, *Jung and Politics: The Political and Social Ideas of C. G. Jung* (New York 1976), pp. 22, 163. See also Edward F. Edinger, *Ego and Archetype: Individuation and the Religious Function of the Psyche* (New York, 1972), esp. pp. 3–36.

44. Carl G. Jung, *Psychology and Alchemy*, trans. R. F. C. Hull, 2d ed. (Princeton, 1968), p. 479.

45. Ernest Becker, *The Denial of Death* (New York, 1973), p. 138, also comments on the frequency with which narcissistic personality attaches to charismatic leaders.

46. My simplified version of Kohut's analysis of narcissism is drawn largely from Paul H. Ornstein's introduction of the work that he edited, *The Search for the Self: Selected Writings of Heinz Kohut, 1950–1978*, 2 vols. (New York, 1978), vol. 1, esp. 85–90.

47. Heinz Kohut, *The Restoration of the Self* (New York, 1977), p. 6.

48. Kohut, "Creativeness, Charisma, Group Psychology: Reflections on the Self-Analysis of Freud," in *Search for the Self*, ed. Paul H. Ornstein (New York, 1978), 2:381–82.

49. Perhaps it is revealing that, according to Alcides Spelucín, Haya from an early age insisted upon playing the role of hero for his peers (Stein, *Populism in Peru*, p. 266 n. 45), evidently expecting compliance, support, and wish fulfillment from them.

50. Karen Horney, *Neurosis and Human Growth: The Struggle toward Self-Realization* (New York, 1970, originally published in 1950), p. 62.

51. Quoted by Eduardo Sierralta Lorca, *El Apra y la sombra* (Mexico City, 1957), p. 365.

52. OC, 5:156.

53. Norman Cohn, *The Pursuit of the Millennium: Revolutionary Millenarians and Mystical Anarchists of the Middle Ages*, rev. ed. (New York, 1970), p. 85, notes that those who attached themselves to a messianic prophet in many medieval millennialist movements saw themselves as a holy people: "and holy just because of their unqualified submission to the saviour and their unqualified devotion to the eschatological mission as defined by him. They were his good children and as a reward they shared in his supernatural power. It was not only that the leader deployed his power for their benefit—they themselves, so long as they clung to him, partook in that power and thereby became more than human, Saints who could neither fail nor fall."

54. Eduardo Jibaja, "Ingreso al cielo interno de Víctor Raúl Haya de la Torre" (Lima, 1945), clipped from an unidentified newspaper, probably *Trinchero Aliada*, in the Benson Latin American Collection of the University of Texas. In this remarkable piece, Jibaja expresses unadulterated adulation and reverence for the god-like Haya de la Torre.

55. Cossío, *Víctor Raúl*, pp. 37, 354.

56. Anna Kingsford and Edward Maitland, *The Perfect Way*, 3d ed. (London, 1890), pp. 333–34. Kingsford and Maitland also hailed the poet's divine personality. "Not merely he sees and examines these Rocks and Trees: these variable Waters, and these glittering Peaks. Not merely he hears this plaintive Wind, these rolling Peals: But he *is* all these: and with them—nay, *in* them—he rejoices and weeps, he shines and aspires, he sighs and thunders. And when he sings, it is not he—the Man—whose Voice is heard: it is the voice of all the Manifold Nature herself." Through his political oratory Haya, I believe, hoped to accomplish what, according to Kingsford and Maitland, the gifted poet accomplished. I first encountered the important material of *The Perfect Way* in Cathy Login Jrade, *Rubén Darío and the Romantic Search for Unity: The Modernist Recourse to the Esoteric Tradition* (Austin, 1983), pp. 74–75.

57. Orrego, quoted by Silva Villacorta, *¿A dónde van las ideas?*, p. 11.

58. Víctor Villanueva reports on his 1947 conversation with Orrego in his *La tragedia de un pueblo y de un partido: Páginas para la historia del Apra* (Santiago de Chile, 1954), p. 50. Villanueva broke with the APRA at the end of the 1940s; he is an honorable man and I believe a credible witness in this instance.

59. Ibid., p. 51. On Neoplatonic concepts of the astral spirit and how these concepts figured in the esoteric tradition, see Carolyn Merchant, *The Death of Nature* (San Francisco, 1980), pp. 119–20. On this and related matters in the esoteric tradition, see also the influential work by Edouard Schuré (b. 1841), *The Great Initiates: A Study of the Secret History of Religions*, trans. Gloria Rasberry (West Nyack, N.Y., 1961). In its earlier French editions this work influenced many Latin American modernist writers, and Haya de la Torre may well have been acquainted with it.

60. Jibaja, "Ingreso al cielo interno."

61. On Haya's interest in horoscopes, see Luis Eduardo Enríquez, *Haya de la Torre: La estafa política más grande de América* (Lima, 1951), p. 145. In the course of a lengthy 1968 interview with Guillermo Thorndike, Haya revealed that the return of Halley's Comet to proximity to the earth had helped stimulate his interest in the heavenly bodies. Halley's Comet reappeared in 1910, when Haya was fifteen. See Thorndike, "Los corazones doblan a difunto," *El Comercio* (Lima), Aug. 5, 1979.

62. Villanueva, *Tragedia de un pueblo*, p. 51.

63. Víctor Villanueva, *El Apra en busca del poder, 1930–1940* (Lima, 1975), p. 58.

64. Marc Edmund Jones, *Astrology: How and Why It Works: An Introduction to Basic Horoscopy* (Stanwood, Wash., 1974, originally published in 1969), pp. 202–203. The fact that he was a Pisces may have helped inspire Haya de la Torre's regenerationist, millenarian convictions. Many of those involved in astrology be-

334

lieved that Pisces, "the twelfth and last age in the zodiacal cycle," contained in its own dissolution the beginning of a new cycle. The sign of the new age was to be Aquarius, the Water Bearer. "Water being a symbol of the unconscious, the sign betokens the emergence from the unconscious of those contents which unified with conscious elements will lead to a union of the opposite polarities." See Frank Waters, *Mexico Mystique: The Coming Sixth World of Consciousness* (Chicago, 1975), p. 281. In order to place Haya de la Torre in the context of his times, it should be recalled that in 1930 London's *Sunday Express* began to publish weekly pieces on horoscopes. Their success touched off the flood of newspaper and popular-publications interest in astrology that has not abated over the years.

65. See Thomas Moore, *The Planets Within: Marsilio Ficino's Astrological Psychology* (Lewisburg, Pa., 1982).

66. See the Davies and Villanueva introduction to their edited book, *300 documentos*, pp. 19–20; and Sierralta, *El Apra y la sombra*, pp. 151–59.

67. Davies and Villanueva, *300 documentos*, pp. 19–20; and Sierralta, *El Apra y la sombra*, pp. 160–63. Jorge Basadre, *La vida y la historia: Ensayos sobre personas, lugares y problemas* (Lima, 1975), p. 554, confirms the incident and accepts the accuracy of the detailed description provided by Sierralta's very often true-to-life historical novel.

68. Davies and Villanueva, *300 documentos*, p. 20.

69. Writing in the *New York Times Book Review*, Oct. 5, 1980, p. 11, Paul Zweig observes: "there is a kind of obsessive fraudulence that is so passionate, so engrossing, that it imposes itself, for all intents and purposes, as fact. Freud knew that lies were often more revealing, and possessed a more satisfying scope, than mere truth-telling."

70. OC, 6:337, from the Dec. 18, 1933, Trujillo address.

71. See Luis Alberto Sánchez, "Garcilaso y Vasconcelos," *Mundial* (Lima) 364 (June 3, 1927), and *Garcilaso Inca de la Vega, primer criollo* (Santiago de Chile, 1939).

72. Sánchez, *Testimonio*, 3:973.

73. Quoted by Gabriel del Mazo, *Vida de un político argentino: Convocatoria de recuerdos* (Buenos Aires, 1976), pp. 250–51.

74. Carlos Manuel Cox, *Dinámica económica del aprismo*, 2d ed. (Lima, 1971), pp. 214–16.

75. See Carlos Manuel Cox, *Utopía y realidad en el Inca Garcilaso: Pensamiento económico, interpretación histórica* (Lima, 1965).

76. Manuel Seoane, *Las seis dimensiones de la revolución mundial* (Santiago de Chile, 1960).

77. OC, 5:336, Dec. 18, 1933, Trujillo address. Similar sentiments are expressed in the Aug. 23, 1931, Plaza de Acho address in Lima. See OC, 5:53–82.

78. Mazo, *Vida de un político*, p. 241.

79. Ibid., p. 240.

80. Ibid., pp. 241–42.

81. Antenor Orrego, El pueblo continente: Ensayos para una interpretación de la América Latina (Santiago de Chile, 1939), pp. 164, 213, 223, 224, 227.

82. Ibid., p. 175.

83. Ibid., p. 178.

84. Lucien Lévy-Bruhl, Primitive Mentality, trans. Lilian A. Clare (Boston, 1966, originally published in 1923), p. 169.

85. Ibid., pp. 98–99.

86. See Garcilaso de la Vega, el Inca, Royal Commentaries of the Incas, and General History of Peru, trans. Harold V. Livermore, 2 vols. (Austin, 1966), 1:68.

87. See Cox, Utopía, pp. 54–58.

88. See Oscar Núñez del Prado, with the collaboration of William Foote Whyte, Kuyo Chico: Applied Anthropology in an Indian Community, trans. Lucy Whyte Russo and Richard Russo (Chicago, 1973), pp. 38–39. See also Juan Víctor Núñez del Prado B., "The Supernatural World of the Quechua of Southern Peru as Seen from the Community of Qotobamba," in Native South Americans: Ethnology of the Least Known Continent, ed. Patricia J. Lyon (Boston, 1974), pp. 238–50; and Billie Jean Isbell, To Defend Ourselves: Ecology and Ritual in an Andean Village (Austin, 1978).

89. See Peter Matthiessen, "Native Earth," Parabola 6 (1981): 14; and Frank Salomon, "Andean Ethnology in the 1970s," LARR 17, no. 2 (1982), esp. pp. 88–94.

90. See James H. Billington, Fire in the Minds of Men: Origins of the Revolutionary Faith (New York, 1980), p. 103.

91. Hints of this are found in Garcilaso de la Vega's Royal Commentaries, although el Inca, good Christian that he professed to be, stopped far short of the implications reached by late descendants of the Incas and by Indianists in general. On aspects of Andean messianism and millennialism through the ages see: Jeffrey Klaiber, "The Posthumous Christianization of the Inca Empire in Colonial Peru," Journal of the History of Ideas 37 (1976): 507–20, and Religion and Revolution in Peru, 1824–1976 (Notre Dame, Ind., 1979), esp. pp. 6–67; Vittorio Lanternari, The Religions of the Oppressed: A Study of Modern Messianic Cults, trans. Lisa Sergio (New York, 1963), and "Nativistic and Socio-Religious Movements: A Reconsideration," Comparative Studies in Society and History 16 (1974): 483–503; Mercedes López-Baralt, "Millenarism as Liminality: An Interpretation of the Andean Myth of Inkarrí," Point of Contact 6 (1979): 65–82; Juan M. Ossio A., ed., Ideología mesiánica del mundo andino (Lima, 1973); Steve J. Stern, Peru's Indian Peoples and the Challenge of Spanish Conquest: Huamanga to 1640 (Madison, 1982). See also James Mooney, The Ghost-Dance Religion and the Sioux Outbreak of 1890, abridged and edited by Anthony F. C. Wallace (Chicago, 1965). Wallace writes (p. 1): "What tribe or people has not had its golden age, be-

fore Pandora's box was loosed, when women were nymphs and dryads and men were gods and heroes? And when the race lies crushed and groaning beneath the alien yoke, how natural is the dream of a redeemer, an Arthur, who shall return from exile or awake from some long sleep to drive out the usurper and win back for his people what they have lost. The hope becomes a faith and the faith becomes the creed of . . . prophets, until the hero is a god and the dream a religion, looking to some great miracle of nature for its culmination." In addition, see Anthony F. C. Wallace, "Revitalization Movements," *American Anthropologist* 58 (1956): 264–81.

92. See Luis Heysen, *Yo soy un Túpac* (Lima, 1962). Through Masonry, Heysen maintained, people can "discover the spiritual powers that reside, even if sleeping, in their being" (p. 5). While in exile in Chile in the 1930s, Manuel Seoane became a Mason (Enríquez, *Haya de la Torre*, p. 52), and Luis Alberto Sánchez was initiated in 1925 into the Lima Lodge "Virtud y Unión, Número 3." Through Masonry, Sánchez attests, he learned discipline and solidarity and to be "more humane and amply ritualistic" (*Testimonio*, 1:226). Much of the crucial work of organizing and disciplining the Peruvian Aprista Party for the 1931 election was entrusted to José Antonio Genit, a Mason who later became Grand Master "of the principal Masonic Lodge in Peru" (Murillo, *Historia del APRA*, p. 121).

93. On Túpac Amaru see Leon G. Campbell, "Recent Research on Andean Peasant Revolts, 1750–1820," LARR 14, no. 1 (1979), esp. pp. 7–22, and "Social Structure of the Túpac Amaru Army in Cuzco, 1780–81," HAHR 61 (1981): 675–93.

94. See Magda Portal, *El aprismo y la mujer* (Lima, 1933), p. 10. Since women suffered a degree of inequality far more intense than their "male comrades," Portal argued, any revolutionary movement had to be primarily concerned with women. One of Peru's greatest Indianist writers was José María Arguedas, who committed suicide in 1969. Coming to Lima in the 1930s, Arguedas saw a clear connection between the liberation of Indians and of women. This theme forms one of the central messages of his moving novel *Deep Rivers*, trans. Frances Horning Barraclough (Austin, 1978). Moreover, Stephen Jay Gould, in *The Panda's Thumb: More Reflections in Natural History* (New York, 1980), p. 158, notes that women are characteristically lumped together, by males, with all the human species—Indians included—that have not yet evolved adequately from nature toward culture. In view of this, Gould concludes: "I do not regard as empty rhetoric the claim that women's battles are fought" for all of society's underlings.

95. Portal, *Aprismo*, pp. 41–43, 48–49. See also Marie Marmo Mullaney, *Revolutionary Women: Gender and the Socialist Revolutionary Role* (New York, 1983). Many of the insights Mullaney provides in her study of five female revolutionaries (Eleanor Marx, Aleksandra Kollantai, Rosa Luxemburg, Angelica Balabanoff, and Dolores Ibarurri) seem applicable also to Magda Portal. The revolutionary woman, according to Mullaney, is motivated by a "craving for free-

dom and independence" (p. 249)—perhaps a somewhat romanticized interpretation of the feminine psyche that is used to distinguish it from the masculine
psyche that drives the revolutionary male to seek power over others. Women revolutionaries, according to Mullaney, tend to be self-effacing and self-sacrificing,
ready to defer to the will of the masses; they are able, when they occupy positions
of power, to exercise authority in an egalitarian way (p. 251). When Portal eventually broke with Aprismo, it was partly on the grounds that Haya had established a
hierarchical, patriarchal party structure that betrayed his early liberationist message. See below, note 103.

96. Portal, *Aprismo*, p. 44.

97. Ibid., pp. 51–54.

98. For the most elementary and succinct description of anima and animus,
see Carl G. Jung, *Memories, Dreams, Reflections*, trans. Richard and Clara Winston, recorded and edited by Aniela Jaffé (New York, 1963), pp. 186f.

99. See Elaine Pagels, *The Gnostic Gospels* (New York, 1979), pp. 80–81.

100. OC, 2:37. Moreover, while in England, Haya may have been struck by
the fact that homosexuals such as Edward Carpenter assumed a natural affinity
between the establishment of rights for women and rights for homosexuals. On
this matter see John Ryle, "Visions of Inversion," *Times Literary Supplement*,
Jan. 25, 1985, p. 95, a review of some of the republished writings of Carpenter (d.
1929).

101. Heysen, *El ABC de la peruanización del Perú* (Lima, 1932), pp. 20–21.

102. Rómulo Meneses, *Aprismo feminino peruano* (Lima, 1934).

103. Haya, before long, was perceived to have a misogynist streak. See Davies
and Villanueva, *300 documentos*, pp. 277, 296. Especially after 1945, Haya did appear inclined to reduce women to subordinate positions within APRA ranks. This
was a contributing factor, but only one among several, that precipitated Portal's
break with the party. See her *¿Quienes traicionaron al pueblo? A los apristas*
(Lima, 1950).

104. In a statement certainly applicable to Peru in the early 1930s, Waldo
Frank, in *America Hispana: A Portrait and a Prospect* (New York, 1931), p. 313, observed: "Rome was always inclined to suppress and persecute its pietistic and
neo-Platonic mystics...." And Pope Leo XIII (1878–1903) in his encyclical *Hu-
manum Genus* had looked upon Masonry as the great center of occult movements and of spiritualist beliefs inimical to the Catholic faith. Apparently he also
saw a connection, one widely and wildly denounced in the early twentieth century, between Masonry, communism, and socialism. Such a connection appeared
beyond question to Peruvian conservatives in the 1930s. Moreover, the APRA's
links to anarcho-syndicalism through its labor connections further incited Catholic suspicions. Another source of contention lay in APRA's advocacy of a totally
state controlled educational structure and of separation of church and state. See

Partido Aprista Peruano, *Programa mínimo* (Lima, 1931), p. 5. Yet another difficulty in the eyes of church officials was Aprista glorification of the nineteenth-century defrocked priest and Mason, Francisco de Paula González Vigil. See OC, 5:207, and Fredrick B. Pike, "Heresy, Real and Alleged, in Peru: An Aspect of the Conservative-Liberal Struggle, 1830–1875, HAHR 47 (1967): 50–74. For background, see Judith Walker, "The Influence of González Prada on the Attitudes toward Religion of Mariátegui and Haya de la Torre," in *Religion in Latin American Life and Literature*, ed. Lyle C. Brown and William F. Cooper (Waco, Tex., 1980).

105. The quoted words are from Gershom Scholem, *Sabbatai Sevi: The Mystical Messiah, 1626–1676*, trans. R. J. Zwi Werblowsky (Princeton, 1973), p. 513, and apply to a seventeenth-century messianic movement. Just as accurately, they could be applied to dozens of other messianic movements, including the APRA.

Chapter 7

1. OC, 3:81.

2. Quoted by Jack J. Roth, *The Cult of Violence: Sorel and the Sorelians* (Berkeley, 1980), p. 22.

3. See Brian H. Smith, "Religion and Social Change: Classical Theories and New Formulations in the Context of Recent Developments in Latin America," LARR 10, no. 2 (1975): 23. See also Philip E. Berryman, "Popular Catholicism in Latin America," *Cross Currents* 21 (1971): 284–301.

4. Victor Brombert, "Perfecting the Art of Deviation," *Times Literary Supplement* (London), July 16, 1982, p. 769, observes that the spiritualist vogue in turn-of-the-century Europe must be seen in part as a stubborn though disguised "nostalgia for a religious faith." The observation is applicable also to Peru in the 1930s.

5. Eric Voegelin, *The New Science of Politics: An Introduction* (Chicago, 1952), pp. 130–37.

6. See Mario Peláez Bazán, *Haya de la Torre y la unidad de América Latina* (Lima, 1977), pp. 437–39.

7. On Haya's use of religious imagery, see Jeffrey L. Klaiber, "Religion and Revolution in Peru: 1920–1945," *The Americas* 31 (1975), esp. pp. 306–7; and Steve Jay Stein, *Populism in Peru: The Emergence of the Masses and the Politics of Social Control* (Madison, 1980), p. 265 n. 36.

8. For the Lima address, see OC, 5, esp. p. 158.

9. Ibid., pp. 332–33.

10. Ibid., p. 333.

11. Víctor Villanueva, *El Apra en busca del poder, 1930–1940* (Lima, 1975), p. 18.

12. Luis F. de las Casas, "Haya de la Torre: Su vida y su obra," in the anonymously edited *Radiografía de Haya de la Torre* (Lima, 1946), p. 33.

13. Luis Alberto Sánchez, *Haya de la Torre o el político: Crónica de una vida sin tregua,* 2d ed. (Santiago de Chile, 1936), p. 185.

14. *Cancionero aprista* (Lima, 1941). For a translation of the entire Aprista hymn, see Harry Kantor, *The Ideology and Program of the Peruvian Aprista Movement* (Berkeley, 1953), p. 133.

15. Juan José Lara, "Canto a las compañeras," in Alberto Hidalgo et al., *Cantos de la revolución* (Lima, 1934), p. 49.

16. Serafín Delmar, "Frente aprista," in ibid., pp. 47–48.

17. Ramiro Prialé, quoted on the frontpiece of Jesús Véliz Lizarraga, *Principios fundamentales del aprismo: Filosofía, doctrina y programa* (Lima, 1956).

18. Quoted by Haya, OC, 1:272.

19. Luis Eduardo Enríquez, *Haya de la Torre: La estafa política más grande de América* (Lima, 1951), pp. 76–77. For the credo of the Sánchez Cerro partisans, see Stein, *Populism in Peru,* p. 108.

20. See Andrés Townsend Ezcurra's prologue to Percy Murillo Garaycochea, *Historia del APRA, 1919–1945* (Lima, 1976), p. 11, specifically referring to Aprismo as a civil religion. Luis Alberto Sánchez, in a 1936 conference in Buenos Aires, stated that APRA's function was to replace the old religious mystique with a social mystique. See Gabriel del Mazo, *Vida de un político argentino: Convocatoria de recuerdos* (Buenos Aires, 197), pp. 250–51.

21. See Haya's March 29, 1943, letter to Luis Alberto Sánchez, in Haya and Sánchez, *Correspondencia, 1924–1976,* 2 vols. (Lima, 1983), 1:435.

22. See William Irwin Thompson, *The Time Falling Bodies Take to Light: Mythology, Sexuality, and the Origins of Culture* (New York, 1981), pp. 102–3.

23. See Murillo, *Historia del APRA,* pp. 141–42. The statement was prompted during the course of Seoane's famous constituent assembly debates with Víctor Andrés Belaúnde, an eloquent spokesman of orthodox Catholic theology.

24. See OC, 2:72, 76.

25. Ibid., 5:148–49, from the *Manifiesto* of Nov. 12, 1933.

26. Antenor Orrego, *El pueblo continente: Ensayos para una interpretación de la América Latina* (Santiago de Chile, 1939), pp. 154–55.

27. Magda Portal, "Palabras de esperanza," in Alberto Hidalgo et al., *Cantos de la revolución* (Lima, 1934) pp. 16–21.

28. Ibid., p. 34.

29. All initiation rites, all conceptions of passages into an altogether different life, involved the notion of dying in order to live, as R. R. Marett observes in *The Threshold of Religion,* rev. ed. (London, 1914), p. 164.

30. OC, 5:338.

340

31. Bronislaw Malinowski, *Magic, Science and Religion, and Other Essays* (Garden City, N.Y., 1954, originally published in 1948), p. 22, draws attention to James Frazer's observation that for primitive man "death has a meaning mainly as a step to resurrection, decay as a stage of rebirth, the plenty of autumn and the decline of winter as preludes to the revival of spring."

32. OC, 5:181.

33. Quoted in Magda Portal, *El aprismo y la mujer* (Lima, 1933), pp. 38–39.

34. Applicable to this aspect of Aprismo is Bruce Mazlish, *The Revolutionary Ascetic: Evolution of a Political Type* (New York, 1976).

35. OC, 7:240.

36. See David E. Apter's probing essay, "Notes on the Underground: Left Violence and the National State," *Daedalus* 108 (Fall 1979), esp. pp. 155–58.

37. Jung quoted by Erich Neumann, *The Origins and History of Consciousness*, trans. R. F. C. Hull, (Princeton, 1970, originally published in 1954), pp. 369–70.

38. OC, 2:323.

39. "Deslumbramiento y alumbramiento," OC, 1:239–41.

40. Jacques Lafaye, *Quetzalcoatl and Guadalupe: The Formation of Mexican National Consciousness, 1531–1813*, trans. Benjamin Keen (Chicago, 1976), pp. 205–6.

41. Carl G. Jung, *Civilization in Transition*, trans. R. F. C. Hull, 2d ed. (Princeton, 1970), p. 91.

42. See OC, 4:321–28.

43. Ibid., 1:134.

44. See Magda Portal, *América Latina frente al imperialismo y Defensa de la revolución mexicana* (Lima, 1931), p. 49.

45. Gabriel del Mazo, *Reforma universitaria y cultura nacional*, 4th ed. (Buenos Aires, 1955), p. 29.

46. Haya, however, had sketched out the concept of East-West fusion in a 1930 article (OC, 2:320–23). In this article he expressed agreement with Romain Rolland's belief that Latin America would effect a union between the spirit of Asia and Europe, becoming the synthesis of the thesis and antithesis. From the early days of his political awareness, Haya had been drawn toward the East, specifically China. Fascinated by the revolution initiated by Sun Yat-sen, Haya believed that it and the Kuomintang that Sun founded in 1912 were precursors of his Peruvian revolution and of the APRA, respectively. He admired both the multiclass aspects of the Kuomintang and its anti-imperialism that did not go to the extreme of totally denying a place to foreign capital but insisted on national control over that capital. For years Haya remained convinced that Aprismo and the Kuomintang were linked in a common type of movement to reintegrate societies whose wholeness had been sundered by the intrusion of unchecked foreign capital. See OC,

1:137, 139–40; 2:361; 3:101–6; 5:353. See also Luis Alberto Sánchez, *Apuntes para una biografía del Apra*, 3 vols. (Lima, 1978–81), 1:14.

47. Orrego, *Pueblo continente*, esp. pp. 68–69, 116–46.

48. Spanish editions of Scott Nearing and Joseph Freeman's *Dollar Diplomacy: A Study in American Imperialism* (New York, 1925) appeared in 1925 (Madrid) and 1926 (Mexico City); at the end of the 1920s Manuel Seoane, in exile in Chile, supervised publication of an abridged, popularized version of the work under the title "La garra yanqui" in *Atenea*, the journal of the University of Concepción. See Sánchez, *Apuntes*, 1:150.

49. OC, 1:74–75.

50. See Víctor Villanueva, *La ideología pequeñoburguesa del Partido Aprista Peruano, primer versión en espanōl de la versión inglesa publicada en "Latin American Perspectives"* (Lima, 1977), pp. 19–23.

51. Aug. 23, 1931, address, OC, 5:59

52. On the anti-imperialist aspects of the Aug. 23 address, see Jorge Guillermo Llosa, *En busca del Perú* (Lima, 1962), pp. 97–98.

53. See Alberto Baeza Flores, *Haya de la Torre y la revolución constructiva de las Américas* (Buenos Aires, 1962), p. 140; and Pablo Silva Villacorta, *¿ A donde van las ideas de Haya de la Torre? Una nueva visión sobre las ideas que conforman la doctrina del APRA* (Lima, 1966), pp. 33–45.

54. See Thomas M. Davies Jr., "Peru," in *The Spanish Civil War, 1936–39: American Hemispheric Perspectives*, ed. Mark Falcoff and Fredrick B. Pike (Lincoln, 1982), p. 212. See also n. 34, ch. 2.

55. Hermann Keyserling, *The Recovery of Truth*, trans. Paul Fohr in collaboration with the author (New York, 1929), pp. 12–16.

56. Ibid., p. 23.

57. The same symbolism was employed by Aprismo's amauta, Antenor Orrego. In *Pueblo continente*, pp. 162–63, Orrego depicted the Indian as the egg, Europe as the sperm. The two had come together originally at the time of conquest to produce a new civilization; but now that civilization had lost its vitality, and the Indian egg awaited the refertilization that would replicate the great cosmic drama not only of conquest but of the much earlier circumstances when Inti or Father Sun, in the role of *logos spermatikus*, had fertilized Pacha Mama, the earth goddess. This preconquest act of fertilization had caused the birth of the Empire of Tahuantinsuyo, and Indians now awaited their new Inti.

58. Hermann Keyserling, *Meditaciones suramericanas*, trans. Luis López-Ballesteros y de Torres (Santiago de Chile, 1931), pp. 233–34.

59. OC, 4:156.

60. See Susan Brownmiller, *Against Our Will: Men, Women and Rape* (New York, 1975).

61. Enríquez, *Haya de la Torre*, p. 21.

342

62. The Fernando de Rojas *Tragicomedia de Calisto y Melibea* is better known as *La Celestina*. See *The Celestina: A Novel in Dialogue*, trans. Lesley Bird Simpson (Berkeley, 1955).

63. In 1970, to demonstrate the constancy of his views, Haya arranged publication of the third edition of *El antimperialismo y el Apra* (Lima). The work was first published in 1935 in Santiago de Chile.

64. Haya, "Reflexiones en un breve viaje," OC, 1:264–67. Written in Rome in 1960, the essay was first published in *Pensamiento político de Haya de la Torre*, 5 vols. (Lima, 1961), 5:199–205.

65. See, for example, Billie Jean Isbell, "La otra mitad esencial: Un estudio de complementariedad sexual andina," *Estudios Andinos* (La Paz) 12 (1976): 37–56. Furthermore, the fusion of male-female principles is well nigh a constant preoccupation in the remarkable seventeenth-century work of Felipe Guamán Poma de Ayala, *El primer nueva corónica y buen gobierno*. See Rolena Adorno, "Paradigms Lost: A Peruvian Indian Surveys Colonial Society," *Studies in the Anthropology of Visual Communication* 5 (1979): 78–96. See also André Leroi–Gourhan, *The Art of Prehistoric Man in Western Europe*, trans. Norbert Guterman (London, 1968). One of the twentieth century's most distinguished archaeologists, Leroi-Gourhan believes that Paleolithic cave art should be interpreted in terms of male-female symbolism. On the constancy of duality among Indians of the Americas and the vision of reconciling opposites (often seen in terms of the male-female polarity) in harmony, see Åke Hultkrantz, *The Religions of the American Indians*, trans. Monica Setterwall (Berkeley, 1979), esp. pp. 53, 113–14, 171, 175, 184–85, 201, 211, 238, 250–52, 259, 262–65.

66. See Robert May, *Sex and Fantasy: Patterns of Male and Female Development* (New York, 1980), p. 166.

67. See Jung, *Psychology and Alchemy*, trans. R. F. C. Hull, 2d ed., rev. (Princeton, 1968), pp. 161–62.

68. See Philip Rawson, *Eastern Erotic Art* (New York, 1981).

69. Wolfgang Riehle, *The Middle English Mystics*, trans. Bernard Standring (Boston, 1981) shows how concepts of mystical love and union with God often are conveyed through sexual metaphors.

70. Felipe Cossío del Pomar, *Víctor Raúl: Biografía de Haya de la Torre* (Mexico City, 1961), p. 34.

71. The androgyne theme is related to the concept of woman as nature, man as culture. See Sherry B. Ortner, "Is Female to Male as Nature Is to Culture," in *Women, Culture, and Society*, ed. Michelle Zimbalist Rosaldo (Stanford, 1974), pp. 67–87. See also Carolyn Merchant, *The Death of Nature* (San Francisco, 1980). One may speculate that woman as nature appeals to man in times of millenarian ferment as a source of salvation. She becomes then the Jungian anima, the feminine aspect within man's nature to which he must be joined to attain wholeness.

In times of normalcy, however, when civilization seems relatively free of over-whelming discontents, woman as nature becomes the Freudian id, which must be kept under suppression so that culture, with its established hegemonic order, can maintain its sway.

72. OC, 6:383–84.

73. Jung, *Psychology and Alchemy*, fig. 23, p. 68. Other depictions of Mercury, pp. 95 and 223, are similar in this respect. Of Mercurius, Jung writes (p. 125): "He is the hermaphrodite that was in the beginning split into the classical brother-sister duality and is reunited in the *coniunctio*, to appear once again at the end in the radiant form of the *lumen novum*, the stone. He is metallic yet liquid, matter yet spirit, cold yet fiery, poison and yet healing draught—a symbol of uniting all opposites...."

74. Antenor Orrego, "Haya de la Torre: El hombre acción," in *Radiografía de Haya de la Torre*, ed. anon. (Lima, 1946), p. 29. Reference to the conjunction of two antithetical worlds seems again to place Haya in the trickster category. Carl G. Jung, *Four Archetypes: Mother, Rebirth, Spirit, Trickster*, trans. R. F. C. Hull (Princeton, 1969), p. 143, writes of the trickster: "Even his sex is optional despite its phallic qualities: he can turn himself into a woman and bear children."

75. The new humanity theme, based on visions of cultural mestizaje, is found also in Carlos Manuel Cox, *Utopía y realidad en el Inca Garcilaso: Pensamiento económico, interpretación histórica* (Lima, 1965), p. 32. Garcilaso himself was interested not only in fusing the outward races of the world but in a Neoplatonic quest for inward harmony. See Harold V. Livermore's introduction to his translation of Garcilaso's *Royal Commentaries of the Incas*, 2 vols. (Austin, 1966), 1:xxiv.

76. James Hillman, *The Dream and the Underworld* (New York, 1979), pp. 70–71.

77. Melvin J. Lasky, *Utopia and Revolution* (Chicago, 1976), p. 47.

78. Basil Davidson, *Let Freedom Come: Africa in Modern History* (Boston, 1978), pp. 49–50. On the tensions between individual liberty and the claims of the communal and holistic life, see Yi-Fu Tuan, *Segmented Worlds and Self: Group Life and Individual Consciousness* (Minneapolis, 1982).

79. See OC, 5:43, 53, drawn from Haya's 1931 campaign oratory in Lima. See also Partido Aprista Peruano, *Programa mínimo* (Lima, 1931), p. 4; Carlos Manuel Cox, *Dinámica económica del aprismo* (Lima, 1948), one of the principal expositions of Aprismo's functional democracy; Luis Heysen, *El ABC de la peruanización del Perú* (Lima, 1932), p. 19; Orrego, *Pueblo continente*, pp. 93–95, 116–46; Javier Pulgar Vidal, *La gea, el hombre y la historia del Perú: Visión aprista del Congreso Económico Nacional en función de nuestra realidad* (Lima, 1947). For an attack against the Aprista-envisioned functional democracy, see Samuel Ramírez del Castillo, *La anti-república: O el Congreso Económico Nacional* (Lima, 1946).

344

80. See G. D. H. Cole, *A Short History of the British Working Class Movement, 1789–1937*, 3 vols. in one, 2nd ed. (London, 1937, originally published 1925–27), 3:75. Cole notes the importance of two mystics, S. G. Hobson and A. R. Orage (see n. 16, ch. 5), in propounding, under the rubric of cooperativism, the restoration of an organic society resting on a guild structure. See also Jośe Antonio Naymlap, *Un pueblo clavado en la cruz* (Lima, 1941). In this plea for functional democracy and cooperativism, Naymlap explains (pp. 31–34) the circumstances leading Haya de la Torre to abandon the term corporatism in favor of cooperativism.

81. OC, 1:279; 4:177.

82. Ibid., 6:308.

83. Ibid., 1:278.

84. Ibid., pp. 286–87.

85. Ibid., 5:114–15.

86. Martin Buber, *Paths in Utopia*, trans. R. F. C. Hull (Boston, 1958), p. 197. Buber's eloquent description of how a society might pass from an inorganic to an organic stage applies in many ways to Aprista conceptions. Buber, a great Jewish scholar (d. 1978), had Israel in mind. On the degree to which Haya was impressed in 1957 by Israel's endeavor to fashion what he saw as an organic society based on a government of four powers, see his "Crónica internacional," OC, 7:299.

87. OC, 3:151–53; 5:78–79. As the ideal Aprista state took shape in Haya's mind by the mid-1940s, he foresaw the coexistence of a Political Parliament along with a National Economic Congress. Parliament's role would be to initiate legislative proposals that would then be decided on by the functionally organized, vertically selected NEC. See the interview with Haya de la Torre in *Oiga* (Lima), Oct. 31, 1975, p. 18.

88. See OC, 2:455–56; 5:70.

89. See Philippe C. Schmitter, "Still the Century of Corporatism?" in *The New Corporatism: Social-Political Structures in the Iberian World*, ed. Fredrick B. Pike and Thomas Stritch (Notre Dame, Ind., 1974), pp. 85–131. See also Antony Black, *Guilds and Civil Society in European Political Thought: From the Twelfth Century to the Present* (Ithaca, 1984), a study that touches often on utopian, and practical, endeavors to combine guild-like associations—with their values of friendship, brotherhood, and mutual aid—with the institutions of the market economy that honor the individualistic, commerical spirit. David Bakan, *The Duality of Human Existence* (Chicago, 1966), explores similar themes as he deals with "agency" (in gender terms, associated with maleness) and "communion" (associated with feminine traits).

90. The coincidence of opposites may be seen as a divinity principle (as, for example, with Wakan Tanka, the supreme being of the Sioux Indians in whom *all* powers or "medicines" inhere); and the quest of reconciling opposites may be

seen as the grail search. As early as 1928, perhaps owing to his being steeped in concepts that in many esoteric circles are traced back to Heraclitus, Haya de la Torre referred to this Greek thinker as the source for the understanding that "unity results from the harmonious resolution of opposites." See OC, 1:161–62. In Haya's opinion, Heraclitus, not Hegel, was the true father of the dialectic. A succinct analysis of the thought of Heraclitus, clearly revealing why it would have appealed to the spiritualist streak in Haya de la Torre, is found in Karl Jaspers, *The Great Philosophers*, vol. 2: *The Original Thinkers: Anaximander, Heraclitus, Parmenides, Plotinus, Lao-Tzu, Nagarjuna*, trans. Ralph Manheim, ed. Hanah Arendt (New York, 1966), pp. 11–18.

91. See Goran Hyden, *Beyond Ujamaa in Tanzania: Underdevelopment and an Uncaptured Peasantry* (Berkeley, 1980), esp. pp. 98–99.

92. See A. James Gregor, "African Socialism, Socialism, and Fascism: An Appraisal," *Review of Politics* 29 (1967): 324–53.

93. Manuel Ugarte's *El destino de un continente (Nice, France, 1923)*, along with the Nearing-Freeman book *Dollar Diplomacy* (see note 48), had helped shape Haya's early anti-imperialism.

94. In *The World in the Making*, trans. Maurice Samuel (New York, 1927), p. 183, Hermann Keyserling wrote: "Nations will . . . no longer play a decisive rôle in in the future, and just as little will the state. New forms of socialization are arising irresistibly. Among the many possible, one finds its futuristic pattern shadowed forth in the Soviet Union, which, in its form of free association of peoples, now realized for the first time, is the inheritor of traditional conquest." Again, in *The Recovery of Truth*, p. 12. Keyserling maintained that the tensions within any one nation state could not be completely resolved within its confines. Rather, the nation had to be brought into rhythm with a larger system that transcended it. The result would be an all-embracing harmony in which previously antagonistic elements would enter into counterpoint relationship.

95. See Orrego, *Pueblo continente*, p. 77. In his view of progress as an ascending spiral (p. 78), Orrego saw nationalism as the spiral of a less advanced age, while people-continents were the spirals of a higher stage of civilization. Haya de la Torre held comparable views (see OC, 6:310, 313). Already in 1925 he declared, "The cult of the *patria chica* is suicide" (ibid., 1:77). In 1926 he intoned: "My life is consecrated to the cause of our generation, which is the cause of revolutionary justice and unity for the people of twenty republics whose frontiers we ought to erase" (ibid., p. 125). The Aprista flag symbolized the dream of uniting the Indo-American people-continent. A circular gold map of Latin America was imposed upon a sea of red. The flag was rich in symbolism. The circle stood, I suppose, for the wholeness of perfection; gold depicted what for the alchemists was the most pure and noble element. Gold could also stand for the sunlight of consciousness. The Incas, moreover, had revered gold as embodying the tears of the sun, which

helped to fertilized Pacha Mama, the supreme earth goddess. The sea of red forming the background suggests purifying blood as well as the blood that accompanies birth and irrigates the soil to produce regeneration in numerous rites and myths.

Haya's rather prosaic explanation, of the flag is presented in the text toward the conclusion of chapter 3 (see n. 64, ch. 3). Introducing the flag in 1924, before his exposure to the mystical and spiritualist currents of Europe, he may have been only subliminally aware of the full symbolic possibilities of the Aprista banner.

Chapter 8

1. Crowd estimates varied enormously throughout the 1931 campaign. The one hundred thousand estimate (Lima's population at the time was about four hundred thousand) came from Luis Alberto Sánchez, *Testimonio personal: Memorias de un peruano del siglo XX*, 4 vols. (Lima, 1969–76), 1:535. In another work, *Haya de la Torre o el político: Crónica de una vida sin tregua*, 2d ed. (Santiago de Chile, 1936), p. 191, Sánchez concedes that most estimates placed the crowd at 80,000. The major rally for Haya's political adversary Sánchez Cerro, held the following month, attracted even more people. According to Sánchez, *Testimonio*, 1:355, the volume was swelled by the busing into Lima from the provinces of market women and people of all sorts "with time on their hands."

2. José María Manzanilla, quoted by Alfredo Moreno Mendiguren, comp., *Repertorio de noticias breves sobre personajes peruanos* (Lima, 1956), p. 523.

3. See *Programa de gobierno del Comandante Luis M. Sánchez Cerro, candidato a la presidencia de la república del Perú* (Lima, 1931).

4. Luis E. Heysen, *El comandante del Oropesa* (Lima, 1931), pp. 24–25.

5. Ibid., p. 13.

6. See the comments of rightist ideologue José de la Riva Agüero in *Revista de la Universidad Católica del Perú* (Lima) 9 (Nov.–Dec. 1941), p. 466.

7. Partido Aprista Peruano, *Llamiento a la nación* (Lima, 1931), p. 5.

8. Luis Heysen, *El ABC de la peruanización del Perú* (Lima, 1932), pp. 16–17.

9. Magda Portal, *América Latina frente al imperialismo y Defensa de la revolución mexicana* (Lima, 1931), p. 42. Two originally separate tracts were bound together in this publication.

10. Ibid., p. 50.

11. E. J. Hobsbawm, *Primitive Rebels: Studies in Archaic Forms of Social Movements in the Nineteenth and Twentieth Centuries* (New York, 1965, originally published in 1959), p. 8.

12. See Thomas M. Davies Jr., "The *Indigenismo* of the Peruvian Aprista Party: A Reinterpretation," HAHR 51 (1971): 643–44, and *Indian Integration in*

Peru: A Half Century of Experience, 1900–1948 (Lincoln, 1974), p. III.

13. Jorge Basadre, *Historia de la República del Perú, 1822–1933*, 6th ed. rev., 17 vols. (Lima, 1968–70), 14:145.

14. For an indication of the dismay experienced by northern sugar estate owners in the face of perceived Aprista radicalism, see Dennis L. Gilbert, "The Oligarchy and the Old Regime in Peru" (Ph.D. diss., Cornell University, 1977), p. 94.

15. Felipe Cossío del Pomar, *Víctor Raúl: Biografía de Haya de la Torre* (Mexico City, 1961), p. 343, makes this estimate. Haya, OC, 5:51, estimates the crowd at forty thousand, although the Plaza de Acho had a seating capacity of only around thirty-two thousand.

16. Romain Rolland, *Mahatma Gandhi: The Man Who Became One with the Universal Being*, trans. Catherine D. Groth (New Delhi, 1968, originally published in London and Paris, 1924), pp. 50–51.

17. OC, 3:157–62. The importance Aprismo attached to organized, collective singing may also have originated in practices of Peruvian anarcho-syndicalism. See Percy Murillo Garaycochea, *Historia del APRA, 1919–1945* (Lima, 1976), p. 22.

18. Felipe Cossío del Pomar, *Haya de la Torre, el indoamericano* (Mexico City, 1939), p. 223.

19. Gustavo Valcárcel, *Apología de un hombre, Haya de la Torre* (Lima, 1945).

20. See Christopher B. Donnan, *Moche Art of Peru: Pre-Columbian Symbolic Communication*, rev. ed. (Los Angeles, 1978), pp. 151–55. On the salute and other aspects of Aprista symbolism and ritual see also Harry Kantor, *The Ideology and Program of the Peruvian Aprista Movement* (Berkeley, 1953), pp. 56–58. Aprista symbolism included a stylized condor (the bird deemed sacred by several pre-Columbian civilizations) with four wings on each side and the letters APRA. Frequently, at least by the 1940s, Apristas wore a lapel pin depicting a condor. Also an Aprista favorite was the five-pointed red star, sometimes with the letters APRA arranged to form a circle within the star.

21. The quotation is from Víctor Villanueva, *La tragedia de un pueblo y de un partido: Páginas para la historia del Apra* (Santiago de Chile, 1954), p. 19. For a description of Aprista mass meetings see also Víctor Villanueva, *El Apra en busca del poder, 1930–1940* (Lima, 1975), p. 63; and Robert J. Alexander, comp. and trans., *Aprismo: The Ideas and Doctrines of Víctor Raúl Haya de la Torre* (Kent, Ohio, 1973), p. 21.

22. Alberto Hidalgo, *Haya de la Torre en su víspera* (Lima, 1931), pp. 10–11.

23. Murillo, *Historia del APRA*, p. 118.

24. See William G. McLoughlin, *Revivals, Awakenings, and Reform* (Chicago, 1978), p. 19.

25. According to D. M. Dooling, "Focus," *Parabola* 7, no. 3 (1982): 2–3, "a person—or community—usually seeks a ceremony at the moment of recognizing human inadequacy in the face of life events.... When help is needed for a diffi-

cult transition, or a blessing or an achievement or a new possibility, one feels the insufficiency of one's own forces, even to be a successful petitioner." In such instances, people will band together, as a herd, hoping thereby to make their wishes more effective, by accumulating a mass force. Moreover, in such instances people feel the need for an intercessor: they look for "a priest or a shaman" to plead for them.

26. Gustave Le Bon, *The Crowd: A Study of the Popular Mind* (London, 1952), pp. 73, 75. The first English version of this enormously influential work appeared in 1896. Le Bon (1841–1931) is reputed to have influenced Mussolini through his publications, and Haya de la Torre in his mastery of crowd psychology seems either to have learned from Le Bon or to have intuited his insights. Le Bon understood that the crowd was predisposed to cede "individual personality to a 'Führer principle' of one kind or another" (publisher's note, p. 4, of the 1952 English ed.). On the man and his importance, see *Gustave Le Bon: The Man and His Works*, edited, translated, and with an introduction by Alice Widener (Indianapolis, 1979); and Susanna Barrows, *Distorting Mirrors: Visions of the Crowd in Late Nineteenth-Century France* (New Haven, 1981), containing an especially perceptive account of Le Bon's views on how a new Caesar, armed with an understanding of crowd psychology, could control the masses. Like Le Bon, Haya seems to have held the uncontrolled, unmanipulated masses in terror.

27. See Volodymir W. Odajnyk, *Jung and Politics: The Political and Social Ideas of C. G. Jung* (New York, 1976), p. 23; and Aristide R. Zolberg, "Moments of Madness," *Politics and Society* 2 (1972): 196.

28. Victor Turner, *Dramas, Fields, and Metaphors: Symbolic Action in Human Society* (Ithaca, 1974), p. 56, notes that "if communities can be developed within a ritual pattern it can be carried over into secular life for a while and help to mitigate or assuage some of the abrasiveness of social conflicts. . . ."

29. Basadre, *Historia de la república*, 14:134.

30. See Fredrick B. Pike, *The Modern History of Peru* (London, 1967), pp. 254–56.

31. Enrique Chirinos Soto, *Historia de la república: 1821-Peru-1978* (Lima, 1977), pp. 462–63.

32. See Pike, *Modern History of Peru*, p. 364, n. 10.

33. Basadre, quoted in Moreno Mendiguren, *Repertorio*, p. 522. See also the reliable study by Orazio A. Ciccarelli, "The Sánchez Cerro Regime in Peru, 1930–1933" (Ph.D. diss., University of Florida, 1969), for a detailed analysis.

34. Steve Jay Stein, *Populism in Peru: The Emergence of the Masses and the Politics of Social Control* (Madison, 1980), pp. 195–96. Stein's entire treatment of the election, pp. 188–202, is masterful.

35. See Karen Horney, *Neurosis and Human Growth: The Struggle toward Self-Realization* (New York, 1970, originally published in 1950), pp. 49, 60.

36. See the Paul H. Ornstein introduction to his edited work, *The Search for the Self: Selected Writings of Heinz Kohut, 1950–1978*, 2 vols. (New York, 1978), 1:69.

37. OC, 1:87–88. This passage of Haya's casts doubt on the contention of Raúl Haya de la Torre de la Rosa, "El aprismo: Doctrina y virajes" (Lima, 1978, Mimeographed), part 1, p. 10, that in his uncle's writings of the 1920s may be found a clear advocacy of violence as the means to accomplish revolution. However, other passages in Haya's early writings tend to justify his nephew's conclusion. Thus in addressing an audience in Mexico City in 1927 Haya contended that violence is a necessary ingredient in working out the dialectical process: the synthesis, or new society that resolves the tensions of the old, was always the result of violence. See Haya, *¿A donde va Indoamérica?* (Santiago de Chile, 1935), pp. 51–66.

38. John A. Mackay, *Los intelectuales y los nuevos tiempos* (Lima, 1923), p. 10.

39. OC, 5:97.

National State," *Daedalus* 108 (Fall 1979): 168–69. See also Meyer Howard Abrams, *Natural Supernaturalism: Tradition and Revolution in Romantic Literature* (New York, 1971), p. 356.

ture (New York, 1971), p. 356.

41. OC, 5:97.

42. Indo-Americans by nature, according to Haya, inclined toward unity and cohesiveness. But the intrusion of capitalism and free-enterprise business practices had produced an unnatural aggressiveness that must be tamed by means of a return to origins. See his June 20, 1925, address to the Latin American Anti-Imperialism Assembly in Paris, ibid., 1:76–77. Manuel Seoane, *Páginas polémicas* (Lima, 1931), pp. 10–11, also wrote of the need to eradicate the individualistic personality that atomizes a national population.

43. As early as 1930, in fact, some Apristas had thought that in Sánchez Cerro they had found the military man who would put them in power. See the single-sheet tract by Aprista militant Gamaliel Churata, *Corad, Sapos* (Puno, Sept. 24, 1930), in the Colección de Hojas, 1930–32, Sala de Investigaciones, Biblioteca Nacional del Perú. They misjudged the lieutenant colonel grievously, and when he spurned them they initiated, with Haya still in Germany, a series of unsuccessful uprisings in Cuzco and elsewhere.

44. See Villanueva, *El Apra en busca del poder*, pp. 54–57. For the text of the address, see OC, 5:87–90, or Haya de la Torre, *Construyendo el aprismo* (Buenos Aires, 1933), pp. 172–75.

45. Gandhi, quoted by Rolland, *Mahatma Gandhi*, pp. 34–35.

46. Norman Cohn, *The Pursuit of the Millennium: Revolutionary Millenarians and Mystical Anarchists of the Middle Ages*, rev. ed. (New York, 1970), p. 160. See also Gershom Scholem, *Sabbatai Sevi: The Mystical Messiah, 1626–1676*, trans. R. J. Zwi Werblowsky (Princeton, 1973), p. 290: "Sabbatai had achieved his

unique power of justifying and condemning through the unspeakable agonies he suffered in behalf of the Israelite nation." Weston La Barre, *The Ghost Dance: Origins of Religion*, rev. ed. (New York, 1972), p. 310, notes that prophesies of catastrophism, preceding an anticipated new and wonderous day, are very nearly a constant in American hemisphere millenarian, regeneration movements.

47. Cohn, *Pursuit of the Millennium*, p. 64.

48. See Robert May, *Sex and Fantasy: Patterns of Male and Female Development* (New York, 1980), p. 155.

49. Ibid., pp. 155–59.

50. Theodor Reik, *Masochism in Modern Man*, trans. Margaret H. Beigel and Gertrude M. Kurth (New York, 1941), pp. 262–63. Alfred Adler saw suffering as meant to gain attention and "attain a devious superiority." See Horney, *Neurosis and Human Growth*, p. 238. On this subject see also Margaret Brenman, "On Teasing and Being Teased: The Problem of 'Moral Masochism,'" in *Psychoanalytic Psychiatry and Psychology*, ed. Cyrus Friedman and Robert Knight (New York, 1954), pp. 29–51; and Leila Lerner, ed., *Masochism and the Emergent Ego: Selected Papers of Esther Menaker* (New York, 1979).

51. Reik, *Masochism*, p. 145.

52. Ibid., p. 138.

53. David E. Stannard, in his devastating attack on psychohistory and psychoanalysis, *Shrinking History: On Freud and the Failure of Psychohistory* (New York, 1980), makes many points which I find altogether persuasive.

54. See "El Proceso Haya de la Torre," in OC, 5:247.

55. Basadre, *Historia de la república*, 14:221.

56. Thomas M. Davies Jr., "Peru," in *The Spanish Civil War: 1936–39: American Hemispheric Perspectives*, ed. Mark Falcoff and Fredrick B. Pike (Lincoln, 1982), p. 214. See also Rogger Mercado, *La revolución de Trujillo y la traición del Apra, 1932* (Lima, 1966). Written from a communist perspective by an eyewitness to the events, this far-fetched work maintains that the APRA had virtually nothing to do with the Trujillo uprising. It emerged, he contends, out of decisions taken by workers and peasants on their own.

57. See the splendid account Murillo presents in *Historia del Apra*, pp. 209–49. Also useful is Guillermo Thorndike, *El año de la barbarie, Perú 1932* (Lima, 1969), its value enhanced by maps and illustrations. My own treatment of the incident in *The Modern History of Peru* is marred by the inaccurate statement (p. 265) that Aprista leaders, before abandoning the besieged Trujillo, left orders for the assassination of sixty hostages. Jorge Basadre, *Historia de la república*, 14:236, properly takes me to task for this statement.

58. Quoted by Dennis L. Gilbert, "The Oligarchy and the Old Regime in Peru" (Ph.D. diss., Cornell University, 1979), p. 103. See also Lorenzo Huertas

Vallejos, *Capital burocrático y lucha de clases en el sector agrario: Lambayegue, Perú, 1920–1950* (Lima, 1974).

59. Carmen Rosa Rivadeneira, quoted by Magda Portal, *El aprismo y la mujer* (Lima, 1933), pp. 38–39.

60. Luis Alberto Sánchez, *Apuntes para una biografía del Apra*, 3 vols. (Lima, 1978–81), 2:27. Contained in this volume, pp. 74–107, are three interesting letters that Jiménez wrote Sánchez and that are published here for the first time. They are included in the collection that Sánchez has left the Pennsylvania State University library. See Donald C. Henderson and Grace R. Pérez, trans. and comps., *Literature and Politics in Latin America: An Annotated Calendar of the Luis Alberto Sánchez Correspondence, 1919–1980* (University Park, Pa., 1982), pp. 289–92.

61. Haya de la Torre letter to Juan Seoane, Dec. 4, 1932, in OC, 7:212–13. See also Seoane's book, based on his prison experience, *Hombres y rejas* (Santiago de Chile, 1937).

62. See n. 26, ch. 4.

63. Nat Freedland, *The Occult Explosion* (New York, 1972), p. 43.

64. See Sánchez, *Haya de la Torre*, p. 222.

65. OC, 7:206.

66. Ibid., 5:137.

67. See Villanueva, *El Apra en busca del poder*, pp. 143–52. Sánchez, *Apuntes*, 2:132–35, remains strangely silent on this point, although he never hesitates to challenge Villanueva's interpretations when able to present evidence against them. On the matter see Murillo, *Historia del APRA*, pp. 292–94.

68. Basadre, *Historia de la república*, 14:421–26.

69. Sánchez, *Apuntes*, 2:164–65.

70. June Nash, "Myth and Ideology," in *Ideology and Social Change in Latin America*, ed. Nash (New York, 1977), p. 116.

71. OC, 5:153.

72. Ibid., p. 154.

73. Ibid., p. 156.

74. Ibid., pp. 155–56.

75. Saint Theresa of Avila, *Interior Castle*, trans. and ed., E. Allison Peers (Garden City, N.Y., 1961), p. 226.

76. Sigmund Freud, *Moses and Monotheism*, trans. Katherine Jones (New York, 1939), p. 109.

77. One finds also echoes of St. John's Book of Revelation. For John, Roman oppression was interpreted to mean that God was inflicting suffering on Christians as punishment for sin and as a test or proof. God's servants were supposed to react to affliction by returning to the virtues Christ had taught, to spurn the

"beast," and to witness for Jesus even unto death. Those who could not resist idolatry or vice were doomed to damnation. If one substitutes oligarchy and Revolutionary Union for Romans and Apristas for Christians, one would approximate Haya de la Torre's implications.

78. Sánchez, *Haya de la Torre*, pp. 333–34.

79. OC, 5:331.

80. Ibid., pp. 332–33.

81. Ibid., p. 334.

82. Ibid., p. 335.

83. Ibid., p. 339.

84. Ibid., p. 340.

85. Quoted by James M. Rhodes, *The Hitler Movement: A Modern Millenarian Revolution* (Stanford, 1980), p. 73.

86. Ibid., p. 74.

87. See *Boletín de la Masonería Boliviana* (La Paz) 26 (1946), pp. 51–56.

88. See Peter Linehan, "Growing Hostility to Gays," *Times Literary Supplement* (London), Jan. 23, 1981, p. 73. See also Caroline Walker Bynum's title essay in her book *Jesus as Mother: Studies in the Spirituality of the High Middle Ages* (Berkeley, 1982); and Wayne A. Meeks, "The Image of the Androgyne: Some Uses of a Symbol in Earliest Christianity," *History of Religions* 13 (1974): 165–208. In medieval crucifixion scenes, moreover, the sun and moon were often depicted flanking the cross, and this tradition continued in Spanish colonial art in America. Perhaps Haya saw such depictions and found them suggestive. In any event, these portrayals of the crucifixion imply the androgynous qualities of Christ: masculine and feminine qualities fuse in him as he undergoes the ordeal that will result in regeneration.

89. Carl G. Jung, *Psychology and Alchemy*, trans. R. F. C. Hull, 2d ed. (Princeton, 1968), pp. 19, 112, and 203 n. 28.

90. For a long time Haya had been fascinated by blood symbolism. In 1926 he wrote that old forms of society were ending in Europe as the twilight of capitalism set in. A new life was beginning to surge in the world, however, and "we will throw down the white glove of the diplomat and show the hand that bleeds from the wounds of the people" (OC, 1:29). In the same year he wrote: "We [the youthful generation] should speak and write with blood on our lips and on the pen . . ." (ibid., p. 126).

91. See André Leroi-Gourhan, *Treasures of Prehistoric Art* (New York, 1967), p. 174.

92. Carl G. Jung, *Four Archetypes: Mother, Rebirth, Spirit, Trickster*, trans. R. F. C. Hull (Princeton, 1969), p. 136.

93. "La última conferencia de Riva Agüero," *Revista de la Universidad Católica del Perú*, 13 (April 1945): 466.

94. According to Sánchez, *Apuntes*, 3:105, Incahuasi was located at no. 221 Calle Carlos Arrieta. Haya spent most of his time underground at that address. Occasionally he also used the house of Rómulo Flores Salcedo on Avenida Chorillos. Flores also provided an automobile for Haya's use.

95. See Murillo, *Historia del APRA*, pp. 459–60.

96. Murillo suggests (ibid., p. 460) that Benavides may have been implicated in the 1939 incident that led to the wounding of Haya's secretary, although he may have sent out his agents to arrest, not to kill, the fugitive.

97. Ibid., pp. 327–30; Sánchez, *Haya de la Torre*, pp. 328–29.

98. See Davies, "Peru," p. 217.

99. Sánchez, *Apuntes*, 2:7, 9–10.

100. Gilbert, "Oligarchy," p. 293.

101. Murillo, *Historia del APRA*, pp. 379–80.

102. See Sánchez, *Apuntes*, 1:78, and *Testimonio*, 2:555. Apristas, among them Alcides Spelucín, were active also in Colombia. See Carlos Showing and Pedro E. Muñiz, *Lo que es el aprismo* (Bogotá, 1932). After spending some time as a teacher in Baranquilla, Spelucín moved on to Ecuador. On Aprista influence in Venezuela, and specifically on Rómulo Betancourt, see Arturo Sosa A. and Eloi Lengrand, *Del garibaldismo estudiantil a la izquierda criolla: Los orígenes marxistas del proyecto de A.D., 1928–1935* (Caracas, 1981). The authors tend to stress the differences between Aprista ideology and the thought of Betancourt. In his introduction to the volume, however, Jesús Sanoja Hernández judges Haya's influence on Betancourt to have been far from negligible. In any event it became part of Aprista lore that their party had exercised decisive influence in shaping the program and ideology of Betancourt's Acción Democrática.

103. *OC*, 7:239.

104. Letter of Haya de la Torre, Aug. 4, 1938, in Thomas M. Davies, Jr., and Víctor Villanueva, eds., *300 documentos para la historia del APRA* (Lima, 1978), p. 277. In the numerous letters that Haya wrote to Luis Alberto Sánchez in Chile he persisted in a nagging, almost whining tone as he harped on his suffering, the constant danger he was in, and his chronic lack of funds. Repeatedly he charged Apristas in exile with not making all-out efforts in the party's behalf. Haya, who described himself as constantly engaged in party business, had to sell his car for funds. On one occasion he was forced to borrow two pounds from a friend and even had to pawn his clothing "and the like." He reminded Sánchez that he had a large "family" for which he must purchase soap, socks, medicine, etc.; and he had to pay for an operation on his companion Jorge Idiáquez. In one letter Haya noted that if money did not arrive he would "soon be dead of hunger." Shortly, two hundred soles reached him, enabling him "at last" to buy new socks. In his letters Haya reported keeping busy writing, or putting the finishing touches on the essays that composed *El antimperialismo y el Apra* (1935), *¿A donde va In-*

354

doamérica? (Santiago de Chile, 1935), and *Ex combatientes y desocupados: Notas sobre Europa* (Santiago de Chile, 1936). All of these works were published in Santiago de Chile, under arrangements made by Sánchez. Haya persistently complained of inadequate advances, of delays in royalty payments, of careless printing and poor quality paper, and of lack of advertising for the books. He also complained of his precarious health, noting he had been forced to give up smoking, go on a vegetarian diet, and consume large quantities of a medicine called mucene. For references to and extracts from this correspondence, see Henderson and Pérez, *Literature and Politics*, pp. 178–235. See also Haya's May 1935 letter to Sánchez, in which he attributes his health problems to "a huge ulcer," in Haya and Sánchez, *Correspondencia, 1924–1976*, 2 vols. (Lima, 1983), 1:60.

105. Letter of Haya de la Torre, Feb. 10, 1939, in Davies and Villanueva, *300 documentos*, p. 313.

106. Letter of Haya de la Torre, 1938 (day and month not specified), OC, 7:240.

107. Cossío del Pomar, *Víctor Raúl*, p. 354.

108. OC, 1:20.

109. Ibid., p. 87.

110. Originally written in 1929, this piece is included in Haya's *Construyendo el aprismo*, pp. 167–70. On integral education, see also a piece Haya wrote while in Dresden in 1930, in OC, 2:303, and his Aug. 30, 1936, communication in Davies and Villanueva, *300 documentos*, esp. p. 75.

111. *Construyendo el aprismo*, p. 191.

112. OC, 2:437.

113. Ibid., 3:162

114. Dearing to Secretary of State, State Department Archives, Jan. 6, 1932, D.C. 823.008/66. This reference was provided by Professor Thomas M. Davies Jr.

115. See Nathan Leites and Charles Wolf Jr., *Rebellion and Authority: An Analytic Essay on Insurgent Conflicts* (Chicago, 1970), p. 56.

116. OC, 1:271–72. The selection dates from 1934.

117. This is an element in the plot around which Eduardo Sierralta Lorca builds his novel *El Apra y la sombra* (Mexico City, 1957). It is not specified whether fornication in which both partners are Apristas is acceptable.

118. Murillo, *Historia del APRA*, pp. 320–21. For a translation of the complete Fajista code of conduct, see Kantor, *Ideology and Program*, pp. 135–37.

119. See Comité Aprista Peruano, Brigada de Organización, *Organización vertical del Partido Aprista Peruano: Comentarios y explicación de la organización por el Jefe del Partido* (Santiago de Chile, 1927). This pamphlet is included in Davies and Villanueva, *300 documentos*, pp. 198–209.

120. Davies and Villanueva, *300 documentos*, p. 204.

121. Ibid., pp. 199–200.

122. Antenor Orrego, *El Pueblo continente: Ensayos para una interpretación de la América Latina* (Santiago de Chile, 1939), p. 158.

123. On the strength of Haya's "hegemonic will" in imposing "total direction" on the PAP, and on his "intransigent anti-Hispanism," see Sánchez, *Apuntes*, 3:60. See also Davies, "Peru," p. 229. Spanish historian and man of letters Salvador de Madariaga complained of Haya's anti-Hispanism as constituting a "postcolonial complex" and opined that Haya was too emotional for a statesman. See Henderson and Pérez, *Literature and Politics*, p. 310. On the subject of Haya and the Spanish Civil War see also Sánchez's Aug. 20, 1935, letter to Haya, and the latter's November 1938 [?] letter to Sánchez, cited and extracted in ibid., pp. 183, 227–28.

124. See Haya de la Torre letter of October 1938 to Manuel Seoane and other Aprista leaders in Santiago de Chile, in Davies and Villanueva, *300 documentos*, pp. 317–18, and the Jan. 4, 1939, letter to Haya from César Enrique Pardo in Santiago, pp. 303–4. Pardo notes that he and Seoane have lost faith in the trustworthiness of the army as an instrument for bringing the PAP to power through a *golpe*. What is necessary is intervention from abroad. The United States is depicted as the source of hope, and it must be appealed to on the basis of delivering Peru from the fascist administration of Benavides, who, allegedly, is favorable to Germany, Italy, and Japan. See also OC, 6:149–52. As an example of the sort of propaganda that Apristas managed to promulgate in the United States, according to which the fascistic leanings of the Benavides administration accounted for its persecution of the APRA, see Jonathan Mitchell, "End of the Conquistadores," *New Republic* 81 (Jan. 2, 1935): 210–12.

125. Peruvian novelist Ciro Alegría (a prominent fallen-away Aprista) wrote in *La Crónica* (Lima) of Oct. 16, 1948: "Moreover, they [Aprista leaders] have believed it was enough to organize and discipline the Party to have power fall into their hands."

126. Horney, *Neurosis and Human Growth*, p. 60.

127. Alberto Baeza Flores, *Haya de la Torre y la revolución constructiva de las Américas* (Buenos Aires, 1962), pp. 168–69.

128. Antenor Orrego, prologue to Alcides Spelucín Vega, *Antología poética*, selection and introduction by Pedro Morán Obiol (Bahía Blanca, Argentina, 1971), p. 27.

129. These words are attributed to the poet Alberto Guillén, who later turned against Haya. See OC, 1:21.

130. Ibid., 2:323, from a June 1930 essay that Haya wrote in Berlin.

131. See Thomas M. Davies Jr. and Víctor Villanueva, eds., *Secretos electorales del APRA: Correspondencia y documentos de 1939* (Lima, 1982), pp. 121–22, passim.

132. See Sánchez, *Apuntes*, 3:105–6. See also this chapter's notes 95 and 96.

133. Luis Alberto Sánchez, *Haya de la Torre y el Apra* (Santiago de Chile, 1955), p. 368, maintains that such a pact was reached. Haya, however, has insisted otherwise. The jefe was furious with Manuel Prado, suspecting him of being behind the 1939 attempt on his life. This, at least, is the implication in Haya's November 1939 letter to Sánchez, cited and extracted in Henderson and Pérez, *Literature and Politics*, p. 234. In the letter Haya relates that at the time of the near assassination he had been reading Ricardo Rojas's *Ollantay*. In the mélée the book had been lost, and he requested Sánchez to send another copy. Haya felt a deep rapport with the Argentine Rojas (1882–1957), a person who viewed Argentine destiny in terms of an eventual amalgamation of European values and Indian traditions, of coastal, commercial Buenos Aires and the rural, interior provinces. In the letter Haya also laments that all his possessions were lost in consequence of the raid, including the treasured *Encyclopaedia Britannica* that John Mackay had contrived to send from the United States. In spite of all, Apristas were quickly back at their posts carrying on their work, and Haya himself claimed not to have lost even a single day.

Chapter 9

1. Herbert Croly, "The Obstacle to Peace," *New Republic* 18 (April 26, 1919): 406.

2. See Roscoe C. Hinkle, *Founding Theory of American Sociology, 1881–1915* (Boston, 1980); and William G. McLoughlin, *Revivals, Awakenings, and Reform* (Chicago, 1978), p. 165.

3. James A. Nuechterlein, "The Dream of Scientific Liberalism: The *New Republic* and American Progressive Thought, 1914–1920," *Review of Politics* 42 (1980), p. 177.

4. See Michael G. Kammen, *People of Paradox: An Inquiry Concerning the Origins of American Civilization* (New York, 1972).

5. See Isaiah Berlin, *Four Essays on Liberty* (New York, 1969), p. 39.

6. See Fredrick B. Pike, "Corporatism and Latin American–United States Relations," in *The New Corporatism: Social-Political Structures in the Iberian World*, ed. Pike and Thomas Stritch (Notre Dame, Ind., 1974), pp. 132–70.

7. The literature on Collier is vast and often polemical. Even-handed treatment is provided by Kenneth R. Philp, *John Collier's Crusade for Indian Reform, 1920–1954* (Tucson, 1977). On Collier's life and multifaceted activities up to 1928, see Lawrence C. Kelly's masterful *The Assault on Assimilation: John Collier and the Origins of Indian Policy Reform* (Albuquerque, 1983), the first of a projected two-volume biography. Kelly sees the 1920s as a watershed in Indian policy, with the old nativist insistence on assimilation giving way to acceptance and even to the welcoming of cultural pluralism. A similar theme is sounded at the conclusion of

Frederick A. Hoxie's splendid study, *A Final Promise: The Campaign to Assimilate the Indians, 1880–1920* (Lincoln, 1984). See esp. pp. 240–44. On the mystical, visionary approach that underlay formulation of Collier's Indian policy, see his short, eloquently written *On the Gleaming Way: Navajos, Eastern Pueblos, Zuñis, Hopis, Apaches and Their Land: And Their Meanings to the World*, 2d ed. (Chicago, 1962). Collier's mystical concepts resembled those that Haya de la Torre brought to his indigenismo—and also the concepts that shaped Waldo Frank's attitudes toward Latin Americans, as discussed toward the conclusion of this chapter.

8. See John J. Johnson, *Latin America in Caricature* (Austin, 1980). This is one of the most important studies I have encountered on underlying United States assumptions concerning the nature of Latin Americans.

9. See Ernest Lee Tuveson, *Redeemer Nation: The Idea of America's Millennial Role* (Chicago, 1968).

10. Robert A. Rosenstone, "Learning from those 'Imitative' Japanese: Another Side of the American Experience in the Mikado's Empire," *American Historical Review* 85 (1980), p. 954, referring to Prof. Ernest F. Fenollosa.

11. Ernest F. Fenollosa, "Chinese and Japanese Traits," *Atlantic Monthly* 69 (1892), p. 774, quoted by Rosenstone, "Learning," p. 594.

12. John Reed (d. 1920) produced a vibrant book, *Insurgent Mexico* (New York, 1914), out of his experiences in Mexico. See also Jim Tuck, *Pancho Villa and John Reed: Two Faces of Romantic Revolution* (Tucson, 1984).

13. Barry Carr, "Marxism and Anarchism in the Formation of the Mexican Communist Party, 1910–19," HAHR 63 (1983): 290–91, describes the "many hundreds" of United States opponents to their country's entry into World War I who made their way to Mexico. Among them were many draft dodgers and also a "few dozen" radicals who soon became connected with Mexico's socialist movement. Among these few was Carleton Beals.

14. At Frank Tannenbaum's suggestion, Moisés Sáenz, who headed Indian reform programs in Mexico, was invited to Washington in 1931 by the U.S. Commissioner of Indian Affairs. At this time John Collier, the future commissioner, was enormously enthusiastic about the prospects of United States–Mexican collaboration on Indian reform policies. Praising the Sáenz programs in Mexico based on cooperative organization and land use and on Indian citizenship and education, Collier in a Sept. 1, 1931, letter to Lewis Meriam observed that the policies directed by the Mexican were the kind "which we all, in the U.S.A., would want for our Indians but . . . haven't anywhere been able to get. . . ." Collier added, "At the same time we have Indian groups richer in their heritage than any in Mexico, and (this is a mere impression of course) more virile than any" (John Collier Papers, Yale University Library, New Haven). I am grateful to my Notre Dame colleague Donald Critchlow for providing me a copy of Collier's letter.

358

15. For information on Beals and Tannenbaum in Mexico during the 1920s I have depended on a carefully researched article by John A. Britton: "In Defense of Revolution: American Journalists in Mexico, 1920–1929," *Journalism History* 5 (1978–79); 124–36. I have also profited from correspondence with Professor Britton.

16. Porter's 1934 story "Hacienda" exhibited many of the themes that the expatriate writers in Mexico concentrated on: exaltation of the Indians as the only true Mexicans; contempt for capitalists whether of the Mexican or United States variety; sympathy for Russia; a conviction that through art one approaches the truth and envisions social justice. "Hacienda" appears in *The Collected Stories of Katherine Anne Porter* (New York, 1965), pp. 135–70. See also in this volume "That Tree," pp. 66–79, a story about an expatriate United States journalist in Mexico who is modeled after Carleton Beals.

17. Beals, *Fire on the Andes* (Philadelphia, 1934), p. 24.

18. Ibid., p. 431. See also Beals, "Aprismo: The Rise of Haya de la Torre," *Foreign Affairs* 13 (1935): 237. From his 1934 association with Beals in Mexico, Haya had learned about Tannenbaum and other North Americans who desired to transform the nature of their country preparatory to the forging of close spiritual, cultural, and political ties with Latin America. In particular, Haya learned more about Ernest Gruening, who had become editor of *The Nation* shortly before his initial journey to Mexico in 1922. The first article to bring Haya to the attention of United States readers was "The Story of Haya de la Torre," published in the April 9, 1924, edition of *The Nation*, pp. 406–10.

19. Beals, *Fire on the Andes*, pp. 426–27. In a Feb. 19, 1935, letter to Luis Alberto Sánchez, Haya commented favorably on Beals's *Fire on the Andes*, observed the growing United States interest in Aprismo, and noted that efforts should be made to intensify the movement's propaganda in North America. In a March 8, 1936, letter to Sánchez, Haya noted appreciatively that Beals's intervention with President Benavides had helped secure Magda Portal's release from prison. Then, in an October (?) 1938 letter to Sánchez, Haya praised Beals's new book, *The Coming Struggle for Latin America* (Philadelphia, 1938). In this work, according to Haya, Beals underscored the fact that, subsequent to the Mexican Revolution, Aprismo had influenced all of Indo-America's important political movements. These letters are cited and extracted in Donald C. Henderson and Grace R. Pérez, trans. and comps., *Literature and Politics in Latin America: An Annotated Calendar of the Luis Alberto Sánchez Correspondence, 1919–1980* (University Park, Pa., 1982), pp. 181, 201, 226.

20. OC, 1:200.

21. On the Nearing-Freeman book *Dollar Diplomacy: A Study in American Imperialism*, and its influence on Haya and Aprismo, see n. 48, ch. 7. Haya referred to *Dollar Diplomacy* as the inspiration of many of his original anti-

imperialist tenets. See Luis Alberto Sánchez, *Apuntes para una biografía del Apra*, 3 vols. (Lima, 1978–81) 1:150.

22. See Thomas M. Davies Jr. and Víctor Villanueva, eds., *Secretos electorales del APRA: Correspondencia y documentos de 1939* (Lima, 1982), pp. 17–19, reproducing documents from the U.S. State Department Archives.

23. See Sánchez, *Apuntes*, 3:62. Haya also conversed personally with delegates representing Mexico, Chile, Uruguay, and Colombia. With delegates from other countries he communicated through third parties. Sánchez, in exile at the time, relies for his information on Haya's companion, chauffeur, and occasional secretary, Jorge Idiáquez.

24. See Waldo Frank, *Dawn in Russia: The Record of a Journey* (New York, 1932). By 1933, the work had appeared in Spanish translation: *Aurora rusa*, published in Madrid. See also Paul Hollander, *Political Pilgrims: Travels of Western Intellectuals to the Soviet Union, China, and Cuba, 1928–1978* (New York, 1981), pp. 107–13, 131–38, 174–76, 240–48.

25. James Webb, *The Harmonious Circle: The Lives and Work of G. I. Gurdjieff, P. D. Ouspensky, and Their Followers* (New York, 1980), pp. 271–72. On Frank see also the perceptive study by Michael Ogorzaly, "Waldo Frank: Prophet of Hispanic Regeneration" (Ph.D. diss., University of Notre Dame, 1982). I am grateful to Dr. Ogorzaly for his advice on this chapter.

26. For development of these themes, see Frank's *The Re-Discovery of America: An Introduction to a Philosophy of American Life* (New York, 1929).

27. According to Van Wyck Brooks, *Days of the Phoenix: The Nineteen-Twenties I Remember* (New York, 1957), pp. 27–28, Frank "was drawn to Latin America because whatever were its defects, 'well-being' was not considered the highest good there. It seemed to him obvious that certain values survived in the Hispanic scene that our country had forgotten. . . . Feeling that the mystical values flourished still in the Hispanic world, he hoped for a cultural union between the North and the South. Believing that this would restore the traditional wholeness of man, he set out to integrate these worlds to one another." Frank himself, in *Re-Discovery of America*, pp. 268–70, commended Latin Americans for their ability to use the mystic tradition in attaining their secular salvation. Moreover, he credited them with understanding the necessity of creating a new world. Thus, he placed them in a position superior to that of his unenlightened fellow citizens of the United States. See Ogorzaly, "Waldo Frank," pp. 113–14.

28. According to the *Literary History of the United States*, ed. Robert Spiller et al. (New York, 1948), 2:1387, Frank was the "only serious North American author who exercised a direct influence in Latin America during the 1920s." Moreover, Frank's reputation endured in Latin America, in contrast to the precipitous decline it suffered in the United States.

29. Frank, *America Hispana: A Portrait and a Prospect* (New York, 1931), p.

370. In *Memoirs of Waldo Frank*, ed. Alan Trachtenberg with an introduction by Lewis Mumford (Amherst, 1973), p. 134, Frank wrote: "How could the Americas become a New World (rather than 'the grave of Europe') unless they produced new men?"

30. This was Frank's message to Argentines, as described by Doris Meyer, *Victoria Ocampo: Against the Wind and the Tide* (New York, 1979), p. 105.

31. *America Hispana*, pp. 339–41

32. Sánchez, quoted in *Waldo Frank in America Hispana*, ed. M. J. Bernardete (New York, 1930), p. 119.

33. Luis Alberto Sánchez, *Testimonio personal: Memorias de un peruano del siglo XX*, 4 vols. (Lima, 1969–76), 1:310.

34. The Waldo Frank–Luis Alberto Sánchez correspondence concerning arrangements for Frank to lecture in Peru is cited and extracted in Henderson and Pérez, *Literature and Politics*, pp. 101–2. For his San Marcos lecture, Frank chose the topic "Los profetas del arte moderno." For Frank's impressions of his impact on Peruvians, see his foreword to Sánchez, *Un sudamericano en Norteamérica: Ellos y nosotros*, 2d ed. (Lima, 1968, originally published in 1943). See also Frank, *Primer mensaje a la América Hispana* (Madrid, 1930), p. 10.

35. Sánchez, "Introduction to Waldo Frank," in *Waldo Frank in America Hispana*, ed. M. J. Bernardete, p. 115. "Jewishness" at the time was widely associated with, among other causes, internationalism. J. H. Talmon, in the section "The Jewish Dimension" in his *The Myth of the Nation and the Vision of Revolution: The Origins of Ideological Polarization in the Twentieth Century* (Berkeley, 1980), suggests that the threat to Jews arising out of European nationalism inclined them toward internationalism. Frank's interpretation, however, like Haya de la Torre's, was constrained by its focus on the American hemisphere. It was here that Frank expected the initial move toward an eventually all-encompassing internationalism to originate. In a way, then, he saw redemption arising out of the sort of people-continent extolled by Haya and Antenor Orrego as a synthesis between limited nationalism and the ineffable universalism of a world order. According to Haya, OC, 6:313, Simón Bolívar had envisaged a similar destiny. Frank, in *Birth of a World: Bolívar in Terms of his Peoples* (Boston, 1951), also depicts Bolívar as caught up in the search for an entity standing midway between the individual nation state and a universal order and partaking of the strengths of each.

36. Sánchez, "Introduction," pp. 115, 126.

37. Sánchez, *Testimonio*, 1:320.

38. *America Hispana*, pp. 173–75.

39. Bernardete, *Waldo Frank in America Hispana*, p. 142.

40. See *America Hispana*, p. 170.

41. Ibid., p. 176.

42. Ibid., p. 176 n. 1. Before its 1931 publication, Frank sent the *America His-*

pana manuscript to Luis Alberto Sánchez, just beginning his involvement with the Peruvian Aprista Party, for corrections. See Henderson and Pérez, *Literature and Politics*, p. 103.

43. OC, 2:107.

44. Frank was by no means an uncritical admirer of Haya in the early 1930s. In a June 13, 1931, letter to Sánchez, written during the course of the Haya–Sánchez Cerro electoral campaign, he recorded the impression that Haya might be "veering toward fascism." In a Jan. 7, 1934, letter to Sánchez, Frank confided that he did not understand certain of Haya's utterances but did appreciate Aprismo's role in general. Then, in a March 26, 1935, letter to Sánchez, Frank denied that he was anti-Aprista and promised to read books by Sánchez and Haya to inform himself better of their "revolutionary politics, methods, and almost everything else." See Henderson and Pérez, *Literature and Politics*, p. 104. In a March 21, 1934, letter to Samuel Glusberg in Buenos Aires (ibid., pp. 459–60), Sánchez opined that neither Glusberg nor Frank understood Aprismo; and he accused them of being "pure intellectuals," not attuned to everyday political and social struggles. Apparently Frank was at times disturbed by the methods, not the ideology, of Aprismo. Probably Haya sought to reassure him in a 1937 letter that he sent via two associates in the United States (see ibid., p. 148). Haya's letter to Frank has not come to light, however, and one can only speculate on its contents.

45. Jonathan Mitchell, "End of the Conquistadors," *New Republic* 81 (Jan. 2, 1935): 210. Careless in its facts, Mitchell's piece is one of blatant propaganda.

46. Frank, *South American Journey* (New York, 1943), p. 383. Translated by León Felipe, the work was published in Mexico City in 1944 as *Viaje por Suramérica*.

47. On Frank's concept of the "Deep War," see his "La guerra simple y la guerra profunda: Prefacio a la edición castellana," in *Rumbos para América (Nuestra misión en el nuevo mundo)*, trans. María Zambrano, Luis Orsetti, and José Basiglio Agosti (Buenos Aires, 1942), pp. 15–21. This is the Spanish version of Frank's *Chart for Rough Water: Our Role in a New World* (New York, 1940).

Chapter 10

1. Luis Alberto Sánchez, *Apuntes para una biografía del Apra*, 3 vols. (Lima, 1978–81), 3:128.

2. Percy Murillo Garaycochea, *Historia del APRA, 1919–1945* (Lima, 1976), p. 462.

3. Sánchez, *Apuntes*, 3:43.

4. OC, 6: 12–13.

5. Ibid., p. 28.

6. Waldo Frank, *South American Journey* (New York, 1943), p. 382.

7. Haya de la Torre, *Y después de la guerra ¿qué?* (Lima, 1946), in OC, 6:204.

8. Haya de la Torre letter of March 8, 1943, to Luis Alberto Sánchez, cited and extracted in Donald C. Henderson and Grace R. Pérez, trans. and comps., *Literature and Politics in Latin America: An Annotated Calendar of the Luis Alberto Sánchez Correspondence, 1919–1980* (University Park, Pa., 1982), p. 240.

9. OC, 6:221.

10. Ibid., p. 204. In particular, Haya hailed Beals's book *America South*, published in the United States in 1937 and in a Santiago de Chile Spanish translation as *América ante América* in 1940.

11. Haya letter of March 8, 1943, to Sánchez, extracted in *Literature and Politics*, Henderson and Pérez, pp. 240–41. Haya also noted that despite their different personalities and despite their political disagreements of the moment, he and Sánchez were united by a shared faith. Haya's references to faith are reminiscent of his utterances in his November 1933 address in Lima following his release from the penitentiary (and quoted toward the beginning of chapter 6). In the November address, Haya had assured his listeners that the most important thing in their lives was the faith that united them and created a means of communication that transcended words: "Our faith has the formidable force to make vibrate all our consciousness, creating authentic sentiment and marvelous intuition, of which refined consciousness can attain scarely an inkling" (OC, 5:154).

12. On Haya's hopes for hemispheric harmony, see his July 1941 essay in *La defensa continental* (Buenos Aires, 1942), in OC, 4:355–57.

13. *Y después*, in OC, 6:238–44.

14. See Haya's Feb. 10, 1939, communication to the secretary general of the Aprista committee of exiles in Santiago de Chile, in *300 documentos para la historia del APRA*, ed. Thomas M. Davies Jr. and Víctor Villanueva (Lima, 1978), p. 316.

15. OC, 6:97, 228–31.

16. See Raoul de Roussy de Sales, *The Making of Tomorrow* (New York, 1942), p. 227.

17. *Y después*, in OC, 6:217–18. In the principal essay of *Y después* (pp. 220–35), "El aprismo en su linea" (1940), Haya places the four freedoms within the mystical context of the merging of opposites.

18. De Sales, *Making of Tomorrow*, p. 331.

19. OC, 5:358. For a more obscurely expressed reference to the linkage between the four freedoms and historical space-time, see OC, 6:228.

20. Haya developed this idea in a 1943 essay in *Y después* (OC, 6:30).

21. Ibid., p. 231.

22. On Haya's belief that Indo-America and China shared a common destiny, see his 1943 essay in ibid., p. 20. See also n. 60, ch. 7.

23. Lin Yutang wrote, in *Between Tears and Laughter* (New York, 1943), p. 20: "The emergence of Asia simply means this: the end of the era of imperialism."

24. Ibid., pp. 215-16.

25. Ibid., pp. 191-92.

26. See n. 43, ch. 7.

27. Lin, *Between Tears and Laughter*, p. 190.

28. Ibid., pp. 69-73.

29. On Haya's conviction concerning the postwar convergence of capitalism and socialism in the United States, see Alberto Baeza Flores, *Haya de la Torre y la revolución constructiva de las Américas* (Buenos Aires, 1962), p. 145. Haya also foresaw a mutual approximation between the socioeconomic systems of the United States and the Soviet Union.

30. OC, 6:46.

31. Henry A. Wallace, *New Frontiers* (New York, 1934), p. 254.

32. Ibid., p. 276.

33. OC, 6:46.

34. Ibid., pp. 77-82.

35. Víctor Villanueva, *El Apra y el ejército, 1940-1950* (Lima, 1977), pp. 32-33.

36. Víctor Villanueva, *El Apra en busca del poder, 1930-1940* (Lima, 1975), p. 45.

37. Villanueva, *El Apra y el ejército*, pp. 30-32. Villanueva's account is based on U.S. State Department documents.

38. See the 1944 essay by Haya in *Y después*, OC, 6:220-35.

39. See Felipe Cossío del Pomar, *Haya de la Torre, el indoamericano* (Lima, 1946), pp. 357-61; and Arthur P. Whitaker, "Pan America in Politics and Diplomacy," *Inter-American Affairs: 1944* (New York, 1945), p. 33.

40. See Luis Eduardo Enríquez, *Haya de la Torre: La estafa política más grande de América* (Lima, 1951), p. 53; and Pablo Silva Villacorta, *¿A dónde van las ideas de Haya de la Torre? Una nueva visión sobre las ideas que conforman la doctrina del APRA* (Lima, 1966), p. 103. According to Enríquez (p. 53), Haya and many of his cohorts began now to abandon Masonry, and Manuel Seoane started once more to receive communion in the Catholic Church.

41. See Allen Gerlach, "Civil-Military Relations in Peru: 1914-1945" (Ph.D. diss., University of New Mexico, 1973), p. 516; Dennis L. Gilbert, "The Oligarchy and the Old Regime in Peru" (Ph.D. diss., Cornell University, 1977), p. 119; and Liisa North, "The Origins and Development of the Peruvian Aprista Party" (Ph.D. diss., University of California, Berkeley, 1973), p. 136.

42. Eduardo Jibaja, "Ingreso al cielo interno de Víctor Raúl Haya de la Torre" (Lima, 1945), clipped from an unidentified newspaper, probably *Trinchero Aliada*, in the Benson Latin American Collection of the University of Texas.

364

43. *Inter-American Affairs: 1945* (New York, 1946), p. 287.
44. Mario Peláez Bazán, *Haya de la Torre y la unidad de América Latina* (Lima, 1977), p. 131.
45. Cossío, *Haya de la Torre*, p. 367.
46. For the May 20, 1945, re-encounter address, see OC, 5:343–55.
47. Víctor Villanueva, *La tragedia de un pueblo y de un partido: Páginas para la historia del Apra* (Santiago de Chile, 1954), p. 16.
48. Karen Horney, *Neurosis and Human Growth: The Struggle toward Self-Realization* (New York, 1950), p. 65.
49. Theodor Reik, *Masochism in Modern Man*, trans. Margaret H. Beigel and Gertrude M. Kurth (New York, 1941), p. 88.
50. OC, 5:146–47.
51. Cossío, *Haya de la Torre*, p. 369.
52. See Weston La Barre, *The Ghost Dance: Origins of Religion*, rev. ed. (New York, 1972), p. 180. In this instance, berdache is not associated with the connotation of male prostitute that it sometimes conveys.
53. Jibaja, "Ingreso al cielo interno." The title of the short piece comes from Jibaja's belief that through the mystical experience of the evening of May 20 he had seen "pieces of the internal heaven of Víctor Raúl."
54. Victor Turner, *Dramas, Fields, and Metaphors: Symbolic Action in Human Society* (Ithaca, 1974), p. 122.
55. Jorge Basadre, *La vida y la historia: Ensayos sobre personas, lugares y problemas* (Lima, 1975), p. 573.
56. Enrique Chirinos Soto, *El Perú frente a junio de 1962* (Lima, 1962), p. 62.
57. The Oct. 9, 1945, address is in OC, 5: 356–93.
58. Ibid., pp. 383–86.
59. See Alberto Yáñez Gómez, "Sentido religioso del símbolo," *Boletín de la Masonería Boliviana* (La Paz) 31 (1950): 41.
60. See Carl G. Jung, *Psychology and Alchemy*, trans. R. F. C. Hull, 2d ed., rev. (Princeton, 1968), p. 169.
61. OC, 5:369. In his toy-car imagery, Haya seems to have been influenced by a man to whom he and, indeed, most Latin American intellectuals referred frequently, the German explorer-naturalist Alexander von Humboldt (1769–1859). In *Cosmos*, the crowning work of a life devoted to exploration and the study of geology, botany, metereology, and astronomy, Humboldt developed a theory of geographical determinism. He asserted that the physical life of an area determined the character of its inhabitants, and that one type of environment would be conducive to slow or arrested development, another to rapid and progressive development. Humboldt also had his occult, esoteric side, attuned to the German idealism and Romanticism of his era. Because of this, and his alleged homosexuality, he may have impressed Haya as a kindred soul and seer.

62. See Jung, *Psychology and Alchemy*, p. 104.

63. OC, 5:387.

64. Ibid., p. 388.

65. Jung, *Psychology and Alchemy*, p. 204.

66. Ibid., p. 22.

67. See Ibid., p. 205.

68. See Frederic V. Grunfeld, *Prophets without Honor: A Background to Freud, Kafka, Einstein, and Their World* (New York, 1979), p. 177, with reference to Arnold Schönberg's "Moses and Aaron." Moreover, the attempt to square the circle represents one of the classic esoteric visions of reconciling opposites. The circle stood for the perfection, the wholeness of the divinity in heaven, while the square, suggesting the cardinal points, represented the earth.

69. In the Teatro Municipal address Haya showed himself once again to be a kindred soul with Count Hermann von Keyserling and to be deeply immersed in the whole esoteric tradition. In *The World in the Making*, trans. Maurice Samuel (New York, 1927), pp. 72–73, Keyserling wrote: "When a group of spiritual values which harmonizes properly in rhythm and quality is apprehended as a unit, we experience something which is qualitatively new and individual. . . . Since it is in my nature to be able to see in the complex the expression of the higher unity, and to determine the right relationship of the part to the whole, I found little difficulty . . . in presenting the higher form of insight, which I had in view of the harmony resulting from the orchestration of the usual, partial points of view."

70. See Felipe Cossío del Pomar, *Víctor Raúl: Biografía de Haya de la Torre* (Mexico City, 1961), p. 313. On the enduring Pythagorean influence within the spiritualist tradition, see Ernest McLain, "Three for Aristotle," *Parabola* 5 (1980): 100–101; Renee Weber, "Philosophical Foundations and Frameworks for Healing," *The American Theosophist* 72 (1984): 180–82, 185, and nn. 52, 60, ch. 5.

71. Manuel Seoane, "Haya de la Torre: El hermano mayor," in the anonymously edited *Radiografía de Haya de la Torre* (Lima, 1946), p. 21. This short work provides striking examples of the sort of adulation that Apristas accorded the jefe as the Party of the People began its legal existence.

72. Enríquez, *Haya de la Torre*, p. 183.

73. Ibid., p. 112.

74. Ibid., p. 161.

75. Manuel Seoane and Luis Barrios Llona letter of June 11, 1954, written in Santiago de Chile to Haya de la Torre. The letter is reproduced in Villanueva, *Tragedia de un pueblo*, pp. 227–47.

76. See the anonymously edited *Haya de la Torre: Su vida y sus luchas* (Lima, 1957), an interesting, illustrated pamphlet without page numbering.

77. See Peláez Bazán, *Haya de la Torre*, pp. 437–39. Jorge Basadre, *Historia de la república del Perú, 1882–1933*, 6th ed., rev., 17 vols. (Lima, 1968–70), 14:241,

notes that the first Día de la Fraternidad celebration occurred on February 21, 1933, when a group of Apristas shot off firecrackers in Lima's Neptune Park, hoping that Haya in the penitentiary would hear this manifestation of their devotion.
78. Gustavo Valcárcel, *Apología de un hombre, Haya de la Torre* (Lima, 1945). The pamphlet is unpaginated. Valcárcel broke with the party in 1952, which prompted Aprista charges that he was a Communist.
79. See Serafino Romualdi, *Presidents and Peons: Recollections of a Labor Ambassador in Latin America* (New York, 1967), pp. 294–95. Chapter 18 in Romualdi's work, "Peru and Haya de la Torre," provides a sympathetic treatment of the APRA and its leader. Romualdi expressed misgivings, however, about the party's vertical organization.
80. *La Tribuna* (Lima), May 27, 1948, p. 1.
81. Ibid., June 4, 1948, p. 1.
82. See the poem "Salutación," in J. H. Chávez's mercifully short book of poems, *Voces de la ruta* (Lima, 1947). Another Chávez poem, "Alborada," concludes with these words: "From the peak of this hour of his glory / The CHIEF can contemplate his spartan work / Which has written his name with blood in history / Redeeming a thousand times this Peruvian land."
83. OC, 5:404.
84. Ibid., pp. 409–11, 418.
85. Ibid., p. 421.
86. See Romualdi, *Presidents and Peons*, p. 293.
87. See Fredrick B. Pike, *The Modern History of Peru* (London, 1967), p. 284.
88. For an even-handed summary of the Aprista-Bustamante confrontation, see Enrique Chirinos Soto, *Historia de la república: 1821-Perú-1978* (Lima, 1977), pp. 490–97.
89. See Pike, *Modern History*, pp. 284–86.
90. See the Aprista-inspired pamphlet *"Documento de Rancagua": El crimen Graña—un caso de provocación; la huelga parlamentaria y el boicot al Contrato de Sechura son partes del plan ruso* (Lima, 1948).
91. Arthur P. Whitaker, "Summary and Prospect," *Inter-American Affairs: 1943* (New York, 1944), pp. 205–6.
92. See William L. O'Neill, *A Better World: The Great Schism: Stalinism and the American Intellectuals* (New York, 1982).
93. See Richard J. Walton, *Henry Wallace, Harry Truman, and the Cold War* (New York, 1976).
94. Philip Gleason, "Identifying Identity: A Semantic History," *Journal of American History* 69 (1983): 924.
95. Basadre, *La vida y la historia*, p. 604.
96. Works by Víctor Villanueva, although not impartial, provide an extremely

valuable coverage of the October 3 uprising and the background to it, including Haya de la Torre's dealings with General Marín. Claiming initially to have enjoyed Haya's backing, Villanueva was instrumental in planning this uprising. He feels that top-level Aprista leaders betrayed the party by failing to back the Callao uprising once it began. See Villanueva's *El militarismo en el Perú* (Lima, 1962) and *Tragedia de un pueblo*, pp. 132–33, 161–62, passim. Although a work that must be used with extreme caution owing to its strong anti-Aprista biases, Enríquez' *Haya de la Torre* provides valuable insights on events that preceded and accompanied the October 3 rebellion. This incident had a great impact on the Party of the People. In the years immediately following it a number of important figures renounced their membership, invariably citing as one of their reasons Haya's alleged betrayal of those who engineered the uprising. See, for example, Magda Portal, *¿Quienes traicionaron al pueblo? A los Apristas* (Lima, 1950). On their part, Haya and his immediate associates placed the blame on underlings who failed to heed orders to abort the golpe. The official party command line is captured by the North American writer Hoffman R. Hays in his novel *The Envoys* (New York, 1953), p. 265. When an Aprista leader in Trujillo is dumbfounded by news of the Callao insurrection, he explodes: "Something has gone wrong again. This was not planned. Traitors, extremists, provocateurs . . . God knows . . . they have destroyed us."

97. José Luis Bustamante y Rivero provides an understandably unfriendly account of the Odría-led golpe that ousted him in his *Tres años de lucha por la democracia en el Perú* (Buenos Aires, 1949), pp. 250–70. This book is especially valuable for the light it casts on the president's three-year duel with the APRA.

Chapter 11

1. Friends of Haya in various parts of the world sought to mobilize international opinion to demand that he be permitted to leave his asylum under safe conduct. Some of the material they issued in the course of their campaign is compiled in *El asilado "silencioso": Antología del caso Haya de la Torre* (Mexico City, 1954). A good insight into the campaign that Apristas waged on an international scale is found in letters and documents in the Luis Alberto Sánchez archives at Pennsylvania State University. For extracts of this material see Donald C. Henderson and Grace R. Pérez, trans. and comps., *Literature and Politics in Latin America: An Annotated Calendar of the Luis Alberto Sánchez Correspondence, 1919–1980* (University Park, Pa., 1982), esp. pp. 14–15, 245–59. During Haya's confinement, a vast literature appeared on the international law aspects of the case, which eventually came before the Permanent Tribunal at the Hague.

368

2. Haya, Nov. 8, 1952, letter to Sánchez, cited and extracted in *Literature and Politics*, Henderson and Pérez, pp. 245–46.

3. Haya, letter of Feb. 23, 1953, to Sánchez, cited and extracted in ibid., p. 248.

4. Haya, March 22, 1954, letter to Sánchez, cited and extracted in ibid., p. 259.

5. Haya's *Toynbee frente a los panoramas de la historia* was published in Buenos Aires in 1955, under the supervision of his old friend Gabriel del Mazo, and is included in OC, 7:11–195. His *Treinta años de aprismo*, another of his principal works written in the embassy, was published in Mexico City in 1956 and is included in OC, 6:249–448. In the latter work, Haya depicted Aprismo as a moderate, even conservative, movement.

6. Haya, Nov. 8, 1952, letter to Sánchez, cited in note 2.

7. Haya, May 21, 1953, letter to Sánchez, cited and extracted in *Literature and Politics*, Henderson and Pérez, pp. 349–50.

8. Haya, Sept. 2, 1953, letter to Sánchez, ibid., p. 251.

9. Haya, Feb. 23, 1953?, letter to Sánchez, ibid., p. 248. Set against the period of the October 3, 1948, Aprista uprising at Callao, *The Envoys* probes the complexity of the Peruvian situation, mainly through the eyes of North Americans living in Peru. The novel effectively brings out the misgivings that many progressive-minded individuals felt over Haya's Mussolini tendencies. Although it highlights the repressiveness of a reactionary oligarchy in dealing with Aprismo, it shows also the bitter class hatred of some Apristas, which gave the oligarchy reason to be repressive. Finally, Hays's novel gives voice to the hope that North Americans, for all their materialism, may begin to concern themselves more with poetry as Latin Americans begin to develop their practical, economic skills. A humanist convinced of the continuum of man and nature and of the need for man to retain a partnership with nature, notwithstanding the threats of technology to that partnership, Hays was capable of responding to the mystical contents of Aprista ideology.

10. Haya, Oct. 12, 1953, letter to Sánchez, cited and extracted in *Literature and Politics*, Henderson and Pérez, pp. 251–52.

11. See p. 62 of Ray Josephs' Oct. 16, 1948, *Colliers* article, "Uncle Sam's Latin Salesman": "They [Apristas] know that Einstein has called Haya one of the twelve men in the world who really understands the theory of relativity." It was part of Aprista lore that Einstein made such a statement; but specifics as to when and where Einstein rendered this judgment are never provided. In any event, Josephs' article, which is analyzed in the preface of this book, brings out very well Haya's frantic efforts to curry United States backing. "Haya's greatest crime," Josephs reports (p. 62), "is that he is Uncle Sam's best friend."

12. Haya, January 23, 1954, letter to Sánchez, cited and extracted in *Literature and Politics*, Henderson and Pérez, p. 258.

13. Eudocio Ravines, *El momento político* (Buenos Aires, 1945), p. 26. On Ra-

vines, who founded the Peruvian Communist Party, but disavowed communism in 1942, see n. 81, ch. 4. While Ravines shows flashes of brilliance as a journalist, his anti-Aprista prejudices must be taken into account.

14. Ibid.

15. See Grant Hilliker, *The Politics of Reform in Peru: The Aprista and Other Mass Parties of Latin America* (Baltimore, 1971), p. 105 n. 5. See also Victor Alba, *Alliance without Allies: The Mythology of Progress in Latin America*, trans. John Pearson (New York, 1965), pp. 88–92; and Harry Kantor, *The Ideology and Program of the Peruvian Aprista Movement* (Berkeley, 1953), p. 57.

16. On the APRA during 1948–54, see the first seven chapters, vol. 3, of Luis Alberto Sánchez's *Testimonio personal: Memorias de un peruano del siglo XX*, 4 vols. (Lima, 1969–76). In a May 13, 1955, letter to Haya, cited and extracted in Henderson and Pérez, *Literature and Politics*, p. 265, Sánchez noted that during the past five years there had been a move within the party to discredit Haya as a future presidential candidate on the grounds that someone with "greater guarantees of triumph" should be the party's standard-bearer.

17. See Luis Eduardo Enríquez, *Haya de la Torre: La estafa política más grande de América* (Lima, 1951).

18. See *Literature and Politics*, Henderson and Pérez, pp. 22–24, 265.

19. See n. 16, ch. 6.

20. Hidalgo, *Por qué renuncié al Apra* (Buenos Aires, 1954). Given its inflammatory tone, the pamphlet scarcely inspires credence.

21. Portal, *¿Quienes traicionaron al pueblo? A los Apristas* (Lima, 1950), p. 28. A useful work dealing in part with the defections from the APRA in the 1940s and 1950s is Alfredo Hernández Urbina, *Los partidos y la crisis del Apra* (Lima, 1956). See also César A. Guardia Mayorga, *Reconstruyendo el aprismo: Exposición i refutación de la doctrina política y filosófica hayista* (Arequipa, 1945).

22. Quoted by Martin Green, *The Challenge of the Mahatmas* (New York, 1978), p. 42.

23. According to Jamake Highwater, *The Primal Mind* (New York, 1981), p. 5, the "primal mind" rejects the universe in favor of a "multi-verse." Native Americans, he continues, "don't believe that there is one fixed and eternal truth; they think there are many different and equally valid truths." In rejecting the typical modern approach to reality, Haya was acting more as the Indo- than as the Latin American.

24. See Víctor Villanueva, *El Apra y el ejército, 1940–1950* (Lima, 1977), p. 81. Villanueva, who stands in the Peruvian anarchist tradition, laments that after 1948 APRA lost its revolutionary thrust, succumbing to bourgeois goals.

25. Isaiah Berlin, *Russian Thinkers* (New York, 1978), p. 140.

26. The essays composing *Toynbee frente a los panoramas de la historia* were written between 1951 and 1954 (see note 5). The first part of *Toynbee* is devoted to

a careful analysis of vol. 1 of *A Study of History*. In the concluding section, Haya relates Toynbee's theories to his own historical space-time concepts. Haya used the Spanish translation of the Toynbee work, published in Buenos Aires beginning in 1950, and derided the 3-volume English abridged edition.

27. On Toynbee, see John Barker, *The Superhistorians: Makers of Our Past* (New York, 1982), pp. 368–99. Among other points, Barker stresses that Toynbee thought the future for humanity lay in a syncretized religion.

28. See Bruce Mazlish, *The Riddle of History: The Great Speculators from Vico to Freud* (New York, 1966), pp. 356, 378.

29. OC, 7:20.

30. Ibid., p. 21.

31. Ibid., pp. 28–29.

32. See esp. ibid., pp. 180–95.

33. Ibid., p. 165.

34. Ibid., pp. 96–98. In this section Haya also provides a full description of Toynbee's conception of the Yin and Yang principles. Toynbee, according to an approving Haya, pictured the Yang in terms of a serpent and also of hardness, movement, fire, and light. The Yin he equated with blandness, undisturbed water (in contrast to falling, moving, or penetrating water, which was Yang-like), shade and quietude. Furthermore, Haya explained (pp. 134–39), Toynbee saw the Yang, in its serpent manifestation, as associated with the devil, whereas the Yin stood for God. In Toynbee's analysis, as presented by Haya, the devil could never be vanquished and was, in fact, as essential to wholeness as God. Similar interpretations appear in most esoteric traditions, in a good deal of Eastern religious thought, in American Indian beliefs, and in Jung's thought.

35. Ibid., pp. 194–95.

36. See n. 20, ch. 4.

37. A sizeable portion of the lengthy Seoane-Barrios letter is reproduced in Villanueva, *El Apra y el ejército*, pp. 227–47.

38. Serafino Romualdi, *Presidents and Peons: Recollections of a Labor Ambassador in Latin America* (New York, 1967), p. 315.

39. Enrique Chirinos Soto, *Historia de la república: 1821-Peru-1978* (Lima, 1977), p. 509.

40. OC, 3:402. See also Alberto Baeza Flores, *Haya de la Torre y la revolución constructiva de las Américas* (Buenos Aires, 1962), p. 145.

41. See *Literature and Politics*, Henderson and Pérez, p. 263. In a letter of June or July 1955 (ibid., pp. 266–67), Haya assured Sánchez that his (Haya's) vision of world peace harmonized with the thinking of Einstein, Bertrand Russell, and Scandinavian and Russian leaders.

42. See the anonymously edited *Haya de la Torre, fundador del aprismo: Rasgos biográficos, opiniones, anécdotas: Homenaje en el Día de la Fraternidad*

(Lima, 1959), p. 21. On the straitened circumstances in which he lived while in Europe, Haya's correspondence with Luis Alberto Sánchez is convincing. See especially his letter of Feb. 4, 1955, written from Geneva, in Haya and Sánchez, *Correspondencia, 1924–1976*, 2 vols. (Lima, 1983), 2:197–204. Many of the other letters written in 1955 and 1956 (pp. 204–301) also refer to impecunious circumstances. Before long, though, the letters lost their querulous, self-pitying tone. Frequently, Haya referred to income deriving from his incessant writing, his main money-earner having been an article published in *Life* about the time he began his exile.

43. *Caretas* (Lima), Dec. 22–Jan. 15, 1961, p. 11.

44. OC, 5:340.

45. Ibid., p. 413.

46. Saint Theresa of Avila, *Interior Castle*, trans. and ed. E. Allison Peers (Garden City, N.Y., 1961), pp. 197–98. The "wound of love" is incurred by the seeker in the "Sixth Mansion," the state in which the seeker's soul is already quite advanced, in which the lover and beloved see each other for long periods as they grow in intimacy, and in which the soul, as lover, receives increasing favors from the beloved. Along with favors, however, come afflictions. The soul, in fact, suffers afflictions of a new intensity, resembling the suffering of souls in purgatory, as it grows apprehensive over the fragility of its bonds with the beloved and the certainty of new periods of the beloved's withdrawal.

47. See nn. 74 and 75, ch. 8.

48. Partido del Pueblo, *¿De qué vive Haya de la Torre? Documentos reveladores* (Lima, 1960), p. 6.

49. Ibid., pp. 25–26.

50. Ibid., pp. 23–24.

51. Haya, "Sobre la revolución intelectual de nuestro siglo," published originally in *Cuadernos Americanos* (Mexico City) 18 (1960); reproduced in OC 1:366–86.

52. Haya, "Reflexiones en un breve viaje," OC 1:264–67. See also Baeza, *Haya de la Torre*, pp. 156–61, for an account of a 1961 lecture that Haya delivered in Paris. In this discourse, Haya dwelt on historical space-time as he envisioned a coming age of cosmic harmony.

53. Baeza, *Haya de la Torre*, pp. 146–48.

54. Chirinos Soto, *Historia de la república*, p. 514.

55. The interview, published in the July 30, 1966, edition of *Time*, is quoted extensively by Víctor Villanueva, *El Apra en busca del poder, 1930–1940* (Lima, 1975), p. 17.

56. See Roy Soto Rivera, "Vida y pasión de un personaje inolvidable," in *La revolución que el Perú necesita: Homenaje póstumo al ilustre político*, by Manuel Seoane (Arequipa, 1965), p. 30.

57. See *Del Apra al Apra Rebelde: Documentos para la historia de la revolución peruana* (Lima, 1980).

58. On declining middle sector support of APRA, see Hilliker, *Politics of Reform*, p. 86.

59. Pedro Roselló, quoted in Hernando Aguirre Gamio, *Liquidación histórica del Apra y del colonialismo neoliberal* (Lima, 1962), p. 10.

60. Patricio Ricketts Rey de Castro, "Personaje proteico," *Caretas*, Aug. 6, 1979, p. 72.

61. Chirinos Soto, *Historia de la república*, p. 523.

62. Ibid., p. 523.

63. Ibid., pp. 523–24.

64. For Haya's cryptic and unsatisfactory explanation of his pact with Odría, see his interview published in *Oiga* (Lima), Oct. 31, 1975, pp. 18–19, 30–32.

65. See Rogger Mercado, *Vida, traición y muerte del movimiento aprista* (Lima, 1970), a Marxist diatribe against the APRA.

66. See Fredrick B. Pike, *The Modern History of Peru* (London, 1967), pp. 302–3.

67. Ibid., pp. 307–10.

68. Robert J. Alexander, comp. and trans., *Aprismo: The Ideas and Doctrines of Víctor Raúl Haya de la Torre* (Kent, Ohio, 1973), p. 18.

69. See *Caretas*, Jan. 30–Feb. 14, 1962, p. 18; and *La Tribuna*, the Aprista daily published in Lima, Jan. 22, 1962.

70. Chirinos Soto, *Historia de la república*, p. 525, speculates that many Peruvians who actually favored Haya did not wish to waste their ballots again, foreseeing another military intervention to prevent his inauguration if he won the election.

71. Sánchez, *Testimonio personal*, 3:1250.

Chapter 12

1. Despite their negative stance on some issues, Apristas could claim credit for inclusion in an agrarian reform law approved by congress of a provision stipulating that bits of land that peasants had been permitted to use for their own purposes would become their actual property.

2. See Adalberto J. Pinelo, *The Multinational Corporation as a Force in Latin American Politics: A Case Study of the International Petroleum Company in Peru* (New York, 1973), pp. 118–19.

3. R. R. Marett, *Head, Heart and Hands in Human Evolution* (New York, 1935), p. 39.

4. See the prologue by Orestes Rodríquez Campos, rector in the 1970s of the

popular universities, in Eduardo Jibaja C. (pseud. Ignacio Campos), *Coloquios de Haya de la Torre* (Lima, 1977), p. 8.

5. Serafino Romualdi, *Presidents and Peons: Recollections of a Labor Ambassador in Latin America* (New York, 1967), p. 321.

6. See Grant Hilliker, *The Politics of Reform in Peru: The Aprista and Other Mass Parties of Latin America* (Baltimore, 1971), p. 107. Hilliker quotes extensively from Townsend's penetrating analysis, published in the newspaper *Correo* (Lima), March 4, 1966, p. 20.

7. Hilliker, *Politics of Reform*, p. 88.

8. Robert J. Alexander, comp. and trans., *Aprismo: The Ideas and Doctrines of Víctor Raúl Haya de la Torre* (Kent, Ohio, 1973), p. 19.

9. Juan Velasco Alvarado, *La revolución peruana* (Buenos Aires, 1973), pp. 26, 66.

10. Ibid., p. 95.

11. Carlos Delgado, *Problemas sociales en el Perú contemporáneo* (Lima, 1971), p. 37.

12. Norman Long and Bryan R. Roberts, eds., *Peasant Cooperation and Capitalist Expansion in Central Peru* (Austin, 1978), effectively discredit the notion that collectivism is a common denominator among Andean peasants or *campesinos*. See also n. 14, ch. 4, and this chapter's n. 52.

13. On the influence of Yugoslavian models on the industrial community see Ismael Frías, *Nacionalismo y autogestión* (Lima, 1971), pp. 183-85. The concept of "communitarian property," associated with leftist currents in Latin American Christian Democracy, also exercised an influence.

14. Velasco Alvarado, *Revolución peruana*, p. 123.

15. See the valuable study by David Scott Palmer, *"Revolution from Above": Military Government and Popular Participation in Peru, 1968-1972*, Cornell University Latin American Studies Program Dissertation Series 47 (Ithaca, 1973), p. 5.

16. Frank Bonilla, "Cultural Elites," in *Elites in Latin America*, ed. Seymour Martin Lipset and Aldo Solari (New York, 1967), p. 250.

17. On the importance of civilians in the military government see Frederick M. Nunn, "Notes on the 'Junta Phenomenon' and the 'Military Regime' in Latin America, with Special Reference to Peru, 1968-1972," *The Americas* 31 (1975): 237-51.

18. Velasco Alvarado, *Revolución peruana*, p. 56. For a good analysis of the populist element in Peru's government see Julio Cotler, "Political Crisis and Military Populism in Peru," *Studies in Comparative International Development* 6 (1970-71): 95-113. In a speech delivered early in 1976, Gen. Francisco Morales Bermúdez, who presided at the time over the Revolutionary Government of the Armed Forces, claimed that "The Armed Forces arise as the only and most faith-

374

ful interpreter of the aspirations of the national majorities." See *Oiga* (Lima), May 21, 1976, p. 11.

19. OC, 7:340–41.

20. Ibid., pp. 374–75.

21. In 1970, there appeared a third edition of what was probably Haya's most revolutionary book, *El antimperialismo y el APRA*—first published in 1935, although the essays composing it had been written principally in the late 1920s. In the 1960s critics often charged the APRA with intentionally keeping Haya's radical book out of circulation. In his book *Aprismo y antimperialismo* (Arequipa, 1970), Aprista Roy Soto Rivera celebrated the appearance of the third edition of Haya's controversial book. The event, he maintained, gave the lie to those who claimed that *Antimperialismo* had been placed on the index of prohibited reading for young Apristas. Not only in Peru but throughout much of the developed world the surge of radical countercultures contributed to a climate of opinion that may have encouraged Haya to revive the revolutionary fervor of early Aprismo. Furthermore, a resuscitation of soft Marxism, as an underlying feature of counterculture radicalism, tended to bring new respectability to Aprismo's pristine ideological position.

22. See Michael Gregory Macaulay, "Ideological Change and Internal Cleavages in the Peruvian Church; Change, Status Quo and The Priest; The Case of ONIS" (Ph.D. diss., University of Notre Dame, 1972).

23. Gustavo Gutiérrez, *A Theology of Liberation: History, Politics, and Salvation*, trans. and ed. Sister Caridad Inda and John Eagleson (Maryknoll, N.Y., 1973), p. 231. For a sympathetic review of some of the theology of liberation literature, see Daniel H. Levine, "Religion, Society, and Politics: States of the Art," LARR 16, no. 3 (1981): 185–209. For a critical approach, see Michael Novak, ed., *Liberation South, Liberation North* (Washington, D.C., 1981).

24. T. Howland Sanks, "Liberation Theology and the Social Gospel: Variations on a Theme," *Theological Studies* 41 (1980): 681.

25. OC, 7:328–29.

26. Alexander, *Aprismo*, p. 20.

27. See the second installment of the two-part interview with Haya de la Torre published in *Oiga*, Oct. 31, 1975, pp. 18–19. The first installment appeared in the Oct. 24 *Oiga*.

28. Feb. 20, 1976, address, in OC, 7:478.

29. Haya, "Crónicas internacionales" (1957), in ibid., p. 299.

30. Ibid., p. 478.

31. Feb. 23, 1973, address in ibid., pp. 400–401. In his 1975 *Oiga* interview (Oct. 31, p. 30), Haya gently chided the Mexicans for having made the mistake in their 1910 Revolution of confining attention to their own country. As a result, Mexicans had allowed themselves to be led astray by chauvinism.

32. See Mario Peláez Bazán, *Haya de la Torre y la unidad de América Latina* (Lima, 1977), p. 559. Throughout this book, Peláez Bazán argues persuasively that Haya, as he approached the end of his life, wished more than anything else to be remembered for his contribution to continental solidarity. Peláez Bazán also provides an impressive chronological bibliography (pp. 579–99) of Haya's writings on themes of Indo-American unity. At various times throughout his life, Haya's lack of chauvinism drew the fire of superpatriots.

33. OC, 7:481.

34. Ibid., p. 478.

35. Sept. 21, 1969, address, ibid., pp. 327–28.

36. Feb. 20, 1971, address, ibid., p. 357.

37. May 7, 1969, address, ibid., p. 494.

38. Feb. 23, 1973, address, ibid., p. 401.

39. Ibid., p. 412.

40. Sept. 21, 1969, address, ibid., p. 330.

41. Sept. 21, 1972, address, ibid., p. 392.

42. Sept. 21, 1969, address, ibid., p. 323.

43. Sept. 21, 1972, address, ibid., p. 391.

44. Sept. 21, 1969, address, ibid., p. 324.

45. Ibid., p. 328.

46. Feb. 23, 1973, address, ibid., p. 411. In Haya's emphasis on youth as he dealt with death and regeneration there seems to lurk something of the archetypal desire, often associated with ancient Greece, of the elderly wise man to communicate enlightenment to a youth through, in the theoretical ideal, a Platonic relationship. In both instances, homosexual proclivities may have been involved. For a comparison of the Greek ideal to Aprismo's concern with the "political treasure" of youth, see Haya's March 29, 1943, letter to Luis Alberto Sánchez, in Haya and Sánchez, *Correspondencia, 1924–1976*, 2 vols. (Lima, 1983), 1:433.

47. *Oiga*, Feb. 27, 1976, estimated the crowd at between 40,000 and 50,000. Apristas claimed between 100,000 and 120,000, while the government's estimate was 15,000.

48. Feb. 20, 1976, address, OC, 7:480.

49. See Donald C. Henderson and Grace R. Pérez, trans. and comps., *Literature and Politics in Latin America: An Annotated Calendar of the Luis Alberto Sánchez Correspondence, 1919–1980* (University Park, Pa., 1982), pp. 70, 72.

50. For appraisals of a small sampling of the enormous body of literature on the Peruvian military revolution, see Luis Pásara, "Diagnosing Peru," LARR 17, no. 1 (1982): 235–43; and Evelyne Huber Stephens, "The Peruvian Military Government, Labor Mobilization, and the Political Strength of the Left," LARR 18, no. 2 (1983): 57–94. The most useful single book on the topic may well be Cynthia

376

McClintock and Abraham F. Lowenthal, eds., *The Peruvian Experiment Reconsidered* (Princeton, 1983).

. See Frits Wils, *Industrialization, Industrialists, and the Nation-State in Peru: A Comparative/Sociological Analysis* (Berkeley, 1979).

52. See Rosemary Thorp and Geoffrey Bertram, *Peru, 1890–1977: Growth and Policy in an Open Economy* (London, 1978), esp. p. 327. See also Cynthia McClintock's fine study, *Peasant Cooperatives and Political Change in Peru* (Princeton, 1981). Although McClintock sees considerable change in peasant attitudes toward political participation and social behavior occurring in consequence of land reform under the generals, she concludes that the government did not score truly notable advances toward a "fully participatory social democracy" in the sierra. Maintaining their traditional suspiciousness toward the national government, sierra campesinos turned their newly developing political solidarity into a weapon against what they regarded as government encroachment on "their" cooperatives (pp. 313–14). See also Peter S. Cleaves and Martin J. Scurrah, *Agriculture, Bureaucracy, and Military Government in Peru* (Ithaca, 1980); and David Guillet, *Agrarian Reform and Peasant Economy in Southern Peru* (Columbia, Mo., 1979). An especially intriguing book not only on agrarian reform under the generals but also on the nature of Indian social and economic structures through the centuries and on Indian relations with non-Indians is Harald O. Skar, *The Warm Valley People: Duality and Land Reform Among the Quechua Indians of Highland Peru* (Oslo, 1982). One of Skar's important conclusions is that Indianists have been quite mistaken in assumptions about the inherent socialism of Indian life. Whether in pre-Columbian or modern times, the Indian's basic social structure actually rested not just on social cooperation but on the competition of moieties within comunidades. Nevertheless, the socialist assumptions characteristic of romantic Indianism found their way into the military approach to agrarian reform.

53. See Enrique Chirinos Soto, *Historia de la república: 1821-Perú-1978* (Lima, 1977), pp. 545–46.

54. On the support that many Peruvian Communists extended Velasco Alvarado, see César Jiménez, *Perú: ¿Revolución popular o reformismo burqués?* (Lima, 1980), pp. 344–46.

55. Feb. 20, 1971, address, OC, 7:340–41.

56. Feb. 18, 1972, address, ibid., pp. 374–75, 360. For an especially eloquent defense of democracy see Haya's Feb. 22, 1974, discourse, ibid., pp. 413–30. Haya maintained a steady but temperate criticism of authoritarian planning, pronouncing at the last rally over which he presided (May 7, 1976) against dictatorship from above and from below. See ibid., p. 491.

57. Sept. 19, 1975, address, ibid., p. 459.

58. Feb. 23, 1973, address, ibid., p. 403.

59. Sept. 19, 1975, address, ibid., p. 459.

60. Feb. 23, 1973, address, ibid., p. 408.

61. Sept. 21, 1972, address, ibid., pp. 378–79.

62. Haya de la Torre interview, *Oiga*, Oct. 24, 1975, p. 20.

63. Ibid., pp. 18–20.

64. "El reto de Haya de la Torre," *Oiga*, Feb. 20, 1976, pp. 8–10, provides a shrewd analysis of the effectiveness of Haya's approach to criticizing the military government.

65. OC, 7:312–15.

66. Heinz Kohut, "Creativeness, Charisma, Group Psychology: Reflections on the Self-Analysis of Freud," in *The Search for the Self: Selected Writings of Heinz Kohut, 1950–1978*, ed. Paul H. Ornstein, 2 vols. (New York, 1978), 2:830–31.

67. Ornstein, "Introduction," ibid., 1:69.

68. Heinz Kohut, *The Restoration of the Self* (New York, 1977), p. 21.

69. Sept. 21, 1972, address, OC 7:391.

70. Feb. 23, 1973, address, ibid., pp. 411–12.

71. *Oiga*, Oct. 24, 1975, p. 22.

72. Ibid., p. 21.

73. See *Caretas* (Lima), June 22, 1978, p. 13. On Haya's enormous popularity in the 1970s, see Chirinos Soto, *Historia de la república*, p. 463.

74. See Steve Jay Stein, *Populism in Peru: The Emergence of the Masses and the Politics of Social Control* (Madison, 1980), p. 202.

75. Obsession with the importance of the number four may very well have sprung from Haya's objective of harmonizing human structures with the structure of the cosmos, with its four-dimensional space-time continuum. Herman Minkowski, a mathematician who had been Einstein's teacher, wrote: "Henceforth space by itself, and time by itself, are doomed to fade into mere shadows, and only a kind of union of the two will preserve an independent reality." Minkowski proceeded to work out the mathematics "of a four-dimensional space-time continuum." See Donald M. Lowe, *History of Bourgeois Perception* (Chicago, 1982), p. 112. The Minkowski quotation is from H. A. Lorentz et al., *The Principle of Relativity*, trans. W. Perrett and G. B. Jeffrey (London, 1923), p. 75.

76. See the final two pages of the unnumbered nine-page *Discurso pronunciado por el Presidente de la Asamblea Constitucional, Dr. Víctor Raúl Haya de la Torre, el 28 de julio de 1978, al instalar las sesiones de la Asamblea* (Lima, 1978).

77. *Caretas*, Sept. 18, 1978, p. 21.

78. Luis Alberto Sánchez, "Notas sobre Haya de la Torre," ibid., Aug. 13, 1979, pp. 24B–24C.

79. Sánchez letter of July 18, 1955, to Haya, cited and extracted in *Literature and Politics*, Henderson and Pérez, p. 267.

80. *Caretas*, July 2, 1979, p. 11.

378

81. Sánchez, "'¿Constitución de que clase?'' ibid., p. 32.
82. Quoted in Luis Eduardo Enríquez, *Haya de la Torre: La estafa política más grande de América* (Lima, 1951), p. 144.
83. *Caretas*, July 23, 1979, p. 17.
84. Ibid., July 30, 1979, p. 11.
85. *El Comercio*, Aug. 3, 1979, pp. 1, 2.
86. Ibid., Aug. 5, 1979, p. 4.
87. See Carlos Bendezu, "Tiempos difíciles," *Caretas*, Aug. 13, 1979, p. 18.
88. See n. 24, ch. 4.
89. On this and related matters, see Peter Charles Hoffer, *Revolution and Regeneration: Life Cycle and the Historical Vision of the Generation of 1776* (Athens, Ga., 1983).
90. See Thomas M. Davies Jr., *Indian Integration in Peru: A Half Century of Experience, 1900–1948* (Lincoln, 1974), esp. pp. 129–39.
91. OC, 7:481, 483.
92. Benjamin Lee Whorf, "An American Indian Model of the Universe" (1936), in *Language, Thought, and Reality: Selected Writings of Benjamin Lee Whorf*, ed. John B. Carroll, (Cambridge, Mass., 1956), pp. 59–60.
93. Lowe, *History of Bourgeois Perception*, pp. 110–11.
94. Ibid., p. 117.
95. The quoted material is from Hayden Herrera's description of the art of Frida Kahlo. See Herrera, *Frida: A Biography of Frida Kahlo* (New York, 1983), p. 256. In Mexico, Kahlo (the third wife of Diego Rivera) was one of the many artists who responded to the same impulses that propelled Haya de la Torre.

Index

Adas, Michael, 21–22
Addams, Jane, 165
Adler, Alfred, 99
African influences on Peru, 20
Agrarianism, 190
Agrarian reform, 258, 262, 263, 273
Albrecht family, 22
Aldana, Julio, 185–86
Alegría, Ciro, 237
Alessandri, Arturo, 45
Alliance for Progress, 252, 255, 258
Amauta (Inca wise man), 125, 139
America Hispana (Waldo Frank),
  196, 197
Amfortas, 174
Anarchism, 275
Anarcho-syndicalism, 16–17, 28–29,
  133
Ancón (Peru), 212
Animism, 6
Animus/anima theory, 127
Anthropology, British, 95–97
Anthropos, 143
Anticapitalism in U.S., 187–88, 191
Anticommunism of Haya, xiv, 70,
  206, 242, 253
Anti-imperialism: of Haya, 49, 72–
  73, 94–95, 153–54, 183, 242; of
  India, 321 n. 43; in U.S., 191, 204
Anti-Imperialist Congress, 70, 73
Antimaterialism, 31, 56
Antimperialismo y el APRA, El
  (Haya), 98, 374 n. 21
APRA (Alianza Popular Revolu-
  cionaria Americana): appeal of,
  92–93; in Central America, 98; in
  congress, 225–26, 250, 258–59;

decline of, 236–38, 244; democracy in, 253; discipline in, 177–82,
  208, 231–32; dissension in, 230,
  242, 251, 261, 284; exclusivism of,
  213; finances of, xii; flag of, 50,
  155, 345 n. 95; foundation of, 50;
  membership of, 117, 120, 130, 131,
  140–41, 158, 184, 262, 306 n. 51;
  middle class in, 72–73, 251–52;
  opposition to, 128–29, 150–51, 154,
  184–85; and organized labor, 225–
  26, 250; organizing state of, 177–
  80, 344 n. 87; in Paris, 94; poetry
  of, 113, 132, 224; program of, 94–
  95, 138–39, 207, 250–51, 264–65,
  276; propaganda by, xi, 177, 181–
  82; repression of, 174–75, 177, 184,
  186, 199, 206–7, 232–33, 241, 242,
  271; symbolism in, xii; totalitarianism in, 221; youth in, 74, 155,
  168, 179–80, 225, 260
Aprismo: appeal of, 92–93, 120, 170;
  asceticism in, 162–64, 166–67;
  Credo of, 92, 132–33, 155; exclusivism of, 133, 224; forgiveness in,
  210, 244; Indianism in, 123–26,
  128; influence of, 235–36; and
  Marxism, 140, 202, 242, 291;
  nonviolence in, 180, 245; and
  regeneration myth, 134–37; as
  religion, 7, 72, 130–33, 69, 157,
  169–72, 210, 260, 265, 287, 339 n.
  20, 362 n. 11; social system of,
  146–49
Aprista Heart, 131
Arbenz, Jacobo, 242
Arciniegas, Germán, 247, 296 n. 5

Arenas y Loayza, Carlos, 36
Arequipa (Peru), 232, 305 n. 43
Arévalo, Juan José, 5, 122
Arévalo, Manual, III, 121, 175, 200
Argentina, 39–40, 45
Arguedas, José María, 336 n. 94
Arias, Harmodio, 49
Arica (Chile), 45
Arielism, 71, 73
Aristotle, 72, 77, 247
Aspíllaga, Luis, 166
Astrology, 119, 124, 333 n. 64
Atkins, Gaius Glenn, 56
Austin, Mary, 51

Baca Rossi, Miguel, 285
Backus, Jacob, 13
Bacon, Francis, 77
Bakunin, Michael, 7, 71
Barmby, Goodwyn, 65
Barreto Cisco, Manuel ("El Bú-
    falo"), 165
Barrios Llona, Luis, 221, 241–42
Basadre, Jorge, 45–46, 158, 168
Beals, Carleton, 189–92; describes
    Peru, 20, 23; praises Aprismo,
    236, 358 n. 19
Belaúnde, Víctor Andrés, 37
Belaúnde Terry, Fernando: in 1957
    election, 244; in 1962 election,
    253; in 1963 election, 256–57; in
    1980 election, 284; Popular
    Action party of, 244, 252, 261; as
    president, 257–59
Benavides, Oscar R.: in 1945 elec-
    tion, 212; APRA propaganda
    against, 181–82; and assassination
    plots, 168, 176; and economic
    recovery, 185; and repression of
    APRA, 120, 174–75
Benavides Canseco, Agustín, 120
Ben Gurion, David, 268
Benlloch y Vivó, Juan, 38
Bergson, Henri, 20–21, 239

Bernstein, Jeremy, 80
Betancourt, Rómulo, 122, 235, 353
    n. 102
Between Tears and Laughter (Lin),
    202
Billington, James, 65
Blavatsky, Helena P., 114, 125
Bogdanov, Alexander A., 64
Bolívar, Simón, 268
Bolivia, 176
Borah, Woodrow, 191, 204
Born, Max, 297 n. 10
Brenner, Anita, 165
Broglie, Louis de, 85
Brownmiller, Susan, 142
Brundage, Burr Cartwright, 62
Bruno, Giordano, 2
Buddhism, 143
Búfalos, 168, 221, 225
Bureau of Conjunctions, 221
Bustamante y Rivero, José Luis, 212,
    213, 225–26, 230–33

Callao (Peru), 232–34, 238, 367 n. 96
Capitalism: in Indo-America, 70, 73,
    95; nature of, 53; rejection of, 52,
    94, 95, 185, 238. See also
    Socialism-Capitalism synthesis
Carpenter, Edward, 97–98, 337 n. 100
Cartesian duality, 78
Casa del Pueblo: APRA meeting
    place, 246, 260, 267; mourning
    for Haya at, 283, 284; speeches at,
    253, 269, 271
Casa Grace, 12, 13, 22, 23
Cassels, Alan, 73–74
Castilla, Ramón, 120
Castro, Fidel, xi, 252
Catholicism: exclusionary thought
    of, 1; liberation theology of, 265–
    66; and the marginal, 286–87; and
    Marxism, 292; mysticism in, 6;
    opposition to APRA, 128–29;
    337 n. 104; popular, 130–31; revival

of, 36–39, 50; traditional, 3, 19, 21, 36, 131; and university students, 38–39
Catholic University (Lima), 36–37
Centro Esotérico Nacional (Lima), 120
Centro Humanista (Lima), 120
Cerro de Pasco Mining Company, 13
Chan-Chan (Peru), 28, 57, 291
Charismatic leadership, 106–16, 118, 123, 170; through esotericism, 5; of Haya, 107–16; 118, 123, 170, 245, 284; power of, 99, 157
Chávez, J. H., 224
Chicama Valley (Peru), 22, 23
China, 202, 340 n. 46
Chirinos Soto, Enrique, 158
Christianity: and Marxism, 67; sex symbolism in, 143. *See also* Catholicism
Clodd, Edward, 95
Club Nacional (Lima), 209
Cochran, William P., 192
Cole, G. D. H., 71–72, 94, 97
Colegio Anglo Peruano de Lima, 47–48, 67
Collectivism of Indians, 263, 373 n. 12
Collectivization, Haya's criticism of, 275
Collier, John, 188, 193, 356 n. 7, 357 n. 14
Colliers, xi
Colombian Embassy in Lima, 233–34, 241
El Comercio, 176–77, 225, 226
Communalism of Indians, 56, 263, 373 n. 12
Communism, 65–69, 95
Communists and APRA, 129, 206, 227, 236, 242
Community, restoration of: for del Mazo, 45; for Haya, 27–28; and myth of lost community, 53–55, 66

Concientización, 265–66
Condor, 222 fig.
Confederación de Trabajadores del Peru, 225
Constituent assembly (1978), 280–82
Constitution of 1978, 282–83
Convivencia, 250–51, 265
Cooperativism, 146, 344 n. 80. *See also* Corporatism
Corporatism: in Aprismo, 146–49, 188, 267–69, 275; of Velasco Alvarado, 262–64
"Cosmic race," 50
Cossío del Pomar, Felipe, 102, 117–118, 250, 301 n. 35
Cox, Carlos Manuel, 101, 121, 199
Croly, Herbert, 187
Cross: of calvary, 172; symbolism of, 41, 139
Crowd psychology, 156–57
Cuadros, Juan de Dios, 231
Cuba, 49, 252
Cultural relativism, 95
Cuzco (Peru): and Haya's spiritual awakening, 57–58, 60–62, 288; Indianism in, 307 n. 1; as source of wisdom, 125
Cyclical ascent theories, 4
Cyclical view of progress, 160, 203

Davies, Thomas M., Jr., xv, 120, 289
Dearing, Fred Morris, 179, 182
"Deep War," 198
De la Bretonne, Restif, 65
De las Casas, Luis F., 132
De la Torre (de Haya), Zoila Victoria, 24, 235
Delgado, Carlos, 262–63
Delmar, Serafin, 101, 113, 126, 132, 199
Del Mazo, Gabriel, 40, 41, 45
De Sales, Raoul de Roussy, 201–3
Dietzgen, Joseph, 64
Dintilhac, Georges, 36

Dissident Committee of Forty Intellectuals of Peru, 195
Dollar Dipolomacy (Nearing and Freeman), 358 n. 21
Dreams, in primitivism, 124
Dreyfus, Louis G., 192

Eastman, Max, 63
East/West dichotomy, 137–38
East-West synthesis, 136–39, 202–3
Edwards Bello, Joaquín, 91
Ego consciousness/unconsciousness, 137, 145–46
Einsten, Albert: and Haya, viii, 223, 236, 248, 368 n. 11; pacifism of, 100; pleas for clemency, 165; and space-time relativity, 85, 88, 90–91, 248; and spiritualism, 80, 81
Elections: of 1931, 147–48, 150–59, 256–57, 346 n. 1; of 1939, 185–86, 199; of 1945, 212; of 1956, 244; of 1962, 252–55; of 1963, 256–57; of 1969, 261; of 1978, 280; of 1980, 284
Engels, Friedrich, 311 n. 47
England: Haya in, 94–98, 244; spiritualism in, 76–77
Enríquez, Luis Eduardo, 10, 237
Envoys, The (Hays), 9, 236, 368 n. 9
Erikson, Erik H., 107
Esotericism, 2–5, 75–77, 91, 219
Espacio-tiempo-histórico (Haya), 213
Europe and world harmony, 243
Export-Import Bank, 272

Fabianism, 94
Fascism, 73–74, 101, 146, 181, 317 n. 100
Federación Aprista Juvenil, 179–80
Federación Obrera Local, 67
"Feminine"/"masculine" characteristics, 55, 56, 137, 141–42, 164–65. *See also* Sex symbolism

Feminism in Aprismo, 126–28, 336 n. 95
Feminism in the United States, 229
Fisher, John, 310 n. 34
Fletcher, William B., 200, 227
Flores Salvedo, Rómulo, 353 n. 94
Foreign investment: in APRA program, 250–52; in Peru, 12–15, 17–18, 35, 102, 272; and university reform movement, 40
Four-dimensional universe, 87–91
Four freedoms, 201, 281
Frank, Waldo: and APRA, 361 n. 44; and Latin American values, 359 n. 27; on Leguía, 35; on Lima, 61–62; on Marx, 69; pleas for clemency, 165; prophet of regeneration, 192–98, 200, 204, 205, 252
Frankfurt school of Marxism, 64–65
Fraternity Day speeches, 264, 268
Frazer, James, 114
Freeman, Joseph, 139, 191, 358 n. 21
Freemasonry, 81, 100, 125–26, 173, 320 n. 41
Freud, Sigmund, 63, 287
Freudian psychology, 55
Functional democracy. *See* Corporatism

Gandhi, Mohandas K.: anti-imperialism of, 321 n. 43; and music, 155; nonviolence of, 162, 238; and spiritual strength, 82
García Pérez, Alan, 293
Garcilaso de la Vega ("el Inca"), 244; and dreams, 124; and *mestisaje*, 57, 100; millennialism of, 121, 310 n. 34; and praise of Indians, 335 n. 91
"Generation of 1905," 37
"Generation of 1919," 39
Germany: esotericism in, 77; Haya in, 98–101

Gildemeister estate, 22, 29–30
Giner de los Ríos, Francisco, 43
Gnostic Gospels, 127
Golpes. See Insurrections
González, Natalicio, 122
González Prada, Adriana de, 235
González Prada, Manuel, 28, 43, 124, 235, 288–89
Good Neighbor policy, 183, 188, 228
Goodwin, Richard, 252
Gouldner, Alvin W., 63
Grace, Michael P., 12–13
Grace, William R., 12–13
Graña Garland, Francisco, 226–27, 230
Graves, Anna Melina, 67–68, 94, 205, 313 n. 69
Great Depression, 74, 130, 187, 262
Gregor, A. James, 74
Guerrero, Julio C., 176
Guevara, Ernesto "Che," i, x, 6
Guillén, Alberto, 112
Gunther, John, 200
Gurdjieff, Georges I., 76, 86, 87, 193, 324 n. 69
Gutiérrez, Gustavo, 266

Harmony: in historical space-time, 89–90; through synthesis of opposites, 84–85
Haya de la Torre, Agustín ("Cucho"), 29
Haya de la Torre, Edmundo, 24, 126
Haya de la Torre, Víctor Raúl: appeal of, xi, xii; appearance of, xii, xiii, 102–4, 209, 329 n. 140; asceticism of, 163–64, 177; attacks on, 199–200; and constituent assembly, 280–82; "cosmic interpretation" of, 121; criticism of, 237–38, 241–42; death of, 282–83; early life of, 24–29, 116; economic program of, 140–41 (*see also* Corporatism); egotism of, 29,

104, 112, 114, 115, 221, 223; and end of military rule, 271, 274–77; in exile, xii, 49–50, 67–69, 82, 94–101; in hiding, 175, 180, 197, 199–200, 233–36, 239–41, 367 n. 1; idealism of, 9; influence of, xiii–xiv, 287–88, 292–93; intellectual curiosity of, xiii, 105, 276; internationalism of, 45; as international statesman, 249, 250, 254; life-style of, 221, 245–47, 276, 353 n. 104; masochism of, 164–65, 210, 279–80; mysticism of, 145, 211, 213; narcissism of, 158–59, 164–65, 177, 182, 233, 235, 277–79; neuroticism of, 165, 167, 209–12; opposition to, xi, 46, 150–51; optimism of, 200, 235, 236; oratorical style of, 91, 104, 135, 138, 156–57, 161, 170–71, 269; as patriarch, 246, 260; pluralism of, 9; political organization plan of, 215–17; as politician, 8–10, 74, 213, 219, 231–32, 242, 252–55, 257, 259–60, 274–77 (*see also* Elections); in prison, 165–68; and racial admixtures, 31–32, 100; tolerance of, 9, 280, 282; totalitarianism of, xvi, 7, 9, 221–22; and use of religion, 47–48; the visionary, 7–8
Haya y Cárdenas, Raúl Edmundo, 23–27, 302 n. 47
Hays, Hoffman R., 236, 368 n. 9
Hegel, Georg Friedrich, 88, 247, 345 n. 90
Hegelianism, 63, 65
Heisenberg, Werner, 247, 297 n. 10
Heraclitus, 2, 81, 247, 345 n. 90
Hermaphrodite symbolism, 164, 173
Hermes Trismegistus, 2
Hermeticism, 4
Hernández Martínez, Maximiliano, 5
Heysen, Luis, 101, 126, 128, 152, 153
Hidalgo, Alberto, 10, 109, 113, 237–38

High Center of Military Studies, 274
High consciousness, leaders of, 88, 89, 274
Hinduism, 143
Hinton, Charles Howard, 90, 324 n. 65
Hispanism, 37–39, 43, 50–51, 181, 303 n. 14
Historical space-time theory, 85; cornerstone of Aprismo, 290; in East-West synthesis, 136; for Haya, 240; and international harmony, 323 n. 56; and Marxism, 242; and North-South synthesis, 142–43; for Toynbee, 239
Hitler, Adolf, 99–100, 173
Hobsbawm, E. J., 16, 153
Hobson, J. A., 139
Homosexuality: of Haya, alleged, 10, 100–101, 117, 328 n. 135; of millennialist leaders, 97–98
Horney, Karen, 182
Huancavelica (Peru), 176
Huancayo (Peru), 176
Huanchaco (Peru), 23
Humboldt, Alexander von, 364 n. 61
Hyperspace philosophy, 87, 88

Idealism, 79
Ideology and Program of the Peruvian Aprista Movement, The (Kantor), 236
Idiáquez, Jorge, 185–86, 210, 221
Immigrants, 22, 25
Imperialism: in East-West synthesis, 202–3; for Haya, 139–42, 153–54, 238; and historical space-time, 92; in North-South synthesis, 144–45; after World War II, 229–30
Incahuasi, 175, 185, 234, 235, 353 n. 94
Incas, 59, 62, 125, 256, 275
Indianism, 52, 54–60; in Aprismo,

123–26, 128; in Cuzco, 307 n. 1; of Henry Wallace, 204; and regeneration, 51, 290–91; socialism in, 376 n. 52; as symbol, 151, 288–89; in U.S., 188–91; and Volk mysticism, 99, 308 n. 9
Indians: in agrarian reform, 263; communalism of, 56, 263, 373 n. 12; consciousness of, 290–91; and "feminine" traits, 142; Haya's concern for, xi–xii; Haya's empathy with, 28, 309 n. 20; social upheaval of, 16; stereotypes of, 79; in utopian scheme, 313 n. 61; witchcraft among, 20
Indigenismo, 50
Individualism, 7, 56, 228
Individualism-collectivism synthesis, 203, 204; in corporatism, 145–48; for Indians, 56; in "organizing state," 178–80; for U.S. thinkers, 187–88; in World War II, 202
Individuation (psychic rebirth), 58–60, 187–88
Indo-America: anti-imperialism in, 70; and corporative synthesis, 149; at crossroads of opposites, 138, 145; and Hispanism, 50–51; and historical space-time, 88–89, 91–92, 136; Indians in, 51, 60; integration of, 268–69, 281; and millennialism, 86; as people-continent, 84; regeneration of, 89, 95; sex symbolism in, 183–84
Industria, La, 24
Infrahistoria, 44, 58, 60
Ingenieros, José, 304 n. 20
Inman, Samuel Guy, 200
Institución Libre de Enseñanza, 43, 305 n. 42
Insurrections: of 1929, 165; of 1932, 110–11, 350 n. 56; of 1933, 165–67; of 1934, 176; of 1939, 185; of 1945, 212; of 1948, 231–33, 238, 367 n. 96;

of 1962, 255; of 1968, 261–62, 289;
of 1975, 274; Haya's part in, 161;
plots of, 70, 153, 174, 176
Integral education, 178
Inter-Americanism, 228
International Petroleum Company,
102, 226, 256, 258, 261–62
Inti (Inca sun deity), 134
Intrahistory (*infrahistoria*), 44, 58, 60
IPC, 102, 226, 256, 258, 261–62

Jeans, James, 78, 79, 202
Jefferson, Thomas, 288
Jibaja, Eduardo, 210–11, 237
Jiménez, Gustavo, 166
Johnson, J. H., 13
Josephs, Ray, xi, xiv, 295 n. 1
Jung, Carl G.: and anima of Indians,
58; and consciousness/uncon-
sciousness, 89, 137; and individ-
uation, 58–59, 288; and Keyser-
ling, 309 n. 25; and Portal's
feminism, 127; and primordial
images, 135–36; and repression,
287; and Toynbee, 309 n. 26
Justicialismo, 5–6
Juventud Aprista Peruana, 225

Kammen, Michael, 187
Kantor, Harry, 236
Karlin, Alma, 20
Kelly, Aileen, 7
Kennedy, John F., 252, 255, 256
Kepler, Johannes, 90, 218
Keyserling, Hermann: and cyclical
progress, 160; and East-West
synthesis, 138; on economic
growth, 141; and feminism, 184,
323 n. 62; and Jung, 59, 309 n. 25;
on Latin America, 111; and sex
symbols in regeneration, 141;
spiritualism of, 83–86, 320 n. 37;
and theory of relativity, 90
Klarén, Peter F., 25

Kohut, Heinz, 115–17, 278–79
Kollantai, Aleksandra, 127
Krausism, 305 n. 42
Kuomintang, 340 n. 46

La Barre, Weston, 99
Labour party, British, 94
Lafaye, Jacques, 136–37
Lang, Andrew, 95
Laserna, Mario, 236
Laski, Harold, 94, 165
Lasky, Melvin J., 61
Latin America, stereotype of, 188–89,
229
Latin American unity, 139, 149
Lawlor, Robert, 85
League for Industrial Democracy, 191
Le Bon, Gustave, 157
Leguía, Augusto B.: and Catholic
Church, 38, 48; *oncenio* of, 33–
36, 226; overthrow of, 151; repres-
sion under, 42, 49, 195
Lenin, Nicolai, 316 n. 90
León de Vivero, Fernando, 221
León Pinelo, Antonio Rodríguez de,
136–37, 203
Lévi-Strauss, Claude, 309 n. 18
Lévy-Bruhl, Lucien, 56, 124
Lewis, Sinclair, 165
Liberation theology, 265–66
Lima (Peru): demonstrations in, 102,
108, 150; description of, 14, 20,
34–36, 41, 57; Haya's dislike of,
60, 61; Haya hides in, 197; Haya's
speeches in, 154, 168–69, 207–8,
213–20, 224, 244–45; violence in,
152, 176
Lin Yutang, 202–3
Lippman, Walter, 187
Lissón, Emilio, 48
London School of Economics, 244
Lowe, Donald M., 291–92
Lumumba, Patrice, 278
Lunacharsky, Anatoly, 64

Luna Vegas, Ricardo, 296 n. 3, 314 n. 79

McCarthy, Joseph, 236
MacDonald, Ramsay, 94
Mackay, John A., 99, 128; and St. John's Revelation, 260–61, 306 n. 53; and spiritual revolution, 47–49, 130, 159
McLoughlin, William G., 19
Madero, Francisco I., 5
Magic in politics, 96, 107–8, 118
Making of Tomorrow, The (de Sales), 201, 202
Malinowski, Bronislaw, 75, 95–96, 130
Malraux, André, 65
Mandala, 62, 214, 218
Marañón, Gregorio, 165
Marett, R. R., 95, 97, 130, 260
Mariátegui, José Carlos: and Dissident Committee, 195; and Haya, 70, 99, 314 n. 79; Indianism of, 55–56, 289; Marxism of, 6, 65–67, 69, 313 n. 59; and Waldo Frank, 196–97
Marín, José del Carmen, 231, 232
Martyrdom in Aprismo, 99, 134–35, 166, 169–73, 176, 208, 271, 281
Marx, Karl, 63, 69–72
Marxism: appeal of, 314 n. 78; in Aprismo, 140, 202, 242, 291; and capitalism, 19; of "Che" Guevara, 6; "hard" version of, 63; of Haya, 63, 67–74, 94; and historical space-time, 91, 242; and Indo-America, 91–92; and materialism, 316 n. 90; in Peruvian military, 373–74; "soft" version of, 63–67, 69–74, 196, 248, 266, 374 n. 21; and spiritualism, 80–81
Masonry, 81, 100, 125–26, 173, 320 n. 41
Materialism: positivist, 36, 79, 81, 93; rejection of, 20–21, 52, 87

Mazo, Gabriel del, 114, 121–22, 138, 326 n. 98
Mead, Margaret, 228
Mella, Julio Antonio, 98
Mendoza Leiva, Abelardo, 168
Meneses, Rómulo, 128
Mercury, duality of, 144, 215, 343 n. 73
Merton, Robert K., 93
Messianism of Haya, 62, 83, 99–100, 102, 109–13, 116–17, 132, 157, 172–75, 210, 271
Mestisaje (fusion of races), 57
Mexican Revolution, 124, 189–91, 321 n. 42
Mexico: Haya in, 49–50; and U.S. intellectuals, 189–91
Millenarianism: and asceticism, 162–64; eclecticism of, 121; feminism in, 123, 127–28; and individual vs. group, 148; and lost-community myth, 45, 54; Peru's receptiveness to, 18–19; and primitivism, 55; in Túpac Amaru uprisings, 126; in university reform movement, 41
Millennialism: appeal of, xvi; of Aprismo, 266–67; in liberation theology, 265–66; in Peruvian sierra, 310 n. 34
"Mind energy," 20–21
Mining, 12–14
Miró Quesada, Antonio, 176, 199
Moche (Peru), 23, 28
Mochica Indians, 156
Morales Bermúdez, Francisco, 274, 277
More, Henry, 87
Mountains as regeneration symbol, 61, 310 n. 34
Murphy, V. J., 200
Music: of APRA, 155; in APRA ritual, 132, 155; and mysticism, 322 n. 52
Myers, Mary Ann, xvi

Myths: of incarnation, 90; of long
march, 52–54; of lost community,
53–55, 66; and religion, 96

Nash, June, 168
National Alliance, 230, 231
National Democratic Front, 212
National Economic Congress, 147,
216, 267, 281
National Front of Democratic
Youth, 244
Nationalization: in APRA program,
94–95, 102, 237; of copper indus-
try, 272; of IPC, 261–62
National Socialism, 99–101
Nature: glorification of, 55; as passiv-
ity symbol, 142; and progress,
51–53
Naumburg, Margaret, 193
Nearing, Scott, 139, 191, 358 n. 21
New Deal, 201
New Fatherland, 35–36, 38
Newton, Isaac, 72, 81
Niebuhr, H. Richard, xv
Nonlinear time, 4
Nonviolence: of Haya, 159–61, 167,
180, 209, 231–32, 238–39; of uni-
versity reform movement, 100
Nonviolent revolution, 159–61
Noriega, Zenón, 233
North-South synthesis: failure of,
205, 227–30; Haya's plan of, 139–
42; sex symbolism in, 183–84;
support for in U.S., 186–98, 200–
201; for Toynbee, 240; of Waldo
Frank, 194–95
Numbers, mystical, 218

Obras completas (Haya de la Torre),
xv
Occultism, 119–20, 125, 130–31
"Oceanic feeling," 115, 138, 270, 288
Odría, Manuel A.: in 1962 election,
252–55; in 1963 election, 257; end
of term, 244; leads golpe, 232–33;
and repression of APRA, 233–36,
241, 242
Officers' Club (Lima), 273
Oiga interview, 275–76, 279–80
Oncenio, 33–36, 226
Opposites, reconciliation of: for
Haya, 31–32; in historical space-
time, 85; in people-continent, 139;
in spiritualism, 4–6, 9; in univer-
sity reform movement, 41
Orage, A. R., 193
Order of the Sun, 283
Organic democracy. See Corporatism
Organizing state (Haya's plan), 178–
80, 344 n. 87
Orient, 80, 82
Oriental character, 56
Orrego, Antenor: defines Aprismo,
180, 184; mysticism of, 122–23;
and people-continents, 82, 84,
139, 269, 345 n. 95; as
philosopher-journalist, 29–31; on
popular universities, 44; praises
Haya, 112–13, 144; and regenera-
tionism, 134
Ortega y Gasset, José, 83–84, 165
Our America (Frank), 193
Ouspensky, P. D., 76–78, 86–88, 193

Pachacútec, xii, 62–63, 175, 239, 311
n. 44
Pacha Mama (earth goddess), 134
Pachter, Henry, 300 n. 28
Palacios, Alfredo, 42
Panama Canal, 14, 94–95, 138–39, 250
Pan American Congress (Lima), 192
PAP (Peruvian Aprista Party): forma-
tion of, 101. See also APRA
Pardo, José, 14
Partido Civilista, 132
Partido del Pueblo, 207. See also
APRA
Patria Nueva, 35–36

Penates (pre-Columbian household gods), 270
People-continent: in Aprismo, 82, 84, 139, 269, 345 n. 95; in Toynbee's vision, 240
Pérez Godoy, Ricardo, 255
Perón, Eva and Juan, xi, 5, 148
Peronism, 235–36
Peru: agriculture in, 14; civil war in (1930s), 175–76; demography of, 34–35; economic improvement in, 185; immigrants to, 14; Indians of, 124; middle class of, 140; politics in, 9, 14. *See also* Elections; positivists in, 14–15, 18–19; socioeconomic decline in, 12–19, 22–23, 25, 26, 33–36, 74, 301 n. 44
Peruvian Aprista party, 101. *See also* APRA
Peruvian University Students Federation, xii, 42
Phelan, John, 295 n. 2
Philosophical idealism, 9
Phoenicia, 98
Pico della Mirandola, Giovanni, 2
Pike, Fredrick B. II, xiv
Planck, Max, 79, 81
Plato, 143
Plaza de Acho (Lima), speeches in: Aug. 23, 1931, 154; Nov. 12, 1933, 168–69; Sept. 7, 1946, 224
Plaza San Martín (Lima), speeches in: May 20, 1945, 207–8; July 25, 1957, 244–45
Pluralism, philosophical, 9
Poetry of APRA, 246
Popular Action party, 244, 252, 261
Popular universities: at Casa del Pueblo, 246, 260; goal of, 306 n. 44; in integral education, 178; origin of, 43–44, 305 n. 40
Populism, 269–70
Portal, Magda, 101; of feminism, 126–28, 336 nn. 94, 95; imprison-

ment of, 358 n. 19; and nonviolence, 238; and regenerationism, 134
Porter, Katherine Anne, 6, 191
Positivism: in Aprismo, 208–9; and Indians, 124; and nature, 53, 55; proponents of, 14–15, 17; and racism, 32; rejection of, 18–21, 37, 51, 52, 56, 87, 91; and spirit-matter connection, 291; and spiritualism, 95
Prado, Manuel: in 1939 election, 185, 186; in 1945 election, 212; in 1956 election, 244; in 1962 election, 254; Convivencia of, 250; and Indian integration, 289; ouster of, 255; propaganda against, 206; and repression of APRA, 199
Prensa, La, 225, 226
Prialé, Ramiro, 199, 243, 250, 268
Primitivism, 54–56, 59–60, 95, 124
Progressive party, 228
Protestantism, 128
Proudhon, Pierre, 71
Pueblo continente (Orrego): 30, 82, 122, 139. *See also* people-continent
Pythagoras, 81, 86, 87, 90, 323 n. 60

Quantum physics: antimaterialism of, 78–80, 202–3; and Marxism, 72, 247–48; and pluralism, 9; and representation of matter, 320 n. 29
Quesada, José, 185
Quinta Mercedes, 276, 283

Racism, 32, 228–29
Railroads, 13, 14, 22
Ravines, Eudocio, 315 n. 81, 368 n. 13
Real and ideal, unity of, 78

Rebel Aprista party, 251
Rebirth (as symbol), 40–41
Reductionism, 2, 3
Reed, John, 189
Regenerationism: and APRA, 120–21, 169, 174, 178; through harmonizing of rhythms, 92; in historical space-time, 93; and Indianism, 58, 59; and Marxism, 64; mythology of, 54–56, 61, 134–38; in Orient, 82; in popular universities, 43–44; psychic source of, 60; symbolism in, 141–44, 154
Regenerationist socialism, 67
Reik, Theodore, 164
Relativity, theory of, 90, 203
Religion: among marginal sectors, 295 n. 2; and myth, 96, 99; Oriental, 122–23, 143; political use of, 130; as revolutionary ideology, 47–48; secular, 133. See also Aprismo as religion; Catholicism; Messianism
Revolutionary Government of the Armed Forces, 262–74, 276
Revolutionary Union, 151, 185, 225
Rhythm: in historical space-time, 88–89; of Indo-America, 51, 60, 92; for spiritualists, 59
Ritual: in APRA rallies, 152, 154–56, 207–8, 168, 260; in crowd psychology, 157; in National Socialism, 99
Riva Agüero, José de la, 174–75
Rodó, José Enrique, 71
Rodríguez, Antonio, 120, 176
Rojas, Ricardo, 356 n. 133
Rolland, Romain: and capitalism, 185; and cyclical progress, 160; and East-West synthesis, 82, 138, 340 n. 46; and Jung, 309 n. 25; and nonviolence, 100; and "oceanic feeling," 115; pleas for clemency, 165; praises Haya, 112; and

relativity, 90; and spiritualism, 80, 81, 83, 86, 321 n. 42
Roma (sugar estate), 22, 29
Romualdi, Serafino, 260
Roosevelt, Franklin D., 183, 187, 201, 281
Russell, Bertrand, 78, 244

Sabroso, Arturo, 113, 132
St. John's Revelation, 100, 260–61, 306 n. 53, 351 n. 77
Saint Theresa, 169–70, 245, 371 n 46
Sánchez, Luis Alberto: as APRA leader, 114, 284; in exile, 234; on Haya's intolerance, 282; as Mason, 336 n. 92; on Peruvian civil war, 176; senator, 257; spiritualism of, 120–21; on Waldo Frank, 194–96
Sánchez Cerro, Luis M: in 1931 election, 131, 151–53, 158; assassination of, 168; corporatism of, 147–48; influence on Haya, 254; as insurrection leader, 101, 153; and repression of APRA, 165, 174, 241; and Unión Revolucionaria, 185
Sandino, Augusto César, xi
Schlesinger, Arthur M., Jr., 252
"Seasap" (Solo el aprismo salvará al Perú), 155
Sechura Contract, 226–27
Seoane, Juan, 113, 176, 199
Seoane, Manuel: as APRA leader, 101, 121, 237, 243; criticizes Haya, 241–42, 251; and Dissident Committee, 195; as Mason, 336 n. 92; opinions of Haya, 220–22; uses religious imagery, 131, 133
"Sermon on the Mount" (Haya), 161, 168
Seven Arts, The, 193
Sex symbolism: in Christianity,

Sex symbolism (continued)
352 n. 88; in four freedoms, 201;
in North-South synthesis, 183–84;
in regenerationism, 141–44
Shamanism, 6, 20, 31
Sierralta Lorca, Eduardo, 311 n. 45
Sinclair, Upton, 165, 191
Social Gospel movement, 47, 100
Socialism-capitalism synthesis: in
corporatism, 145–48; in Europe,
243; in Haya's "multiverse," 238;
in the United States, 203, 228,
230, 253; in World War II, 202
Socialism of Indians, 376 n. 52
Socialist party, 191
Sorel, Georges, 69–70
South American Meditations (Keyserling), 86
Soviet Union, 67–69, 127, 202, 248
Space-time relativity, 85, 90, 248–49,
290
Spanish Civil War, 181
Spelucín, Alcides, 29–31, 113, 185–86,
210
Spengler, Oswald, 85, 90, 98–99,
323 n. 56
Spirit and matter, unity of: in esotericism, 91; for Haya, 59, 326 n.
93; for Marxists, 65, 71–72; in
new physics, 78
Spiritualism: appeal of, 5, 6, 19–20;
in Aprismo, 118, 121–23; and
capitalism, 299 n. 24; cyclical
determinism in, 160; description
of, 1–4; effects of, 286–88; in
Europe, 76–86; of Haya, 7–8, 120;
and Indianism, 124–26; and
Marxism, 292; and Masonry, 126;
in Mexican Revolution, 321 n. 42;
in Peru, 233; and power of spirit
over matter, 59–60; and racism,
32; in the United States, 204–5, 228
Steer, Carlos, 176
Stein, Steve Jay, 25, 27, 158

Strikes of 1918–19, xii–xiii, 17, 42
Structuralism, 96
Study of History, A (Toynbee),
239, 243
Sugar production, 14, 22, 272
Sun Yat-sen, 340 n. 46
Switzerland, Haya in, 81

Tahuantinsuyo (Inca capital; Four
Corners), 57, 62, 270
Talara (Peru), 102
Tannenbaum, Frank, 189–90, 192,
200
Taoism, 202, 203
Taos (New Mexico), 193
Teatro Municipal speech (Lima, Oct.
9, 1945), 213–20
Teatro Popular speech (Trujillo, Dec.
18, 1933), 170–73, 245
Tertium Organum (Ouspensky), 77
Theosophism, 94, 125
Thomas, Norman, 191
Time, circular conception of, 124–25
Townsend Ezcurra, Andrés, 261
Toynbee, Arnold, 235, 239–41, 243,
370 n. 34
Treinta años del aprismo (Haya), 235
Trotsky, Leon, 68
Trujillo (Peru): economic change in,
22–23; Haya's speech in, 170–73,
245; insurrection in, 110–11, 165–
67; and mixing of opposites, 31–
32; shamanism in, 31
Trujillo Bohemians, 26–27, 29
Tupac Amarú, 126, 273
Turner, Victor W., 19, 211

Ugarteche, Pedro, 46
Unamuno, Miguel de, 44, 58, 165
Unión Revolucionaria (UR). See
Revolutionary Union
United States: 1940s thought in,
200–201, 227–28; as ally of APRA,
181–84, 205–6, 229–30, 236, 242,

368 n. 11; Haya in, 191, 223; opposes Haya, 98; and Soviet Union, 202, 248. *See also* North-South synthesis
University of Córdoba (Argentina), 39
University of San Marcos (Lima), 31, 36, 42, 46, 195, 225
University of Trujillo, 29, 30
University reform movement, 39–46, 41–46, 130; goal of, 292; influence on Peruvian military, 274; Marxism in, 70–71; nonviolence of, 100; young people in, 74
Ureta, Eloy, 212

Valcárcel, Gustavo, 223, 366 n. 78
Valdelomar, Abraham, 83
Vallejo, César, 29–31, 69
Vanguardia Aprista de Choque, 221
Vanity Triumphant (Haya), 31, 42
Vargas Llosa, Mario, 295 n. 2
Vasconcelos, José, 10, 49–50, 100
Velasco Alvarado, Juan, 262–64, 272–75
Velasco Ibarra, José María, 5
"Vertical Organization of the Peruvian Aprista Party," 180, 182
Villanueva, Armando, 284
Villanueva, Víctor, 120, 132
Violence in APRA politics, 152–53, 184–85, 225, 227

Virgin Spain (Frank), 194, 195
Vitarte (Peru), 276
Vivekananda, 80, 82
Voegelin, Eric, 131
Völkisch movement, 99, 308 n. 9

Wallace, Henry A., 203–5, 228
Wallas, Graham, 75
Ward, Lester Frank, 187
Webb, James, 77
Weber, Max, 106
Wells, H. G., 85, 94
Whitaker, Arthur P., 227–28
Whitaker, John T., 200
Whitehead, Alfred North, 78, 247
Williams, Robert C., 64
Witchcraft, 20
Wolfe, Bertram and Ella, 191
World Congress of Communist Youth, 67
Wound symbolism, 173–74, 245

Yanca ayllu ("worthless people"), 62
Yin-Yang principle, 370 n. 34
Youth: in APRA, 221, 225; and Belaúnde, 244; for Haya, 74; and National Socialism, 99
Yrigoyen, Hipólito, 5, 45, 122, 262

Zukav, Gary, 79